Building Real-Time Marvels with Laravel

Create Dynamic and Interactive Web Applications

Sivaraj Selvaraj

Apress®

Table of Contents

About the Author

 **Sivaraj Selvaraj**'s work is focused on modern technologies and industry best practices. His experience includes frontend development approaches such as HTML5, CSS3, and JavaScript frameworks, as well as creating responsive web design to optimize user experience across devices. He specializes in developing dynamic web applications with server-side languages such as PHP, WordPress, and Laravel, as well as managing and integrating databases with SQL and MySQL. Sivaraj is enthusiastic about sharing his significant expertise and experience, empowering readers to solve tough challenges and create highly functional, visually appealing websites.

About the Technical Reviewer

Yogesh Kamal Sharma is an application developer enthusiast, consultant, and avid paperback reader. He is presently associated with NICE Actimize to modernize AML programs by bringing together machine learning and domain expertise to combat money laundering and terrorist financing. He graduated from VSIT Mumbai, is a father of one, and enjoys his free time golfing.

Acknowledgments

I am indebted to my mentors and fellow developers in the Laravel community. Your guidance, insights, and shared knowledge have been pivotal in my growth as a Laravel developer. The open collaboration and spirit of learning in the community have inspired me to strive for continuous improvement.

I extend my gratitude to the reviewers and editors who diligently reviewed and refined the content, ensuring its accuracy and clarity.

To my friend Divya Modi, thank you for your unwavering camaraderie and encouragement throughout this journey. Your insights and discussions have enriched my understanding of book development as a whole.

To all the readers and supporters of this book, thank you for your interest in learning and mastering Laravel. Your passion for growth and dedication to honing your skills motivate me to share my knowledge and experiences.

This book would not have been possible without the contributions of each individual mentioned here. Your belief in this project and your unwavering support have been integral to its success.

With sincere appreciation

Introduction

Welcome to *Building Real-Time Marvels with Laravel: Create Dynamic and Interactive Web Applications.* This book will introduce you to the exciting world of Laravel, a powerful PHP framework that allows developers to create cutting-edge web apps with real-time functionality. Whether you're a seasoned developer or just starting out, this thorough tutorial will provide you with the knowledge and skills you need to create remarkable and engaging web experiences with Laravel.

Because of its elegance, simplicity, and feature-rich environment, Laravel has garnered enormous appeal in the online development community. It gives developers a strong collection of tools and conventions that help streamline the development process, letting them focus on creating novel features and great user experiences.

We will cover the Laravel framework in a logical and organized manner, chapter by chapter, throughout this book. Each chapter delves further into the Laravel environment, covering fundamental principles, advanced techniques, and best practices to help you become an expert Laravel developer.

Our goal is to provide you with the knowledge and confidence you need to create real-time miracles—online applications that engage users with dynamic information, interactive interfaces, and seamless communication. This book will walk you through the process of creating a real-time chat application, a collaborative dashboard that displays real-time data, or any other interactive online application.

If you're new to Laravel, don't worry! We'll start with an overview of the Laravel ecosystem, covering its key principles, architecture, and vital components. You will learn how to configure your development environment so that you have everything you need to begin developing Laravel applications.

Fear not, those who are already familiar with Laravel! There are numerous advanced topics available to challenge and extend your knowledge. This book covers a wide range of subjects, from learning complicated routing strategies to fine-tuning database interactions with Eloquent Object-Relational Mapping (ORM) to adding real-time features with WebSockets to improving performance and scaling your applications.

Throughout the journey, you will experience practical examples, real-world use cases, and hands-on exercises to help you understand the ideas covered. Each chapter builds on the one before it, steadily increasing the level of intricacy of the topics discussed. By the end of this book, you will have the knowledge and confidence to create sophisticated online applications that will astound users and advance your Laravel developer career.

So whether you are a curious beginner or a seasoned developer seeking to unlock the full potential of Laravel, fasten your seatbelt as we embark on this exhilarating journey of building real-time marvels with Laravel. Let's dive in!

What Is in This Book?

In this book, *Building Real-Time Marvels with Laravel: Create Dynamic and Interactive Web Applications*, you will

- Master Laravel's fundamentals and set up your development environment

- Explore advanced routing techniques and database management with Eloquent ORM

- Implement user authentication, authorization, and Application Programming Interface (API) building with Laravel

- Learn real-time application development with WebSockets and Laravel Echo

- Enhance performance with caching, optimize database queries, and scale Laravel applications

Throughout the book, you'll find practical examples of testing, security, and integration with third-party services, empowering you to build impressive real-time web applications using Laravel.

Development Environment

The development environment for this book includes

- PHP and Composer for the Laravel framework

- A web server (e.g., Apache or Nginx)

- A database (e.g., MySQL or SQLite)

- An integrated development environment (IDE) (e.g., Visual Studio Code)

- Git for version control

- Laravel's built-in local development server

Chapters at a Glance

Chapter 1, "Understanding the Laravel Ecosystem": In this introductory chapter, we'll take a closer look at the Laravel framework, learning its key features, architecture, and philosophy that make it stand out among other PHP frameworks. You'll discover how to set up your development environment and get ready to embark on a journey through the Laravel ecosystem.

Chapter 2, "Advanced Routing Techniques": Routing is a fundamental aspect of any web application, and Laravel provides a robust routing system. In this chapter, we'll delve into advanced routing techniques, such as working with route parameters and wildcards, route model binding, and route caching. You'll also explore how to group routes using middleware to enhance code organization and maintainability.

Chapter 3, "Database Management and Eloquent ORM": A crucial part of web application development is managing databases effectively. Laravel's Eloquent ORM simplifies database interaction and makes querying and relationship management a breeze. We'll explore database migrations, learn how to create and modify tables, and dive deep into Eloquent relationships, including one-to-one, one-to-many, and many-to-many relationships.

Chapter 4, "Authentication and Authorization": Security is paramount in any web application. In this chapter, we'll cover user authentication, including registration, login, and logout functionality. Additionally, you'll learn how to implement authorization, user roles, and permissions using Laravel's robust authentication and authorization systems.

Chapter 5, "Building APIs with Laravel": APIs play a vital role in modern web application development. In this chapter, we'll explore the world of API development with Laravel, including building RESTful APIs. You'll discover how to handle API authentication and security, rate limiting, and effective error handling to create robust and reliable API endpoints.

Chapter 6, "Caching and Performance Optimization": Performance is a critical aspect of web applications, and Laravel offers powerful caching mechanisms to improve response times. In this chapter, we'll explore Laravel's cache system, learn to implement caching using Redis and Memcached, and discuss cache tagging and cache invalidation strategies. Additionally, you'll discover performance optimization techniques to speed up your Laravel applications.

Chapter 7, "Advanced Middleware Techniques": Middleware plays a vital role in request processing and application logic. In this chapter, we'll go beyond the basics and explore creating custom middleware, understanding the middleware pipeline, and implementing terminable middleware. You'll also learn about middleware parameters and dependencies, along with best practices and performance considerations.

Chapter 8, "Real-Time Applications with Laravel": Real-time features can significantly enhance user experiences. This chapter introduces you to real-time application development with Laravel. We'll explore Laravel WebSockets, Laravel Echo for broadcasting events, and building real-time notifications and chat applications.

Chapter 9, "Testing and Test-Driven Development": Testing is a crucial aspect of building robust and reliable applications. In this chapter, you'll learn the fundamentals of testing in Laravel, including writing unit tests with PHPUnit and testing HTTP requests and responses. We'll also dive into the Test-Driven Development (TDD) workflow, ensuring that your applications are thoroughly tested and bug-free.

Chapter 10, "Queues and Job Scheduling": Laravel's queuing system enables asynchronous processing of tasks, making your application more scalable and efficient. This chapter introduces you to queues and workers, setting up queue drivers and connections, creating and dispatching jobs, and managing failed jobs and retries. You'll also explore Laravel's task scheduler for automating routine tasks.

Chapter 11, "Advanced Package Development": Laravel's robust package development system allows you to create reusable and distributable components. In this chapter, we'll dive into package development, learn to create custom service providers, publish configuration and assets, and test and version your packages for distribution.

Chapter 12, "Performance Monitoring and Debugging": Monitoring the performance of your Laravel applications is essential for identifying bottlenecks and improving efficiency. In this chapter, we'll explore profiling Laravel applications, debugging techniques, and leveraging Laravel Telescope for performance monitoring. We'll also discuss best practices for logging and monitoring application errors.

Chapter 13, "Scaling Laravel Applications": As your application grows, scalability becomes crucial. In this chapter, we'll discuss scaling strategies and considerations, load balancing, horizontal scaling, and database scaling techniques. We'll also explore caching and Content Delivery Networks (CDNs) for better performance.

Chapter 14, "Advanced Error Handling and Exception Management": Effective error handling is crucial for maintaining the stability of your application. In this chapter, you'll learn how to customize error pages and handle exceptions gracefully. We'll explore logging and monitoring application errors, implementing error reporting and alerting systems, and debugging production errors with remote logging and tracing.

Chapter 15, "Building Internationalized Applications with Laravel": As the world becomes more interconnected, building internationalized applications is essential. In this chapter, we'll introduce you to internationalization and localization in Laravel. You'll learn to configure language files, translate database content and user input, and manage locale-specific views and assets.

Chapter 16, "Advanced Frontend Development with Laravel": Seamless integration between the backend and frontend is vital for modern web applications. In this chapter, we'll explore integrating Laravel with modern frontend frameworks, building single-page applications (SPAs) using Laravel and JavaScript, enhancing the user experience with Asynchronous JavaScript and XML (AJAX) and Vue.js components, and implementing real-time updates with Laravel Echo and WebSockets.

Chapter 17, "Advanced Database Techniques and Optimization": Databases are the heart of most web applications, and optimizing database performance is crucial for a seamless user experience. In this chapter, we'll delve into database indexing, query optimization techniques, advanced database relationships, and performance considerations. You'll also learn about implementing database replication and failover strategies for high availability.

Chapter 18, "Laravel and Serverless Computing": Serverless architecture is gaining popularity for its scalability and cost-efficiency. In this chapter, you'll explore integrating Laravel with serverless platforms, leveraging Function as a Service (FaaS), and scaling Laravel applications with serverless autoscaling and event triggers. We'll also cover monitoring and debugging serverless Laravel applications.

Chapter 19, "Building Progressive Web Applications (PWAs) with Laravel": Building PWAs with Laravel provides an enhanced user experience, especially on mobile devices. In this chapter, you'll learn about PWAs and service workers, converting Laravel applications into PWAs, and implementing offline support and caching strategies. We'll also explore push notifications and background sync for improved user engagement.

Chapter 20, "Advanced UI/UX Design Patterns for Laravel": The user interface and user experience are critical for the success of your application. In this chapter, you'll discover how to design user-friendly interfaces with Laravel's Blade templating engine, implement responsive design and mobile optimization techniques, enhance the user experience with CSS animation and transition effects, and design accessible applications. We'll also cover user feedback and usability testing in Laravel applications.

Chapter 21, "Advanced Analytics and Reporting in Laravel": Understanding user behavior and application performance is essential for making informed decisions. In this chapter, you'll explore integrating analytics tools with Laravel, collecting and analyzing application metrics and user behavior, building custom dashboards and reports, and implementing A/B testing and conversion tracking. We'll also discuss using data visualization libraries with Laravel.

Chapter 22, "Advanced Third-Party Integrations": Modern web applications often rely on third-party services for payment processing, authentication, and more. In this chapter, you'll explore integrating Laravel with payment gateways, implementing social media and authentication (OAuth) integrations, connecting Laravel with email marketing services, integrating Laravel with cloud storage providers, and building custom API integrations.

Chapter 23, "Securing Laravel Applications": Security is a top priority in web application development. In this chapter, you'll learn how to implement two-factor authentication (2FA) in Laravel, secure user input and form validation, prevent Cross-Site Scripting (XSS) and Cross-Site Request Forgery (CSRF) attacks, and secure API endpoints with API keys and rate limiting. We'll also explore implementing Content Security Policies (CSPs) and Secure Sockets Layer/ Transport Layer Security (SSL/TLS) encryption for enhanced security.

Chapter 24, "Advanced DevOps and Infrastructure Automation": Automating infrastructure management and deployment pipelines is essential for efficient development workflows. In this chapter, you'll explore Infrastructure as Code (IaC) with Laravel and tools like Terraform, automating deployment pipelines with Laravel and CI/CD tools, implementing application monitoring and log management, and continuous performance optimization and auto-scaling. We'll also discuss building highly available and fault-tolerant Laravel infrastructures.

Chapter 25, "New Features and Updates in Laravel 10": Laravel is continuously evolving, introducing new features and improvements with each release. In this final chapter, we'll explore the latest updates in Laravel, ensuring you stay up to date with the cutting-edge technologies and tools available for building real-time marvels.

Each chapter is thoughtfully crafted to equip you with practical knowledge and real-world skills that you can immediately apply to your own projects. Throughout the book, we provide hands-on examples and code snippets, ensuring you gain a clear understanding of the topics covered.

Prepare to unlock the full potential of Laravel and embark on a journey of building real-time marvels that leave a lasting impression on your users. Let's get started!

CHAPTER 1

Understanding the Laravel Ecosystem

Welcome to this comprehensive guide to the Laravel framework. In this chapter, we will embark on a journey to explore the various aspects of the Laravel ecosystem, gaining insights into one of the most popular and powerful PHP frameworks in the web development world.

Introduction to the Laravel Ecosystem

In this section, we will provide an overview of Laravel, delving into its history, development philosophy, and rise to prominence in the web development community. You'll gain a clear understanding of why Laravel has become the go-to choice for developers seeking a robust and elegant solution for building web applications.

Setting Up the Development Environment

Before we dive into the depths of Laravel, it's essential to set up a proper development environment. Here, we will walk you through the steps required to configure your local environment for Laravel development, ensuring a smooth and productive coding experience.

Key Concepts and Principles of Laravel

Laravel is built upon a set of core principles and concepts that make it unique and efficient. In this section, we will explore these foundational ideas, such as the MVC architecture, Eloquent ORM, routing, middleware, and more. Understanding these concepts is crucial for harnessing the full potential of Laravel.

Exploring the Laravel Ecosystem

Laravel is more than just a framework; it comes with an extensive ecosystem of packages, libraries, and tools that enhance its capabilities. In this section, we will take a closer look at some of the most popular Laravel packages and extensions, demonstrating how they can elevate your development process and make your projects even more powerful.

© Sivaraj Selvaraj 2024
S. Selvaraj, *Building Real-Time Marvels with Laravel*, https://doi.org/10.1007/978-1-4842-9789-6_1

Throughout this chapter, we aim to equip you with a solid understanding of the Laravel ecosystem, setting the stage for deeper exploration and mastery in the chapters to come. So let's begin this exciting journey into the world of Laravel!

Introduction to the Laravel Ecosystem

Taylor Otwell created Laravel in 2011 as an open source PHP web application framework. It quickly gained popularity and is now one of the most popular choices for developing modern web applications. Laravel simplifies and streamlines the web development process with its expressive syntax, developer-friendly features, and elegant design.

The Laravel ecosystem extends beyond the core framework, offering a diverse set of tools and libraries that enhance and supplement its functionality. Laravel Mix for frontend asset compilation, Laravel Horizon for managing and monitoring queues, Laravel Nova for building administration panels, and Laravel Passport for API authentication are all part of the ecosystem. Furthermore, numerous community-driven packages covering a wide range of functionalities and integrations are available through platforms such as Packagist.

Laravel remains at the forefront of web development frameworks, making it a top choice for developers that place a premium on project productivity, maintainability, and scalability. Whether you are a novice or an experienced developer, the Laravel ecosystem provides a comprehensive and powerful toolkit for quickly creating impressive web applications. Figure 1-1 illustrates the Model-View-Controller (MVC) architectural pattern.

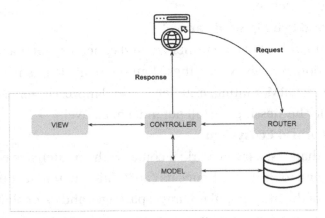

Figure 1-1. *MVC diagram*

MVC Pattern

Routes: Routes define the URLs and corresponding controller actions. They map incoming requests to the appropriate controller method.

Controllers: Controllers handle user requests and manage the flow of data. They receive input from users, interact with models, and return responses. Controllers contain methods (actions) that define the logic for each route.

Models: Models represent the data and business logic of the application. They interact with the database and provide an abstraction layer for retrieving, creating, updating, and deleting data. Models encapsulate the application's data structure and define relationships between entities.

Views: Views are responsible for presenting data to users. They contain the HTML templates and UI components that render the final output. Views can access data from models and controllers to display information.

Structure of the Framework

The 'app' directory contains the core application code, including console commands, exception handlers, HTTP-related classes (controllers, middleware, requests, and resources), and models.

The 'bootstrap' directory contains the bootstrap files responsible for bootstrapping the Laravel application.

The 'config' directory contains configuration files for various aspects of the application, such as database connections, caching, session management, etc.

The 'database' directory houses files related to the database, including factories for generating dummy data, migrations for managing database schema changes, and seeders for populating the database with initial data.

The 'public' directory serves as the document root for the application. It contains the front controller ('index.php') and publicly accessible assets like CSS, JavaScript, and image files.

The 'resources' directory holds non-PHP resources, including JavaScript files, CSS stylesheets, and views (Blade templates) used for rendering HTML.

The 'routes' directory contains route definitions that map URLs to corresponding controllers and actions.

The 'storage' directory is used for storing various types of data generated by the application, such as uploaded files, cached data, logs, etc.

The 'tests' directory houses the application's automated tests.

The 'vendor' directory contains the dependencies installed via Composer.

The '.env' file stores environment-specific configuration settings.

The 'artisan' file is the command-line interface for interacting with the Laravel application.

The 'composer.json' file defines the project's dependencies and provides metadata about the application.

This structure is a standard layout for a Laravel application, although you may find some additional files and directories depending on the specific requirements of your project. Figure 1-2 illustrates the Laravel application structure diagram.

Figure 1-2. *Laravel application structure diagram*

Its philosophy revolves around developer productivity, with a focus on reducing repetitive tasks and providing convenient solutions for common web development challenges.

One of the key strengths of Laravel is its vibrant and active community. The community actively contributes to the framework by developing packages; sharing knowledge through documentation, tutorials, and forums; and continuously improving the overall Laravel ecosystem.

Setting Up the Development Environment

Before diving into Laravel development, it's essential to set up the development environment. This involves installing the necessary software and tools to run Laravel applications. Let's explore the steps involved in setting up the development environment.

PHP (Hypertext Preprocessor)

PHP is a server-side scripting language for web development. It's commonly used to build dynamic web pages and web apps. PHP code is run on the server, which generates HTML, which is then transmitted to the client's web browser.

Install PHP

Download and install PHP 7.4 or higher from the official PHP website (`www.php.net/downloads.php`). Verify the installation by running 'php -v' in the command prompt. You should see the PHP version displayed.

Web Server

A web server is a piece of software that runs on a server computer and monitors incoming HTTP requests from clients (web browsers). It processes these requests and returns to the customers the necessary web pages or resources. Web servers that are often used include Apache, Nginx, and Microsoft IIS.

Install a Web Server

Configure the web server to serve PHP files. For example, in Apache, you can enable the 'mod_php' module. Verify the web server installation by accessing 'http://localhost' in your web browser. You should see a default web page.

Database (DB)

A database is a systematic collection of data that has been arranged and stored in order to be easily retrieved and manipulated. It is used to store and manage application data such as user information, product details, and other information. Databases commonly used in web development include MySQL, PostgreSQL, and SQLite.

Install a Database

Choose a database management system like MySQL, PostgreSQL, or SQLite and install it on your machine. Create a new database for your Laravel application.

Configure the database connection in the Laravel '.env' file.

For Illustration, refer to the following snippet:

```
DB_CONNECTION=mysql
DB_HOST=127.0.0.1
DB_PORT=3306
DB_DATABASE=your_database
DB_USERNAME=your_username
DB_PASSWORD=your_password
```

Composer

Composer is a PHP dependency management tool. It makes it easier to manage PHP packages and libraries in your project. It lets you declare the libraries on which your project depends and then installs and updates them automatically, delivering a consistent and reliable development environment.

Install Composer:

Installation for Linux, Unix, or macOS

Users using Linux, Unix, or macOS can install Composer by following the instructions in the URL provided (https://getcomposer.org/doc/00-intro.md#installation-linux-unix-macos).

Installation for Windows

For Windows users, the installation process is slightly different. Follow these steps to install Composer:

Download and install Composer from the official website (https://getcomposer.org/download/).

Verify the installation by running 'composer --version' in the command prompt. You should see the Composer version displayed.

Install Laravel

Open a command prompt, navigate to the desired directory for your Laravel project, and run the following command:

```
composer create-project --prefer-dist laravel/laravel your-project-name
```

Replace 'your-project-name' with the desired name for your Laravel project.

Composer will download and install Laravel and its dependencies.

Configure Environment Variables

Duplicate the '. env.example' file in the root of your Laravel project and rename it to '.env'.

Update the '.env' file with your database connection details and other configuration settings, such as the application key.

Generate an Application Key

The application key in Laravel is a random 32-character string that is used for different security purposes such as encryption, hashing, and cookie signing. It is generated during the initial setup of a Laravel application and must be kept secure.

Run the following command within your project directory to generate an application key:

```
php artisan key: generate
```

This command will produce a random key and store it in your Laravel project's .env file, specifically in the APP_KEY variable. The key will resemble the following:

```
bash base64 copy code:QqRchgn5/23n+js1FIoMBy3V9T2tYsa9vnruOHdr2Ns=
```

Keep the application key private and avoid distributing it publicly or storing it in version control repositories. If you need to regenerate the key for whatever reason, simply run the key:generate command again, and a new key will be generated and saved in the .env file.

Run the Development Server

Start the Laravel development server by running the following command:

```
php artisan serve
```

Access your Laravel application at 'http://localhost:8000' in your web browser.

Your Laravel development environment is now set up. You can start developing your web application by creating routes, controllers, models, and views using the Laravel framework.

Key Concepts and Principles of Laravel

Laravel is built around several key concepts and principles that contribute to its effectiveness and ease of use. Understanding these concepts is essential for working efficiently with the framework. Let's explore these key concepts in brief.

Routing

Routing in Laravel refers to defining how incoming HTTP requests should be handled. Routes define the URLs and map them to specific controller actions. For example, you can define a route that maps the "/users" URL to a UserController's index action. Routes provide a clean and expressive way to handle different HTTP methods (GET, POST, PUT, and DELETE) and parameters.

For Illustration, refer to the following snippet:

```
Route::get('/users', 'UserController@index');
```

CRUD Routing

Let's now create CRUD (Create, Read, Update, Delete) routes for managing blog posts:

```
// routes/web.php
use App\Http\Controllers\BlogController;
// Show the list of blog posts
Route::get('/posts', [BlogController::class, 'index']);
// Show the form for creating a new blog post
Route::get('/posts/create', [BlogController::class, 'create']);
// Store a newly created blog post
Route::post('/posts', [BlogController::class, 'store']);
// Show a specific blog post
Route::get('/posts/{id}', [BlogController::class, 'show']);
// Show the form for editing a blog post
Route::get('/posts/{id}/edit', [BlogController::class, 'edit']);
```

```
// Update a specific blog post
Route::put('/posts/{id}', [BlogController::class, 'update']);
// Delete a specific blog post
Route::delete('/posts/{id}', [BlogController::class, 'destroy']);
```

In the preceding example, we constructed routes for complete CRUD actions on blog posts. These pathways correspond to the actions listed in the following:

> index: This function displays a list of all blog posts.

> create: Display a form for creating a new blog post.

> store: Save the freshly created blog post to the database.

> show: Display a certain blog post.

> edit: Show a form for editing an existing blog entry.

> update: In the database, update an existing blog post.

> destroy: Removes a particular blog post from the database.

Controllers

Controllers in Laravel are responsible for handling user requests and managing the flow of data in the application. Controllers contain methods, also known as actions, that are invoked when a specific route is accessed. They receive user input, interact with models and services, and return responses to the user. Controllers help separate the logic of an application from the routing layer.

For Illustration, refer to the following snippet:

```
class UserController extends Controller {
    public function index() {
        $users = User::all();
        return view('users.index', ['users' => $users]);
    }
}
```

Now navigate to the app/Http/Controllers directory and double-click the newly created BlogController. Define the mechanisms for dealing with CRUD operations:

```
// app/Http/Controllers/UserController.php
namespace App\Http\Controllers;
use Illuminate\Http\Request;
use App\Models\User;
class UserController extends Controller
{
    // Show the list of users
    public function index()
    {
        $users = User::all();
        return view('users.index', ['users' => $users]);
    }
    // Show the form for creating a new user
    public function create()
    {
        return view('users.create');
    }
    // Store a newly created user in the database
    public function store(Request $request)
    {
        $validatedData = $request->validate([
            'name' => 'required|string|max:255',
            'email' => 'required|email|unique:users,email',
            'password' => 'required|string|min:8',
        ]);
        $user = User::create($validatedData);
        return redirect()->route('users.show', ['user' => $user->id]);
    }
    // Show a specific user
    public function show(User $user)
    {
        return view('users.show', ['user' => $user]);
    }
```

11

```
// Show the form for editing a user
public function edit(User $user)
{
    return view('users.edit', ['user' => $user]);
}
// Update a specific user in the database
public function update(Request $request, User $user)
{
    $validatedData = $request->validate([
        'name' => 'required|string|max:255',
        'email' => 'required|email|unique:users,email,' . $user->id,
        'password' => 'nullable|string|min:8',
    ]);
    $user->update($validatedData);
```

We've added extra methods for the remaining CRUD activities in this modified UserController example:

create: This function returns a view with a form for creating a new user.

store: This method handles the form submission from the create view. It validates the user input, creates a new user record in the database, and then redirects to the show page of the newly created user.

show: This method provides information about a certain user. It takes a User model instance as an argument, which is resolved automatically from the URL parameter (user).

edit: This function produces a view with a form for editing an existing user. It also accepts a parameter of a User model instance, which will be resolved from the URL parameter (user).

update: This function handles the form submission from the edit view. It checks user input, updates the user record in the database, and then redirects to the revised user's show page.

destroy: Removes a specific user from the database. It also makes use of the User model object made available by Laravel's route model binding.

Views

Views in Laravel are responsible for presenting data to the user. They provide an HTML representation of the application's output. Laravel uses the Blade templating engine, which offers a concise and expressive syntax for working with HTML and PHP. Views can receive data from controllers and display it to the user, allowing for a clear separation between presentation and logic.

For Illustration, refer to the following snippet:

```
<!DOCTYPE html>
<html>
<head>
    <title>User List</title>
</head>
<body>
    <h1>User List</h1>
    <ul>
        @foreach($users as $user)
            <li>{{ $user->name }}</li>
        @endforeach
    </ul>
</body>
</html>
```

You would perform the following to display this view from the UserController's index method:

```
// app/Http/Controllers/UserController.php
namespace App\Http\Controllers;
use Illuminate\Http\Request;
use App\Models\User;
class UserController extends Controller
{
    public function index()
```

```
    {
        $users = User::all();
        return view('users.index', ['users' => $users]);
    }
    // Other methods (create, store, show, edit, update, destroy) can be
defined here as well
}
```

We get all the users from the database using User::all() in the UserController's index method and then provide the $users collection to the view using the view() function. The view() function takes two arguments: the path to the view and an associative array with keys representing the variable names accessible in the view and values representing the data that will be available in those variables. In this scenario, we provide the $users collection to the view's users variable.

Models

Models in Laravel represent the data and business logic of the application. They interact with the database through Laravel's Object-Relational Mapping (ORM) called Eloquent.

Models provide an abstraction layer that allows you to work with database records as objects.

Eloquent assumes that the associated database table for the User model is named users by default. If your table name is different, you can indicate it in the model by setting the $table property.

For Illustration, refer to the following snippet:

```
class User extends Model
{
    protected $table = 'custom_users_table';
}
```

Eloquent in Laravel will utilize this custom_users_table as the table for the User model by default.

Migrations

Migrations in Laravel provide a convenient way to manage database schema changes using code. They allow you to create and modify database tables in a structured manner, keeping track of versioning. Migrations make it easier to collaborate with other developers and deploy changes to different environments. Laravel's migration system abstracts the database-specific syntax, making it portable across different database systems.

For Illustration, refer to the following snippet:

```
class CreateUsersTable extends Migration {
    public function up() {
        Schema::create('users', function (Blueprint $table) {
            $table->increments('id');
            $table->string('name');
            $table->string('email')->unique();
            $table->timestamps();
        });
    }
    public function down() {
        Schema::dropIfExists('users');
    }
}
```

We have a migration called CreateUsersTable in this example. The up method is in charge of generating the users table with the necessary columns, and the down method is in charge of removing the users table if the migration is rolled back.

The migration is broken down as follows:

Schema::create('users', ...): users is a new table that is created.

$table->increments('id'): Inserts an auto-incrementing primary key column id into the table.

$table->string('name'): Inserts a column of type VARCHAR named name.

$table->string('email')->unique(): Inserts and makes a column named email of type VARCHAR unique.

$table->timestamps(): Adds two columns for recording timestamps when a record is generated or updated: created_at and updated_at.

Middleware

Middleware in Laravel acts as a bridge between the incoming HTTP request and your application. It can intercept requests and perform tasks such as authentication, authorization, input validation, and more.

Middleware allows you to modify the request and response objects, making it a powerful tool for handling cross-cutting concerns. Laravel provides various middleware out of the box, and you can create custom middleware as per your application's needs.

For Illustration, refer to the following snippet:

```
class AuthenticateMiddleware {
    public function handle($request, $next) {
        if (!Auth::check()) {
            return redirect('/login');
        }
        return $next($request);
    }
}
```

The middleware is broken out as follows:

The handle method: In Laravel, every middleware must implement a handle method that takes two parameters: $request and $next.

Auth::check(): Determines whether or not the user is authenticated. If the user is authorized, the Auth::check() method returns true; otherwise, it returns false.

return redirect('/login'): The middleware returns the user to the login page if they are not authenticated.

return $next($request): If the user is authenticated, the middleware uses the $next closure to transfer the request to the next middleware in the pipeline. This permits the request to go to the desired route or controller action.

These key concepts form the foundation of Laravel and provide a solid structure for building web applications. By understanding and leveraging these concepts, you can develop robust and maintainable applications using Laravel's powerful features and conventions.

Exploring the Laravel Ecosystem

The Laravel ecosystem extends beyond the core framework and includes a wide range of components, packages, tools, and resources that enhance the development experience. Let's explore some important components of the Laravel ecosystem.

Laravel Packages

Laravel has a vibrant community that develops and maintains numerous packages, which are available through Composer. These packages offer additional functionality and can be easily integrated into Laravel projects.

They cover a wide range of areas such as authentication, caching, queuing, image manipulation, payment gateways, API integrations, and more. Some popular Laravel packages include Laravel Debugbar, Laravel Telescope, Laravel Cashier, and Laravel Passport.

For Illustration, refer to the following snippet.

To integrate a package like Laravel Debugbar into your Laravel project, you can simply require it using Composer:

```
composer require barryvdh/laravel-debugbar
```

Then, follow the package's documentation to configure and use it in your application.

Laravel Forge

Laravel Forge is a server provisioning and deployment platform specifically designed for Laravel applications. It simplifies the process of setting up and managing servers, configuring databases, and deploying Laravel projects to production environments.

Forge provides a user-friendly web interface and automates tasks such as server configuration, SSL certificate management, and scheduled backups. It supports popular cloud hosting providers like DigitalOcean, AWS, Linode, and more.

With Laravel Forge, you can quickly provision a server, select your desired cloud provider, configure the server settings, and deploy your Laravel application with just a few clicks.

Laravel Valet

Laravel Valet is a development environment for macOS that provides a lightweight and convenient way to run Laravel applications locally.

Valet configures your system to automatically serve your Laravel projects without the need for complex server configurations like Apache or Nginx.

It uses Dnsmasq and Nginx under the hood to create a seamless development experience.

After installing Valet, you can simply navigate to your Laravel project's directory and access it through a local domain like '`http://project-name.test`'.

Laravel Homestead

Laravel Homestead is a pre-packaged Vagrant box that provides a complete development environment for Laravel. It includes all the necessary software, tools, and configurations to quickly get started with Laravel development.

Homestead abstracts the complexities of setting up a local development environment, allowing you to focus on building your Laravel applications.

After installing Homestead, you can define your Laravel projects in the 'Homestead. yaml' file, and Homestead will automatically configure the virtual machine with the necessary software and mappings to run your projects.

Laravel Mix

Laravel Mix is a wrapper around the popular JavaScript build tool Webpack. It simplifies the process of managing and compiling frontend assets such as CSS, JavaScript, and image files.

Laravel Mix provides a clean and intuitive API for defining frontend asset build tasks, enabling you to leverage the power of Webpack without the need for complex configuration.

Using Laravel Mix, you can define tasks in your 'webpack.mix.js' file to compile Sass to CSS, bundle JavaScript modules, optimize images, and more. Running the 'npm run dev' command will trigger the asset compilation.

Laravel Documentation and Community

Laravel has extensive and well-documented resources available online, including official documentation, tutorials, and forums. The official Laravel documentation provides in-depth explanations of Laravel's features, concepts, and usage.

The Laravel community is active and supportive, with many developers sharing their knowledge and experiences through blog posts, tutorials, forums, and social media platforms. Engaging with the Laravel community can provide valuable insights, assistance, and opportunities for collaboration.

Summary

In this chapter, we delved into the vast Laravel environment. The chapter introduced Laravel, a popular PHP framework, as well as its various components, emphasizing their roles and significance in modern web development. You learned about the fundamental Model-View-Controller (MVC) architectural paradigm that underpins Laravel. The benefits of using Laravel in web application development were discussed, including its expressive syntax and developer-friendly features. The chapter also emphasized the significance of Composer, a sophisticated dependency management tool.

CHAPTER 2

Advanced Routing Techniques

In the previous chapter, we looked at the fundamentals of the Laravel ecosystem, gaining valuable insight into the framework's core concepts and principles. We also discovered a plethora of packages and tools that can help us improve our development process and efficiently build powerful web applications.

Now, building on what we learned in the previous chapter, we're ready to delve into the complexities of Laravel's routing system. This chapter will guide us through the process of mastering advanced routing techniques that will enable us to create flexible, dynamic, and efficient routes for our web applications.

In this chapter, we will cover the following:

Route Parameters and Wildcards

Laravel's route parameters and wildcards are essential tools for handling dynamic segments in our URLs. We will explore how to define and use route parameters and wildcards to accept various user inputs and create routes that adapt to different scenarios seamlessly.

Route Model Binding

Route model binding is a powerful feature that simplifies data retrieval from the database by automatically injecting model instances into our route closures or controller methods. By learning route model binding, we can streamline our code and enhance the readability of our routes while effortlessly working with database records.

Route Caching

Route caching is a performance optimization technique that significantly improves the response time of our applications by converting route definitions into a cached file. We will discover how to leverage route caching to minimize the overhead of route registration, resulting in faster and more responsive web applications.

© Sivaraj Selvaraj 2024
S. Selvaraj, *Building Real-Time Marvels with Laravel*, https://doi.org/10.1007/978-1-4842-9789-6_2

Middleware and Route Grouping

Middleware plays a vital role in Laravel's HTTP processing, providing an elegant way to filter incoming requests. This section will guide us through the effective use of middleware and route grouping, enabling us to apply middleware to specific groups of routes, enhance security, and maintain a well-organized codebase.

By the end of this chapter, we will have honed our skills in advanced routing techniques, equipping us with the expertise to design sophisticated, user-friendly, and high-performance routes for our Laravel applications. So let's embark on this journey to unlock the full potential of Laravel's routing system and elevate our web development capabilities!

Route Parameters and Wildcards

In Laravel, creating dynamic and flexible routes is vital for building robust web applications. Route parameters and wildcards are two key features that play a significant role in enabling this flexibility.

Route parameters are placeholders within the route definition that allow developers to capture specific segments from a URL. By defining these parameters, developers can extract dynamic values from the URL and use them as inputs for their application logic.

On the other hand, wildcards offer even more flexibility by matching multiple URL segments. They enable capturing variable or arbitrary parts of the URL, making it possible to handle various dynamic scenarios efficiently.

Leveraging route parameters and wildcards in Laravel routes empowers developers to build dynamic web applications that respond to different user inputs, enhancing the user experience with seamless and intuitive interactions. These features enable developers to create adaptable and powerful routes, catering to a wide range of use cases.

Route Parameters

Route parameters allow for the definition of dynamic segments within a URL pattern. Instead of specifying a fixed value for a segment, a placeholder is used to match any value in that position. This enables the extraction of relevant information from the URL to be used in the application logic.

The most common syntax for defining route parameters is to enclose them in curly braces '{}'.

For Illustration, refer to the following snippet:

```
/users/{id}
Route::get('/hello/{name}', function ($name) {
    return 'Hello, ' . $name . '!';
});
```

In this example, '{id}' is a route parameter that matches any value in that segment of the URL. When a URL matches this pattern, the actual user ID can be extracted and utilized in the application code to retrieve the corresponding user data.

When you visit a URL like http://yourdomain.com/hello/Divya, Laravel will extract the value "Divya" from the name segment and provide it to the closure as the $name parameter. The closure will then return the message, "Hello, Divya!"

Route parameters provide a powerful way to handle dynamic segments in URLs, allowing for more flexible and customizable routing. By capturing specific values from the URL, applications can respond accordingly and provide dynamic content or functionality.

Wildcards

Wildcards offer even greater flexibility in handling URL patterns. They allow for the matching of multiple segments or entire sections of a URL, accommodating more complex and hierarchical routing scenarios.

There are two common types of wildcards:

- Single-segment wildcard

- Multi-segment wildcard

Single-Segment Wildcard

The single-segment wildcard is denoted by an asterisk '*' or a double asterisk '**'. It matches a single segment within the URL:

```
-------------------------------------------------------------------
/products/*
-------------------------------------------------------------------
```

This pattern will match any URL that starts with '/products/' followed by any segment. The matched segment can then be extracted and used for further processing, such as retrieving product information or applying specific routing logic.

For Illustration, refer to the following snippet:

```
-------------------------------------------------------------------
Route::get('/products/{any}', function ($any) {
    return 'You are viewing the product: '. $any;
});
-------------------------------------------------------------------
```

Save the file.

When you visit a URL like http://yourdomain.com/products/laptop, Laravel will extract the value "laptop" from any segment and provide it to the closure as the $any parameter. The closing will then return the message "You are viewing the product: laptop".

Similarly, if you go to http://yourdomain.com/products/smartphone, Laravel will extract "smartphone", and the closure will return "You are viewing the product: smartphone".

The single-segment wildcard * allows you to catch any value following /products/ and utilize it in your application logic for processing or routing.

Multi-segment Wildcard

The multi-segment wildcard, denoted by a double asterisk '**', matches multiple segments or an entire section of a URL.

For Illustration, refer to the following snippet:

```
-------------------------------------------------------------------
/content//images
-------------------------------------------------------------------
```

This pattern will match any URL that contains '/content/' followed by any number of segments and ends with '/images'. The matched segments can be extracted and used as needed, allowing for more dynamic routing and handling of hierarchical data structures.

Wildcards provide a powerful mechanism for handling diverse and evolving URL patterns. By using wildcards, applications can handle a wide range of URLs without explicitly defining each possible variation, resulting in more adaptable and maintainable routing systems.

Both route parameters and wildcards enhance the versatility of routing mechanisms, providing developers with the tools to build robust and adaptable web applications. By leveraging these advanced routing techniques, applications can accommodate dynamic URL structures and handle complex routing scenarios effectively.

Route Model Binding

Route model binding is a strong Laravel framework feature that streamlines the process of retrieving model data from the database and binding it to route parameters. It enables you to automatically inject model objects into route callbacks or controller functions, resulting in clearer, more expressive, and more efficient code.

Route Binding

You frequently need to retrieve data from the database based on route parameters when designing routes in Laravel.

Consider the following route, which displays a specific post based on its ID:

```
// Retrieve and display a specific post
Route::get('posts/{id}', function ($id) {
    $post = App\Models\Post::findOrFail($id);
    return view('post.show', compact('post'));
});
```

The route parameter id is manually used in this example to fetch the relevant Post model from the database. This approach, however, becomes considerably simpler with route model binding.

There are two types of route model binding in Laravel:

- Implicit route model binding

- Explicit route model binding

Implicit Route Model Binding

Implicit route model binding allows you to automatically bind route parameters to model instances without any additional configuration. Laravel chooses which model to fetch depending on the name of the route parameter and the type hint in the route callback or controller method.

You may use implicit route model binding by simply hinting at the model class in the route closure or controller method, for example:

```
use App\Models\Post;
Route::get('posts/{post}', function (Post $post) {
    return view('post.show', compact('post'));
});
```

Laravel will retrieve the Post model instance based on the post route argument, provided your Post model has a primary key named ID. If the provided post does not exist, Laravel will generate a 404 error.

Explicit Route Model Binding

Explicit route model binding allows you to define the binding behavior for certain route parameters. It allows you more flexibility over model instance retrieval.

To use explicit route model binding, create a binding in the RouteServiceProvider's boot method. This method may be found in the file app/Providers/RouteServiceProvider.php.

For the Post model, here's an example of explicit route model binding:

```
use App\Models\Post;
public function boot()
{
    parent::boot();
    Route::model('post', Post::class);
    // Alternatively, you can use a closure to resolve the model instance:
    // Route::bind('post', function ($value) {
```

```
//      return Post::where('slug', $value)->firstOrFail();
//  });
}
```

With explicit binding, if you have a route parameter named post, Laravel will automatically fetch the associated Post model instance based on the provided value (e.g., post slug). In the preceding example, we assume that the database recognizes postings by their slug column.

When you use explicit route model binding, you may add additional logic to the model retrieval process, which can be handy for dealing with special instances where the route parameter does not correlate exactly to the primary key.

Customizing Route Model Binding

The explicit route model binding technique allows you to define the route model binding behavior for certain route parameters. This enables you to build custom logic for retrieving the model instance based on the route parameter value provided. Additional database queries can be run, or the model instance can be retrieved depending on various columns or criteria.

To personalize route binding for a given model, add a binding callback to the RouteServiceProvider class's boot function, which is normally located at app/Providers/RouteServiceProvider.php. Assume you have an Article model and wish to tie it to the slug route parameter instead of the default main key binding.

Here's how you can customize route binding for the **Article** model:

```
use App\Models\Article;
public function boot()
{
    parent::boot();
    Route::bind('article', function ($value) {
        // Your custom logic to retrieve the Article instance based on 'slug'
        return Article::where('slug', $value)->firstOrFail();
    });
}
```

In this example, we use the **bind** method on the **Route** facade to define a custom binding for the **article** route parameter. The closure receives the value of the route parameter (in this case, the **slug**) and returns the corresponding **Article** model instance. We use **firstOrFail** to automatically handle the case when no matching article is found, and Laravel will return a 404 response if needed.

With this customization, when you define a route that contains **{article}** in its URI, Laravel will automatically retrieve the **Article** model instance based on the provided **slug** value.

For Illustration, refer to the following snippet:

```
Route::get('articles/{article}', function (Article $article) {
    return view('articles.show', compact('article'));
});
```

Now, when you visit a URL like **/articles/my-article-slug**, Laravel will automatically fetch the corresponding **Article** model based on the provided **slug**, and you can directly use the **$article** variable in your route closure.

Remember that the route parameter name (in this case, **article**) in the **bind** method should match the parameter name in your route definition and the type hint in the route closure.

Custom Route Keys

By default, route model binding assumes that the route parameter name matches the primary key of the model. However, if the model uses a different attribute as its key, developers can define a route key on the model to specify which attribute should be used for binding.

For Illustration, let's assume a Post model has a unique 'slug' attribute that serves as the key:

```
class Post extends Model
{
    public function getRouteKeyName()
    {
```

```
        return 'slug';
    }
}
```

By implementing the 'getRouteKeyName()' method in the 'Post' model, developers can specify that the 'slug' attribute should be used as the route key for model binding. This means that when a URL contains a 'Post' slug in the route parameter, the route model binding will retrieve the corresponding 'Post' instance using the 'slug' attribute instead of the primary key.

Custom Binding Resolution

In some cases, route model binding default resolution logic may not be sufficient for retrieving models. Developers might need to customize how the models are fetched. This can be achieved by defining a binding resolution callback in the route definition:

```
Route::get('/posts/{post}', function (Post $post) {
    // Custom resolution logic for retrieving the post
});
```

In this example, the closure function receives the resolved 'Post' model instance as an argument. Developers can apply their own resolution logic within the closure to fetch the model instance based on the provided route parameter.

This allows for more flexibility in retrieving models according to specific requirements.

Assuming you have a Post model that represents your post table, proceed as follows:
Navigate to your routes/web.php file.
Define the custom binding resolution route:

```
use App\Models\Post;
Route::get('/posts/{post}', function (Post $post) {
    // Custom resolution logic for retrieving the post
    // For example, you can add additional processing or fetch related data
        before returning a response.
```

```
    $comments = $post->comments;
    $author = $post->author;
    // Now, you can return a view with the post and related data.
    return view ('post.show', compact ('post', 'comments', 'author'));
});
```

Save the file.

When a GET request is made to the URL /posts/1, Laravel's route model binding mechanism will automatically download the associated Post model instance with an ID of 1 and provide it to the closure as the $post parameter.

Within the closure, you can use your unique resolution logic to retrieve related data, apply certain filters, or perform any other necessary processing before delivering a response. In this example, we retrieved the comments and author of the post to utilize in the view.

Finally, the closure provides a view (in this case, post.show) that displays the post as well as any relevant data that was retrieved using your custom resolution logic.

By including the anonymous function in the route design, you get the ability to adjust the model retrieval to the unique requirements for each route, resulting in a more tailored and efficient way to manage your application's needs.

Benefits of Route Model Binding

Route model binding offers several benefits:

Convenience: By automatically fetching and injecting model instances based on route parameters, route model binding eliminates the need for manual retrieval, reducing boilerplate code.

Readability: By directly injecting model instances into route handlers or controllers, the code becomes more expressive and easier to understand, as the intention is clear.

Flexibility: Developers can customize the binding behavior to match specific requirements by defining custom route keys or implementing custom resolution logic for fetching models.

Consistency: Route model binding promotes consistency by enforcing a standardized approach to retrieving models throughout the application, enhancing maintainability.

Route model binding is a powerful feature that streamlines the process of retrieving and injecting model instances in web applications.

By leveraging this technique, developers can improve code readability, reduce redundant code, and create more efficient and maintainable routing systems.

Route Caching

Routing is a critical aspect of web applications as it determines how incoming requests are directed to specific handlers or controllers. As applications grow in complexity, the process of parsing and interpreting route configurations on each request can introduce performance overhead. To address this, advanced routing techniques include route caching, a mechanism for precompiling and storing route definitions to optimize routing lookups and enhance application performance.

How does route caching work?

In a typical web application, the routing system reads route definitions from files or configuration files for each incoming request. This process involves parsing the route definitions, building a routing table, and matching the requested URL against the defined routes to determine the appropriate handler or controller.

Route caching streamlines this process by precomputing the routing information and storing it in a cached file. During the route caching step, the application compiles the route definitions into a format that can be quickly accessed and searched during runtime. This compilation step is typically performed during the deployment process or when the route definitions are modified.

When the application is in production mode and route caching is enabled, the routing system reads the precompiled routes from the cache file instead of parsing the route files on each request. This allows for much faster routing lookups as the application can quickly search the cached routes and determine the appropriate handler or controller for a given URL.

A number of factors and considerations influence the decision to utilize or deactivate route caching in a Laravel application. The following are some instances in which route caching should be enabled or disabled.

Ideal Cases for Enabling Route Caching

Production setting: Enabling route caching is strongly advised in a production setting when performance and response times are crucial. It reduces the overhead of route parsing and increases the application's overall speed and scalability.

Stable routes: If your application's routes are pretty stable and do not change frequently, route caching becomes more advantageous. Caching routes during deployment or after revisions ensures speedier routing lookups during normal operation.

High-traffic applications: Route caching might be useful for applications that experience high traffic and a large number of incoming requests. It reduces the computational overhead of parsing routes on each request, resulting in improved performance under high demand.

Resource-constrained setups: Enabling route caching can help conserve resources and improve application responsiveness in circumstances when server resources are limited, such as shared hosting setups.

Ideal Scenarios to Disable Route Caching

Development environment: It is advisable to disable route caching during development and debugging. Developers frequently change routes, and having to delete the cache each time can be inconvenient. Laravel automatically recompiles routes in the development environment with each request, enabling faster testing of route changes.

Dynamic routes: Disabling route caching is recommended if your application extensively relies on dynamic routes with changing parameters or patterns. Frequent route changes may result in excessive cache cleaning, limiting the benefits of caching.

Routes with middleware groups: Disabling route caching may be preferable if your routes use middleware groups and these groups change frequently. Middleware groups can have an impact on route behavior, and recompiling the cache every time they change can be inconvenient.

Debugging and troubleshooting: Disabling route caching is useful for analyzing routing difficulties or debugging route-related problems. You may verify that the application reads the most recent route definitions directly from the route files this way.

Enabling and Disabling Route Caching

The process of enabling route caching varies depending on the web framework or routing system being used. Typically, a specific command or configuration option is used to generate the route cache file.

For Illustration, in Laravel, a popular PHP framework, route caching can be enabled by running the following command:

```
php artisan route:cache
```

This command compiles the route definitions into a cache file, enhancing the application's routing performance.

To disable route caching and revert to dynamic route parsing, a corresponding command or configuration option is used:

```
php artisan route:clear
```

This command clears the route cache file and allows the application to read and interpret the route definitions dynamically again.

Benefits of Route Caching

Route caching provides several benefits to web applications:

Improved performance: By precompiling and caching route definitions, route caching significantly reduces the overhead of dynamic route parsing on each request. This leads to faster routing lookups and improved response times for the application.

```
// Laravel route caching example
// routes/web.php
Route::get('/users', 'UserController@index');
Route::get('/users/{id}', 'UserController@show');
Route::post('/users', 'UserController@store');
```

Without route caching, on each request, Laravel would need to parse the 'web. php' file to determine the appropriate handler for the requested URL. With route caching enabled, the parsing step is skipped, and the application directly looks up the precompiled routes, significantly improving performance.

Optimized resource utilization: With route caching, the application can focus more on processing requests and serving content rather than repeatedly parsing and interpreting route configurations. This allows for better utilization of server resources and improved scalability.

```php
use App\Http\Controllers\UserController;
// Route for listing all users
Route::get('/users', [UserController::class, 'index']);
// Route for showing a single user by ID
Route::get('/users/{id}', [UserController::class, 'show']);
// Route for creating a new user
Route::post('/users', [UserController::class, 'store']);
```

With route caching enabled, Laravel will directly use the precompiled routes instead of reading and parsing the web.php file on every request, resulting in increased performance, optimized resource utilization, and greater scalability.

Enhanced scalability: Route caching enhances the scalability of web applications by reducing the processing time required for route lookups. This enables the application to handle a larger number of concurrent requests without sacrificing performance.

```php
// Laravel route caching example continued
// After enabling route caching with "php artisan route:cache"
// routes/web.php.cache
return [
  '/users' => 'UserController@index',
  '/users/{id}' => 'UserController@show',
  '/users' => 'UserController@store',
];
```

With route caching, the Laravel application uses the precompiled cache file instead of parsing the 'web.php' file. This allows the application to quickly match the requested URL to the appropriate handler, enabling efficient handling of a high volume of concurrent requests.

Enhanced security: Caching route definitions can improve the security of the application by reducing the exposure of route configuration files. With route caching enabled, the application does not expose the route files, making it harder for potential attackers to gain insight into the application's internal structure.

By preventing direct access to route configuration files, route caching adds an extra layer of security. Attackers would have a harder time gathering information about the application's endpoints and potential vulnerabilities.

Considerations and Limitations

While route caching offers significant performance benefits, there are a few considerations to keep in mind:

Dynamic routes: Route caching is most effective for applications with static or unchanging route configurations. If routes need to be modified dynamically at runtime, such as for dynamic route parameters or custom routing logic, route caching may not be suitable.

For Illustration, an ecommerce application that generates dynamic routes based on product availability or user preferences may require dynamic route parsing. In such cases, it's essential to carefully evaluate the caching strategy to ensure dynamic routes are handled correctly.

Maintenance and deployment: When making changes to the route definitions, the route cache must be cleared and regenerated to reflect the updated routes. This requires appropriate maintenance and deployment processes to ensure that the route cache is consistently up to date.

It is important to incorporate a clear process for clearing and regenerating the route cache whenever changes to the route definitions occur. This ensures that the application accurately reflects the latest routes and avoids potential issues caused by outdated or invalid route cache files.

Route caching is a valuable technique for optimizing the routing performance of web applications. By precompiling and caching route definitions, applications can significantly reduce routing overhead and improve overall response times.

However, it is important to consider the dynamic nature of the routes and incorporate appropriate maintenance processes when enabling route caching. When used effectively, route caching can greatly enhance the performance and scalability of web applications.

Middleware and Route Grouping

Middleware and route grouping are advanced routing techniques that allow developers to apply shared functionalities, such as authentication, authorization, and request preprocessing, to multiple routes in a concise and organized manner. These techniques improve code maintainability and reusability and provide a structured approach to handling common tasks across multiple routes.

Middleware

Middleware acts as a bridge between the incoming requests and the application's route handlers, or controllers. It intercepts the request, performs certain operations or checks, and then either passes the request to the next middleware in the pipeline or returns a response directly.

Middleware can be used to perform various tasks, such as the following:

Authentication: Middleware can check if a user is authenticated before allowing access to protected routes. If the user is not authenticated, the middleware can redirect them to a login page or return an appropriate response.

```
// Laravel authentication middleware example
namespace App\Http\Middleware;
use Closure;
use Illuminate\Support\Facades\Auth;
class Authenticate
{
    public function handle($request, Closure $next)
    {
        if (Auth::guest()) {
            return redirect()->route('login');
        }
```

```
        return $next($request);
    }
}
```

In this example, the Laravel authentication middleware checks if the user is authenticated. If the user is not authenticated, it redirects them to the login page.

Authorization: The middleware can verify if the authenticated user has the necessary permissions to access a particular route or perform a specific action. If the user is not authorized, the middleware can return an error response or redirect them to an unauthorized page.

```
// Express.js authorization middleware example
function authorizeUser(req, res, next) {
    if (!req.user.isAdmin) {
        return res.status(403).json({ error: 'Unauthorized' });
    }
    next();
}
// Apply authorization middleware to a route
app.get('/admin/dashboard', authorizeUser, adminController.dashboard);
```

In this Express.js example, the 'authorizeUser' middleware checks if the user is an admin. If not, it returns a 403 error response, indicating unauthorized access.

Request preprocessing: Middleware can preprocess the request by modifying the request data, attaching additional information, or performing data validation. This can include tasks like parsing request headers, sanitizing input, or transforming data for easier consumption by route handlers.

```
// Laravel request preprocessing middleware example
namespace App\Http\Middleware;
use Closure;
```

```
class SanitizeRequest
{
    public function handle($request, Closure $next)
    {
        $input = $request->all();
        // Sanitize input data
        $sanitizedInput = sanitizeInput($input);
        // Attach sanitized input to the request
        $request->merge($sanitizedInput);
        return $next($request);
    }
}
```

In this Laravel example, the 'SanitizeRequest' middleware sanitizes the incoming request data and attaches the sanitized data to the request object for further processing by the route handler.

Middleware can be applied globally to all routes or selectively to specific routes or route groups. By organizing middleware into groups, developers can easily manage and apply them to multiple routes, enhancing code readability and maintainability.

Route Grouping

Route grouping provides a way to group related routes together and apply common middleware or route attributes to all the routes within the group. This is particularly useful when multiple routes require the same middleware or share common URL prefixes or attributes.

By grouping routes, developers can

Apply middleware: Grouping routes allows the application of middleware to a specific set of routes in a single place.

This reduces redundancy and ensures the consistent application of middleware to related routes.

```
// Laravel route grouping with middleware example
Route::middleware(['auth'])->group(function () {
    Route::get('/dashboard', 'DashboardController@index');
    Route::get('/profile', 'ProfileController@show');
    Route::post('/profile', 'ProfileController@update');
});
```

In this Laravel example, all routes within the group are protected by the 'auth' middleware. This ensures that only authenticated users can access these routes.

Share attributes: Route grouping enables the sharing of common attributes, such as URL prefixes, route names, or route parameters, among multiple routes. This simplifies route definition and maintenance.

```
// Express.js route grouping example
const adminRoutes = express.Router();
adminRoutes.get('/dashboard', adminController.dashboard);
adminRoutes.get('/users', adminController.users);
adminRoutes.get('/products', adminController.products);
app.use('/admin', adminRoutes);
```

In this Express.js example, all routes within the 'adminRoutes' group have the '/admin' prefix. This simplifies the route definition and makes it clear that these routes are related to the admin section of the application.

Organize routes: Grouping related routes provides a logical structure to the application's route definitions, making it easier to navigate and understand the routing system.

Route grouping improves code organization and simplifies the application of middleware and route attributes, leading to cleaner and more maintainable routing configurations.

Benefits of Middleware and Route Grouping

Using middleware and route grouping in routing configurations offers several benefits:

Code reusability: Middleware allows developers to encapsulate common functionalities and apply them to multiple routes. This promotes code reuse and reduces redundancy by avoiding the need to define the same logic in multiple places.

Code maintainability: Middleware and route grouping provide a structured approach to handling common tasks, making the codebase more organized and easier to maintain. Modifications or additions to shared functionalities can be made in a single place, simplifying updates and ensuring consistency across the application.

Improved readability: Middleware and route grouping enhance the readability of routing configurations by grouping related routes and making it clear which middleware is applied to specific routes or route groups. This improves overall code comprehension and maintainability for developers.

Centralized configuration: Middleware and route grouping centralize the configuration of shared functionalities. This allows developers to manage middleware and route attributes in a single location, reducing the chances of errors and ensuring consistency across the application.

Enhanced security: Middleware can be used to enforce authentication, authorization, and other security checks at a global or route-specific level. This helps in protecting sensitive routes or resources and ensures that the appropriate security measures are consistently applied.

Middleware and route grouping are powerful techniques for managing shared functionalities and organizing routes in web applications. They enhance code maintainability and reusability and provide a structured approach to handling common tasks across multiple routes. By leveraging these techniques, developers can create more efficient and manageable routing systems.

Route Model Binding for Polymorphic Relations

Route model binding is a powerful feature that allows developers to automatically resolve route parameters into model instances. It simplifies the process of fetching related models based on route parameters, enhances code readability, and reduces boilerplate code. In the context of polymorphic relations, where a single relationship can belong to multiple models, route model binding becomes even more valuable.

Understanding Polymorphic Relations

Polymorphic relations are a database design pattern where a single relationship can be associated with multiple models. This is useful when different models can participate in the same relationship. For Illustration, consider a scenario where a comment can belong to either a post or a video. In this case, the Comment model has a polymorphic relationship with both the Post and Video models.

The database structure for such a polymorphic relationship typically includes three columns:

'commentable_id': The ID of the related model instance.

'commentable_type': The type of the related model.

commentable: The relationship method defined in the Comment model. Figure 2-1 illustrates the polymorphic relationship structure.

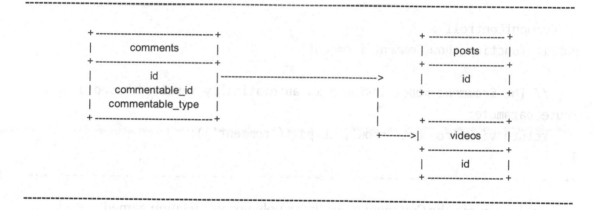

Figure 2-1. *A visual representation of the polymorphic relationship structure*

In this example, the 'commentable_id' column stores the ID of the related model instance (post or video), and the 'commentable_type' column stores the class name of the related model.

Route Model Binding with Polymorphic Relations

To resolve route parameters into model instances for polymorphic relations, route model binding can be customized to handle the dynamic nature of the relationship.

Here's an example in Laravel:

```php
// Comment model
class Comment extends Model
{
    public function commentable()
    {
        return $this->morphTo();
    }
}
// CommentController
public function show(Comment $comment)
{
    // The $comment model instance is automatically resolved based on the
route parameter
    return view('comments.show', compact('comment'));
}
```

In this example, the Comment model has a polymorphic relation named 'commentable'. When defining the route, Laravel route model binding automatically resolves the route parameter into the appropriate model instance based on the 'commentable_type' and 'commentable_id' values.

For Illustration, if the route is defined as follows

```php
Route::get('/comments/{comment}', 'CommentController@show');
```

when the URL '/comments/1' is requested, Laravel will automatically query the Comment model for a record where the 'id' matches 1. It will then resolve the related model instance based on the 'commentable_type' and 'commentable_id' values, allowing you to directly use the '$comment' variable in your controller method.

This automatic resolution simplifies the code by eliminating the need to manually fetch related models based on route parameters.

Customizing Polymorphic Route Model Binding

Sometimes, you may need to customize the route model binding for polymorphic relations to handle specific scenarios or modify the query logic. Laravel provides a way to define custom route model bindings using the 'resolveRouteBinding' method in the model class.

```
// Comment model
class Comment extends Model
{
    public function resolveRouteBinding($value, $field = null)
    {
        // Custom logic to resolve the model instance based on polymorphic
relations
        return $this->where('id', $value)
            ->where('commentable_type', 'App\Post')
            ->firstOrFail();
    }
}
```

In this example, the 'resolveRouteBinding' method is overridden in the Comment model. It provides a custom implementation for resolving the model instance based on the polymorphic relations. In this case, it retrieves the Comment model instance where the 'id' matches the provided value and the 'commentable_type' is set to 'App\Post'.

By customizing the route model binding, you have full control over how the model instances are resolved for polymorphic relations.

Benefits of Route Model Binding for Polymorphic Relations

Route model binding for polymorphic relations offers several benefits:

Simplifies code: Route model binding simplifies the code by automatically resolving route parameters into model instances. This eliminates the need to manually fetch related models based on route parameters, reducing boilerplate code and enhancing code readability.

Dynamic resolution: With polymorphic relations, the route model binding dynamically resolves the appropriate model instance based on the 'commentable_type' and 'commentable_id' values. This flexibility allows you to seamlessly handle multiple models participating in the same relationship.

Customization: Route model binding can be customized to handle specific scenarios or modify the query logic. You can define custom logic in the model's 'resolveRouteBinding' method to control how the model instance is resolved for polymorphic relations.

Consistency: Route model binding ensures consistency in resolving model instances throughout the application. Regardless of the relationship type or model involved, the same route model binding mechanism can be used, providing a unified approach to resolving route parameters.

Using route model binding for polymorphic relations simplifies the process of fetching related models based on route parameters. It eliminates the need for manual queries and allows for dynamic resolution of model instances. By leveraging this feature, you can create more streamlined and maintainable routing systems in your web applications.

In the provided example, the Comment model has a polymorphic relationship with the Post and Video models. The 'commentable_id' column stores the ID of the related model, and the 'commentable_type' column indicates the type of the related model.

Route model binding automatically resolves the route parameter '{comment}' into the appropriate Comment model instance based on the 'commentable_type' and 'commentable_id' values.

The benefits of using route model binding for polymorphic relations include simplified code, dynamic resolution of related models, customization possibilities, and consistency in resolving model instances throughout the application.

Summary

In this chapter, you learned advanced routing approaches in web development using the Laravel framework. The chapter also covered the complexities of routing and showed how to design dynamic and custom routes to improve the flexibility and functionality of web applications. You learned about route parameters, regular expression limitations, and how to use middleware on routes to efficiently manage and filter incoming requests. Additionally, you gained an introduction to route grouping, which enables developers to organize routes more efficiently.

In the next chapter, we will cover database management and Eloquent ORM.

CHAPTER 3

Database Management and Eloquent ORM

In the previous chapter, we explored the intricacies of advanced routing techniques, equipping ourselves with the skills to create dynamic and efficient routes for our Laravel applications. Now, as we continue our journey through Laravel's ecosystem, we will dive deep into the realm of database management and the powerful Eloquent ORM.

Working with Database Migrations

Database migrations are a vital aspect of Laravel development, allowing us to version and manage the database schema effortlessly. In this section, we will learn how to create and execute database migrations, enabling seamless collaboration among developers and efficient database schema changes.

Querying the Database with Eloquent

Laravel's Eloquent ORM is a feature-rich and expressive tool for interacting with databases. We will discover how to use Eloquent to perform various database queries, ranging from simple CRUD operations to more advanced techniques that harness the full power of this ORM.

Eloquent Relationships: One-to-One, One-to-Many, and Many-to-Many

Eloquent relationships are the heart of database modeling in Laravel. Here, we will explore three primary relationship types: one-to-one, one-to-many, and many-to-many. Understanding these relationships is crucial for designing efficient and maintainable database structures.

Advanced Eloquent Techniques: Polymorphic Relations and Query Scopes

Laravel's Eloquent goes beyond basic querying and relationships. This section will introduce us to two advanced Eloquent techniques: polymorphic relations and query scopes. We will discover how polymorphic relations enable more flexible relationships, and query scopes allow us to encapsulate common query logic for reuse throughout our application.

© Sivaraj Selvaraj 2024
S. Selvaraj, *Building Real-Time Marvels with Laravel*, https://doi.org/10.1007/978-1-4842-9789-6_3

Using Eloquent Collections and Serialization

Eloquent collections provide a powerful way to work with sets of models, allowing us to perform various transformations and aggregations. Additionally, we will explore serialization techniques to present our data in different formats, such as JSON or XML.

Throughout this chapter, we will gain a comprehensive understanding of database management in Laravel and learn to harness the full potential of Eloquent ORM. By mastering these essential techniques, we will be well-equipped to build robust, maintainable, and high-performing database-driven applications. So let's dive into the world of database management and Eloquent ORM to elevate our Laravel development skills to the next level!

Working with Database Migrations

Working with database migrations in Laravel refers to the process of managing and version-controlling the database schema using code-based migration files. In Laravel, database migrations allow developers to define changes to the database structure, such as creating new tables, modifying existing ones, adding or removing columns, and defining relationships, all within the application's codebase.

Database Migrations Provide Several Benefits

Version control: Migrations enable developers to keep track of changes made to the database schema over time. Each migration file represents a specific set of changes, and Laravel ensures that these changes can be applied in sequence, making it easy to roll back or move forward through different versions of the database schema.

Collaborative development: With migrations, developers can share and collaborate on the database schema changes effectively. Each developer can create their own migrations, and these changes can be merged into a shared code repository, ensuring a consistent database structure across the team.

Simplified deployment: By using migrations, the process of deploying database changes becomes more straightforward. The migration files can be run in the production environment, applying the necessary changes to the database without affecting existing data.

Data consistency: Migrations allow you to define the structure of the database in code, reducing the risk of errors and inconsistencies that may arise when manually executing SQL queries.

The process of working with database migrations involves creating migration files, which contain instructions to modify the database schema. These migration files are executed using Laravel's Artisan command-line tool, which applies the changes to the database. Laravel also provides a way to roll back migrations in the case of errors or when changes need to be undone.

Overall, database migrations in Laravel offer a powerful and efficient way to manage database changes, ensuring that the application's data remains organized, version-controlled, and consistent throughout its development lifecycle.

Creating Migrations

To create a new migration in Laravel, you can use the 'make:migration' Artisan command. This command generates a new migration file in the 'database/migrations' directory, where you can define the desired changes to the database schema.

For Illustration, let's create a migration that adds a new 'users' table to the database. Run the following command:

```
php artisan make:migration create_users_table
```

This will create a new migration file with a timestamp prefix, such as '2022010100000_create_users_table.php'.

Open the generated file and define the desired schema changes within the 'up' method using the Schema Builder:

```
use Illuminate\Database\Schema\Blueprint;
use Illuminate\Support\Facades\Schema;
class CreateUsersTable extends Migration
{
    public function up()
    {
        Schema::create('users', function (Blueprint $table) {
```

```
        $table->id();
        $table->string('name');
        $table->string('email')->unique();
        $table->string('password');
        $table->timestamps();
    });
}
public function down()
{
    Schema::dropIfExists('users');
}
}
```

In this example, the 'up' method creates a 'users' table with columns for 'name', 'email', 'password', and timestamps ('created_at' and 'updated_at'). The 'down' method defines the rollback operation for the migration, which drops the 'users' table if needed.

Running Migrations

To apply the database migrations and create the corresponding tables in the database, you can use the 'migrate' Artisan command:

```
php artisan migrate
```

This command will execute all pending migrations that have not been run before. Laravel keeps track of the executed migrations using a migrations table in the database.

You can also roll back or undo the last batch of migrations using the 'migrate:rollback' command:

```
php artisan migrate:rollback
```

This command will revert the last batch of migrations, effectively rolling back the changes made to the database schema.

Modifying Migrations

As your application evolves, you may need to modify existing migrations or create new ones to update the database schema. However, it's important to note that modifying a migration file that has already been executed can lead to inconsistencies in the database. In such cases, you should create a new migration to handle the desired changes.

To create a new migration file for modifying an existing table, you can use the 'make:migration' command with a descriptive name:

```
php artisan make:migration add_role_to_users_table
```

This will generate a new migration file that you can open and define the necessary changes, such as adding a new column to the 'users' table:

```php
use Illuminate\Database\Schema\Blueprint;
use Illuminate\Support\Facades\Schema;
class AddRoleToUsersTable extends Migration
{
    public function up()
    {
        Schema::table('users', function (Blueprint $table) {
            $table->string('role')->nullable();
        });
    }
    public function down()
    {
        Schema::table('users', function (Blueprint $table) {
            $table->dropColumn('role');
        });
    }
}
```

In this example, the 'up' method adds a new nullable 'role' column to the 'users' table, while the 'down' method defines the rollback operation, which drops the 'role' column if needed.

Once the new migration is defined, you can run the migrations again using the 'migrate' command:

```
php artisan migrate
```

This will apply the new migration and update the database schema accordingly.

Migration Rollback and Refresh

Laravel provides additional commands for rolling back migrations and refreshing the database.

To roll back the last batch of migrations, you can use the 'migrate:rollback' command:

```
php artisan migrate:rollback
```

This will revert the last batch of migrations, effectively rolling back the changes made to the database schema.

If you want to roll back all migrations and then rerun them, you can use the 'migrate:refresh' command:

```
php artisan migrate:refresh
```

This command will roll back all migrations and then reapply them, effectively resetting the database to its initial state.

Warning   Incorrect use of 'migrate:refresh' may result in data loss.

When working with Laravel migrations, be cautious when using the 'migrate:refresh' command. It undoes all migrations and then reapplies them, restoring the database to its original state. However, improper use may result in irreversible data loss.

To Avoid Unwanted Consequences

Back up your data: Always build a complete database backup before running 'migrate:refresh' to restore data if necessary.

Verify migration files: Check the migration files to verify that they will not cause data loss during the refresh process.

Understand the implications: 'migrate:refresh' is a dramatic step that resets the database. Understand the repercussions and have a good purpose for utilizing it.

Restrict use to development: Use 'migrate:refresh' primarily in development situations where data loss is less critical.

Thoroughly test: Before using 'migrate:refresh' in production or staging, thoroughly test it in a controlled environment to detect and fix errors.

Seeding the Database

In addition to defining the database structure, migrations can also be used to seed the database with initial data. Database seeding allows you to insert predefined data into the tables during the migration process.

To create a new seeder, you can use the 'make:seeder' Artisan command:

```
php artisan make:seeder UsersTableSeeder
```

This will generate a new seeder file that you can open and define the data to be inserted into the 'users' table:

```
use Illuminate\Database\Seeder;
use Illuminate\Support\Facades\DB;
class UsersTableSeeder extends Seeder
{
    public function run()
```

```
    {
        DB::table('users')->insert([
            'name' => 'John Doe',
            'email' => 'john@example.com',
            'password' => bcrypt('password'),
        ]);
    }
}
```

In this example, the 'run' method inserts a new user record into the 'users' table.

To run the seeder and populate the database, you can use the 'db:seed' Artisan command:

```
php artisan db:seed
```

This command will execute all the seeders defined in the 'database/seeds' directory.

Benefits of Database Migrations

Working with database migrations provides several benefits:

Version control: Migrations enable version control of the database schema. Each migration file represents a specific change, allowing you to track and manage schema modifications over time.

Database portability: Migrations make it easier to set up and replicate the database structure across different environments or when collaborating with other developers. The database structure can be easily recreated by running the migrations.

Schema evolution: Migrations allow for easy and controlled modifications to the database schema as the application evolves. You can add, modify, or delete tables and columns, keeping the database structure in sync with the application's requirements.

Database seeding: Migrations can also include seeders to populate the database with initial data. This is particularly useful for setting up development or testing environments with predefined data.

Code consistency: Migrations define the database structure using code, ensuring consistency and eliminating manual steps in the database setup process. This improves maintainability and reduces the chances of errors.

Using database migrations in Laravel simplifies the process of managing database schema changes and version control.

This process allows you to manage and control database schema changes effectively, ensuring consistency and version control in your Laravel application.

Querying the Database with Eloquent

Eloquent is Laravel's ORM (Object-Relational Mapping) that provides a convenient and expressive way to interact with the database. It allows you to perform database queries using a fluent and intuitive syntax, making it easier to retrieve, manipulate, and persist data.

Retrieving Models

To retrieve models from the database using Eloquent, you can use the 'get' method on the model class. This method returns a collection of model instances that match the specified query conditions:

```
$users = User::get ();
```

In this example, the 'get' method retrieves all user records from the 'users' table and returns them as a collection of 'User' model instances.

You can also use various query methods to filter and customize the retrieval process.

For example, you can use the 'where' method to add conditions to your query:

```
$admins = User::where('role', 'admin')->get ();
```

This query retrieves all user records where the 'role' column is set to "admin".

Query Constraints

Eloquent provides a wide range of query constraints to help you retrieve specific data from the database. Some commonly used query constraints include

'where': Adds a basic where clause to the query.

'orWhere': Adds an "or" where clause to the query.

'whereIn': Adds a where in clause to the query.

'whereBetween': Adds a where between clause to the query.

'orderBy': Orders the query results by a specified column.

'limit': Limits the number of records returned by the query.

Here's an example that combines multiple query constraints:

```
$users = User::where('role', 'admin')
          ->orWhere('role', 'editor')
          ->orderBy('created_at', 'desc')
          ->limit(10)
          ->get ();
```

This query retrieves the ten most recent user records where the 'role' column is either "admin" or "editor". The results are ordered by the 'created_at' column in descending order.

Relationships

Eloquent makes working with database relationships seamless and intuitive. You can define relationships between your models, such as one-to-one, one-to-many, and many-to-many relationships. These relationships allow you to easily retrieve related data without writing complex SQL queries.

For example, consider a scenario where you have a 'User' model and a 'Post' model with a one-to-many relationship (a user can have multiple posts). You can define the relationship in the 'User' model:

```
class User extends Model
{
    public function posts()
    {
        return $this->hasMany(Post::class);
    }
}
```

Now, you can retrieve all posts belonging to a specific user like this:

```
$user = User::find(1);
$posts = $user->posts;
```

In this example, '$user->posts' retrieves all posts associated with the user with an ID of 1.

Creating and Updating Models

Eloquent also provides simple and straightforward methods for creating and updating models.

To create a new model instance and save it to the database, you can use the 'create' method:

```
$user = User::create([
    'name' => 'John Doe',
    'email' => 'john@example.com',
    'password' => bcrypt('password'),
]);
```

This code creates a new 'User' model with the specified attributes and saves it to the database.

To update an existing model, you can retrieve it from the database, modify its attributes, and call the 'save' method:

```
$user = User::find(1);
$user->name = 'Jane Smith';
$user->save();
```

In this example, the user with an ID of 1 is retrieved, its 'name' attribute is modified, and the changes are saved to the database.

Deleting Models

To delete a model from the database, you can call the 'delete' method on the model instance:

```
$user = User::find(1);
$user->delete();
```

This code deletes the user with an ID of 1 from the database.

Lazy Loading and Eager Loading

In Laravel's Eloquent ORM, relationships between database tables are defined using Eloquent models. When querying related data, there are two approaches:

1. Eager loading: Eager loading allows you to retrieve the main model along with its related models in a single query. It uses the 'with ()' method to specify the relationships to be loaded up front, reducing the number of database queries and improving performance:

```
// Eager loading example
$users = User::with('posts')->get();
```

2. Lazy loading: Lazy loading, on the other hand, loads related models only when they are accessed for the first time. It avoids loading unnecessary data but may lead to the N+1 query problem, where additional queries are executed when accessing related data in a loop, causing potential performance issues:

```
// Lazy loading example
$users = User::all();
foreach ($users as $user) {
    $posts = $user->posts; // Lazy loading the 'posts' relationship for
    each user
}
```

Advantages of Eager Loading

Performance improvement: Eager loading reduces database queries by fetching all required data in one query, resulting in better performance.

Reduced N+1 query problem: Eager loading fetches related data in advance, preventing extra queries when accessing relationships later.

Cons of Eager Loading

Increased initial query time: Eager loading may lead to complex and time-consuming initial queries, affecting response time for some requests.

Overfetching data: Eager loading retrieves all related data, potentially transferring unnecessary data over the network, increasing payload size.

Resource consumption: Fetching large datasets with eager loading can consume more server resources, especially with deeply nested relationships.

Complicating code logic: Eager loading may complicate code logic, making it harder to maintain, especially in complex relationship scenarios.

Advantages of Lazy Loading

Reduced memory usage: Lazy loading conserves memory by loading related models only when needed, which is ideal for large datasets where not all related data is required.

Faster initial querying: Lazy loading initial queries are faster as only the main model's data is retrieved, which is beneficial when related data is not always needed.

Cons of Lazy Loading

N+1 query problem: Lazy loading can lead to the N+1 query problem, resulting in multiple database hits and reduced performance when accessing related data in a loop.

Performance overhead during access: Lazy loading introduces performance overhead when accessing related data for the first time, as each lazy-loaded relationship triggers a separate query.

Code logic complexity: Lazy loading can complicate code logic, making it harder to optimize and maintain. Developers must be cautious when accessing related data to avoid performance issues.

Potential debugging challenges: Debugging issues related to lazy loading, such as the N+1 query problem, can be more challenging compared with eager loading, requiring a deeper understanding of data access patterns.

Choosing the Right Approach

Choosing the right loading approach (eager or lazy) depends on your specific needs, data size, and how often you access related data. Aim for a balance between both methods to ensure efficient data retrieval, and monitor query performance regularly for optimization. Figure 3-1 illustrates the Eloquent querying process.

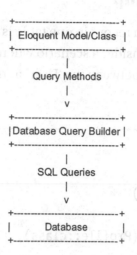

Figure 3-1. *Eloquent querying process*

In this representation, the Eloquent model/class is at the top, representing your application's data structure. The model interacts with the database through the Database Query Builder, which provides various query methods for retrieving, updating, and deleting data.

These query methods generate SQL queries that are executed on the database, resulting in data retrieval or modification.

Using Eloquent in Laravel simplifies the process of interacting with the database by providing an expressive and intuitive syntax. It enhances productivity and readability, making database operations more manageable in your web applications.

Eloquent Relationships: One-to-One, One-to-Many, and Many-to-Many

Eloquent provides powerful features for managing relationships between database tables. These relationships define how the tables are related to each other, allowing you to easily retrieve, create, update, and delete related records.

One-to-One Relationship

In a one-to-one relationship, each record in one table is associated with only one record in another table. For example, consider a scenario where a user has one profile. You can define a one-to-one relationship between the 'User' and 'Profile' models.

In the 'User' model:

```
class User extends Model
{
    public function profile()
    {
        return $this->hasOne(Profile::class);
    }
}
```

In the 'Profile' model:

```
class Profile extends Model
{
    public function user()
    {
        return $this->belongsTo(User::class);
    }
}
```

With this relationship defined, you can easily access the profile of a user or retrieve the user associated with a profile:

```
// Retrieve the profile of a user
$user = User::find(1);
$profile = $user->profile;
```

```
// Retrieve the user associated with a profile
$profile = Profile::find(1);
$user = $profile->user;
```

In this representation, the 'User' model has a 'profile' method defined, representing the one-to-one relationship with the 'Profile' model. The 'Profile' model has a 'user' method defined, representing the inverse side of the relationship.

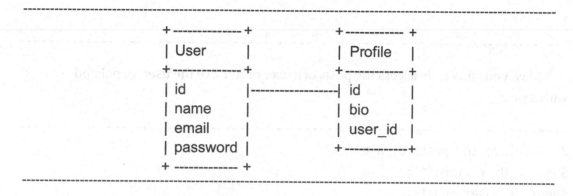

Figure 3-2. *One-to-one relationships*

One-to-Many Relationship

In a one-to-many relationship, a record in one table can be associated with multiple records in another table. For example, consider a scenario where a user has multiple posts. You can define a one-to-many relationship between the 'User' and 'Post' models.

In the 'User' model:

```
class User extends Model
{
    public function posts()
    {
        return $this->hasMany(Post::class);
    }
}
```

In the 'Post' model:

```
class Post extends Model
{
    public function user()
    {
        return $this->belongsTo(User::class);
    }
}
```

Now, you can easily access the posts of a user or retrieve the user associated with a post:

```
// Retrieve the posts of a user
$user = User::find(1);
$posts = $user->posts;
// Retrieve the user associated with a post
$post = Post::find(1);
$user = $post->user;
```

Figure 3-3 illustrates one-to-many relationships.

```
+----------------+          +--------------------+        +------------------------+
| User           |          | Post               |        | Category               |
+----------------+          +--------------------+        +------------------------+
| id             |          | id                 |        | topic                  |
| name           |----------| title              |<---    | title                  |
| email          |    |     | content            |   |    | content                |
| password       |    |---->| user_id            |   |----| category               |
+----------------+          +--------------------+        +------------------------+
```

Figure 3-3. *One-to-many relationships*

In this representation, the 'User' model has a 'posts' method defined, representing the one-to-many relationship with the 'Post' model. The 'Post' model has a 'user' method defined, representing the inverse side of the relationship.

Many-to-Many Relationship

In a many-to-many relationship, records in one table can be associated with multiple records in another table and vice versa. For example, consider a scenario where a user can have multiple roles, and a role can be associated with multiple users. You can define a many-to-many relationship between the 'User' and 'Role' models.

In the 'User' model:

```
class User extends Model
{
    public function roles()
    {
        return $this->belongsToMany(Role::class);
    }
}
```

In the 'Role' model:

```
class Role extends Model
{
    public function users()
    {
        return $this->belongsToMany(User::class);
    }
}
```

With this relationship defined, you can easily access the roles of a user or retrieve the users associated with a role:

```
// Retrieve the roles of a user
$user = User::find(1);
$roles = $user->roles;
// Retrieve the users associated with a role
$role = Role::find(1);
$users = $role->users;
```

In this representation, the 'User' model has a 'roles' method defined, representing the many-to-many relationship with the 'Role' model. The 'Role' model has a 'users' method defined, representing the inverse side of the relationship. The intermediate table ('RoleUser' or 'UserRole') stores the associations between users and roles.

Eloquent relationship features simplify managing complex database relationships and provide a convenient way to access related data. By defining the relationships between models, you can efficiently retrieve, create, update, and delete records across related tables in your Laravel application.

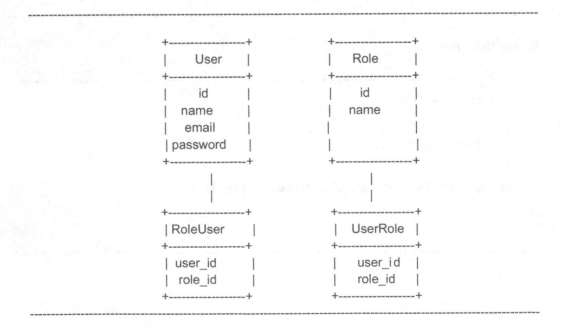

Figure 3-4. *Many-to-many relationships*

Advanced Eloquent Techniques: Polymorphic Relations and Query Scopes

Eloquent, Laravel's ORM (Object-Relational Mapping), offers advanced techniques that enable you to handle complex relationships and perform customized queries. In this section, we will explore two powerful features: polymorphic relations and query scopes.

Polymorphic Relations

Polymorphic relations allow a model to be associated with multiple other models in a single relationship. This is useful when a single model needs to have a relationship with various other models, but the specific model is not known in advance. It allows for flexibility and dynamic relationships between models.

Key points:

Polymorphic relations allow a model to have relationships with multiple other models.

It is useful when a single model needs to be associated with different models.

Three database columns are required: foreign key column, the related model's ID column, and the related model's type column.

Here's an example to illustrate polymorphic relations:

Consider a scenario where you have a 'Comment' model that can be associated with either a 'Post' model or a 'Video' model. The 'Comment' model can have multiple comments associated with different types of content.

In the 'Comment' model:

```
class Comment extends Model
{
    public function commentable()
    {
        return $this->morphTo();
    }
}
```

In the 'Post' model:

```
class Post extends Model
{
    public function comments()
    {
        return $this->morphMany(Comment::class, 'commentable');
    }
}
```

In the 'Video' model:

```
class Video extends Model
{
    public function comments()
    {
        return $this->morphMany(Comment::class, 'commentable');
    }
}
```

With this polymorphic relationship defined, you can easily retrieve comments for either a post or a video, for example:

```
$post = Post::find(1);
$comments = $post->comments;
$video = Video::find(1);
$comments = $video->comments;
```

In this picture representation, the 'Comment' model has a polymorphic relationship defined with the 'Post' and 'Video' models. The 'commentable_id' column represents the ID of the related model, and the 'commentable_type' column stores the class name of the related model.

Query Scopes

Query scopes are a powerful tool in Eloquent that allows you to define reusable query constraints. Scopes enable you to encapsulate commonly used query conditions into methods, improving code organization and reusability. They help keep your code DRY (Don't Repeat Yourself) and make it easier to maintain.

Key points:

Query scopes allow you to define reusable query constraints.

They improve code organization and reusability.

Scopes are defined as methods in the model, prefixed with 'scope.'

Here's an example to illustrate query scopes:

Consider a scenario where you frequently need to retrieve only active users from the 'User' model. You can define a scope to encapsulate this condition.

In the 'User' model:

```
class User extends Model
{
    public function scopeActive($query)
    {
        return $query->where('active', true);
    }
}
```

With this scope defined, you can easily retrieve active users:

```
$users = User::active()->get ();
```

You can also chain multiple scopes together:

```
$users = User::active()->orderBy('name')->get ();
```

In this picture representation, the 'User' model has a query scope 'active' defined, which applies a constraint to retrieve only active users. The scope is called using the 'active()' method, and additional methods like 'orderBy()' can be chained to further customize the query.

In addition to local scopes, you can also define global scopes that are automatically applied to all queries for a specific model. Global scopes can be useful when you always need to apply certain conditions to queries across the entire application.

Advanced Eloquent Techniques Summary

Polymorphic relations: Polymorphic relations allow a model to be associated with multiple other models in a single relationship. It is useful when a model needs to have relationships with various other models. The relationship is defined by using a foreign key column, the related model's ID column, and the related model's type column.

Query scopes: Query scopes allow you to define reusable query constraints by encapsulating them within methods. Scopes improve code organization and reusability, making it easier to compose complex queries. Scopes can be defined at the local level within a specific model or as global scopes applied to all queries for a specific model.

These advanced Eloquent techniques provide flexibility and customization options when working with relationships and queries in Laravel. By leveraging polymorphic relations and query scopes, you can handle complex scenarios, write cleaner and more maintainable code, and streamline your database management tasks efficiently.

Using Eloquent Collections and Serialization

Eloquent provides powerful features for working with query results as collections and serializing data in various formats. In this section, we will explore how to leverage Eloquent collections and serialization capabilities.

Eloquent Collections

Eloquent collections are objects that represent sets of Eloquent models returned from queries. Collections provide a variety of useful methods for manipulating and transforming data. Here are some key points:

Eloquent collections are objects that represent a set of Eloquent models. They provide an array-like interface with additional helpful methods.

Collections can be used to perform operations on query results, such as filtering, mapping, and sorting.

Let's consider an example to understand the use of Eloquent collections:

```
-----------------------------------------------------------------------
$users = User::where('active', true)->get ();
// Filter users based on a condition
$activeUsers = $users->filter(function ($user) {
    return $user->age > 18;
});
// Map the users' names to uppercase
$upperCaseNames = $users->map(function ($user) {
    return strtoupper($user->name);
});
// Sort the users by their age in descending order
$sortedUsers = $users->sortByDesc('age');
-----------------------------------------------------------------------
```

In this example, we retrieve a collection of active users using the 'get ()' method. We then utilize collection methods like 'filter()', 'map()', and 'sortByDesc()' to perform operations on the collection. These methods help us filter the users based on a condition, transform the users' names to uppercase, and sort the users by their age in descending order.

Eloquent collections provide a convenient way to work with query results and perform various data manipulations, saving you time and effort.

Serialization

Serialization refers to the process of converting objects or data structures into a format that can be stored or transmitted. Eloquent provides built-in serialization capabilities to convert Eloquent models and collections into JSON or array representations.

Here are some key points:

Eloquent models and collections can be serialized into JSON or arrays.

Serialization allows you to convert complex Eloquent objects into a simpler format for storage or transmission.

Consider the following example to understand serialization in Eloquent:

```
$user = User::find(1);
// Serialize the user model into JSON
$json = $user->toJson();
// Serialize the user model into an array
$array = $user->toArray();
```

In this example, we retrieve a User model using the 'find()' method and serialize it into JSON and an array. The ' toJson() ' method converts the model into a JSON string, while the ' toArray() ' method converts the model into an array representation.

Serialization is particularly useful when you need to pass Eloquent data to APIs, store it in a cache, or send it as a response from your application.

Using Eloquent Collections and Serialization Summary

Eloquent collections: Eloquent collections are objects that represent sets of Eloquent models. They provide a variety of methods to manipulate and transform data, making it easier to work with query results and perform operations like filtering, mapping, and sorting.

Serialization: Eloquent provides built-in serialization capabilities to convert Eloquent models and collections into JSON or array representations. Serialization allows you to convert complex Eloquent objects into a simpler format for storage, transmission, or integration with external systems.

By leveraging Eloquent collections and serialization, you can easily manipulate and transform query results, as well as convert Eloquent models into different formats. These features enhance the flexibility and versatility of working with data in your Laravel application.

Summary

In this chapter, you took your first steps in database administration and learning how to harness the power of Eloquent ORM within the Laravel framework. The chapter covered basic database principles and demonstrated how to set up and configure database migrations in Laravel and introduced you to Eloquent ORM, a powerful tool that facilitates database interactions using object-oriented techniques. It also delved into a variety of Eloquent topics, such as model construction, data retrieval, data manipulation, and database table relationships.

In the next chapter, we will cover authentication and authorization.

CHAPTER 4

Authentication and Authorization

In the previous chapter, we delved into the realm of database management and explored the powerful Eloquent ORM in Laravel. We learned how to work with database migrations, execute various database queries using Eloquent, and establish relationships between different database models. Armed with this knowledge, we are now ready to tackle one of the most critical aspects of web development—authentication and authorization.

User Authentication: Registration, Login, and Logout

Authentication is a fundamental aspect of any web application, ensuring that only authorized users can access specific resources. In this section, we will dive into the world of user authentication. We will learn how to implement user registration, login, and logout functionalities, enabling users to securely access and interact with our web application.

Authentication Guards and Providers

Laravel provides a flexible authentication system with various authentication guards and providers. Here, we will explore how to configure and utilize different guards and providers to handle various authentication scenarios, such as user authentication via API tokens or session-based authentication.

Managing User Roles and Permissions

In many applications, user roles and permissions play a crucial role in determining what actions a user can perform within the system. We will learn how to manage user roles and permissions effectively, allowing us to control access to specific functionalities based on the user's role.

Advanced Authorization Techniques: Gates and Policies

Beyond simple role-based authorization, Laravel offers more fine-grained control through gates and policies. In this section, we will uncover the power of gates and policies to define complex authorization logic and manage access to resources based on custom conditions.

© Sivaraj Selvaraj 2024
S. Selvaraj, *Building Real-Time Marvels with Laravel*, https://doi.org/10.1007/978-1-4842-9789-6_4

Throughout this chapter, we will explore the ins and outs of authentication and authorization in Laravel, equipping ourselves with the knowledge to build secure and access-controlled web applications. By the end of this chapter, we will have a firm grasp on implementing user authentication, managing roles and permissions, and mastering advanced authorization techniques. So let's begin our journey into the world of authentication and authorization in Laravel!

User Authentication: Registration, Login, and Logout

User authentication is a fundamental aspect of modern web applications that ensures the security and privacy of user data while providing personalized experiences. It involves three primary processes: registration, login, and logout.

During the registration process, users create new accounts by providing essential information such as a unique username, email address, and password. This data is validated and securely stored in the application's database.

Upon subsequent visits to the application, users go through the login process. They enter their credentials, such as username, email, and password, to verify their identity. If the credentials are valid, users gain access to their personalized accounts and any restricted features.

The logout process allows users to terminate their authenticated session, preventing unauthorized access to their accounts when they are not actively using the application.

User authentication is a critical component in building secure and user-centric web applications, ensuring that sensitive data remains protected while offering a tailored experience to each individual user.

User Registration

User registration allows users to create new accounts on your application. Laravel's authentication system provides pre-built registration functionality that you can easily incorporate into your application.

Here's an example of implementing user registration in Laravel.

Define the Routes for Registration

To define the routes for user registration in a Laravel web application, you normally need to construct routes for displaying the registration form and processing form submission. In Laravel, you can define the routes for user registration as follows:

Let's assume you're using Laravel's built-in authentication scaffolding.

Navigate to the routes/web.php file in your Laravel project.

Include the route for showing the registration form:

```
// routes/web.php
Route::get('/register', 'App\Http\Controllers\Auth\RegisterController
@showRegistrationForm')->name('register');
Route::post('/register', 'App\Http\Controllers\Auth\RegisterController
@register');
```

Create a 'RegisterController' to handle the registration logic.

To create a RegisterController to handle registration logic in a Laravel application, follow these steps:

Launch your terminal and navigate to the Laravel project directory.

Create the RegisterController with the php artisan make:controller command:

```
php artisan make:controller Auth/RegisterController
```

After running the command, a new file will be created at app/Http/Controllers/ Auth/RegisterController.php. Open this file with your preferred code editor.

Inside the RegisterController, you can use Laravel's built-in RegistersUsers trait to handle the registration logic. Update the controller code as follows:

```php
<?php
namespace App\Http\Controllers\Auth;
use App\Http\Controllers\Controller;
use Illuminate\Foundation\Auth\RegistersUsers;
use Illuminate\Support\Facades\Validator;
```

```php
use Illuminate\Http\Request;
use App\Models\User; // Assuming you have a User model
class RegisterController extends Controller
{
    use RegistersUsers;
    // Where to redirect users after registration.
    protected $redirectTo = '/home'; // Change '/home' to the desired
    redirect URL after successful registration.
    // Show the registration form.
    public function showRegistrationForm()
    {
        return view('auth.register'); // Replace 'auth.register' with the
        actual view path for your registration form.
    }
    // Handle a registration request for the application.
    protected function register(Request $request)
    {
        $this->validator($request->all())->validate();
        $user = $this->create($request->all());
        // You can add any additional logic or actions here after the user
        is successfully registered.
        return redirect($this->redirectPath());
    }
    // Get a validator for an incoming registration request.
    protected function validator(array $data)
    {
        return Validator::make($data, [
            'name' => 'required|string|max:255',
            'email' => 'required|string|email|max:255|unique:users',
            'password' => 'required|string|min:8|confirmed',
        ]);
    }
```

```
// Create a new user instance after a valid registration.
protected function create(array $data)
{
    return User::create([
        'name' => $data['name'],
        'email' => $data['email'],
        'password' => bcrypt($data['password']),
    ]);
}
}
```

Make sure to substitute the exact view path for your registration form for 'auth. register'. Additionally, modify the $redirectTo parameter to point to the URL you want to direct people to following a successful registration.

You now have a RegisterController in charge of the registration logic. The controller makes use of the RegistersUsers trait, which provides methods for user registration, validation, and the creation of new user instances. You can further customize this controller by adding more logic to meet your specific registration needs.

Create a Registration Form

To construct a registration form view in a Laravel application, follow these steps:

Create a new file called register.blade.php in the resources/views/auth directory (if the auth directory does not already exist, create it).

Open the register.blade.php file in your favorite code editor.

To build the registration form, enter the following code:

```
<!-resources/views/auth/register.blade.php -->
<form method="POST" action="{{ route('register') }}">
    @csrf
    <!-Registration form fields -->
    <button type="submit">Register</button>
</form>
```

User Login

User login allows registered users to authenticate themselves and access protected resources on your application. Laravel provides built-in login functionality that you can easily incorporate into your application.

Here's an example of implementing user login in Laravel.

Define the Routes for login

In order to design the routes for user login in a Laravel web application, you must first define the routes for displaying the login form and processing form submission. In Laravel, you can define the routes for user login as follows:

You only need to provide a particular route for login if you're using Laravel's built-in authentication scaffolding, which contains the Auth::routes() method.

In your Laravel project, navigate to the routes/web.php section.

Add the following route to display the login form:

```
// routes/web.php
Route::get('/login', 'App\Http\Controllers\Auth\LoginController@
showLoginForm')->name('login');
Route::post('/login', 'App\Http\Controllers\Auth\LoginController@login');
```

These routes use Laravel's built-in authentication controller (**LoginController**) to handle the login process. The **showLoginForm** method displays the login form, and the **login** method processes the form submission and authenticates the user.

Create a 'LoginController' to Handle the Login Logic

To create a LoginController to handle login logic in a Laravel application, follow these steps:

Navigate to the directory containing your Laravel project in your console.

Create the LoginController with the PHP artisan make:controller command:

```
php artisan make:controller Auth/LoginController
```

After running the command, a new file called app/Http/Controllers/Auth/ LoginController.php will be created. Use your chosen code editor to open this file.

To handle the login logic, you can utilize Laravel's built-in AuthenticatesUsers trait inside the LoginController. The controller code should be updated as follows:

```php
namespace App\Http\Controllers\Auth;
use App\Http\Controllers\Controller;
use Illuminate\Foundation\Auth\AuthenticatesUsers;
use Illuminate\Http\Request;
class LoginController extends Controller
{
    use AuthenticatesUsers;
    protected function authenticated(Request $request, $user)
    {
        // Customize authenticated behavior if needed
    }
    protected function loggedOut(Request $request)
    {
        // Customize logged out behavior if needed
    }
}
```

Create a Login Form View

To create a login form view in a Laravel application, follow these steps:

Create a new file called login.blade.php in the resources/views/auth directory (if it does not already exist, create it).

Open the login.blade.php file in your favorite code editor.

To construct the login form, enter the following code:

```blade
<! -resources/views/auth/login.blade.php -->
<form method="POST" action="{{route('login')}}">
    @csrf
```

```
<! -Login form fields -->
<button type="submit">Login</button>
</form>
```

User Logout

User logout allows authenticated users to end their session and log out of your application. Laravel provides built-in logout functionality that you can easily incorporate into your application.

Here's an example of implementing user logout in Laravel.

Define the Route for Logout

To define the user logout route in a Laravel web application, construct a route that points to a controller method that is responsible for logging the user out. In Laravel, you can define the route for user logout as follows:

In your Laravel project, navigate to the routes/web.php section.

Add the following route to handle user logout:

```
// routes/web.php
Route::post('/logout', 'App\Http\Controllers\Auth\LoginController@logout')->
name('logout');
```

This route points to the **logout** method in the **LoginController** to handle the logout process.

With this route defined, users can log out by submitting a **POST** request to **/logout**. You can implement a logout button or link in your views that makes a POST request to this URL when clicked. For example, you can use the following code in your Blade views:

```
<form id="logout-form" action="{{ route('logout') }}" method="POST"
style="display: none;">
    @csrf
</form>
```

```
<a href="#" onclick="event.preventDefault(); document.
getElementById('logout-form').submit();">
    {{ __('Logout') }}
</a>
```

In this case, selecting the "Logout" link will send a POST request to the /logout route, logging the user out of the application.

Add a Logout Button or Link to Your Application's Navigation or User Interface

You can add a logout button or link to your application's navigation or user interface by doing the following:

Open your main layout file (e.g., resources/views/layouts/app.blade.php) or any relevant view file where the logout button/link should be included.

To insert the logout button or link, add the following code:

```
<!-resources/views/layouts/app.blade.php -->
<!-Your existing navigation or user interface code goes here -->
<!-Add the Logout button or link -->
@if(Auth::check())
    <form id="logout-form" action="{{ route('logout') }}" method="POST"
style="display: none;">
        @csrf
    </form>
    <a href="#" onclick="event.preventDefault(); document.
getElementById('logout-form').submit();">
        {{ __('Logout') }}
    </a>
@endif
```

Save the document.

The @if(Auth::check()) condition determines whether or not the user is authenticated (logged in). If the user is logged in, the logout button or link will be displayed.

The logout button or link is implemented as a form that contains a single button (or link). When the user selects the "Logout" button or link, a POST request to the /logout route is sent, and the user is logged out of the application.

When making a POST request, the @csrf directive generates a CSRF token field inside the form, which is essential for security reasons.

After completing these steps, the logout button or link will be placed to the navigation or user interface of your program. The user can successfully log out of the application by clicking the "Logout" link.

By implementing user registration, login, and logout functionalities in your Laravel application, you can provide a secure and seamless user authentication experience. Laravel's authentication system simplifies the process and helps you focus on building other features for your application.

Authentication Guards and Providers

Authentication guards and providers are essential components of Laravel's authentication system. They play a crucial role in determining how users are authenticated and where user information is stored. Understanding authentication guards and providers is key to effectively implementing user authentication in your Laravel application.

To summarize:

Authentication is the process of validating a user's identity and giving access to the system.

Authorization is the process of identifying which actions or resources an authenticated user is permitted to access.

Here's a quick reminder:

Set up several methods of confirming user identification using authentication guards and providers (e.g., session-based authentication for web applications, token-based authentication for APIs).

Use roles and permissions to restrict what certain users or user groups can do within the application once they have been authenticated.

Authentication Guards

Authentication guards define how users are authenticated in your application. Laravel provides multiple guard drivers out of the box, such as session, token, and API guards. Each guard driver has its own configuration and authentication mechanism, allowing you to choose the most suitable option based on your application's requirements.

Authentication Guard Drivers

Session guard: The session guard driver uses session-based authentication. It stores the authenticated user's information in the session, allowing the user to access protected resources until the session expires or the user logs out. This guard is commonly used for web applications that rely on sessions for user authentication.

Sample configuration:

```
'guards' => [
    'web' => [
        'driver' => 'session',
        'provider' => 'users',
    ],
],
```

Token guard: The token guard driver is used for API authentication. It authenticates users based on tokens passed with API requests. Tokens can be generated for each user and used to verify their identity for subsequent API requests. This guard is commonly used for stateless API authentication.

Sample configuration:

```
'guards' => [
    'api' => [
        'driver' => 'token',
        'provider' => 'users',
    ],
],
```

API guard: The API guard driver is designed specifically for stateless authentication using API tokens. It is suitable for building APIs that require user authentication without relying on sessions. This guard is commonly used for mobile applications or API-driven systems.

Sample configuration:

```
'guards' => [
    'api' => [
        'driver' => 'passport',
        'provider' => 'users',
    ],
],
```

To configure an authentication guard, you need to define it in the 'config/auth. php' configuration file. You can specify the guard to be used in your routes or controller middleware. For example, to protect a route with the 'web' guard, you can use the 'auth:web' middleware.

Authentication guards provide the flexibility to define different authentication mechanisms based on your application's requirements. By configuring the appropriate guard, you can ensure that users are authenticated using the desired method.

Authentication Providers

Authentication providers determine where user information is stored and how it is retrieved. Laravel provides various authentication providers, including database, Eloquent, and LDAP providers. These providers interact with your chosen storage mechanism to store and retrieve user information.

Authentication Provider Options

Database provider: The database provider retrieves user information from a database table. It allows you to store and retrieve user credentials, such as email and password, from your database. This provider is commonly used for applications that store user information in a relational database.

Sample configuration:

```
'providers' => [
    'users' => [
        'driver' => 'database',
        'table' => 'users',
    ],
],
```

Eloquent provider: The Eloquent provider is a subset of the database provider specifically designed for working with Eloquent models. It simplifies the storage and retrieval of user information using Eloquent ORM. This provider is commonly used when your application uses Eloquent models for managing user data.

Sample configuration:

```
'providers' => [
    'users' => [
        'driver' => 'eloquent',
        'model' => App\Models\User::class,
    ],
],
```

LDAP provider: The LDAP provider retrieves user information from an LDAP server. It is useful when your application's user data is stored in an LDAP directory. This provider is commonly used in enterprise environments where user information is managed using LDAP directories.

Sample configuration:

```
'providers' => [
    'users' => [
        'driver' => 'ldap',
```

```
        'model' => App\Models\User::class,
    ],
],
```

To configure an authentication provider, you need to define it in the 'config/auth.php' configuration file. You can customize the provider's behavior by creating a corresponding model and configuring it accordingly.

Authentication providers allow you to choose the appropriate storage mechanism for user information. By configuring the provider and model, you can seamlessly store and retrieve user data.

Customizing Authentication Guards and Providers

Laravel provides the flexibility to customize authentication guards and providers to suit your application's specific requirements. You can create custom guard drivers and authentication providers to integrate with external systems or implement custom authentication logic.

Customization Options

Custom guard drivers: You can create custom guard drivers by implementing the 'Guard' contract and defining the authentication logic. This allows you to authenticate users using a custom mechanism or integrate with third-party authentication services. For example, you might create a custom guard driver that authenticates users via social media platforms like Facebook or Google.

Example custom guard driver:

```
namespace App\Guards;
use Illuminate\Auth\SessionGuard;
class MyCustomGuard extends SessionGuard
{
    // Custom authentication logic goes here
}
```

Custom authentication providers: Laravel also allows you to create custom authentication providers by implementing the 'UserProvider' contract. This enables you to store and retrieve user information from alternative sources or systems. For instance, you might create a custom authentication provider that retrieves user data from a remote API.

Example custom authentication provider:

```
namespace App\Providers;
use Illuminate\Auth\EloquentUserProvider;
class MyCustomProvider extends EloquentUserProvider
{
    // Custom retrieval and storage logic goes here
}
```

Customizing authentication guards and providers gives you the ability to adapt to unique authentication scenarios. Whether it's integrating with a third-party authentication service or implementing custom authentication logic, Laravel's extensibility allows you to tailor the authentication system to your specific needs.

Authentication Guards and Providers Summary

Authentication guards: Authentication guards define how users are authenticated in your application. Laravel provides multiple guard drivers, such as session, token, and API guards, each with its own configuration and authentication mechanism. By choosing the appropriate guard, you can authenticate users using the desired method.

Authentication providers: Authentication providers determine where user information is stored and how it is retrieved. Laravel offers various authentication providers, including database, Eloquent, and LDAP providers. By configuring the appropriate provider, you can seamlessly store and retrieve user data.

Customization: Laravel allows you to customize authentication guards and providers to match your application's requirements. You can create custom guard drivers and authentication providers to integrate with external systems or implement custom authentication logic.

Understanding authentication guards and providers is crucial for implementing secure and efficient user authentication in your Laravel application. By configuring the appropriate guard and provider, you can ensure that users are authenticated using the desired method and that user information is stored and retrieved correctly.

Managing User Roles and Permissions

Managing user roles and permissions is an essential aspect of building secure and robust applications. Laravel provides a flexible and convenient way to implement role-based access control (RBAC) to control user permissions and access levels. In this section, we will explore how to manage user roles and permissions in Laravel.

User Roles

User roles define the access levels and permissions assigned to different types of users in your application. Roles help determine what actions a user can perform and what resources they can access. By categorizing users into roles, you can effectively manage permissions and restrict access based on user roles.

Key Points

- User roles define access levels and permissions for different types of users.

- Roles help manage user permissions and restrict access to specific resources.

- Users can be assigned one or multiple roles based on their privileges.

To Manage User Roles in Laravel, You Typically Follow These Steps

Define the roles: Identify the different types of users or access levels in your application and create corresponding role definitions. For example, you might have roles like "admin", "moderator", and "user."

Create a roles table: Create a database table to store the role definitions. The table can include fields like 'id', 'name', and 'description' to store role information.

Here's an example of a roles table structure:

```
|----||----------------------||------------------------|
| id || name                 || description            |
|----||----------------------||------------------------|
| 1  || admin                || Administrator          |
| 2  || moderator            || Moderator              |
| 3  || user                 || Regular User           |
|----||----------------------||------------------------|
```

Figure 4-1. *Roles table structure*

Assign roles to users: Implement a mechanism to assign roles to users. This can be done through a user interface, where an administrator can assign roles to users, or through code, where you assign roles programmatically. For example, you might have a User model with a 'roles' relationship:

```
public function roles()
{
    return $this->belongsToMany(Role::class);
}
```

Check user roles for authorization: When performing authorization checks, verify the user's role(s) to determine if they have the necessary permissions to access a resource or perform a specific action. You can define methods in your User model to check roles, for example:

```
public function hasRole($role)
{
    return $this->roles->contains ('name', $role);
}
```

Then, you can use the 'hasRole' method to check if a user has a specific role:

```
if ($user->hasRole('admin')) {
    // User has the 'admin' role
}
```

By managing user roles, you can control access to various parts of your application and ensure that users only have permissions based on their assigned roles.

User Permissions

User permissions determine the specific actions or operations that a user can perform within your application. Permissions are often associated with specific resources, such as CRUD operations on certain models or access to specific routes or functionalities. By managing user permissions, you can fine-tune the access levels and actions available to different users.

Key Points

- User permissions define the specific actions a user can perform.

- Permissions are often associated with specific resources or functionalities.

- Users can have multiple permissions based on their role or specific access needs.

To Manage User Permissions in Laravel, Consider the Following Steps

Define the permissions: Identify the specific actions or operations that users can perform within your application. For example, you might have permissions like "create_post", "edit_post", or "delete_post."

Create a permissions table: Create a database table to store the permissions. The table can include fields like 'id', 'name', and 'description' to store permission information.

Here's an example of a permissions table structure:

---

id	Name	description
1	create_post	Create a new post
2	edit_post	Edit a post
3	delete_post	Delete a post

Figure 4-2. *Permissions table structure*

Assign permissions to roles: Associate permissions with specific roles. Define which permissions are allowed for each role. This can be done through a user interface or programmatically in your code.

For example, you might have a 'permissions' relationship with your Role model:

```
public function permissions()
{
    return $this->belongsToMany(Permission::class);
}
```

Check user permissions for authorization: When performing authorization checks, verify if the user has the necessary permissions to perform a specific action or access a particular resource. You can define methods in your User model to check permissions, for example:

```
public function hasPermission($permission)
{
    return $this->roles->flatMap(function ($role) {
        return $role->permissions;
    })->contains('name', $permission);
}
```

Then, you can use the 'hasPermission' method to check if a user has a specific permission:

```
if ($user->hasPermission('edit_post')) {
    // User has the 'edit_post' permission
}
```

By managing user permissions, you can control what actions users can perform and ensure that they have appropriate access to different parts of your application.

Implementing Role-Based Access Control (RBAC)

Laravel provides convenient features and tools to implement role-based access control (RBAC) in your application. RBAC allows you to assign roles and permissions to users and control access based on those roles and permissions. Laravel's RBAC implementation is typically done using middleware and authorization gates.

Middleware and Authorization Gates

Middleware: Middleware acts as a filter that intercepts requests and performs actions before passing them to the intended route or controller. In the context of RBAC, middleware can be used to check if a user has the necessary role or permissions to access a specific route or perform an action.

Authorization gates: Authorization gates provide a way to define authorization logic within your application. Gates can be used to check if a user has specific permission to perform an action. By defining authorization gates, you can easily check permissions throughout your application.

Here's an example of using middleware and authorization gates to implement RBAC in Laravel:

Define middleware: Create a custom middleware that checks if the authenticated user has the required role to access a specific route.

```
namespace App\Http\Middleware;
use Closure;
use Illuminate\Support\Facades\Auth;
class CheckRole
{
    public function handle($request, Closure $next, $role)
    {
        if (!Auth::check() || !Auth::user()->hasRole($role)) {
            abort(403, 'Unauthorized');
        }
        return $next($request);
    }
}
```

Register middleware: Register the custom middleware in the 'app/Http/Kernel. php' file.

```
protected $routeMiddleware = [
    // Other middleware definitions
    'role' => \App\Http\Middleware\CheckRole::class,
];
```

Use middleware in routes: Apply the middleware to the routes that require specific roles.

```
Route::group(['middleware' => 'role:admin'],
function () {
    // Routes accessible only for users with the 'admin' role
});
```

Define authorization gates: Define authorization gates to check permissions for specific actions or operations.

```
Gate::define('edit-post', function ($user, $post) {
    return $user->hasPermission('edit_post') && $user->id === $post-
    >user_id;
});
```

Use authorization gates: Utilize authorization gates in your application logic to check permissions.

```
if (Gate::allows('edit-post', $post)) {
    // User has permission to edit the post
} else {
    // User is not authorized to edit the post
}
```

By implementing RBAC using middleware and authorization gates, you can control access to different parts of your application based on user roles and permissions.

Managing User Roles and Permissions Summary

Managing user roles and permissions is crucial for building secure and controlled applications. By assigning roles and permissions to users, you can control access levels and determine what actions they can perform.

Here's a summary of the key points covered in this section:

User roles: User roles define access levels and permissions for different types of users. By categorizing users into roles, you can effectively manage permissions and restrict access based on user roles.

User permissions: User permissions determine the specific actions or operations that a user can perform within your application. By managing user permissions, you can fine-tune the access levels and actions available to different users.

Implementing role-based access control (RBAC): Laravel provides features like middleware and authorization gates to implement RBAC. Middleware can be used to check user roles for access control, while authorization gates allow you to define and check permissions throughout your application.

By effectively managing user roles and permissions in your Laravel application, you can ensure that users have appropriate access levels and maintain the security and integrity of your application.

Advanced Authorization Techniques: Gates and Policies

In addition to basic authentication and role-based access control (RBAC), Laravel provides advanced authorization techniques such as gates and policies. These features allow you to define fine-grained authorization rules and apply them to different parts of your application. Let's dive into how to use gates and policies for advanced authorization in Laravel.

Gates

Gates are authorization callbacks that define the authorization logic for specific actions or operations in your application. By defining gates, you can have granular control over what users can and cannot do. Gates are typically used to check permissions based on specific conditions or criteria.

To define a gate, you need to register it in the 'AuthServiceProvider' class, which can be found in the 'app/Providers' directory. In the 'boot' method of the service provider, you can use the 'Gate' facade to define your gates.

Here's an example of defining a gate to check if a user is authorized to update a post:

```
use Illuminate\Support\Facades\Gate;
public function boot()
{
    $this->registerPolicies();
```

```
Gate::define('update-post', function ($user, $post) {
    return $user->id === $post->user_id;
});
}
```

In this example, the gate is named "update-post", and it takes a callback function that receives the authenticated user and the post being checked for authorization. The callback function returns 'true' if the user is authorized to update the post and 'false' otherwise.

To use the gate for authorization, you can use the 'Gate' facade or the 'authorize' method in your controllers or routes:

```
use Illuminate\Support\Facades\Gate;
if (Gate::allows('update-post', $post)) {
    // User is authorized to update the post
} else {
    // User is not authorized to update the post
}
```

Gates provides a powerful way to define custom authorization rules based on specific conditions. You can define gates for various actions or operations in your application and use them to check user permissions throughout your code.

Policies

Policies are classes that encapsulate authorization logic for a particular model. Policies define authorization rules for multiple actions related to the model, such as creating, viewing, updating, or deleting records. Policies provide a structured and organized way to manage authorization rules for a specific model.

To create a policy, you can use the 'make:policy' Artisan command:

```
php artisan make:policy PostPolicy --model=Post
```

This command generates a new policy class named 'PostPolicy' and associates it with the 'Post' model. The generated policy class can be found in the 'app/Policies' directory.

In the policy class, you can define authorization methods for different actions:

```
namespace App\Policies;
use App\Models\User;
use App\Models\Post;
class PostPolicy
{
    public function view(User $user, Post $post)
    {
        // Authorization logic for viewing a post
    }
    public function update(User $user, Post $post)
    {
        // Authorization logic for updating a post
    }
    public function delete(User $user, Post $post)
    {
        // Authorization logic for deleting a post
    }
}
```

In each authorization method, you can define the specific authorization logic based on the user and the post being checked.

To use the policy for authorization, you can call the 'authorize' method in your controllers or routes:

```
$this->authorize('update', $post);
```

This will check if the authenticated user is authorized to update the given post using the 'update' method defined in the associated policy.

Policies provide a convenient way to organize and centralize authorization logic for a specific model. By using policies, you can encapsulate authorization rules and easily apply them to different actions related to the model.

Resource Controllers and Implicit Model Binding

Laravel provides resource controllers that offer convenient methods for handling CRUD operations on resources. When using resource controllers, you can leverage implicit model binding to automatically resolve model instances based on route parameters.

Implicit model binding allows you to type-hint the model in the controller method, and Laravel will automatically resolve the instance using the route parameter. This can be useful for authorization purposes as well, as you can directly authorize the model instance without manually fetching it from the database.

Here's an example of using a resource controller with implicit model binding and authorization:

```
Route::resource('posts', PostController::class);
```

In the 'PostController' class, you can define methods for various actions like 'index', 'show', 'store', 'update', and 'destroy'.

For authorization, you can use the 'authorizeResource' method in the controller's constructor:

```
use App\Models\Post;
public function __construct()
{
    $this->authorizeResource(Post::class, 'post');
}
```

In this example, the 'authorizeResource' method associates the 'Post' model with the resource controller and specifies that the route parameter for the model is named "post". Laravel will automatically resolve the 'Post' instance using implicit model binding and authorize the user's actions based on the defined policy for the 'Post' model.

By using resource controllers and implicit model binding, you can streamline your code and simplify authorization by leveraging Laravel's powerful features.

Advanced Authorization Techniques Summary

Gates: Authorization callbacks that allow for fine-grained rules for individual actions. Examine permits depending on requirements or criteria.

Policies: Classes that encapsulate a model's authorization logic. Manage permissions for numerous model actions.

Resource controllers and implicit model binding: Convenient techniques for doing CRUD actions on resources. Implicit model binding streamlines authorization by explicitly authorizing the resolved model instance based on route parameters.

These techniques provide flexibility and control over authorization rules and allow for efficient management of user permissions and access control.

Summary

Over the course of this chapter, you learned about the critical features of authentication and authorization in the Laravel framework. The chapter covered protecting web applications through the implementation of user authentication and the control of access to various portions of the program based on user roles and permissions. You also learned how to use authentication techniques such as user registration, login, and password reset. Also discussed were user authorization approaches such as setting roles, rights, and policies to limit user access to certain actions and resources.

In the next chapter, we'll explore building APIs with Laravel.

CHAPTER 5

Building APIs with Laravel

In the previous chapter, we explored the crucial aspects of authentication and authorization in Laravel, empowering our web applications with secure user access and fine-grained control over resource permissions. Now, we are ready to take our skills to the next level by venturing into the world of API development with Laravel.

Introduction to API Development

In this section, we will get acquainted with the concept of API development and understand its significance in modern web applications. We will explore the fundamental principles of building APIs, such as statelessness, endpoint design, and request-response patterns, setting the stage for our journey into building robust APIs with Laravel.

Building RESTful APIs with Laravel

Representational State Transfer (REST) is a widely adopted architectural style for designing APIs. We will learn how to implement RESTful APIs in Laravel, defining resourceful endpoints, handling HTTP methods, and structuring responses using best practices.

API Authentication and Security

Securing APIs is of paramount importance to protect sensitive data and prevent unauthorized access. In this section, we will explore various authentication methods like OAuth, token-based authentication, and API keys, ensuring that our APIs are well-protected against potential threats.

API Rate Limiting and Throttling

Rate limiting and throttling are essential techniques to control the rate at which clients can access our APIs. We will learn how to implement rate limiting and throttling mechanisms in Laravel, preventing abuse and ensuring fair usage of API resources.

© Sivaraj Selvaraj 2024
S. Selvaraj, *Building Real-Time Marvels with Laravel*, https://doi.org/10.1007/978-1-4842-9789-6_5

Handling API Errors and Exceptions

Effective error handling is crucial for providing meaningful responses to API clients when things go wrong. In this final section, we will discover how to handle errors and exceptions gracefully, delivering informative error messages to aid API consumers in debugging and troubleshooting.

Throughout this chapter, we will immerse ourselves in the world of API development using Laravel. By the end of this journey, we will have the knowledge and skills to build robust, secure, and efficient APIs, enabling seamless integration with various clients and expanding the reach and usability of our applications. So let's embark on this exciting adventure of building APIs with Laravel!

Introduction to API Development

In today's interconnected world, building APIs (Application Programming Interfaces) has become a crucial aspect of web development. APIs allow different applications and systems to communicate and exchange data seamlessly. Laravel provides powerful tools and features to simplify the development of robust and efficient APIs. In this chapter, we will explore the fundamentals of API development using Laravel.

What is an API?

An API, or Application Programming Interface, is a set of rules and protocols that define how different software components should interact with each other. APIs provide a standardized way for applications to exchange data and perform specific actions. They enable developers to build modular and scalable systems by decoupling different components and allowing them to communicate through a well-defined interface.

Why use APIs?

APIs offer several benefits in the development of modern web applications:

Modularity: APIs allow developers to break down complex systems into smaller, modular components that can be developed, tested, and maintained independently. This promotes code reusability and simplifies the development process.

Scalability: APIs enable horizontal scaling by allowing multiple instances of an application to communicate with each other through the API layer. This allows applications to handle increasing traffic and distribute the workload effectively.

Integration: APIs facilitate the integration of different systems and services. They enable applications to leverage the functionality and data provided by external services, making it easier to build feature-rich applications.

Compatibility: APIs provide a standardized interface that allows different applications to work together regardless of the technologies or programming languages used. This promotes interoperability and simplifies the integration of third-party services.

Building RESTful APIs with Laravel

RESTful APIs are a popular approach for designing web APIs that follow the principles of the REST architectural style. Laravel provides a robust framework for building RESTful APIs, making it easy to create endpoints for performing CRUD (Create, Read, Update, Delete) operations on resources. In this section, we will explore how to build RESTful APIs with Laravel.

Resourceful Routing

Laravel's resourceful routing allows you to define routes for a resource in a concise and consistent manner. Resourceful routes automatically map to corresponding controller methods for CRUD operations.

The following is an illustration of this feature:

```
Route::resource('users', 'UserController');
```

This single line of code will generate the following routes:

```
GET       /users                UserController@index
POST      /users                UserController@store
GET       /users/{user}         UserController@show
PUT       /users/{user}         UserController@update
DELETE    /users/{user}         UserController@destroy
```

Controller and Model Setup

In building RESTful APIs, controllers act as intermediaries between the routes and the database. They handle the logic for processing incoming requests, fetching or manipulating data, and returning responses.

The following is an illustration of this feature:

```php
namespace App\Http\Controllers;
use App\Models\User;
use Illuminate\Http\Request;
class UserController extends Controller
{
    public function index()
    {
        $users = User::all();
        return response()->json($users);
    }
    public function store(Request $request)
    {
        $user = User::create($request->all());
        return response()->json($user, 201);
    }
    public function show($id)
    {
        $user = User::findOrFail($id);
        return response()->json($user);
    }
    public function update(Request $request, $id)
    {
        $user = User::findOrFail($id);
        $user->update($request->all());
        return response()->json($user);
    }
```

```php
    public function destroy($id)
    {
        $user = User::findOrFail($id);
        $user->delete();
        return response()->json(null, 204);
    }
}
```

Route Model Binding

Laravel's route model binding allows you to automatically inject model instances into your controller methods based on route parameters. This simplifies the code by eliminating the need to manually fetch the model from the database.

The following is an illustration of this feature:

```php
Route::get('users/{user}', 'UserController@show');
```

In the preceding Illustration, Laravel will automatically retrieve the 'User' model with the corresponding ID and inject it into the 'show' method of the 'UserController'.

Request Validation

Validating incoming API requests is crucial to ensuring data integrity and security. Laravel provides convenient ways to validate requests using form request classes.

The following is an illustration of this feature:

```php
namespace App\Http\Requests;
use Illuminate\Foundation\Http\FormRequest;
class CreateUserRequest extends FormRequest
{
    public function authorize()
    {
        return true;
    }
```

```
    public function rules()
    {
        return [
            'name' => 'required',
            'email' => 'required|email|unique:users',
            'password' => 'required|min:8',
        ];
    }
}
```

You can use the preceding form request class to validate the data sent in the request before it reaches the controller method.

Response Transformers

Response transformers allow you to format and structure API responses according to specific requirements. Transformers can convert raw data into a consistent and standardized format, enhancing the API's usability.

The following is an illustration of this feature:

```
namespace App\Transformers;
use App\Models\User;
use League\Fractal\TransformerAbstract;
class UserTransformer extends TransformerAbstract
{
    public function transform(User $user)
    {
        return [
            'id' => $user->id,
            'name' => $user->name,
            'email' => $user->email,
        ];
    }
}
```

You can use the preceding transformer class to transform the 'User' model into a desired format before returning the response.

Folder Structure (API-Specific)

When building APIs with Laravel, you may adopt a folder structure that separates API-specific code from traditional web application code. This separation helps keep your codebase organized and easier to maintain. Figure 5-1 illustrates the API directory.

```
├── app
│   ├── API
│   │   ├── Controllers
│   │   ├── Middleware
│   │   ├── Requests
│   │   ├── Resources
│   │   └── Transformers
│   ├── ...
│   └── ...
├── routes
│   ├── api.php
│   └── ...
├── ...
└── ...
```

Figure 5-1. *'API' directory*

In this structure, the 'API' directory contains API-specific code, such as controllers, middleware, requests, resources, and transformers. This separation keeps the API-related code organized and makes it easier to maintain and update the API independently.

Building RESTful APIs with Laravel provides a structured and efficient approach to exposing and managing your application's data and functionality. Laravel's built-in features for routing, controllers, request validation, and response transformation streamline the development process, making it easier to create robust and scalable APIs.

API Authentication and Security

API authentication and security are crucial aspects of building secure and protected APIs. Laravel provides various mechanisms and features to implement authentication and ensure the security of your API endpoints. In this section, we will explore different authentication methods and security measures you can implement in your Laravel APIs.

Token-Based Authentication

Token-based authentication is a commonly used method for API authentication. It involves issuing a unique token to authenticated users, which they then send with each API request to authenticate themselves. Laravel provides a built-in token-based authentication system called "Laravel Sanctum" (formerly known as Laravel Airlock).

The following is an illustration of this feature:

```
// Generating API Tokens
$user = User::find(1);
$token = $user->createToken('API Token')->plainTextToken;
```

In the preceding Illustration, we retrieve the user and generate an API token using Laravel Sanctum. The token is then associated with the user and can be used for subsequent API requests.

```
// Authenticating Requests
Route::middleware('auth:sanctum')->group(function () {
    // API Routes Here
});
```

To protect your API routes with token-based authentication, you can apply the 'auth:sanctum' middleware. This ensures that only authenticated users with valid tokens can access the protected endpoints.

JWT Authentication

JSON Web Tokens (JWTs) are another popular authentication method for APIs. It involves issuing a digitally signed token to authenticated users that contains encoded user information. Laravel provides packages like "tymon/jwt-auth" that make it easy to implement JWT authentication in your Laravel APIs.

The following is an illustration of this feature:

```
// Generating JWT Tokens
$user = User::find(1);
$token = JWTAuth::fromUser($user);
```

In the preceding Illustration, we retrieve the user and generate a JWT token using the "tymon/jwt-auth" package. The client can use the token to authenticate subsequent API requests.

```
// Authenticating Requests
Route::middleware('jwt.auth')->group(function () {
    // API Routes Here
});
```

To protect your API routes with JWT authentication, you can apply the 'jwt.auth' middleware. This middleware validates the JWT token and authenticates the user for each request.

Best Practices for Using JWT in Laravel

Use ephemeral tokens: JWTs typically have a longer lifespan, so consider using ephemeral or short-lived tokens. Set a short expiration time for the token to minimize the risk of unauthorized access if the token is compromised.

For example, set the token expiration to 15 minutes:

```
$token = JWTAuth::factory()->setTTL(15)->fromUser($user);
```

Secure token storage: Store JWT tokens securely on the client side. Avoid storing sensitive information in the token payload, as JWTs are decoded on the client side and can be read by anyone:

```
$token = JWTAuth::fromUser($user);
return response ()->json (['token' => $token])->cookie('token', $token,
$minutes = 15, '/', null, false, true);
```

HTTPS only: Ensure that your API endpoints are accessible only via HTTPS to prevent token interception during transmission.

Use refresh tokens: Implement a refresh token mechanism to obtain new access tokens without requiring the user to re-enter their credentials. Refresh tokens should have a longer lifespan than access tokens.

Here's an example using the Laravel JWT package:

```
$refreshToken = JWTAuth::factory()->setTTL(60 * 24 * 30)->refresh($token);
return response()->json(['token' => $refreshToken]);
```

Protect sensitive routes: Use Laravel middleware to protect sensitive routes that require authentication. Apply the JWT middleware to ensure that only authenticated users can access these routes:

```
Route::middleware('jwt.auth')->group(function () {
    // Protected routes here
});
```

Implement token revocation: Provide an option for users to revoke their tokens (e.g., logout functionality). Maintain a token blacklist to prevent the use of revoked tokens. For example, use Laravel's cache to store blacklisted tokens:

```
// To blacklist a token
Cache::put('token_blacklist_' . $tokenId, true, $minutes);
// To check if a token is blacklisted
if (Cache::has('token_blacklist_' . $tokenId)) {
    // Token is blacklisted, deny access
}
```

Add token expiry validation: Validate the token expiration during the authentication process. If the token is expired, return an appropriate error message and prompt the user to log in again.

Encrypt sensitive token data: If necessary, encrypt sensitive data within the token payload to add an extra layer of security.

Limit token scopes: Include only necessary user information in the token payload. Avoid adding unnecessary data that might compromise user privacy:

```
$payload = [
    'sub' => $user->id,
    'role' => $user->role,
    // other data as needed
];
$token = JWTAuth::encode($payload);
```

Regularly review token usage: Monitor and review token usage patterns to identify any suspicious activities or potential security breaches.

Remember to keep your JWT implementation up to date and follow security best practices to ensure a robust and secure authentication system for your Laravel API.

API Throttling

API throttling is essential to prevent abuse and protect your API from excessive requests. Laravel provides a built-in rate limiting mechanism that allows you to define rate limits for API endpoints.

The following is an illustration of this feature:

```
// Applying API Throttling
Route::middleware('throttle:60,1')->group(function () {
    // API Routes Here
});
```

In the preceding Illustration, we apply the 'throttle' middleware to the API routes, which limits the requests to 60 requests per minute with a rate limit of 1 request per second. You can adjust the rate limits based on your application's requirements.

CORS (Cross-Origin Resource Sharing)

CORS is a security mechanism that prevents unauthorized access to resources by restricting cross-origin requests. Laravel provides middleware to handle CORS and ensure secure communication between client-side applications and your API.

The following is an illustration of this feature:

```
// Enabling CORS
Route::middleware('cors')->group(function () {
    // API Routes Here
});
```

By applying the 'cors' middleware to your API routes, you can allow cross-origin requests from specific domains or configure more advanced CORS settings as per your requirements.

API Versioning

API versioning allows you to introduce changes to your API without breaking existing client integrations. Laravel provides features to manage API versioning using route grouping and middleware.

The following is an illustration of this feature:

```
// Versioning API Routes
Route::prefix('v1')->group(function () {
    // Version 1 API Routes Here
});
Route::prefix('v2')->group(function () {
    // Version 2 API Routes Here
});
```

In the preceding Illustration, we define separate route groups for different API versions. API routes for version 1 are grouped under the '/ v1' prefix, while API routes for version 2 are grouped under the '/ v2' prefix. This allows you to maintain different versions of your API simultaneously.

Implementing authentication mechanisms, security measures, and best practices in your Laravel APIs helps ensure the integrity and privacy of your data. Laravel's built-in features make it easier to incorporate authentication and security measures, allowing you to develop secure and reliable APIs.

API Rate Limiting and Throttling

Rate limiting and throttling are essential techniques used to control and limit the number of API requests made by clients. These techniques help ensure fair usage of API resources, prevent abuse, and maintain system stability. Laravel provides convenient features to implement rate limiting and throttling on your API endpoints. In this section, we will explore how to apply rate limiting and throttling to your Laravel APIs.

Rate Limiting

Rate limiting allows you to restrict the number of requests that can be made to your API within a certain time frame. This helps prevent abuse and ensure fair usage of your API resources. Laravel offers a built-in rate limiting mechanism that you can easily configure.

The following is an illustration of this feature:

```
// Applying Rate Limiting to API Routes
Route::middleware('throttle:60,1')->group(function () {
    // API Routes Here
});
```

In the preceding Illustration, we apply rate limiting to the API routes using the 'throttle' middleware. The parameters '60' and '1' represent the maximum number of requests allowed per minute and the time window for the rate limit, respectively.

Laravel's rate limiting mechanism uses a sliding window approach. It tracks the number of requests made by a client within the specified time window and responds with an error if the rate limit is exceeded.

You can also customize the rate limit configuration based on factors like API keys, user IDs, or any custom logic by creating a custom rate limiter.

Throttling

Throttling limits the rate at which requests can be made to your API by enforcing a delay between consecutive requests. This technique helps prevent excessive API usage and provides a smoother experience for both clients and servers.

The following is an illustration of this feature:

```
// Applying Throttling to API Routes
Route::middleware('throttle:10,1')->group(function () {
    // API Routes Here
});
```

In the preceding Illustration, we apply throttling to the API routes using the 'throttle' middleware. The parameters '10' and '1' represent the maximum number of requests allowed per minute and the number of seconds to wait between requests, respectively.

Laravel's throttling mechanism uses a "leaky bucket" algorithm to regulate the flow of requests. If a client exceeds the defined throttle limit, Laravel will return a response with a status code indicating that the client should retry after a certain time.

You can also customize the throttle configuration by creating a custom throttle middleware and specifying the throttle limits based on your application's needs.

Customizing Rate Limiting and Throttling

Laravel allows you to customize the rate limiting and throttling behavior according to your specific requirements. You can modify the rate limit and throttle settings in the 'App\Http\Kernel' class.

The following is an illustration of this feature:

```
// Modifying Rate Limit and Throttle Settings
protected $middlewareGroups = [
    'api' => [
        'throttle:100,1',
        'bindings',
    ],
];
```

In the preceding Illustration, we modify the rate limit and throttle settings for the 'api' middleware group. The parameters '100' and '1' represent the new rate limit values.

You can define different rate limits and throttling rules for specific API routes or user groups based on your application's needs. Laravel's flexible middleware system allows you to apply rate limiting and throttling to specific routes or groups of routes easily.

Handling Rate Limit Exceeded Responses

When a client exceeds the rate limit or throttle limit, Laravel automatically handles the response. By default, Laravel will return a JSON response with the HTTP status code '429 Too Many Requests' and the appropriate headers indicating the time when the client can retry the request.

117

You can customize the response returned when the rate limit is exceeded by implementing the 'render' method in your exception handler. This allows you to provide a more meaningful response to the client.

Implementing rate limiting and throttling in your Laravel APIs helps protect your resources, maintain system stability, and ensure fair usage of your APIs. By controlling the rate and frequency of API requests, you can prevent abuse and provide a reliable experience for your API consumers.

Handling API Errors and Exceptions

Handling errors and exceptions effectively is crucial for building robust and reliable APIs. When an error occurs during API processing, it's essential to provide meaningful error responses to clients. Laravel provides features and techniques to handle API errors and exceptions gracefully. In this section, we will explore how to handle API errors and exceptions in Laravel.

Exception Handling

Laravel's exception handling mechanism allows you to catch and handle exceptions that occur during API processing. The 'App\Exceptions\Handler' class is responsible for handling exceptions and generating appropriate responses.

The following is an illustration of this feature:

```
-------------------------------------------------------------------
namespace App\Exceptions;
use Exception;
use Illuminate\Foundation\Exceptions\Handler as ExceptionHandler;
use Illuminate\Http\JsonResponse;
use Symfony\Component\HttpKernel\Exception\NotFoundHttpException;
use Illuminate\Validation\ValidationException;
class Handler extends ExceptionHandler
{
    public function render($request, Exception $exception): JsonResponse
    {
```

```
        if ($exception instanceof NotFoundHttpException) {
            return response()->json(['message' => 'Resource not found'], 404);
        }
        if ($exception instanceof ValidationException) {
            return response()->json(['message' => 'Validation error',
            'errors' => $exception->errors()], 422);
        }
        return parent::render($request, $exception);
    }
}
```

In the preceding Illustration, we override the 'render' method in the exception handler to handle specific exceptions. If a 'NotFoundHttpException' occurs, we return a JSON response with a 404 status code and a message indicating that the resource was not found. If a 'ValidationException' occurs, we return a JSON response with a 422 status code, a message indicating a validation error, and the validation errors.

By customizing the exception handling logic, you can provide meaningful and consistent error responses to clients.

Error Formatting

Laravel allows you to format error responses consistently across your API endpoints. You can define error formats using the 'format' method in the exception handler.

The following is an illustration of this feature:

```
protected function formatValidationErrors(Validator $validator): array
{
    return [
        'message' => 'Validation error',
        'errors' => $validator->errors(),
    ];
}
```

In the preceding Illustration, we define the format for validation errors.

The 'formatValidationErrors' method is responsible for formatting validation errors in a consistent structure. By customizing this method, you can format error responses according to your API's requirements.

Error Responses

When handling API errors and exceptions, it's important to provide informative responses to clients. Laravel's 'response' helper allows you to create and return JSON responses with appropriate status codes.

The following is an illustration of this feature:

```
return response()->json(['message' => 'Internal Server Error'], 500);
```

In the preceding Illustration, we return a JSON response with a 500 status code and a message indicating an internal server error. You can customize the response content, status codes, and headers based on the specific error or exception being handled.

Logging and Debugging

Logging and debugging play a vital role in identifying and resolving API errors and issues. Laravel provides a robust logging system that allows you to log API errors and exceptions for debugging purposes.

The following is an illustration of this feature:

```
try {
    // API Logic Here
} catch (Exception $e) {
    Log::error($e->getMessage());
    // Handle the Exception
}
```

In the preceding Illustration, we catch an exception and log the error message using Laravel's 'Log' facade. By logging errors, you can track and review them later to diagnose issues and troubleshoot your API.

Error Handling for Validation Errors

When handling validation errors, Laravel's 'ValidationException' provides convenient methods to access the validation errors and generate appropriate error responses.

The following is an illustration of this feature:

```
try {
    // Validate Request
    $validatedData = $request->validate([
        'name' => 'required',
        'email' => 'required|email',
    ]);
    // API Logic Here
} catch (ValidationException $e) {
    return response()->json(['message' => 'Validation error', 'errors' =>
$e->errors()], 422);
}
```

In the preceding Illustration, we catch a 'ValidationException' and return a JSON response with a 422 status code, a message indicating a validation error, and the validation errors obtained from the exception.

Handling API errors and exceptions effectively improves the user experience and helps identify and resolve issues in your API.

By customizing exception handling, formatting error responses, and logging errors, you can provide meaningful and consistent responses to clients while facilitating debugging and troubleshooting.

Summary

In this chapter, you learned how to develop APIs with the Laravel framework. The chapter emphasized developing APIs that are both strong and scalable in order to enable seamless communication between web applications and external clients. You also learned RESTful API concepts and how to create clean, user-friendly API endpoints and gained insight into how to handle HTTP requests and answers, as well as data serialization and authentication procedures for API access. We also covered API-specific validation, error handling, and versioning procedures.

In the next chapter, we will delve into caching and performance optimization.

CHAPTER 6

Caching and Performance Optimization

In the previous chapter, we delved into the world of API development with Laravel, learning how to build robust and secure APIs to cater to the demands of modern web applications. Now, as we continue our exploration of Laravel's capabilities, we shift our focus to another critical aspect—caching and performance optimization.

Understanding Laravel's Cache System

Caching is a powerful technique to enhance the performance of our applications by storing frequently accessed data in memory. In this section, we will gain a comprehensive understanding of Laravel's caching system, exploring the underlying principles and how caching can significantly improve the response time and overall user experience of our applications.

Implementing Caching with Redis and Memcached

Laravel provides support for various caching drivers, with Redis and Memcached being popular choices for high-performance caching. We will dive into the implementation of caching with Redis and Memcached, discovering how to leverage their features to further boost the speed and efficiency of our applications.

Cache Tagging and Cache Invalidation

Cache tagging is a sophisticated feature that allows us to organize and invalidate cached data efficiently. Here, we will learn how to utilize cache tagging to manage cached data more effectively and gracefully handle cache invalidation when data changes or expires.

Optimizing Database Queries with Eager Loading

Database queries can be a significant bottleneck in application performance. We will explore how to optimize database queries in Laravel by using eager loading, reducing the number of queries executed and mitigating the "N+1" query problem.

© Sivaraj Selvaraj 2024
S. Selvaraj, *Building Real-Time Marvels with Laravel*, https://doi.org/10.1007/978-1-4842-9789-6_6

Performance Optimization Techniques for Laravel Applications

In this final section, we will delve into a collection of performance optimization techniques for Laravel applications. From optimizing code to leveraging caching, database optimization, and server configuration, we will uncover various strategies to ensure our applications run at peak performance.

Throughout this chapter, we will unravel the art of caching and performance optimization in Laravel, empowering us to create high-performing and scalable applications. By adopting these techniques, we can deliver responsive and efficient experiences to our users while maintaining the ability to scale our applications as they grow. So let's embark on this journey of optimizing Laravel applications for speed and performance!

Understanding Laravel's Cache System

In modern web development, performance and responsiveness are paramount. To optimize the efficiency of web applications, developers often rely on caching mechanisms to store and retrieve frequently accessed data more quickly. Laravel, a popular PHP framework, offers a robust and versatile cache system designed to enhance the performance of applications significantly.

Understanding Laravel's cache system is essential for developers seeking to harness the full potential of caching and deliver faster, more responsive web experiences to their users. This system provides a seamless and intuitive way to store various types of data, such as database query results, rendered views, and expensive computations, in temporary storage.

In this exploration, we will delve into the fundamental concepts of Laravel's cache system, gaining insights into its working principles and the multiple cache drivers it supports. We will learn how to leverage caching to improve response times, reduce database queries, and alleviate server load. Furthermore, we'll discover strategies for cache invalidation and managing cache tags to keep data up to date and relevant.

Cache Drivers

Laravel supports multiple cache drivers, including file, database, Redis, and Memcached. These drivers determine where the cached data is stored. By default, Laravel uses the file cache driver, which stores the data in files on the disk. However, you can easily configure Laravel to use other cache drivers based on your application's needs.

Storing Data in the Cache

Storing data in the cache is a straightforward process in Laravel. You can use the 'Cache' facade to store data with a specified key and expiration time. The expiration time is optional, and if not provided, the data will be stored indefinitely.

For Illustration, refer to the following snippet:

```
Cache::put('key', $data, $minutes);
```

In the preceding example, we store the '$data' variable in the cache with the key "key" and an expiration time of '$minutes'.

Retrieving Data from the Cache

Retrieving cached data is equally simple. You can use the 'Cache' facade to retrieve data by providing the corresponding key. If the data is found in the cache, it will be returned; otherwise, you can specify a default value to be returned.

The following is an illustration of this feature:

```
$data = Cache::get('key', $default);
```

In the preceding example, we retrieve the cached data with the key "key". If the data is not found in the cache, the value of '$default' will be returned.

Cache Tags

Laravel's cache system provides a powerful feature called cache tagging. It allows you to group related cached data using tags, making it easier to manage and invalidate specific sets of cached data. You can associate multiple tags with cached data and then perform operations on those tags, such as flushing or invalidating them.

The following is an illustration of this feature:

```
Cache::tags(['tag1', 'tag2'])->put('key', $data, $minutes);
```

In the preceding example, we store the '$data' variable in the cache with the key "key" and associate it with the tags "tag1" and "tag2".

Cache Invalidation

Cache invalidation involves removing or updating specific cached data. Laravel provides various methods for cache invalidation, such as removing data by key, flushing the entire cache, or invalidating data associated with specific tags.

The following is an illustration of this feature:

```
Cache::forget('key');
Cache::flush();
Cache::tags(['tag1'])->flush();
```

In the preceding examples, we remove the cached data with the key 'key', flush the entire cache (removing all cached data), and flush all data associated with the tag 'tag1', respectively.

Understanding Laravel's cache system is crucial for optimizing the performance of your applications. By effectively utilizing caching techniques and leveraging the appropriate cache drivers, you can significantly reduce the load on your database and improve response times.

Figure 6-1 illustrates the basic structure of Laravel's cache system. The cache serves as temporary storage for frequently accessed data, enabling faster retrieval and reducing the load on the underlying data sources.

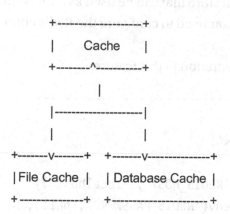

Figure 6-1. *Basic structure of Laravel's cache system*

By employing caching techniques effectively, you can greatly enhance the performance of your Laravel applications, resulting in improved user experiences and optimized server resources.

Implementing Caching with Redis and Memcached

Caching plays a crucial role in optimizing the performance of web applications. While Laravel's default file-based caching system is suitable for many scenarios, utilizing more advanced caching systems like Redis or Memcached can further enhance the speed and efficiency of your application. In this section, we will explore how to implement caching with Redis and Memcached in Laravel.

Configuring Redis as the Cache Driver

Redis is an in-memory data store that can be used as a cache driver in Laravel. To use Redis as the cache driver, you need to configure the Redis connection in the 'config/database.php' file.

The following is an illustration of this feature:

```
'redis' => [
    'client' => 'predis',
    'default' => [
        'host' => env('REDIS_HOST', 'localhost'),
        'password' => env('REDIS_PASSWORD', null),
        'port' => env('REDIS_PORT', 6379),
        'database' => 0,
    ],
],
```

In the preceding example, we configure Redis as the cache driver by specifying the Redis connection details. The 'client' option is set to "predis", which uses the Predis library to connect to Redis. You can customize the host, port, password, and database values based on your Redis configuration.

Configuring Memcached as the Cache Driver

Memcached is another popular in-memory caching system that can be used as a cache driver in Laravel. To use Memcached as the cache driver, you need to configure the Memcached connection in the 'config/cache.php' file.

The following is an illustration of this feature:

```
'memcached' => [
    [
        'host' => env('MEMCACHED_HOST', '127.0.0.1'),
        'port' => env('MEMCACHED_PORT', 11211),
```

```
        'weight' => 100,
    ],
],
```

In the preceding example, we configure Memcached as the cache driver by specifying the Memcached server details. You can customize the host, port, and weight values based on your Memcached configuration.

Using Redis or Memcached for Caching

Once you have configured Redis or Memcached as the cache driver, Laravel will automatically use the configured cache store for caching.

The following is an illustration of this feature:

```
// Storing Data in Redis Cache
Cache::store('redis')->put('key', $data, $minutes);
// Retrieving Data from Memcached Cache
$data = Cache::store('memcached')->get('key');
```

In the preceding examples, we store data in the Redis cache using the 'store' method and the "redis" cache store. Similarly, we retrieve data from the Memcached cache using the "memcached" cache store.

For Illustration using the Redis cache:

```
// Store an item in the Redis cache indefinitely.
Cache::store('redis')->forever('key', 'value');
// Retrieve the item from the Redis cache.
$value = Cache::store('redis')->get('key');
// Check if an item exists in the Redis cache.
if (Cache::store('redis')->has('key')) {
    // Item exists, do something with it.
} else {
```

```
    // Item doesn't exist, do something else.
}
// Remove an item from the Redis cache.
Cache::store('redis')->forget('key');
```

The Redis cache driver saves cached objects to a Redis server. Cache::store('redis')
specifies the Redis cache driver explicitly. The cached item is stored eternally with the
key 'key' by the forever technique. The get function retrieves the cached item using
its key, while the has method determines whether the item exists. The forget method
deletes the cached object.

For Illustration using the Memcached cache:

```
// Store an item in the Memcached cache for 120 seconds.
Cache::store('memcached')->put('key', 'value', now()->addSeconds(120));
// Retrieve the item from the Memcached cache.
$value = Cache::store('memcached')->get('key');
// Check if an item exists in the Memcached cache.
if (Cache::store('memcached')->has('key')) {
    // Item exists, do something with it.
} else {
    // Item doesn't exist, do something else.
}
// Remove an item from the Memcached cache.
Cache::store('memcached')->forget('key');
```

The Memcached cache driver saves cached items in the Memcached memory store.
Cache::store('memcached') specifies the Memcached cache driver explicitly. Using
the put method, the cached item with the key 'key' will be saved for 120 seconds. The
get function retrieves the cached item using its key, while the has method determines
whether the item exists. The forget method deletes the cached object.

By utilizing Redis and Memcached as cache drivers, you can take advantage of their
fast in-memory data storage and retrieval capabilities. These caching systems offer
improved performance and scalability compared with the default file-based caching in
Laravel. Figure 6-2 illustrates integration of Redis and Memcached.

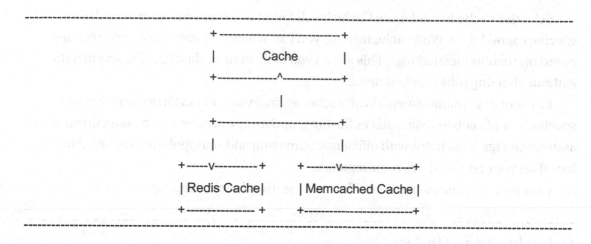

Figure 6-2. *The integration of Redis and Memcached*

The preceding diagram illustrates the integration of Redis and Memcached as cache drivers in Laravel. The cache driver acts as an interface between Laravel and the caching system, facilitating efficient storage and retrieval of cached data.

By implementing caching with Redis or Memcached, you can further optimize the performance of your Laravel applications, resulting in faster response times and improved scalability.

Cache Tagging and Cache Invalidation
Cache Tagging

Cache tagging is a powerful feature in Laravel's cache system that allows you to organize and manage cached data more efficiently. With cache tagging, you can associate one or more tags with specific cached data, making it easier to group related data together and perform operations on specific sets of cached data.

Cache Tagging Provides Several Benefits

Logical grouping: By assigning tags to cached data, you can logically group related data together. This makes it easier to organize and manage data based on specific categories, contexts, or relationships.

Selective cache invalidation: Cache invalidation involves removing or updating specific cached data. With cache tagging, you can selectively invalidate cache entries based on their associated tags. This allows you to flush or update specific sets of data without affecting other cached items.

Efficient data management: With cache tagging, you can perform operations on specific sets of cached data, such as flushing, updating, or retrieving, by targeting the associated tags. This helps with efficiently managing and manipulating cached data based on your application's requirements.

Let's look at some examples to illustrate the use of cache tagging:

```
// Storing Data with Tags
Cache::tags(['users', 'roles'])->put('key', $data, $minutes);
```

In this example, we store the '$data' variable in the cache with the key "key" and associate it with the tags "users" and "roles". This allows us to group the cached data based on users and their roles.

```
// Retrieving Data by Tag
$data = Cache::tags(['users', 'roles'])->get('key');
```

In this example, we retrieve the cached data with the key "key" by specifying the tags "users" and "roles". Laravel will retrieve the cached data if it matches any of the specified tags.

```
// Flushing Cache by Tag
Cache::tags(['users'])->flush();
```

In this example, we flush all cached data associated with the tag "users". This clears the cache for the specified tag, allowing fresh data to be fetched from the data source.

Cache tagging provides a convenient and efficient way to manage and manipulate cached data in Laravel. It allows you to group related data together, perform operations on specific sets of data, and selectively invalidate cache entries based on tags. This level of control over cached data helps optimize performance and improve data management in your Laravel applications.

Retrieving Data by Tag

Laravel's cache system provides a useful feature of retrieving data by tag when using cache tagging. It allows you to retrieve specific sets of cached data based on the associated tags, making it convenient to fetch related data in a grouped manner. Here's how you can retrieve data by tag in Laravel:

```
// Retrieving Data by Tag
$data = Cache::tags(['users', 'roles'])->get('key');
```

In the preceding example, we retrieve the cached data with the key "key" by specifying the tags "users" and "roles" using the 'tags' method. Laravel will retrieve the cached data if it matches any of the specified tags.

By using cache tags, you can easily fetch specific sets of cached data without having to retrieve all cached items. This can be particularly useful when you want to retrieve data related to a specific category, context, or relationship.

Here's another example to demonstrate retrieving data by tag:

```
// Storing Data with Tags
Cache::tags(['products', 'featured'])->put('key', $data, $minutes);
// Retrieving Data by Tag
$data = Cache::tags(['featured'])->get('key');
```

In this example, we store the '$data' variable in the cache with the key "key" and associate it with the tags "products" and "featured". Later, we retrieve the cached data by specifying the "featured" tag. Laravel will fetch the cached data with the given key if it is associated with the specified tag.

Retrieving data by tag allows you to efficiently fetch specific subsets of cached data, reducing the need to retrieve and process all cached items. It provides a convenient way to access related data and enables more targeted data retrieval in your Laravel applications.

Flushing Cache by Tag

Flushing the cache by tag allows you to selectively remove or invalidate specific sets of cached data based on the associated tags. This can be useful when you want to clear or update a group of cached items that share common tags. Here's how you can flush the cache by tag in Laravel:

```
// Flushing Cache by Tag
Cache::tags(['users'])->flush();
```

In the preceding example, we use the 'tags' method to specify the tag "users". By calling the 'flush' method on the cache instance, Laravel will remove all cached data associated with the specified tag, in this case "users". This clears the cache for the specified tag, allowing fresh data to be fetched from the data source.

You can also flush multiple tags at once by passing an array of tags to the 'tags' method:

```
// Flushing Cache by Multiple Tags
Cache::tags(['users', 'roles'])->flush();
```

In this example, we flush all cached data associated with the tags "users" and "roles". This removes all cached items that are associated with any of the specified tags.

By flushing the cache by tag, you have the flexibility to selectively invalidate and update specific sets of cached data. This is particularly useful when you want to clear or refresh cached items that belong to a certain category or context without affecting other cached data in your Laravel application. Figure 6-3 illustrates the concept of cache tagging.

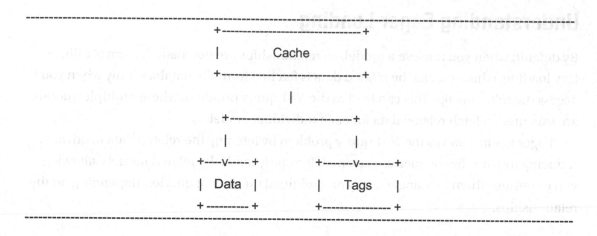

Figure 6-3. *Concept of cache tagging*

The preceding diagram illustrates the concept of cache tagging in Laravel. Cached data can be associated with one or more tags, allowing for efficient management and invalidation of specific sets of data.

By leveraging cache tagging and cache invalidation techniques, you can have better control over your cached data. You can group related data together, retrieve specific sets of data based on tags, and invalidate only the necessary cache entries when needed. This allows you to keep your cached data up to date and consistent with the underlying data source, leading to improved performance and efficient data management in your Laravel applications.

Optimizing Database Queries with Eager Loading

Optimizing database queries is crucial for improving the performance of your Laravel applications. One technique to reduce the number of database queries is eager loading. Eager loading allows you to load relationships along with the main model, reducing the need for separate queries to fetch related data. This can significantly improve the efficiency and speed of your application. Let's explore eager loading in more detail.

Understanding Eager Loading

By default, when you retrieve a model, its relationships are not loaded. Laravel utilizes lazy loading, which means the related data is fetched from the database only when you access the relationship. This can lead to the N+1 query problem, where multiple queries are executed to fetch related data for each individual model.

Eager loading solves the N+1 query problem by fetching the related data in advance, reducing the number of queries executed. It eagerly loads the related models, allowing you to retrieve them in a single query or a minimal number of queries, depending on the relationships.

Eager Loading Syntax

When using eager loading in Laravel, you can specify the relationships you want to load using the 'with' method. The 'with' method accepts an array of relationship names as its argument. Here's an example of the eager loading syntax:

```
$users = User::with('posts')->get();
```

In the preceding example, we are eager-loading the 'posts' relationship for the 'User' model. This means that when we retrieve the users, their associated posts will be fetched as well. The 'with' method instructs Laravel to preload the 'posts' relationship, optimizing the query to fetch the related data.

You can also eager-load multiple relationships by passing an array of relationship names to the 'with' method:

```
$users = User::with(['posts', 'comments'])->get();
```

In this example, we are eager-loading both the 'posts' and 'comments' relationships for the 'User' model. This will fetch the posts and comments associated with each user in a single query, instead of executing separate queries for each user.

Additionally, you can eager-load nested relationships by using dot notation:

```
$users = User::with('posts.comments')->get();
```

In this example, we are eager-loading the 'posts' relationship along with its nested 'comments' relationship for the 'User' model. This will fetch the users, their posts, and the comments for each post in an optimized way, reducing the number of queries executed.

By using the 'with' method and providing the appropriate relationship names, you can efficiently load related data in Laravel using eager loading. This helps minimize the number of queries and improve the performance of your application.

Eager-Loading Nested Relationships

In Laravel, you can eager-load nested relationships using dot notation. This allows you to retrieve multiple levels of related data with optimized queries. Let's look at an example to understand how to eager-load nested relationships:

```
$users = User::with('posts.comments')->get();
```

In this example, we are eager-loading the 'posts' relationship along with its nested 'comments' relationship for the 'User' model. The dot notation "posts.comments" indicates that we want to load the 'comments' relationship nested within the 'posts' relationship.

By eager-loading nested relationships, Laravel optimizes the queries to fetch the related data in a more efficient way. It retrieves the users, their posts, and the comments for each post using a minimal number of queries.

You can nest relationships as deep as necessary to retrieve the desired data. For example, if the 'comments' relationship has another nested relationship called 'replies', you can eager-load it as follows:

```
$users = User::with('posts.comments.replies')->get();
```

In this case, Laravel will retrieve the users, their posts, the comments for each post, and the replies for each comment. The nested relationships can be extended further based on your application's needs.

Eager loading of nested relationships helps avoid the N+1 query problem and improves the performance of your application by reducing the number of database queries executed. It allows you to efficiently retrieve related data in a hierarchical structure, making it easier to work with and manipulate the data in your Laravel application.

Eager Loading Constraints

Eager loading constraints allow you to further optimize your database queries by applying conditions or filters to the eager-loaded relationships. This helps in fetching only the necessary related data that meets specific criteria.

Let's explore how to apply eager loading constraints in Laravel:

```
$users = User::with(['posts' => function ($query) {
    $query->where('is_published', true);
}])->get();
```

In this example, we are eager-loading the 'posts' relationship for the 'User' model, but with a constraint. The constraint is defined using a closure function within the 'with' method. Inside the closure, we can specify conditions using the '$query' variable, which represents the query builder for the 'posts' relationship.

In the example, we apply a constraint to retrieve only the posts where the 'is_ published' column is 'true'. This means that only the published posts will be eager-loaded for each user.

You can apply more complex constraints by utilizing the full power of the query builder. For example, you can use methods like 'where', 'orWhere', 'whereIn', etc., to add additional conditions to the eager-loaded relationships:

```
$users = User::with(['posts' => function ($query) {
    $query->where('is_published', true)
          ->where('category_id', 1);
}])->get();
```

In this example, we apply multiple constraints to the 'posts' relationship. The eager loading will fetch only the posts that are published and belong to the category with ID 1.

By using eager loading constraints, you can optimize the retrieval of related data by filtering out unnecessary records. This reduces the amount of data transferred from the database to your application, resulting in improved performance.

Eager loading constraints are a powerful tool for optimizing your database queries in Laravel. They allow you to selectively fetch related data based on specific conditions, ensuring that only the relevant records are loaded, improving the efficiency of your application. Figure 6-4 illustrates the interaction between models and relationships in Laravel.

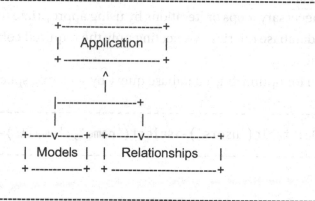

Figure 6-4. *Interaction between models and relationships in Laravel*

The preceding diagram represents the interaction between models and relationships in Laravel's eager loading mechanism. Eager loading optimizes the retrieval of related data, reducing the number of queries and improving the efficiency of your application.

By employing eager loading techniques, you can minimize database queries and enhance the performance of your Laravel applications, resulting in faster response times and improved user experiences.

Performance Optimization Techniques for Laravel Applications

Performance optimization is crucial for ensuring fast and efficient Laravel applications. Here are some techniques and best practices to optimize the performance of your Laravel applications.

Code Optimization

Use efficient data structures and algorithms to minimize memory usage and improve execution speed.

Avoid unnecessary loops or iterations by using appropriate functions and methods.

Optimize database queries by selecting only the required columns and optimizing complex queries.

Illustration for optimizing a database query by selecting specific columns:

```
$users = DB::table('users')->select('name', 'email')->get();
```

Caching

Use Laravel's caching system to store frequently accessed data in cache, reducing the need to fetch it from the database repeatedly.

Illustration for caching a database query result for improved performance:

```
$users = Cache::remember('users', $minutes, function () {
    return DB::table('users')->get();
});
```

Database Optimization

Utilize indexes to improve query performance.

Avoid unnecessary joins and optimize complex queries.

Illustration for adding an index to a frequently used column for faster querying:

```
Schema::table('users', function ($table) {
    $table->index('email');
});
```

Lazy Loading vs. Eager Loading

Understand the trade-offs between lazy loading and eager loading.

Eager loading can improve performance by reducing the number of database queries, but be mindful of loading unnecessary data.

Illustration for eager-loading relationships to reduce database queries:

```
$users = User::with('posts')->get();
```

Code Profiling and Monitoring

Use profiling and monitoring tools to identify performance bottlenecks.

Laravel provides debugging tools like Telescope for monitoring and analyzing application performance.

Illustration for using Laravel Telescope to monitor database queries:

```
php artisan telescope:install
```

Asset Optimization

Minify and combine CSS and JavaScript assets to reduce the number of HTTP requests and improve page load times.

Utilize Laravel Mix or other asset compilation tools to streamline asset management.

Illustration for compiling and minifying assets using Laravel Mix:

```
mix.js('resources/js/app.js', 'public/js')
    .sass('resources/sass/app.scss', 'public/css')
    .version();
```

HTTP Caching

Leverage HTTP caching mechanisms to cache responses on the client side and reduce server load.

Use caching headers like 'ETag' and 'Last-Modified'.

Illustration for setting cache control headers in Laravel:

```
return response($content)
    ->header('Cache-Control', 'public, max-age=3600');
```

Optimized Configurations

Tune the configuration settings of your Laravel application for optimal performance.

Adjust database connections, caching drivers, and session storage based on your application's needs. Illustration for configuring database connections in Laravel:

```
'connections' => [
    'mysql' => [
        'driver' => 'mysql',
        'host' => env('DB_HOST', '127.0.0.1'),
        'database' => env('DB_DATABASE', 'forge'),
        'username' => env('DB_USERNAME', 'forge'),
        'password' => env('DB_PASSWORD', ''),
        'charset' => 'utf8mb4',
        'collation' => 'utf8mb4_unicode_ci',
        'prefix' => '',
```

```
            'strict' => true,
            'engine' => null,
        ],
    ],
```

Queue Optimization

Utilize Laravel's queue system for processing time-consuming tasks asynchronously.

Offload tasks to queues to improve response times and handle spikes in traffic efficiently.

Illustration for dispatching a job to a queue in Laravel:

```
ProcessPodcast::dispatch($podcast)->onQueue('processing');
```

Server Optimization

Optimize your server environment by configuring caching mechanisms, enabling compression, leveraging opcode caching, and using a reverse proxy.

Illustration for configuring Redis as a caching mechanism in Laravel:

```
'default' => env('CACHE_DRIVER', 'redis'),
'stores' => [
    'redis' => [
        'driver' => 'redis',
        'connection' => 'cache',
    ],
],
'connections' => [
    'cache' => [
        'url' => env('REDIS_URL'),
        'host' => env('REDIS_HOST', '127.0.0.1'),
        'password' => env('REDIS_PASSWORD', null),
        'port' => env('REDIS_PORT', '6379'),
```

```
            'database' => env('REDIS_CACHE_DB', '0'),
    ],
 ],
```

By implementing these performance optimization techniques, you can enhance the speed, scalability, and responsiveness of your Laravel applications. Remember to analyze the specific needs of your application, measure the impact of optimizations, and continually monitor and fine-tune performance for the best results.

Summary

In this chapter, we covered caching and performance optimization in the context of Laravel web development. We focused on improving the performance and efficiency of web applications through the efficient use of caching strategies. We also explored Laravel's caching mechanisms, including page caching, query caching, and Redis caching, and how to incorporate caching for database queries, views, and other components to improve response times and server load. You additionally learned about performance optimization tactics such as code profiling, database indexing, and utilizing the Laravel Horizon dashboard to monitor queues and tasks.

The next chapter will focus on advanced middleware techniques.

CHAPTER 7

Advanced Middleware Techniques

In the previous chapter, we delved into the critical aspects of caching and performance optimization in Laravel, equipping ourselves with the knowledge and tools to create high-performing applications. As we continue our exploration of Laravel's advanced features, we now turn our attention to middleware—a powerful mechanism that enables us to intercept and process HTTP requests at various stages of the application's lifecycle.

Creating Custom Middleware

In this section, we will learn how to create custom middleware in Laravel. Custom middleware allows us to inject custom logic into the request-response flow, enabling us to perform tasks such as authentication, logging, or modifying incoming requests. We will explore the process of writing and registering custom middleware to add new layers of functionality to our applications.

Middleware Pipeline and Terminable Middleware

Laravel's middleware pipeline provides a structured way to manage the flow of incoming requests through multiple middleware layers. We will explore how to use middleware groups and apply middleware conditionally based on various criteria. Additionally, we will uncover the concept of terminable middleware, which allows us to perform actions after the response has been sent.

Middleware Parameters and Dependencies

Middleware can also accept parameters and dependencies, allowing us to pass additional information or services to the middleware during its execution. In this section, we will learn how to define and utilize middleware parameters and dependencies effectively, enhancing the flexibility and reusability of our middleware.

© Sivaraj Selvaraj 2024
S. Selvaraj, *Building Real-Time Marvels with Laravel*, https://doi.org/10.1007/978-1-4842-9789-6_7

Global Middleware vs. Route Middleware

Laravel supports two types of middleware—global middleware that applies to all routes and route-specific middleware that targets specific routes or groups of routes. We will explore the differences between these two approaches and understand when to use each to achieve our desired outcomes.

Middleware Best Practices and Performance Considerations

As with any powerful tool, using middleware requires careful consideration and adherence to best practices. In this final section, we will discuss various best practices for creating, organizing, and managing middleware effectively. Additionally, we will explore performance considerations to ensure that our middleware does not introduce unnecessary overhead in our application.

Throughout this chapter, we will dive into the world of advanced middleware techniques in Laravel, honing our skills to intercept, process, and modify HTTP requests with precision and control. By mastering middleware, we can create more robust, modular, and maintainable applications, tailored to meet the unique requirements of our projects. So let's embark on this journey of advanced middleware techniques and further expand our Laravel expertise!

Creating Custom Middleware

Middleware is a crucial component in Laravel that allows developers to intercept and process HTTP requests and responses. Laravel's built-in middleware provides essential functionalities like authentication, session management, and CSRF protection. However, there are scenarios where you may need specific, application-specific middleware to perform custom tasks during the request-response cycle.

Creating custom middleware in Laravel empowers developers to extend the framework's capabilities and tailor the middleware stack according to their application's unique requirements. Custom middleware allows you to perform additional processing, validation, or any other specific tasks for incoming requests or outgoing responses.

In this guide, we will delve into the world of custom middleware in Laravel, understanding the underlying concepts and the step-by-step process to create and register your middleware. We will explore various use cases, such as logging, request modification, and role-based access control, to demonstrate the versatility and power of custom middleware.

Throughout this journey, we will learn how to define middleware classes, integrate them seamlessly into the application's middleware stack, and harness their potential to enhance security, performance, and overall application behavior.

Creating Custom Middleware

Custom middleware in Laravel enables you to define your own logic to be executed during the HTTP request lifecycle. Here's how you can create custom middleware.

Generate a New Middleware

To generate new middleware in Laravel, you can use the artisan command 'make:middleware'. Here's how you can generate new middleware:

Open your terminal or command prompt.

Navigate to your Laravel project's root directory.

Run the following command to generate new middleware:

```
php artisan make:middleware CustomMiddleware
```

This command will generate a new middleware class named 'CustomMiddleware' in the 'app/Http/Middleware' directory.

Once the command is executed successfully, you can find the newly created 'CustomMiddleware' class in the specified directory.

The generated 'CustomMiddleware' class will have a 'handle' method where you can define your custom logic to be executed during the HTTP request lifecycle.

Here's an Illustration of the generated 'CustomMiddleware' class:

```
namespace App\Http\Middleware;
use Closure;
class CustomMiddleware
{
    public function handle($request, Closure $next)
```

```
        {
            // Perform your custom logic here
            return $next($request);
        }
    }
}
```

The new middleware class is now ready for you to add your custom logic. You can modify the 'handle' method to perform any operations you need, such as checking authentication, manipulating request data, or adding headers to the response. Remember to register the middleware in the 'app/Http/Kernel.php' file and apply it to routes or controllers as needed.

Implement the Middleware Logic

After creating custom middleware in Laravel, you can implement your custom logic in the 'handle' method.

Here's an Illustration of how you can implement the middleware logic:

```php
<?php
namespace App\Http\Middleware;
use Closure;
class CustomMiddleware
{
    public function handle($request, Closure $next)
    {
        // Perform your custom logic here
        // Illustration: Check if the request has an API key
        if (!$request->has('api_key')) {
            return response()->json(['error' => 'Unauthorized'], 401);
        }
        // Illustration: Modify the request data
        $request->merge(['modified_data' => 'some value']);
        // Illustration: Add a custom header to the response
        $response = $next($request);
```

```
    $response->header('X-Custom-Header', 'Custom Value');
    return $response;
  }
}
```

In the 'handle' method, you can write your custom logic based on the requirements of your application. Here are a few Illustrations of common use cases:

Authentication: You can check if the request has valid authentication credentials and handle unauthorized requests accordingly.

Data manipulation: You can modify the request data or add additional data before it reaches the controller.

Authorization: You can perform authorization checks to ensure the user has the necessary permissions to access a specific route or resource.

Response manipulation: You can modify the response or add custom headers to the response before it is sent back to the client.

The preceding Illustration demonstrates a few scenarios. It checks if the request has an API key and returns an error response if it doesn't. It also modifies the request data by adding a new key-value pair. Additionally, it adds a custom header to the response using the 'header' method.

You can customize the middleware logic based on your specific requirements. The 'handle' method acts as a middleware pipeline, allowing you to perform operations before passing the request to the next middleware or controller.

Remember to register the middleware in the 'app/Http/Kernel.php' file and apply it to the desired routes or controllers to trigger the execution of your custom logic.

Register the Middleware

After creating a custom middleware in Laravel, you need to register it in the 'app/Http/Kernel.php' file. This registration step allows Laravel to recognize and apply your middleware to the desired routes or controllers. Here's how you can register the middleware:

Open the 'app/Http/Kernel.php' file in your Laravel project.

Inside the 'App\Http\Kernel' class, you will find the '$routeMiddleware' property. This property contains an array of middleware aliases and their corresponding class names.

Add an entry for your custom middleware in the '$routeMiddleware' array. The key should be a unique alias name for your middleware, and the value should be the fully qualified class name of your middleware.

Here's an Illustration of registering the 'CustomMiddleware':

```
protected $routeMiddleware = [
    // Other middleware aliases...
    'custom' => \App\Http\Middleware\CustomMiddleware::class,
];
```

Save the 'Kernel.php' file after adding the entry for your custom middleware.

By registering your middleware in the 'Kernel.php' file, you make it available to be used in your routes or controllers using the middleware alias.

You can now apply the middleware to routes or controllers by using the middleware alias you specified during registration.

For Illustration, to apply the 'CustomMiddleware' to a route, you can use the 'middleware' method in your route definition:

```
Route::get('/Illustration', function () {
    // Route logic
})->middleware('custom');
```

You can also apply the middleware to a group of routes by using the 'middleware' method in a route group definition.

Remember to clear the cache after registering a new middleware by running the following command in your terminal:

```
php artisan cache:clear
```

By properly registering your custom middleware, you can easily apply it to routes or controllers in your Laravel application.

Apply the Middleware

The Console Kernel is critical for handling console commands and operations. It is the entry point for all Artisan commands, which are Laravel's command-line utilities.

Artisan commands enable developers to do a variety of operations, such as database migrations, running scheduled tasks, cleaning the cache, and generating code scaffolding.

Once you have registered a custom middleware in Laravel by adding it to the '$routeMiddleware' array in the 'app/Http/Kernel.php' file, you can apply the middleware to routes or controllers in your application.

Here's how you can apply the middleware:

Open the 'routes/web.php' or 'routes/api.php' file in your Laravel project.

Define a route and use the 'middleware' method to specify the middleware to be applied:

```
Route::get('/Illustration', function () {
    // Route logic
})->middleware('custom');
```

In this Illustration, the 'custom' middleware is applied to the '/Illustration' route. You can replace 'custom' with the alias of your actual middleware.

Here's how to apply the middleware to a group of routes:

Open the 'routes/web.php' or 'routes/api.php' file in your Laravel project.

Use the 'middleware' method in a route group definition to apply the middleware to multiple routes:

```
Route::middleware('custom')->group(function () {
    // Routes within this group will use the custom middleware
});
```

In this Illustration, the 'custom' middleware is applied to all routes within the group.

Here's how to apply the middleware to a controller:

Open the controller file where you want to apply the middleware.

Add the middleware to the controller's constructor method using the 'middleware' method:

```
public function __construct()
{
    $this->middleware('custom');
}
```

In this Illustration, the 'custom' middleware is applied to all methods within the controller.

By applying the middleware to routes or controllers, you ensure that the middleware's logic is executed before the request reaches the route or controller logic. The middleware can perform operations such as authentication, authorization, request manipulation, and more.

Note that the middleware is executed in the order it is applied. You can define multiple middleware, and they will be executed sequentially.

Ensure that the middleware alias matches the one you registered in the 'Kernel. php' file.

By applying custom middleware, you can add specific functionality to your routes or controllers, allowing you to perform tasks at various stages of the HTTP request lifecycle.

Creating custom middleware allows you to add functionality and perform tasks such as authentication, authorization, data manipulation, and more, at various stages of the HTTP request lifecycle. It provides flexibility and reusability, enabling you to customize the behavior of your Laravel application to suit your specific needs.

Middleware Pipeline and Terminable Middleware

In Laravel, middleware can be executed as part of a middleware pipeline. The middleware pipeline allows you to define a sequence of middleware that will be executed in the order they are specified. Additionally, Laravel provides the concept of terminable middleware, which allows you to perform tasks after the response has been sent to the client. Let's explore the middleware pipeline and terminable middleware in more detail.

Middleware Pipeline

In Laravel, a middleware pipeline is a sequence of middleware that is executed in the order it is defined. Each middleware in the pipeline can perform operations on the incoming request or modify the outgoing response. The middleware pipeline is a fundamental concept in Laravel's request processing flow.

Here's How the Middleware Pipeline Works

Your Laravel application receives a request, and it passes through the middleware pipeline before reaching the intended route or controller.

The middleware pipeline is defined in the 'app/Http/Kernel.php' file. It contains two arrays: '$middleware' and '$middlewareGroups':

a. The '$middleware' array holds the global middleware that will be applied to every request.

b. The '$middlewareGroups' array allows you to define sets of middleware that can be applied to specific groups of routes.

The middleware pipeline is executed in the order specified. Each middleware is responsible for processing the request and optionally passing it along to the next middleware in the pipeline.

Middleware can perform various tasks such as authentication, authorization, input validation, logging, and more. They can modify the request or response objects, terminate the request processing, or even return a response immediately.

If a middleware passes the request to the next middleware in the pipeline, it calls the '$next' closure or handler. This allows the next middleware to continue processing the request.

If a middleware chooses not to pass the request to the next middleware, it can return a response immediately, effectively terminating the middleware pipeline.

Once the request has passed through all the middleware in the pipeline, it reaches the intended route or controller, where the final processing occurs.

By utilizing the middleware pipeline, you can implement cross-cutting concerns and apply common functionality to multiple routes or controllers in a modular way. It allows you to handle tasks such as request filtering, validation, and authorization in a centralized manner.

Illustration: Middleware Pipeline

Let's consider an Illustration where you have three middleware: 'FirstMiddleware', 'SecondMiddleware', and 'LastMiddleware'. They are registered in the 'app/Http/Kernel. php' file in the desired order.

When a request enters your Laravel application, it goes through the middleware pipeline as follows:

The request first enters 'FirstMiddleware', where you can perform initial operations or checks.

If 'FirstMiddleware' decides to pass the request to the next middleware, it calls the '$next($request)' method or closure.

The request then enters 'SecondMiddleware', where further processing can occur. Again, the middleware can pass the request to the next middleware or return a response.

Finally, the request reaches 'LastMiddleware', which can perform the last set of operations or modifications before the response is sent.

If 'LastMiddleware' passes the request to the next middleware, the response flows back through the middleware pipeline in reverse order, allowing each middleware to handle the response.

Once the response reaches 'FirstMiddleware', it is returned to the client.

By understanding and utilizing the middleware pipeline effectively, you can modularize your application's logic, implement reusable middleware, and centralize common operations for improved code organization and maintainability.

Terminable Middleware

In Laravel, terminable middleware is a special type of middleware that allows you to perform tasks after the response has been sent to the client. Terminable middleware provides a convenient way to execute cleanup or finalization tasks once the request-response cycle is completed.

Here's how terminable middleware works:

Terminable middleware in Laravel should implement the 'TerminableMiddleware' interface. This interface requires the implementation of a single method, 'terminate'.

The 'terminate' method is called automatically by Laravel after the response has been sent to the client. It allows you to perform any necessary cleanup or finalization tasks.

Inside the 'terminate' method, you have access to both the request and response objects, allowing you to perform any operations based on the information contained within them.

Terminable middleware is registered and used in the same way as regular middleware, but with the added benefit of the 'terminate' method being automatically invoked.

Illustration: Terminable Middleware

Let's consider an Illustration where you have 'LoggingMiddleware' that logs some information after the response has been sent. Here's how you can create terminable middleware:

Create a new middleware class, such as 'LoggingMiddleware', in the 'app/Http/Middleware' directory.

Implement the 'TerminableMiddleware' interface and define the 'terminate' method:

```php
<?php
namespace App\Http\Middleware;
use Closure;
use Illuminate\Contracts\Routing\TerminableMiddleware;
use Log;
class LoggingMiddleware implements TerminableMiddleware
{
    public function handle($request, Closure $next)
    {
        // Perform actions before the request is handled
        return $next($request);
    }
    public function terminate($request, $response)
    {
        // Perform actions after the response has been sent
        Log::info('Request completed.');
    }
}
```

In this Illustration, the 'LoggingMiddleware' class implements the 'TerminableMiddleware' interface and provides the 'terminate' method. Inside the 'terminate' method, we log a message indicating that the request has been completed.

Register the middleware in the 'app/Http/Kernel.php' file, similar to other middleware.

Apply the middleware to the desired routes or controllers using the middleware alias.

Once the response is sent to the client, Laravel will automatically invoke the 'terminate' method of any registered terminable middleware. In this case, the 'LoggingMiddleware' will log the message to indicate that the request has been completed.

Terminable middleware provides a convenient way to execute tasks after the response has been sent, allowing you to perform cleanup, logging, or any other necessary actions.

It is useful for scenarios where you need to handle operations that should occur after the request-response cycle.

By understanding the middleware pipeline and terminable middleware, you can effectively manage the execution flow of your middleware and perform tasks before and after the request-response cycle.

Middleware pipelines provide a powerful way to process requests and responses with flexibility and control.

Middleware Parameters and Dependencies

In Laravel, middleware can accept parameters and dependencies, allowing you to customize their behavior and access additional resources. By leveraging middleware parameters and dependencies, you can enhance the flexibility and functionality of your middleware. Here's how you can work with middleware parameters and dependencies in Laravel.

Middleware Parameters

In Laravel, middleware parameters allow you to pass additional data or values to your middleware during registration. This can be useful when you need to customize the behavior of your middleware based on specific values or configurations. Here's how you can work with middleware parameters in Laravel.

Define Middleware Parameters

To define parameters for your middleware, you can pass them when applying the middleware to routes or controllers. After specifying the middleware name, separate the parameters by a colon.

Illustration for applying middleware with parameters in routes/web.php or routes/api.php:

```
Route::get('/Illustration', function () {
    // Route logic
})->middleware('custom:parameter1,parameter2');
```

In this Illustration, the 'custom' middleware is applied with two parameters: 'parameter1' and 'parameter2'. You can pass any number of parameters, separated by commas.

Access Middleware Parameters

To access the parameters within your middleware, you need to modify the 'handle' method of your middleware class to include additional arguments corresponding to the parameters.

Illustration for retrieving middleware parameters:

```
public function handle($request, Closure $next, $parameter1,
$parameter2)
{
    // Access the parameters here
    // Perform middleware logic
    return $next($request);
}
```

In the 'handle' method, you can access the parameters as additional arguments. The values of the parameters will be automatically passed when the middleware is executed.

Use Middleware Parameters

Once you have access to the parameters in your middleware, you can utilize them in your middleware logic as needed. The parameters can be used to customize the behavior of the middleware based on the provided values.

Illustration for using middleware parameters:

```
public function handle($request, Closure $next, $parameter1,
$parameter2)
    {
        if ($parameter1 === 'value1') {
            // Perform specific actions based on the value of $parameter1
        }
        // Perform other middleware logic
        return $next($request);
    }
```

In this Illustration, the middleware checks the value of '$parameter1' and performs specific actions based on its value. You can use the parameters to conditionally execute certain parts of your middleware logic.

By utilizing middleware parameters, you can pass dynamic values to your middleware and customize its behavior based on those values. This allows you to create more flexible and reusable middleware that can be configured to suit different scenarios within your Laravel application.

Middleware Dependencies

In Laravel, middleware can have dependencies on other classes or services, allowing you to access additional functionality or resources within your middleware. By leveraging middleware dependencies, you can enhance the capabilities and flexibility of your middleware.

Here's how you can work with middleware dependencies in Laravel.

Define Middleware Dependencies

To define dependencies for your middleware, you can utilize Laravel's dependency injection feature. This allows you to specify the required dependencies in the constructor of your middleware class.

Illustration for injecting dependencies into middleware:

```
use App\Services\CustomService;
class CustomMiddleware
{
    protected $customService;
    public function __construct(CustomService $customService)
    {
        $this->customService = $customService;
    }
    public function handle($request, Closure $next)
    {
        // Access the custom service here
        // Perform middleware logic
        return $next($request);
    }
}
```

In this Illustration, the 'CustomMiddleware' class has a dependency on the 'CustomService' class. The dependency is injected through the middleware's constructor. The 'CustomService' can be any custom class or Laravel service that you want to utilize within your middleware.

Automatic Dependency Resolution

Laravel's service container will automatically resolve the dependencies for your middleware when it is instantiated. It will look for the binding or resolution of the required class or service within the container.

To ensure that Laravel can resolve the dependencies, make sure the required classes or services are registered in the service container or bound in the 'AppServiceProvider'.

Using Middleware Dependencies

Once the dependencies are injected into your middleware, you can access them within your middleware's methods. You can utilize the injected dependencies to perform specific tasks or access additional functionality.

Illustration for using middleware dependencies:

```
public function handle($request, Closure $next)
{
    // Access the injected dependency
    $result = $this->customService->performAction();
    // Perform other middleware logic
    return $next($request);
}
```

In this Illustration, the 'CustomMiddleware' class can access the 'CustomService' dependency and utilize its methods or properties. Within your middleware logic, you can leverage the functionality provided by the injected dependencies.

By utilizing middleware dependencies, you can leverage other classes or services within your middleware and enhance its capabilities. This approach promotes code reusability and separation of concerns, as you can delegate specific tasks to the injected dependencies. Additionally, it allows you to easily swap out or mock dependencies for testing purposes.

Ensure that the parameters are properly separated and provided when applying middleware to routes or controllers. Additionally, make sure the dependencies are properly injected into the middleware's constructor or methods.

Middleware parameters and dependencies offer a powerful way to extend the capabilities of your middleware and build more robust and flexible middleware pipelines in your Laravel applications.

Global Middleware vs. Route Middleware

In Laravel, middleware can be classified into two main types: global middleware and route middleware. Understanding the difference between these two types is crucial for properly applying middleware to your application. Here's a comparison between global middleware and route middleware.

Global Middleware

Global middleware in Laravel is applied to every HTTP request that enters your application. It allows you to perform common operations or apply functionality universally across all routes. Here's what you need to know about global middleware:

Definition: Global middleware is defined in the '$middleware' property of the 'app/Http/Kernel.php' file in your Laravel application.

Execution order: Global middleware is executed for every incoming request in the order it is defined in the '$middleware' property.

Modification of request and response: Global middleware has access to both the incoming request and the outgoing response. This means you can modify the request object before it reaches the route or modify the response object before it is sent back to the client.

Common use cases: Global middleware is commonly used for functionality that needs to be applied to every request, such as authentication, CORS (Cross-Origin Resource Sharing) handling, HTTPS redirection, logging, or setting default headers.

Registration: To add global middleware, you need to add the middleware class to the '$middleware' property in 'app/Http/Kernel.php'.

The following is an illustration of this feature:

```
protected $middleware = [
    // Other global middleware...
    \App\Http\Middleware\CustomMiddleware::class,
];
```

In this Illustration, 'CustomMiddleware' is a global middleware that will be executed for every request.

Order of execution: The order of global middleware matters. Middleware defined earlier in the '$middleware' array will be executed before those defined later. So consider the order carefully if you have multiple global middleware registered.

Note   Middleware that modifies the response should be placed after middleware that modifies the request.

Caution   Since global middleware is executed for every request, it can have an impact on the performance of your application. Be cautious when adding global middleware and ensure that it is necessary and optimized for performance.

Global middleware provides a convenient way to apply common functionality to every request in your Laravel application. It allows you to centralize operations that are required across multiple routes, reducing code duplication and improving maintainability. However, be mindful of the performance implications and use global middleware judiciously.

Route Middleware

Route middleware in Laravel allows you to selectively apply middleware to specific routes or groups of routes in your application. It provides a way to add functionality or restrictions to certain routes based on your application's requirements. Here's what you need to know about route middleware:

Definition: Route middleware is defined in the '$routeMiddleware' property of the 'app/Http/Kernel.php' file in your Laravel application.

Selective application: Route middleware is only applied to routes or groups of routes that explicitly specify the middleware.

Execution order: Route middleware is executed in the order it is specified in the route definition.

Granularity: Route middleware allows you to apply specific functionality or restrictions to certain routes. You can define different middleware for different routes or groups of routes based on your application's needs.

Common use cases: Route middleware is commonly used for tasks such as authentication, role-based access control, rate limiting, request validation, API token verification, and more.

Registration: To add route middleware, you need to add the middleware class or alias to the '$routeMiddleware' property in 'app/Http/Kernel.php'.

The following is an illustration of this feature:

```php
protected $routeMiddleware = [
    // Other route middleware...
    'auth' => \App\Http\Middleware\Authenticate::class,
];
```

In this Illustration, 'auth' is a middleware alias associated with the 'Authenticate' middleware class.

Application to routes: Route middleware can be applied to routes in different ways:

Route-level application: You can apply middleware to individual routes by using the 'middleware' method within the route definition.

The following is an illustration of this feature:

```php
Route::get('/Illustration', function () {
    // Route logic
})->middleware('auth');
```

Group-level application: You can apply middleware to a group of routes by using the 'middleware' method within a route group definition.

The following is an illustration of this feature:

```php
Route::middleware('auth')->group(function () {
    // Routes within this group will have the 'auth'
      middleware applied
});
```

Multiple middleware: You can apply multiple route middleware to a single route or group of routes by specifying them as an array.

The following is an illustration of this feature:

```
Route::get('/Illustration', function () {
    // Route logic
})->middleware(['auth', 'role:admin']);
```

In this Illustration, both the 'auth' and 'role' middleware will be applied to the '/Illustration' route.

Route middleware provides a way to selectively apply middleware to specific routes or groups of routes, giving you fine-grained control over the functionality and restrictions within your application. It allows you to keep your middleware focused and avoid applying unnecessary middleware to routes where it is not needed.

By understanding the distinction between global middleware and route middleware, you can apply the appropriate middleware type based on the scope and requirements of your application.

Middleware Best Practices and Performance Considerations

Middleware plays a crucial role in handling incoming requests and responses in Laravel applications. To ensure efficient and maintainable code, it is important to follow best practices and consider performance aspects when working with middleware. Here are some best practices and performance considerations to keep in mind.

Keep Middleware Focused

Each middleware should have a specific responsibility and perform a single task.

Avoid creating monolithic middleware that handles multiple unrelated tasks.

Split complex functionality into multiple middleware for better organization and reusability.

Order of Middleware Matters

The order in which middleware is applied is significant.

Middleware that modifies the request should be placed early in the pipeline.

Middleware that modifies the response should be placed toward the end of the pipeline.

Use Middleware Groups

Middleware groups allow you to group related middleware and apply it to multiple routes at once.

Define middleware groups in the '$middlewareGroups' property of 'app/Http/Kernel.php'.

Utilize middleware groups for common functionality such as API authentication, web authentication, etc.

Apply Middleware Selectively

Apply middleware only to routes that require it.

Avoid applying middleware to routes where it is not necessary.

Be mindful of the performance impact of applying unnecessary middleware.

Middleware Parameters and Dependencies

Use middleware parameters to customize the behavior of middleware based on specific values or configurations.

Leverage middleware dependencies to access additional functionality or resources.

Carefully manage and test middleware parameters and dependencies for correctness and maintainability.

Performance Considerations

Be aware of the potential performance impact of middleware.

Avoid adding unnecessary middleware that adds overhead to every request.

Optimize middleware code to ensure it executes efficiently.

Cache expensive operations or computations performed within middleware.

Monitor and profile your application's performance to identify any bottlenecks related to middleware.

Error Handling and Exceptions

Handle exceptions and errors gracefully within middleware.

Use appropriate HTTP response codes and error messages.

Log any errors or exceptions for debugging purposes.

Testing Middleware

Write unit tests for your middleware to ensure its functionality and correctness.

Test different scenarios and edge cases to cover all possible paths within the middleware code.

Mock dependencies as needed for effective testing.

By following these best practices and considering the performance implications of middleware, you can ensure that your middleware code is well-organized and efficient and provides the desired functionality within your Laravel application.

Summary

This chapter covered advanced middleware approaches in the context of the Laravel framework. You gained insight into middleware's tremendous features and its role in intercepting and altering HTTP requests and answers. The chapter also demonstrated how to write custom middleware to fulfill certain jobs and imparted knowledge of global middleware, route middleware, and group middleware. We also examined conditional middleware applications based on dynamic factors and approaches for chaining various middleware. You also learned how to use middleware to manage exceptions and error responses.

In the next chapter, we'll dive into developing real-time applications with Laravel.

CHAPTER 8

Real-Time Applications with Laravel

In the previous chapter, we explored the fascinating world of advanced middleware techniques in Laravel, empowering ourselves with the ability to intercept and process HTTP requests effectively. As our journey through Laravel's vast capabilities continues, we now venture into the realm of real-time applications—an exciting and dynamic space that allows us to create interactive and engaging user experiences.

Real-Time Applications: An Overview

In this section, we will delve into the concept of real-time applications and understand the significance of delivering data and updates to clients instantaneously. We will explore the challenges and opportunities in building real-time features and the benefits they offer in enhancing user engagement and interaction.

Building Real-Time Features with Laravel WebSockets

Laravel WebSockets provides the foundation for building real-time applications by enabling bidirectional communication between clients and the server. We will learn how to set up and configure Laravel WebSockets to create dynamic and responsive applications that push real-time updates to connected clients.

Broadcasting Events with Laravel Echo

Laravel Echo is a powerful tool that simplifies the process of broadcasting and listening to real-time events in your application. We will uncover how to use Laravel Echo to broadcast events and consume them on the client side, allowing us to deliver real-time updates to users seamlessly.

Creating Real-Time Notifications and Chat Applications

In this final section, we will put our knowledge into practice by building real-time notifications and chat applications using Laravel WebSockets and Laravel Echo. We will explore how to implement features that provide instant notifications to users and enable real-time chat conversations, fostering a sense of immediacy and interactivity within our applications.

© Sivaraj Selvaraj 2024

S. Selvaraj, *Building Real-Time Marvels with Laravel*, https://doi.org/10.1007/978-1-4842-9789-6_8

Throughout this chapter, we will embark on an exciting journey into the world of real-time applications with Laravel. By mastering real-time communication techniques, we can create immersive and responsive user experiences that leave a lasting impression on our audience. So let's dive into the realm of real-time applications, where we bring our Laravel applications to life with dynamic and interactive features!

Real-Time Applications: An Overview

Real-time applications are a type of application that requires instant data updates and communication between the client and server.

These applications enable users to receive and send data in real time without the need for manual page refreshes. Laravel provides several tools and libraries to build real-time applications efficiently.

This chapter introduces the concept of real-time applications and covers the key aspects you need to know.

Here are the main points covered in this chapter:

Real-time communication: Real-time applications involve bidirectional communication between the client and server, allowing them to exchange data instantly. This is achieved through techniques such as WebSockets, AJAX long polling, or server-sent events (SSE).

Laravel Echo: Laravel Echo is a JavaScript library that simplifies real-time communication in Laravel applications. It provides an elegant API to listen for events and broadcast messages over channels using WebSockets or other broadcasting technologies.

Broadcasting: Broadcasting in Laravel allows you to send events from the server to connected clients in real time. Laravel supports broadcasting over various drivers, including Pusher, Redis, and Socket.io.

Pusher: Pusher is a popular real-time messaging service that provides WebSocket-based communication channels. Laravel integrates seamlessly with Pusher, making it easy to implement real-time functionality in your applications.

Event broadcasting: Laravel's event broadcasting feature allows you to define events and broadcast them to interested listeners. This enables real-time updates and notifications across different clients or devices.

Channels and presence channels: Channels in Laravel provide a way to categorize events and broadcast them to specific groups of clients. Presence channels allow you to track the presence of users within a channel, making them useful for building features like chat systems or collaborative applications.

Authentication and security: Real-time applications require proper authentication and security measures to ensure that only authorized users can access and participate in real-time communication. Laravel provides authentication guards and middleware to handle these aspects.

Building real-time applications with Laravel opens up a wide range of possibilities for interactive and responsive user experiences.

Whether you're building a chat application, a live dashboard, or a collaborative editing tool, understanding the foundations of real-time communication and the tools Laravel provides will empower you to create powerful and engaging applications.

Building Real-Time Features with Laravel WebSockets

Laravel WebSockets is a powerful package that allows you to integrate real-time features into your Laravel applications using WebSockets. It provides a simple and efficient way to broadcast events and enable real-time communication between the server and clients. Here's an overview of building real-time features with Laravel WebSockets.

Installation and Configuration

Install the Laravel WebSockets package using Composer.

Configure the broadcasting driver in your Laravel application to use WebSockets.

Configure the WebSocket server, which can be a dedicated server or run within your Laravel application.

Defining Events

Define events that you want to broadcast to clients using Laravel's event system.

Create event classes that extend the 'Illuminate\Contracts\Broadcasting\ ShouldBroadcast' interface.

Define the necessary data and logic within your event classes.

Broadcasting Events

Within your application's logic, trigger events using the 'event ()' helper function or the 'Event' facade.

Events can be broadcast globally or to specific channels, depending on your application's requirements.

Listening to Events on the Client

Use Laravel Echo on the client side to listen for and handle incoming events.

Configure Laravel Echo to connect to your WebSocket server.

Use the 'channel ()' method to join the desired channel(s) and listen for specific events.

Presence Channels

Laravel WebSockets supports presence channels, which allow you to track the presence of users within a channel.

Implement the 'PresenceChannel' interface in your event classes to provide user presence information.

Utilize the 'joining', 'leaving', and 'here' event callbacks to handle user presence–related logic.

Authentication and Security

Secure your WebSocket connections and channels by implementing authentication.

Use Laravel's authentication guards and middleware to authenticate WebSocket connections.

Authenticate users within presence channels to ensure that only authorized users can access them.

Advanced Configuration and Features

Laravel WebSockets offers various configuration options to customize your setup.

Explore additional features such as private channels, authorization headers, and client events.

Laravel WebSockets provides a WebSocket dashboard for you to monitor and manage your WebSocket server.

Laravel WebSockets simplifies the process of building real-time features in Laravel applications. It provides an intuitive API and handles the complexities of managing WebSocket connections and broadcasting events. By leveraging Laravel WebSockets, you can create engaging real-time experiences for your users and enable seamless communication between the server and clients.

Broadcasting Events with Laravel Echo

Laravel Echo is a JavaScript library that simplifies the process of listening for and handling real-time events in your Laravel applications. It works seamlessly with Laravel's broadcasting system, allowing you to easily broadcast events from the server and receive them on the client side. Here's an overview of broadcasting events with Laravel Echo.

Setting Up Laravel Echo

To get started with Laravel Echo, you need to set up the necessary dependencies and configure it to connect to your Laravel application's broadcasting server. Here's a step-by-step guide to setting up Laravel Echo.

Install Laravel Echo

Install Laravel Echo using npm or Yarn in your JavaScript project.

Open your terminal and navigate to your project's directory.

Run the following command to install Laravel Echo:

```
npm install laravel-echo
```

Install Socket.io or Pusher

Laravel Echo requires a broadcast driver for real-time communication.

You can choose between Socket.io and Pusher as your broadcasting driver.

Install the appropriate package based on your choice. For Socket.io:

```
npm install socket.io-client
```

For Pusher:

```
npm install pusher-js
```

Configure Laravel Echo

In your JavaScript code, import Laravel Echo and configure it with the necessary options.

Configure Broadcasting in Laravel

Open the **config/broadcasting.php** file and set the **default** driver to **socket.io**. Also, configure the connection options for your Socket.io server.

The following is an illustration of this feature:

```
return [
    'default' => 'socket.io',
    // ...
    'connections' => [
        'socket.io' => [
            'driver' => 'socket.io',
            'url' => env('APP_URL'), // URL of your Socket.io server
            'client_locations' => [
                'web' => 'web', // The channel for web clients
                // Add more client locations if required
            ],
        ],
    ],
];
```

Initialize Echo in Your Application

Create a new JavaScript file (e.g., **socket.js**) in your **resources/js** directory. In this file, you'll initialize Echo with the Socket.io connection:

```
import Echo from 'laravel-echo';
import { io } from 'socket.io-client';
window.io = io;
window.Echo = new Echo({
    broadcaster: 'socket.io',
    host: window.location.hostname + ':6001', // Replace with the URL of
your Socket.io server
    auth: {
        headers: {
            // If you're using Laravel Sanctum or another authentication
                method, add the necessary headers here
            // 'Authorization': 'Bearer ' + Your_Authentication_Token,
        },
    },
});
// Optionally, you can listen to global events (e.g., 'connect',
'disconnect', etc.)
window.Echo.connector.socket.on('connect', () => {
    console.log('Connected to Socket.io server');
});
window.Echo.connector.socket.on('disconnect', () => {
    console.log('Disconnected from Socket.io server');
});
```

Include the socket.js file in your Laravel views.

Add the following script tag to your main layout file (e.g., **resources/views/layouts/app.blade.php**) to include the **socket.js** file:

```
<!-- resources/views/layouts/app.blade.php -->
<!DOCTYPE html>
<html>
<head>
    <!-- ... -->
</head>
<body>
    <!-- ... -->
    <!-- Include the socket.js file -->
    <script src="{{ asset('js/socket.js') }}"></script>
</body>
</html>
```

Use Laravel Echo in Your JavaScript Code

Now that Laravel Echo is set up, you can use it in your JavaScript files to listen for events and send messages through Socket.io.

The following is an illustration of this feature:

```
// resources/js/main.js
// Example: Listening for events on a channel
window.Echo.channel('public-events')
    .listen('.new-event', (data) => {
        console.log('Received new event:', data);
    });
// Example: Broadcasting an event
window.Echo.private('private-channel')
    .whisper('new-message', {
        user: 'Divya',
        message: 'Hello there!',
    });
```

Remember to run your Socket.io server independently and to make sure it's listening on the correct port (6001 by default, as indicated in the socket.js file). With this configuration, Laravel Echo will enable real-time broadcasting and event listening in your Laravel application using Socket.io.

Configure the Broadcasting Driver in Laravel

In your Laravel application, open the 'config/broadcasting.php' file.

Update the 'default' value to the broadcasting driver you're using (e.g., 'pusher' or 'redis').

Set the configuration options for the chosen broadcasting driver, including credentials and connection details.

Authenticate and Authorize Channels

Laravel Echo requires authentication and authorization to access private and presence channels.

Implement the necessary authentication and authorization logic on your Laravel backend, ensuring that only authorized users can access protected channels.

Laravel provides authentication guards and middleware to handle this, so you can leverage them in your application.

Once you've set up Laravel Echo, you can start listening for events and handling real-time communication in your Laravel application. Remember to refer to Laravel Echo's documentation for more advanced configuration options and features, as well as how to use it with specific broadcasting drivers like Pusher or Socket.io.

Listening for Events with Laravel Echo

Once you have Laravel Echo set up in your JavaScript project, you can start listening for events broadcasted from your Laravel application. Here's how you can listen for events using Laravel Echo.

Joining Channels

Before listening for events, you need to join the desired channel(s) using Laravel Echo's 'channel ()' method.

The 'channel ()' method accepts the channel name as a parameter and returns a channel instance.

Use the channel instance to listen for events on that channel:

```
const channel = window.Echo.channel('channel-name');
```

Listening for Events

Once you have joined the channel, you can use the 'listen()' method to listen for specific events.

The 'listen()' method accepts two parameters: the event name and a callback function to handle the event data:

```
channel.listen('event-name', (data) => {
    // Handle the event data
});
```

The callback function receives the event data as an argument. You can then perform actions based on the received data.

Binding Event Listeners

Another way to listen for events is by binding event listeners directly to specific DOM elements.

You can use Laravel Echo's 'listenForWhisper()' method or Vue.js components to bind event listeners:

```
channel.listenForWhisper('event-name', (data) => {
    // Handle the event data
});
```

This method allows you to bind event listeners to elements and respond to specific events triggered by user interactions or other actions.

Handling Event Data

Inside the event listener callback function, you can access the event data and perform actions based on it.

The event data may include any information you broadcast from your Laravel application.

Update the UI, manipulate data, or trigger other actions based on the received event data:

```
channel.listen('event-name', (data) => {
    // Handle the event data
    console.log(data); // Log the received event data
    // Update the UI or perform other actions based on the data
});
```

Cleaning Up Event Listeners

It is important to clean up event listeners when they are no longer needed to avoid memory leaks.

Laravel Echo provides the 'stopListening()' method to unsubscribe from events and stop listening on a channel:

```
channel.stopListening('event-name');
```

Call the 'stopListening()' method with the event name to unsubscribe from that specific event.

By listening for events with Laravel Echo, you can receive real-time updates from your Laravel backend and take appropriate actions on the client side. Remember to replace "channel-name" and "event-name" with the actual names of your channels and events. Additionally, refer to Laravel Echo's documentation for more advanced features, such as presence channels, private channels, and authentication mechanisms.

Joining Channels

When using Laravel Echo, joining channels allows you to subscribe to specific channels and start receiving events broadcast on those channels. Here's how you can join channels using Laravel Echo.

Public Channels

Public channels are accessible to all users and do not require authentication.

To join a public channel, use the 'channel ()' method provided by Laravel Echo.

Pass the channel name as the parameter to the 'channel ()' method:

```
const channel = window.Echo.channel('public-channel');
```

In this example, "public-channel" is the name of the public channel you want to join.

Private Channels

Private channels require authentication to access and participate in real-time communication.

To join a private channel, use the 'private()' method provided by Laravel Echo.

Pass the channel name as the parameter to the 'private()' method:

```
const channel = window.Echo.private('private-channel');
```

Replace "private-channel" with the name of the private channel you want to join.

Presence Channels

Presence channels allow you to track the presence of users within a channel.

To join a presence channel, use the 'join()' method provided by Laravel Echo.

Pass the channel name as the parameter to the 'join()' method:

```
const channel = window.Echo.join('presence-channel');
```

Replace "presence-channel" with the name of the presence channel you want to join.

Listening for Channel Events

Once you have joined a channel, you can listen for events specific to that channel.

Use the 'listen()' method provided by Laravel Echo to listen for events on the channel instance:

```
channel.listen('event-name', (data) => {
    // Handle the event data
});
```

Replace "event-name" with the name of the event you want to listen for on the joined channel.

Leaving Channels

If you no longer need to receive events from a channel, you can leave the channel to unsubscribe.

Use the 'leave()' method provided by Laravel Echo to leave the joined channel:

```
channel.leave();
```

Calling the 'leave()' method will unsubscribe from the channel and stop receiving events from it.

By joining channels using Laravel Echo, you can start listening for events on specific channels and receive real-time updates in your application. Make sure to replace "public-channel", "private-channel", and "presence-channel" with the actual names of your channels. Additionally, refer to Laravel Echo's documentation for more advanced features, such as presence channel events and channel authentication.

Handling Events

Define event listeners to handle specific events that are broadcast.

Event listeners can be registered using Laravel Echo's 'listen' method or through Vue. js components.

Inside the event listener, you can access the event's data and perform actions based on the received data.

Presence Channels

Presence channels in Laravel Echo allow you to track the presence of users within a channel. This is useful for building real-time features such as online user lists, chat systems, or collaborative applications where you need to know who is currently active in a channel. Here's how you can work with presence channels using Laravel Echo.

Joining a Presence Channel

To join a presence channel, use the 'join()' method provided by Laravel Echo.

Pass the name of the presence channel as the parameter to the 'join()' method:

```
const channel = window.Echo.join('presence-channel');
```

Replace "presence-channel" with the name of the presence channel you want to join.

Listening for Presence Events

Once you have joined a presence channel, you can listen for presence-related events.

Laravel Echo provides event callbacks for presence channel events like 'joining', 'leaving', and 'here':

```
channel.here((users) => {
    // Handle initial presence data (list of users currently in the
        channel)
});
```

```
channel.joining((user) => {
    // Handle a user joining the channel
});
channel.leaving((user) => {
    // Handle a user leaving the channel
});
```

The 'here ()' event callback is triggered when initially joining the channel and provides an array of users currently in the channel.

The 'joining ()' event callback is triggered when a new user joins the channel and provides the user object.

The 'leaving ()' event callback is triggered when a user leaves the channel and provides the user object.

Accessing Presence Data

Inside the event callbacks, you can access the presence data, including user information.

The presence data provides information about the users currently present in the channel:

```
channel.here((users) => {
    // Loop through the users array and access their information
    users.forEach((user) => {
        console.log(user.id); // User ID
        console.log(user.name); // User name
        // ...
    });
});
channel.joining((user) => {
    console.log(user.id); // User ID
    console.log(user.name); // User name
    // ...
});
```

```
channel.leaving((user) => {
    console.log(user.id); // User ID
    console.log(user.name); // User name
    // ...
});
```

The user object contains various properties, such as 'id', 'name', and any additional user-specific data you may have included.

Handling User Presence Updates

Presence channels automatically handle joining and leaving events when users connect to or disconnect from the channel.

You can update the UI or perform other actions based on these events to reflect the presence status of users:

```
channel.here((users) => {
    // Update the online user list or display the number of active users
});
channel.joining((user) => {
    // Update the online user list or display a user joining
        notification
});
channel.leaving((user) => {
    // Update the online user list or display a user leaving
notification
});
```

Based on these events, you can update the UI to display the list of online users or trigger other actions to reflect the presence status of users.

By utilizing presence channels with Laravel Echo, you can track the presence of users within a channel and build real-time features that require knowledge of who is currently active. Make sure to replace "presence-channel" with the actual name of your presence channel. Additionally, refer to Laravel Echo's documentation for more advanced features, such as presence channel authentication and presence channel events.

Private Channels

Private channels in Laravel Echo provide a secure way to transmit sensitive data and restrict access to specific users or authorized individuals. By using private channels, you can ensure that only authenticated users with the appropriate permissions can listen to events on those channels. Here's how you can work with private channels using Laravel Echo.

Joining a Private Channel

To join a private channel, use the 'private()' method provided by Laravel Echo.
   Pass the name of the private channel as the parameter to the 'private()' method.

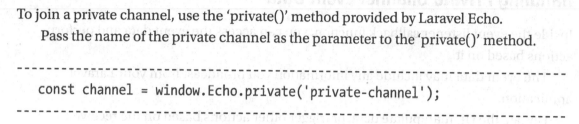

```
const channel = window.Echo.private('private-channel');
```

   Replace "private-channel" with the name of the private channel you want to join.

Authenticating Private Channels

Private channels require authentication to ensure that only authorized users can access them.
   Laravel provides authentication guards and middleware to handle this process.
   Authenticate the user on your Laravel backend and authorize their access to the private channel.
   Laravel Echo automatically handles the authentication process based on your Laravel application's authentication configuration.

Listening for Private Channel Events

Once you have joined a private channel, you can listen for events specific to that channel.
   Use the 'listen()' method provided by Laravel Echo to listen for events on the private channel instance:

```
channel.listen('event-name', (data) => {
    // Handle the event data
});
```

Replace "event-name" with the name of the event you want to listen for on the joined private channel.

Handling Private Channel Event Data

Inside the event listener callback function, you can access the event data and perform actions based on it.

The event data may include any information you broadcast from your Laravel application.

Update the UI, manipulate data, or trigger other actions based on the received event data:

```
channel.listen('event-name', (data) => {
    // Handle the event data
    console.log(data); // Log the received event data
    // Update the UI or perform other actions based on the data
});
```

Cleaning Up Private Channel Listeners

When you no longer need to receive events from a private channel, you can leave the channel to unsubscribe.

Use the 'leave()' method provided by Laravel Echo to leave the joined private channel:

```
channel.leave();
```

Calling the 'leave()' method will unsubscribe from the private channel and stop receiving events from it.

By utilizing private channels with Laravel Echo, you can ensure the security of your real-time communication by restricting access to authorized users. Make sure to replace "private-channel" with the actual name of your private channel. Additionally, refer to Laravel Echo's documentation for more advanced features, such as private channel authentication and authorization mechanisms.

Additional Features

Laravel Echo provides a range of additional features that enhance the functionality and flexibility of real-time communication in your application. These features allow you to customize your real-time implementation and provide a more interactive user experience. Here are some of the additional features offered by Laravel Echo.

Client Events

Laravel Echo allows you to trigger events directly from the client side, which can be received by other clients or the server.

Use the 'socketId()' method to retrieve the unique socket ID of the client.

Trigger a client event using the 'whisper()' method, specifying the event name and data:

```
window.Echo.socketId((socketId) => {
    // Use the socket ID for client-specific operations
    console.log(socketId);
});
window.Echo.whisper('event-name', {
    // Data to be sent with the client event
    // ...
});
```

Private Channels with Authorization Headers

Laravel Echo allows you to authenticate private channels using authorization headers.

Set the authorization headers on the Echo instance using the 'withHeaders()' method.

Pass an object with the headers to be sent with the authentication request:

```
window.Echo.private('private-channel')
    .withHeaders({
        Authorization: 'Bearer ' + authToken,
    })
    .listen('event-name', (data) => {
        // Handle the event data
    });
```

Subscribing to Channels Dynamically

Laravel Echo provides the 'subscribe()' and 'unsubscribe()' methods to dynamically subscribe to and unsubscribe from channels.

This is useful when you need to change the channel subscriptions based on user actions or application logic:

```
const channelName = 'channel-name';
// Subscribe to a channel dynamically
window.Echo.subscribe(channelName).listen('event-name', (data) => {
    // Handle the event data
});
// Unsubscribe from a channel dynamically
window.Echo.unsubscribe(channelName);
```

Binding Events to DOM Elements

Laravel Echo allows you to bind event listeners directly to specific DOM elements.

Use the 'listenForWhisper()' method or Vue.js components to bind event listeners to elements.

Trigger specific events based on user interactions or other actions:

```
window.Echo.listenForWhisper('event-name', (data) => {
    // Handle the event data
});
// Bind event listeners to specific DOM elements
document.getElementById('element-id').addEventListener('click', () => {
    // Trigger a client event or perform other actions
    window.Echo.whisper('event-name', {
        // Data to be sent with the client event
        // ...
    });
});
```

Presence Channel Events

Presence channels in Laravel Echo provide additional event callbacks for handling user presence-related logic.

Use the 'here()', 'joining()', and 'leaving()' event callbacks to respond to user presence updates within presence channels:

```
const presenceChannel = window.Echo.join('presence-channel');
presenceChannel.here((users) => {
    // Handle initial presence data (list of users currently in the
        channel)
});
presenceChannel.joining((user) => {
    // Handle a user joining the channel
});
presenceChannel.leaving((user) => {
    // Handle a user leaving the channel
});
```

These additional features offered by Laravel Echo give you more control and flexibility when working with real-time communication in your application. Explore the Laravel Echo documentation for further details on these features and how to leverage them to enhance your real-time functionality.

Laravel Echo simplifies real-time event handling by providing an intuitive API for listening to events and performing actions in response. It integrates seamlessly with Laravel's broadcasting system and allows you to build engaging real-time features in your applications.

By utilizing Laravel Echo, you can easily implement real-time communication between your Laravel backend and the client side, providing a smooth and interactive user experience.

Creating Real-Time Notifications and Chat Applications

Real-time notifications and chat applications are common use cases for real-time communication in web applications. Laravel provides the necessary tools and features to build such applications easily. Here's an overview of creating real-time notifications and chat applications using Laravel.

Real-Time Notifications

Real-time notifications provide a way to instantly notify users about important events happening in your application. By using Laravel Echo, you can easily implement real-time notifications and deliver them to the users in real time. Here's how you can set up real-time notifications with Laravel Echo.

Define Notification Events

In your Laravel application, define the notification events that should trigger real-time notifications.

These events can represent various actions or updates in your application, such as new messages, friend requests, or order updates.

Use Laravel's event system to define and dispatch these notification events.

Create Notification Classes

Create notification classes that extend Laravel's 'Illuminate\Notifications\
Notification' class.

Define the necessary methods in the notification class, such as 'via()', 'toMail()',
'toDatabase()', etc.

Implement the 'via()' method to specify the notification channels, including the
broadcasting channel for real-time notifications.

Broadcast Notification Events

Use Laravel's broadcasting system to broadcast the notification events to interested
listeners.

In the notification class, override the 'broadcastOn()' method and return the
broadcasting channel you want to use for real-time notifications:

```
public function broadcastOn()
{
    return new Channel('notifications');
}
```

Listen for Notification Events with Laravel Echo

In your JavaScript code, use Laravel Echo to listen for the notification events and handle
them in real time.

Join the broadcasting channel used for real-time notifications:

```
const channel = window.Echo.channel('notifications');
channel.listen('.notification-event', (notification) => {
    // Handle the notification event data
    // Update the UI or display a notification to the user
});
```

The '.notification-event' is the event name used for the real-time notifications.
Replace it with the actual event name you use in your Laravel application.

Triggering Notifications

When an event occurs in your Laravel application that should trigger a notification, dispatch the notification event.

Pass any necessary data to the notification event constructor to customize the notification content:

```
event(new NotificationEvent($user, $data));
```

'NotificationEvent' is the event class representing the notification event, and '$user' and '$data' are the user and data objects needed for the notification.

Handling Notifications on the Client Side

When a notification event is received by Laravel Echo, handle the event data on the client side.

Update the UI or display a notification to the user based on the received event data:

```
channel.listen('.notification-event', (notification) => {
    // Handle the notification event data
    console.log(notification.title); // Notification title
    console.log(notification.message); // Notification message
    // Update the UI or display a notification to the user
});
```

Access the notification data properties, such as 'title', 'message', or any other custom data you included in the notification event.

By implementing real-time notifications with Laravel Echo, you can instantly notify users about important events happening in your application. Users can receive the notifications in real time and stay updated with the latest information. Make sure to replace "notifications" with the actual broadcasting channel name you used for real-time notifications. Additionally, refer to Laravel Echo's documentation for more advanced features, such as private notifications and event listener binding to specific DOM elements.

Chat Applications

Building a chat application involves real-time communication between users, allowing them to send and receive messages instantly. Laravel Echo, along with Laravel's broadcasting capabilities, provides a powerful foundation for creating chat applications. Here's how you can leverage Laravel Echo to build a chat application.

User Authentication and Authorization

Implement user authentication and authorization in your Laravel application.

Use Laravel's authentication system to authenticate users and manage their access to the chat application.

Ensure that only authenticated users can access the chat features.

Database Setup for Chat Messages

Set up a database table to store the chat messages.

Create a migration to define the table structure, including columns like 'sender_id', 'receiver_id', 'message', 'timestamp', etc.

Run the migration to create the chat messages table in your database.

Real-Time Broadcasting Configuration

Configure your Laravel application to use a broadcasting driver like Pusher or Redis.

Set up the broadcasting driver credentials in your Laravel application's '.env' file or broadcasting configuration file ('config/broadcasting.php').

Ensure that your broadcasting server is properly configured and running.

Creating Chat Models and Relationships

Create models for the chat messages and user entities in your Laravel application.

Define relationships between the models to establish associations.

For example, you may have a 'User' model and a 'ChatMessage' model, where a user can send multiple chat messages and a chat message belongs to a sender and a receiver.

Sending and Storing Chat Messages

Implement a form or interface in your chat application for users to compose and send messages.

On the server side, when a user sends a message, store it in the chat messages table with the appropriate sender and receiver IDs.

You can use Laravel's Eloquent ORM to perform database operations, such as creating and storing chat messages.

Receiving and Displaying Chat Messages

Use Laravel Echo on the client side to listen for new chat messages in real time.

Join the channel specific to the authenticated user or the conversation between two users.

When a new message event is received, update the chat interface to display the new message to the appropriate users.

Updating the UI in Real Time

Use JavaScript frameworks like Vue.js or React to handle dynamic UI updates in response to real-time events.

Update the chat interface to display new messages, show typing indicators, or indicate the online/offline status of users.

Leverage Laravel Echo's event callbacks to handle various chat-related events and update the UI accordingly.

By following these steps and leveraging Laravel Echo, you can build a fully functional chat application that enables real-time communication between users. Remember to handle authentication and authorization properly to ensure the security of your chat application. Additionally, refer to Laravel Echo's documentation for more advanced features and techniques to enhance your chat application, such as presence channels for online/offline status or private channels for secure conversations.

Real-Time Presence

Real-time presence functionality allows you to track the online/offline status of users and provide real-time updates on their presence within your application. Laravel Echo, in combination with presence channels, provides the tools to implement real-time presence features. Here's how you can leverage Laravel Echo for real-time presence.

Configure Presence Channels

Set up presence channels in your Laravel application.

Presence channels allow you to track the presence of users in real time.

Configure your broadcasting driver (e.g., Pusher or Redis) to enable presence channel functionality.

Joining Presence Channels

When a user authenticates and logs in to your application, join the corresponding presence channel.

Use Laravel Echo's 'join()' method to join the presence channel, passing the channel name as the parameter:

```
const channel = window.Echo.join('presence-channel');
```

Replace "presence-channel" with the actual name of the presence channel.

Listening for Presence Events

Once a user has joined a presence channel, you can listen for presence-related events.

Laravel Echo provides event callbacks for presence channel events, such as 'here', 'joining', and 'leaving':

```
channel.here((users) => {
    // Handle the initial presence data (users currently in the channel)
});
channel.joining((user) => {
    // Handle a user joining the channel
});
channel.leaving((user) => {
    // Handle a user leaving the channel
});
```

The 'here ()' event callback is triggered when initially joining the channel, providing an array of users currently in the channel.

The 'joining ()' event callback is triggered when a new user joins the channel, providing information about the joining user.

The 'leaving ()' event callback is triggered when a user leaves the channel, providing information about the leaving user.

Updating User Presence Status

When a user authenticates and joins a presence channel, update their presence status in your application.

Store the user's presence status in the database or cache, indicating that they are currently online.

Handling Presence Updates

Inside the presence event callbacks, handle the presence data and update the UI or perform other actions accordingly.

Update the online user list, display the number of active users, or show presence indicators.

Leaving Presence Channels

When a user logs out or leaves your application, make sure they leave the presence channel to unsubscribe.

Use the 'leave()' method provided by Laravel Echo to leave the joined presence channel:

```
channel.leave();
```

Calling the 'leave ()' method will unsubscribe the user from the presence channel.

By utilizing presence channels and Laravel Echo, you can implement real-time presence functionality in your application, providing real-time updates on the online/offline status of users. Ensure that you handle authentication and authorization properly to protect the privacy and security of user presence information. Additionally, refer to Laravel Echo's documentation for more advanced features, such as presence channel events and presence channel member information.

Private Messaging

Private messaging functionality allows users to communicate privately with each other in real time. With Laravel Echo, you can easily implement private messaging features in your application. Here's how you can leverage Laravel Echo for private messaging.

User Authentication and Authorization

Implement user authentication and authorization in your Laravel application.

Use Laravel's authentication system to authenticate users and manage their access to private messaging features.

Ensure that only authenticated users can access the private messaging functionality.

Database Setup for Private Messages

Set up a database table to store private messages between users.

Create a migration to define the table structure, including columns like 'sender_id', 'receiver_id', 'message', 'timestamp', etc.

Run the migration to create the private messages table in your database.

Real-Time Broadcasting Configuration

Configure your Laravel application to use a broadcasting driver like Pusher or Redis.

Set up the broadcasting driver credentials in your Laravel application's '.env' file or broadcasting configuration file ('config/broadcasting.php').

Ensure that your broadcasting server is properly configured and running.

Creating Private Message Models and Relationships

Create models for private messages and user entities in your Laravel application.

Define relationships between the models to establish associations.

For example, you may have a 'User' model and a 'PrivateMessage' model, where a user can send multiple private messages and a private message belongs to a sender and a receiver.

Sending and Storing Private Messages

Implement a form or interface in your private messaging feature for users to compose and send private messages.

On the server side, when a user sends a private message, store it in the private messages table with the appropriate sender and receiver IDs.

You can use Laravel's Eloquent ORM to perform database operations, such as creating and storing private messages.

Receiving and Displaying Private Messages

Use Laravel Echo on the client side to listen for new private messages in real time.

Join a private channel specific to the authenticated user or the conversation between two users.

When a new message event is received, update the private messaging interface to display the new message to the appropriate users.

Updating the UI in Real Time

Use JavaScript frameworks like Vue.js or React to handle dynamic UI updates in response to real-time events.

Update the private messaging interface to display new messages, show typing indicators, or indicate message delivery/read status.

Leverage Laravel Echo's event callbacks to handle various private messaging events and update the UI accordingly.

By following these steps and utilizing Laravel Echo, you can build a robust private messaging system that allows users to communicate privately in real time. Remember to handle authentication and authorization properly to ensure the privacy and security of private messages.

Additionally, refer to Laravel Echo's documentation for more advanced features and techniques to enhance your private messaging functionality, such as message encryption or message status updates.

Building real-time notifications and chat applications with Laravel enables instant communication and enhances user engagement. Laravel's broadcasting system, combined with Laravel Echo, simplifies the implementation of real-time features and provides a seamless experience for users.

Summary

In this chapter, you learned about the intriguing realm of real-time applications with Laravel. The chapter focused on developing interactive and dynamic web applications that can efficiently manage real-time data and events. You learned about Laravel's built-in WebSocket support via technologies such as Pusher and Laravel Echo, how to set up and configure real-time event broadcasting, and how to create event listeners and broadcast events to connected clients. You also saw how to use Laravel's real-time features to create real-time chat applications and live notifications.

The next chapter will introduce you to testing and Test-Driven Development.

CHAPTER 9

Testing and Test-Driven Development

In the previous chapter, we delved into the captivating world of real-time applications with Laravel, harnessing the power of WebSockets and Laravel Echo to create dynamic and interactive user experiences. As we continue our journey through Laravel's diverse toolkit, we now focus on an essential aspect of modern software development—testing and Test-Driven Development (TDD).

Introduction to Testing in Laravel

In this section, we will explore the significance of testing in Laravel applications. Testing ensures the reliability, correctness, and maintainability of our codebase, giving us the confidence to make changes without fear of breaking existing functionalities. We will understand the different types of tests and why testing is an integral part of the development process.

Writing Unit Tests with PHPUnit

Unit testing is the foundation of testing in Laravel, where we validate the functionality of individual units or methods in isolation. We will learn how to write unit tests using PHPUnit, Laravel's testing framework, and discover how to verify the correctness of our code's behavior at the granular level.

Testing HTTP Requests and Responses

Web applications often rely on HTTP requests and responses to function correctly. In this section, we will explore how to test HTTP requests and responses in Laravel, ensuring that our routes and controllers handle incoming requests and return the expected responses.

© Sivaraj Selvaraj 2024

S. Selvaraj, *Building Real-Time Marvels with Laravel*, https://doi.org/10.1007/978-1-4842-9789-6_9

Test-Driven Development (TDD) Workflow

Test-Driven Development (TDD) is a development approach that emphasizes writing tests before implementing the actual code. We will understand the principles and benefits of TDD and walk through the TDD workflow in Laravel, guiding us to write testable and maintainable code from the outset.

Testing API Endpoints and Integrations

APIs are a vital component of modern applications, and testing them thoroughly is essential to ensure their reliability. We will learn how to test API endpoints and integrations in Laravel, validating the correctness of data transmitted and received by our APIs.

Throughout this chapter, we will unravel the art of testing and Test-Driven Development in Laravel, equipping ourselves with the knowledge and skills to build robust, stable, and maintainable applications. By adopting testing best practices and implementing TDD, we can create high-quality software that meets our users' needs and exceeds their expectations. So let's dive into the world of testing and Test-Driven Development to elevate our Laravel development process to new heights!

Introduction to Testing in Laravel

Testing is an integral and critical aspect of software development, as it ensures the dependability and overall quality of the code. In the Laravel PHP framework, testing is made more accessible and efficient, thanks to the integration of PHPUnit, a widely used testing framework in the PHP community. Laravel comes with a testing environment, allowing developers to quickly and easily write and execute tests.

Laravel's testing suite supports various types of tests, including unit tests, integration tests, and feature tests. With these testing options, developers can validate the functionality of different aspects of their applications, such as individual components, HTTP requests, database interactions, and even API endpoints.

By leveraging the testing capabilities provided by Laravel, developers can confidently identify and address bugs early in the development process, maintain the stability of their applications, and ensure the smooth operation of their software in real-world scenarios. This introduction to testing in Laravel will explore these testing concepts further, equipping developers with the knowledge and tools to create reliable and robust applications with ease.

Writing Unit Tests with PHPUnit

Writing unit tests with PHPUnit is an essential part of ensuring the correctness and reliability of your code in a Laravel application. Unit tests focus on testing individual units or components of your code in isolation. These units can be methods, functions, or classes, allowing you to verify that they behave as expected. Let's explore how to write unit tests with PHPUnit in Laravel.

Generating a Test Class

To create a unit test class in Laravel, you can use the 'php artisan make:test' command with the '--unit' option. This will generate a test class in the 'tests/Unit' directory:

```
php artisan make:test YourUnitTest --unit
```

Writing Test Methods

Within the generated test class, you define test methods that correspond to the units or functions you want to test. PHPUnit automatically discovers and executes test methods that start with the word "test."

Let's take a simple example of testing a basic math utility class that performs addition and subtraction:

```
// app/Utils/MathUtility.php
class MathUtility
{
    public function add($a, $b)
    {
        return $a + $b;
    }
}
```

201

```
    public function subtract($a, $b)
    {
        return $a $b;
    }
}
```

Now, let's write unit tests for this 'MathUtility' class:

```php
// tests/Unit/MathUtilityTest.php
use Tests\TestCase;
use App\Utils\MathUtility;
class MathUtilityTest extends TestCase
{
    public function testAddition()
    {
        $mathUtility = new MathUtility();
        $result = $mathUtility->add(2, 3);
        $this->assertEquals(5, $result);
    }
    public function testSubtraction()
    {
        $mathUtility = new MathUtility();
        $result = $mathUtility->subtract(5, 3);
        $this->assertEquals(2, $result);
    }
}
```

In this example, we have two test methods, 'testAddition' and 'testSubtraction', which test the 'add' and 'subtract' methods of the 'MathUtility' class, respectively. We use PHPUnit's assertion methods, such as 'assertEquals', to verify that the expected results match the actual results returned by the methods.

Running Unit Tests

To run the unit tests in Laravel, you can use the 'phpunit' command:

```
vendor/bin/phpunit
```

PHPUnit will automatically discover and execute all the unit tests present in the 'tests/Unit' directory.

Mocking Dependencies

Unit tests should test individual units of code in isolation, which means that they should not rely on external dependencies. If a unit depends on external resources or services, you can use mocking to create fake objects or stubs to simulate the behavior of those dependencies.

In Laravel, you can use the 'Mockery' library, which is included by default, to create mock objects. Alternatively, you can use PHPUnit's built-in mocking features for simpler cases.

Here's an example of using mocking to test a class that depends on an external service:

```
// app/Services/WeatherService.php
class WeatherService
{
    public function getTemperature($city)
    {
        // Code to make an external API request and fetch temperature
        // For testing purposes, we'll mock the response
        return 25;
    }
}
```

```
--------------------------------------------------------------------
// app/WeatherReporter.php
use App\Services\WeatherService;
class WeatherReporter
{
    protected $weatherService;
    public function __construct(WeatherService $weatherService)
    {
        $this->weatherService = $weatherService;
    }
    public function getWeatherReport($city)
    {
        $temperature = $this->weatherService->getTemperature($city);
        return "The current temperature in $city is $temperature degrees
        Celsius.";
    }
}
--------------------------------------------------------------------
--------------------------------------------------------------------
// tests/Unit/WeatherReporterTest.php
use Tests\TestCase;
use App\Services\WeatherService;
use App\WeatherReporter;
use Mockery;
class WeatherReporterTest extends TestCase
{
    public function testGetWeatherReport()
    {
        $weatherService = Mockery::mock(WeatherService::class);
        $weatherService->shouldReceive('getTemperature')
            ->with('London')
            ->andReturn(20);
        $weatherReporter = new WeatherReporter($weatherService);
        $result = $weatherReporter->getWeatherReport('London');
```

```
    $this->assertEquals('The current temperature in London is 20
    degrees Celsius.', $result);
  }
}
```

In this example, we use mocking to simulate the response of the 'WeatherService' dependency, ensuring that our test remains independent of the actual external API request.

Best Practices for Unit Testing

Test each method or function in isolation and ensure they return the correct outputs for various inputs.

Name your test methods descriptively to indicate what they are testing.

Use PHPUnit's assertion methods like 'assertEquals', 'assertTrue', 'assertFalse', etc. to validate expected results.

Avoid testing methods or functions that solely contain framework-specific logic (e.g., view rendering in Laravel).

Mock external dependencies or services to focus on the unit being tested.

Always run your unit tests before deploying changes to production to catch any regressions.

By writing unit tests, you can validate the behavior of individual units of code in your Laravel application, which helps maintain a reliable and maintainable codebase. Properly tested code is less prone to bugs and easier to refactor and enhance over time.

Testing HTTP Requests and Responses

Testing HTTP requests and answers is critical for verifying that your Laravel application behaves correctly, especially when dealing with routes, controllers, and middleware. Laravel provides a strong testing environment for feature tests, allowing you to replicate HTTP queries and validate the results. Let's get started with HTTP requests and responses in Laravel.

Writing Feature Tests

Feature tests are intended to simulate the behavior of your application from the user's point of view. They imitate HTTP queries for your application and allow you to inspect the results to ensure they fulfill your expectations.

To construct a feature test, use 'php artisan make:test' with the '--feature' option:

```
php artisan make:test YourFeatureTest --feature
```

This command will create a test class in the directory 'tests/Feature'. Within this class, you can then define test methods to test certain features of your application.

Simulating HTTP Requests

Laravel provides a collection of testing aids in feature tests to imitate HTTP queries to your site. You can use these testing aids to make GET, POST, PUT, PATCH, DELETE, and other forms of requests.

For example, let's assume you have a simple Laravel route that returns a JSON response:

```
// routes/web.php
Route::get('/api/users/{id}', function ($id) {
    $user = App\Models\User::find($id);
    return response()->json($user);
});
```

In your feature test, you can use the 'get' method to simulate a GET request to this route and examine the response:

```
namespace Tests\Feature;
use Tests\TestCase;
use App\Models\User;
class UserApiTest extends TestCase {
```

```php
public function testGetUserById() {
    $user = User::factory()->create();
    $response = $this->get('/api/users/' . $user->id);
    $response->assertStatus(200)
            ->assertJson([
                'id' => $user->id,
                'name' => $user->name,
                'email' => $user->email,
            ]);
}
}
```

In this example, we create a user using Laravel's model factory, make a GET request to the '/api/users/{id}' endpoint with the user's ID, and then use assertions to verify that the response has a status code of 200 (indicating success) and that the JSON data in the response matches the user's attributes.

Making POST Requests

You can also make POST requests in feature tests to test the behavior of your application when handling form submissions or API endpoints that expect data to be sent via POST.

For instance, let's assume you have a route that handles a POST request to create a new user:

```php
// routes/web.php
Route::post('/api/users', function (Illuminate\Http\Request $request) {
    $data = $request->validate([
        'name' => 'required|string',
        'email' => 'required|email|unique:users,email',
        'password' => 'required|string|min:8',
    ]);
    $user = App\Models\User::create($data);
    return response()->json($user);
});
```

In your feature test, you can use the 'post' method to simulate a POST request with data:

```
namespace Tests\Feature;
use Tests\TestCase;
class UserApiTest extends TestCase {
    public function testCreateUser() {
        $userData = [
            'name' => 'John Doe',
            'email' => 'john.doe@example.com',
            'password' => 'secretpassword',
        ];
        $response = $this->post('/api/users', $userData);
        $response->assertStatus(200)
                ->assertJson($userData);
    }
}
```

In this example, we simulate a POST request to the '/api/users' endpoint with user data and use assertions to verify that the response has a status code of 200 (indicating success) and that the JSON data in the response matches the user data we sent.

Handling Form Submissions

When testing form submissions, you can use the 'post' method and pass an array of form data as the second argument to the method. Laravel's testing environment will handle the form submission and route the request to the appropriate controller method.

Verifying Responses

Laravel's testing environment provides various assertion methods that allow you to verify the content of the responses. Some common assertions include

'assertStatus': Verifies the HTTP status code of the response

'assertJson': Verifies that the response contains specific JSON data

'assertSee': Verifies that a given string is present in the response content 'assertDontSee': Verifies that a given string is not present in the response content

'assertRedirect': Verifies that the response is a redirect

'assertViewIs': Verifies that the response corresponds to a specific view

By using these assertions in your feature tests, you can ensure that your application's HTTP responses are behaving as expected.

Testing Middleware

Feature tests are also useful for testing middleware that intercepts and processes requests before they reach the controller. To test middleware, you can use the 'withoutMiddleware' and 'withMiddleware' methods in your test to disable or enable specific middleware for a particular test scenario.

Running Feature Tests

To run your feature tests, use the 'phpunit' command in the terminal:

```
vendor/bin/phpunit
```

PHPUnit will automatically discover and execute all the feature tests present in the 'tests/Feature' directory.

You may comprehensively test the behavior of your application's HTTP requests and responses by writing feature tests and utilizing Laravel's testing aids, ensuring that your routes, controllers, middleware, and API endpoints perform as intended. These tests provide vital insights into the functionality of your application and can help detect and resolve issues before deploying it to production.

Test-Driven Development (TDD) Workflow

Test-Driven Development (TDD) is a software development approach where tests are written before the actual code is implemented. The TDD workflow follows a simple and iterative process that helps ensure the quality and correctness of the code. TDD is widely used in Agile development methodologies and has become a fundamental practice for many software development teams. Let's explore the steps of the TDD workflow.

Write a Test

The first step in the TDD workflow is to write a test that defines the behavior or functionality you want to implement. This test is written before any code is written to fulfill the requirement. The test initially fails because there is no code to make it pass yet.

In TDD, a test should be concise and specific and address a single requirement. The test should be a small and focused unit test or feature test, depending on the scope of the functionality being tested.

The following is an illustration of this feature:

```php
// tests/Unit/CalculatorTest.php
use PHPUnit\Framework\TestCase;
class CalculatorTest extends TestCase
{
    public function testAddition()
    {
        $calculator = new Calculator();
        $result = $calculator->add(2, 3);
        $this->assertEquals(5, $result);
    }
}
```

In this example, we constructed a CalculatorTest test class. The testAddition method validates the Calculator class's add method. The test determines whether combining 2 and 3 yields the predicted result of 5.

Run the Test

After writing the test, you run the test suite to execute all the tests, including the new test you just created. Since the code to satisfy the test has not been implemented yet, the test will fail. This failure serves as a reminder that the functionality is not yet implemented and motivates you to write the code to make it pass.

When we run the tests using PHPUnit, we'll see an output like this:

```
PHPUnit 9.5.10 by XYZ and contributors.
Time: 00:00.001, Memory: 4.00 MB
There was 1 failure:
1) CalculatorTest::testAddition
Failed asserting that 0 matches the expected 5.
```

The failure indicates that the test did not pass because the expected result is 5, but the actual result is 0.

Write the Code

With the failing test in place, you start writing the code to implement the functionality needed to make the test pass. The primary goal at this stage is to write the simplest code necessary to pass the test. This approach keeps the code focused and minimizes the risk of over-engineering.

The code may not be the most optimized or complete solution at this point, but it should be enough to satisfy the test case you wrote earlier.

Illustrative implementation:

```php
// app/Calculator.php
class Calculator
{
    public function add($a, $b)
    {
        return $a + $b;
    }
}
```

Run the Test Again

Once you have written the code, you run the test suite again. This time, the test you created earlier should pass because the code you wrote fulfills the requirements of the test:

```
PHPUnit 9.5.10 by XYZ and contributors
Time: 00:00.001, Memory: 4.00 MB
OK (1 test, 1 assertion)
```

The test passed successfully, indicating that our implementation of the **add** method is correct.

If the test passes, it gives you confidence that the code you just wrote is working as expected. If the test fails, it means there is an issue with the code and you need to make further adjustments to correct it.

Refactor the Code (Optional)

After the test has passed, you can take a moment to refactor the code and improve its design without changing its behavior. Refactoring helps keep the codebase clean, maintainable, and extensible.

The refactoring step is optional in the TDD workflow, but it is an essential practice in software development to continuously improve the quality of the code.

Repeat the Process

With the first test completed, you can repeat the process by writing another test for a different functionality or edge case. The new test will initially fail since you have not implemented the corresponding code yet.

You continue the cycle of writing a test, running the test (which fails), writing the code to make it pass, running the test again (which passes), and optionally refactoring the code.

The following is an illustration of this feature:

```php
// tests/Unit/CalculatorTest.php
use PHPUnit\Framework\TestCase;
class CalculatorTest extends TestCase
{
    public function testAddition()
    {
        $calculator = new Calculator();
        $this->assertEquals(5, $calculator->add(2, 3));
    }
    public function testSubtraction()
    {
        $calculator = new Calculator();
        $this->assertEquals(1, $calculator->subtract(3, 2));
    }
}
```

In this new test, we see if subtracting two from three yields the predicted answer of one.

We now run the test suite again, which should fail because we haven't yet created the subtract method in the Calculator class. The method is then implemented, and the test is passed.

By continuously writing tests before writing code, you ensure that your codebase is well-tested and that each piece of functionality is thoroughly verified. The TDD workflow encourages a fast feedback loop, reduces the likelihood of introducing bugs, and promotes a robust and maintainable codebase.

Advantages of Test-Driven Development (TDD)

Improved code quality: TDD promotes the construction of cleaner and more maintainable code since it begins with tests that explain the anticipated behavior.

Faster bug detection: TDD helps catch bugs early in the development process, making it easier and less costly to fix issues.

Increased confidence: Comprehensive test coverage gives developers confidence in their code changes, making them more willing to refactor or extend the codebase.

Better documentation: Tests serve as living documentation of the expected behavior of the code, making it easier for other developers to understand how the code works.

Design guidance: TDD encourages writing code in small increments, which can lead to better software design and architecture.

Reduces debugging time: Writing tests before implementing code can help identify issues early, reducing the time spent on debugging later.

Facilitates collaboration: Tests serve as a common understanding between developers and stakeholders about the behavior of the application.

While TDD might initially slow down the development process due to writing tests before code, the overall benefits of improved code quality, faster bug detection, and increased confidence make it a powerful and valuable practice for building robust software.

Testing API Endpoints and Integrations

Testing API endpoints and integrations is a critical part of ensuring that your web applications function correctly and communicate effectively with external services or APIs. In Laravel, you can use feature tests to simulate HTTP requests and examine responses from your API endpoints. Additionally, you can use mocking to simulate external API responses during testing. Let's explore how to test API endpoints and integrations in Laravel.

Writing Feature Tests for API Endpoints

To test API endpoints, you can use feature tests in Laravel. Feature tests allow you to make HTTP requests to your application and verify the responses returned by your API routes.

Suppose we have a simple API endpoint in our Laravel application that returns a list of users in JSON format:

```
// routes/api.php
Route::get('/users', function () {
    $users = App\Models\User::all();
    return response()->json($users);
});
```

Now, let's create a feature test to ensure that this API endpoint works correctly:

```php
// tests/Feature/UserApiTest.php
use Illuminate\Foundation\Testing\RefreshDatabase;
use Tests\TestCase;
class UserApiTest extends TestCase
{
    use RefreshDatabase;
    public function testGetAllUsers()
    {
        $users = User::factory()->count(3)->create();
        $response = $this->get('/api/users');
        $response->assertStatus(200)
                ->assertJson($users->toArray());
    }
}
```

In this example, we use the `RefreshDatabase` trait to reset the database before running the test. The `testGetAllUsers` method tests the `/api/users` endpoint, ensuring it returns a valid JSON response containing the users created in the test.

Mocking External API Responses

When testing integrations with external services or APIs, it's essential to avoid making actual requests to those services during testing. Instead, you can use mocking to simulate the responses from the external APIs.

Laravel provides a powerful mocking system that allows you to create mock objects and define the expected behavior of external dependencies. This ensures that your tests are consistent and not affected by the availability or state of external services.

Let's assume our application interacts with an external weather API to fetch weather information. We'll create a service class that handles this interaction and then use mocking to simulate the API responses during testing:

```
-----------------------------------------------------------------------
// app/Services/WeatherService.php
class WeatherService
{
    public function getWeatherData($city)
    {
        // Code to make a request to the external weather API and
fetch data
        // For testing purposes, we'll mock the response
        return [
            'temperature' => 25,
            'conditions' => 'Sunny',
        ];
    }
}
-----------------------------------------------------------------------
```

Now, let's create a test to verify that our `WeatherService` behaves correctly:

```
-----------------------------------------------------------------------
// tests/Unit/WeatherServiceTest.php
use Tests\TestCase;
use App\Services\WeatherService;
class WeatherServiceTest extends TestCase
{
    public function testGetWeatherData()
    {
        // Create an instance of the WeatherService
        $weatherService = new WeatherService();
        // Mock the API response
        $this->mock(WeatherService::class, function ($mock) {
            $mock->shouldReceive('getWeatherData')
                ->with('London')
                ->andReturn([
                    'temperature' => 25,
```

```
                'conditions' => 'Sunny',
            ]);
        });
        // Perform the test
        $data = $weatherService->getWeatherData('London');
        // Assert the response
        $this->assertEquals([
            'temperature' => 25,
            'conditions' => 'Sunny',
        ], $data);
    }
}
```

In this example, we create a mock of the `WeatherService` using Laravel's `mock` method. We then define the expected behavior of the `getWeatherData` method to return specific data when called with the city name "London." During the test, the actual API request is not made; instead, the mocked response is returned.

Running the Tests

To run your tests in Laravel, you can use the `phpunit` command in the terminal:

```
vendor/bin/phpunit
```

PHPUnit will automatically discover and execute all the tests present in the `tests` directory, including both feature tests and unit tests.

By writing feature tests to validate API endpoints and using mocking to simulate external API responses, you can thoroughly test your Laravel application's interactions with external services, ensuring robust and reliable integrations. This approach helps catch issues early in the development process and ensures that your application works as expected when interacting with various APIs and external dependencies.

Summary

This chapter covered testing and Test-Driven Development (TDD) using the Laravel framework. It emphasized the importance of writing tests to verify the dependability and stability of web applications and demonstrated several Laravel-supported testing tools and approaches, such as PHPUnit and Laravel Dusk for browser testing. It also covered how to create unit tests, feature tests, and browser tests to validate various components of the program.

The next chapter focuses on queues and job scheduling.

CHAPTER 10

Queues and Job Scheduling

In the previous chapter, we explored the essential world of testing and Test-Driven Development (TDD) in Laravel, ensuring the reliability and quality of our codebase. As we venture further into Laravel's advanced features, we now immerse ourselves in the realm of queues and job scheduling—powerful tools that enhance the performance and scalability of our applications.

Introduction to Queues and Workers

In this section, we will gain an understanding of queues and workers in Laravel. Queues enable us to defer time-consuming tasks and process them asynchronously in the background, freeing up the main application to respond to user requests quickly. We will explore how workers handle queued jobs, ensuring that our application can handle a high volume of tasks efficiently.

Setting Up Queue Drivers and Connections

Laravel supports multiple queue drivers, such as Redis, database, Beanstalkd, and more. We will learn how to set up queue drivers and connections, choosing the appropriate driver to best suit the requirements of our application and infrastructure.

Creating and Dispatching Jobs

Jobs are the heart of the queue system, representing the tasks we want to execute asynchronously. In this section, we will discover how to create and dispatch jobs, effectively offloading time-consuming processes to the queue and maintaining the responsiveness of our application.

Managing Failed Jobs and Retries

Handling failed jobs is an essential aspect of a robust queue system. We will explore how to manage failed jobs and configure automatic retries to ensure that critical tasks eventually get executed successfully.

© Sivaraj Selvaraj 2024
S. Selvaraj, *Building Real-Time Marvels with Laravel*, https://doi.org/10.1007/978-1-4842-9789-6_10

Scheduling Jobs with Laravel's Task Scheduler

Laravel's task scheduler allows us to automate the execution of recurring tasks at predefined intervals. We will learn how to schedule jobs using the task scheduler, enabling us to perform periodic maintenance tasks and other scheduled activities.

Throughout this chapter, we will dive deep into the world of queues and job scheduling in Laravel, mastering the art of background processing to optimize the performance and scalability of our applications. By utilizing queues and job scheduling effectively, we can create high-performing applications that handle tasks efficiently and provide a seamless user experience. So let's embark on this journey of queues and job scheduling to enhance the capabilities of our Laravel applications!

Introduction to Queues and Workers

In modern web applications, it is common to encounter tasks that are time-consuming and resource-intensive, such as sending emails, processing large files, or interacting with external APIs. Executing these tasks synchronously within the same request-response cycle can lead to slow response times and a poor user experience.

Laravel's queues and workers offer an efficient way to perform such time-consuming activities asynchronously. Queues allow you to postpone job processing to a later time, while workers are responsible for doing those tasks in the background.

Here's How the Process Works

Task queuing: When a task needs to be completed, Laravel places it in a queue instead of performing it immediately. A queue serves as a buffer, storing tasks until they are ready to be processed. These jobs can be saved in a database, Redis, Beanstalkd, Amazon Simple Queue Service (SQS), or any other Laravel-supported queue service.

Queue workers: Workers are distinct processes or threads that constantly monitor the queues for awaiting jobs. When a worker discovers a job in the queue, it retrieves it and processes it independently of the main application.

Benefits of Using Queues and Workers

Improved responsiveness: Delegating time-consuming activities to background workers allows the main program to respond to user requests faster, resulting in a better user experience.

Scalability: Queues and workers allow for horizontal scaling. You can add extra workers to manage the increasing number of queued jobs, allowing your application to handle a higher burden.

Fault tolerance: If a task fails during execution, the queue system can automatically retry the task a predefined number of times. If the task continues to fail, you can monitor and investigate the failures separately from the main application.

Task prioritization: Queues often support prioritizing tasks, ensuring critical tasks are processed before less critical ones.

Laravel's Integration of Queues and Workers

Laravel provides a comprehensive queue system that seamlessly integrates with various queue drivers. Out of the box, Laravel supports queue drivers like 'sync' (for synchronous execution, useful for development and testing), 'database', 'redis', 'beanstalkd', and 'sqs' (Amazon Simple Queue Service). You can choose the most suitable queue driver based on your application's requirements and infrastructure.

With Laravel's clean and expressive syntax, you can easily define and dispatch jobs to the queue, making it straightforward to implement asynchronous processing for different parts of your application.

Setting Up Queue Drivers and Connections

Laravel allows you to use various queue drivers to process queued jobs. Each driver has its own advantages and is suitable for different scenarios. In this section, we'll walk through the process of setting up queue drivers and connections in Laravel.

Choose a Queue Driver

Before setting up the queue connections, you need to choose a queue driver that fits your application's requirements:

'sync': The 'sync' driver executes the queued jobs immediately within the same request-response cycle. It is suitable for development and testing environments but not recommended for production.

'database': The 'database' driver stores queued jobs in a database table. It allows you to process jobs asynchronously using a separate queue worker process.

'redis': The 'redis' driver uses Redis as the queue store. Redis is an in-memory data structure store, and using it for queues can significantly improve performance.

'beanstalkd': The 'beanstalkd' driver uses the Beanstalkd queue service, which is a fast and simple queue system.

'sqs' (Amazon Simple Queue Service): The 'sqs' driver is used for integrating with Amazon SQS, a fully managed message queuing service.

'rabbitmq': The 'rabbitmq' driver allows you to use RabbitMQ as the queue driver. RabbitMQ is a powerful and highly scalable message broker that enables reliable message delivery between applications.

'null': The null driver is primarily used for testing or when you want to disable the queue system entirely. It discards all queued jobs and doesn't perform any processing.

Configure the Queue Connection

CloudAMQP is a managed message queue service that provides RabbitMQ instances in the cloud, making it easy to set up and scale message queuing for your applications.

To use CloudAMQP with Laravel, you'll typically follow these steps.

Sign Up for CloudAMQP

Go to the CloudAMQP website (www.cloudamqp.com/) and sign up for an account. You'll need to choose a plan that suits your needs and get the connection details for your RabbitMQ instance.

Install the Required Package

Laravel uses the "php-amqplib/php-amqplib" package to interact with RabbitMQ. Make sure this package is installed in your Laravel project.

You can install it via Composer using the following command:

```
composer require php-amqplib/php-amqplib
```

Configure the Queue Connection

In your **config/queue.php** file, add a new connection using the CloudAMQP details you obtained earlier.

For Illustration, refer to the following snippet:

```
'connections' => [
    'cloudamqp' => [
        'driver' => 'rabbitmq',
        'host' => env('CLOUDAMQP_HOST'),
        'port' => env('CLOUDAMQP_PORT', 5672),
        'vhost' => env('CLOUDAMQP_VHOST'),
        'login' => env('CLOUDAMQP_LOGIN'),
        'password' => env('CLOUDAMQP_PASSWORD'),
        'queue' => env('CLOUDAMQP_QUEUE'),
        'options' => [
            'ssl_options' => [
                'cafile' => env('CLOUDAMQP_CAFILE'),
            ],
        ],
    ],
    // Other connections go here...
],
```

Make sure to set the appropriate environment variables in your .env file or your server's environment, such as CLOUDAMQP_HOST, CLOUDAMQP_PORT, etc.

Migrate the Queue Table (for the Database Driver)

If you're using the 'database' driver, you need to run the migration to create the necessary table to store the queued jobs. Run the following Artisan commands:

```
php artisan queue:table
php artisan migrate
```

This will create a table named 'jobs' in your database.

Dispatching Jobs

To add jobs to the queue, you can dispatch them using the 'dispatch' function or one of its shortcuts. The jobs will be pushed to the CloudAMQP queue.

For Illustration, refer to the following snippet:

```
use App\Jobs\ProcessPodcast;
ProcessPodcast::dispatch($podcast);
```

Start the Queue Worker

To process the jobs, start the queue worker for the CloudAMQP connection.

Use the queue:work Artisan command:

```
php artisan queue:work --queue=cloudamqp --tries=3
```

This command will start the queue worker for the "cloudamqp" connection, and it will attempt to execute failed jobs up to three times.

Creating and Dispatching Jobs

In Laravel, a job is a unit of work that can be queued for later execution. It allows you to defer time-consuming tasks, such as sending emails, processing data, or interacting with external services, to be executed in the background, outside the typical request-response cycle. This helps improve the performance and responsiveness of your application.

Laravel provides a built-in queuing system that allows you to create and dispatch jobs easily. Here's a step-by-step explanation of how to create and dispatch jobs in Laravel.

Create the Job Class

To create a job class in Laravel, you can use the 'make:job' Artisan command. For example, let's create a job class to handle the task of sending a welcome email to new users:

```
php artisan make:job SendWelcomeEmail
```

This will generate a new job class named 'SendWelcomeEmail' in the 'app/Jobs' directory.

Define the Job Logic

Open the newly generated 'SendWelcomeEmail' job class ('app/Jobs/SendWelcomeEmail.php') and implement the 'handle' method. This method contains the logic that will be executed when the job is processed:

```php
namespace App\Jobs;
use Illuminate\Bus\Queueable;
use Illuminate\Contracts\Queue\ShouldQueue;
use Illuminate\Foundation\Bus\Dispatchable;
use Illuminate\Queue\InteractsWithQueue;
use Illuminate\Queue\SerializesModels;
use Mail;
class SendWelcomeEmail implements ShouldQueue
{
    use Dispatchable, InteractsWithQueue, Queueable, SerializesModels;
    protected $user;
    public function __construct($user)
    {
        $this->user = $user;
    }
```

225

```
    public function handle()
    {
        // Logic to send the welcome email to $this->user
        Mail::to($this->user->email)->send(new WelcomeEmail($this->user));
    }
}
```

In this example, we have defined a 'SendWelcomeEmail' job class with a constructor that receives the user data. The 'handle' method sends the welcome email to the user using Laravel's built-in Mail facade.

Dispatch the Job

To add the job to the queue and initiate background processing, you need to dispatch it from your application code. This typically happens when certain events occur in your application, such as a user registering, a new item being added, or any other task that should be processed asynchronously.

For instance, let's assume you have a controller method to handle user registration, and after a successful registration, you want to send a welcome email:

```
use App\Jobs\SendWelcomeEmail;
public function registerUser(Request $request)
{
    // Your user registration logic...
    // Dispatch the SendWelcomeEmail job with the newly registered
user data
    SendWelcomeEmail::dispatch($user);
}
```

In this example, we import the 'SendWelcomeEmail' job class and dispatch it, passing the newly registered user data as an argument to the 'dispatch' method. Laravel will automatically serialize the job and its data, add it to the queue, and process it in the background.

The job will be picked up by the queue worker, and the 'handle' method within the job class will be executed asynchronously, sending the welcome email to the new user without delaying the response to the user's registration request.

Remember to start the queue worker using the 'queue:work' Artisan command to ensure the jobs are executed:

```
php artisan queue:work --queue=database
```

In this command, we specify the 'database' queue connection, which is the default queue connection for the 'database' queue driver. You may need to adjust the queue connection based on your setup (e.g., 'redis', 'beanstalkd', etc.).

By creating and dispatching jobs, you can efficiently process time-consuming tasks in the background, improving the responsiveness and performance of your Laravel application.

Illustration: Image Processing

Suppose you allow users to upload images to your application, and you want to process these images to create thumbnails in the background.

Create the Job Class

Generate a job class to handle the image processing task:

```
php artisan make:job ProcessImage
```

Define the Job Logic

Open the 'ProcessImage' job class (located at 'app/Jobs/ProcessImage.php') and implement the 'handle' method. This method will contain the logic for image processing:

```
namespace App\Jobs;
use Illuminate\Bus\Queueable;
use Illuminate\Contracts\Queue\ShouldQueue;
use Illuminate\Foundation\Bus\Dispatchable;
use Illuminate\Queue\InteractsWithQueue;
use Illuminate\Queue\SerializesModels;
use Image;
class ProcessImage implements ShouldQueue
    /*process_image(ch, method, properties, body):*/
{
    use Dispatchable, InteractsWithQueue, Queueable, SerializesModels;
    protected $imagePath;
    public function __construct($imagePath)
    {
        $this->imagePath = $imagePath;
    }
    public function handle()
    {
        // Logic to process the image and create thumbnails
        $image = Image::make($this->imagePath);
        $thumbnailPath = '/path/to/thumbnails/';
        $image->fit(100)->save($thumbnailPath . 'thumbnail_' .
        basename($this->imagePath));
    }
}
```

In this example, we're using the Intervention Image package (https://image.intervention.io/) to handle image processing.

Dispatch the Job

When a user uploads an image, dispatch the 'ProcessImage' job to process it in the background:

```
use App\Jobs\ProcessImage;
public function uploadImage(Request $request)
{
    // Save the uploaded image to a temporary location
    // Dispatch the ProcessImage job
    ProcessImage::dispatch($uploadedImagePath);
}
```

The 'ProcessImage' job will now process the image and create thumbnails without delaying the response to the user.

In both examples, the jobs are dispatched to the queue, and the queue worker processes them in the background, allowing your application to handle other tasks without waiting for time-consuming processes to complete.

Remember to start the queue worker using the 'queue:work' Artisan command to ensure the jobs are executed:

```
php artisan queue:work --queue=database
```

The preceding command starts the queue worker for the 'database' queue connection, which is the default queue connection for the 'database' queue driver.

Remember to handle any potential errors or exceptions that may occur during task processing and to implement appropriate error handling and retry mechanisms to ensure the robustness and reliability of your queue-based system.

Managing Failed Jobs and Retries

Managing failed jobs and retries is an essential aspect of using queues and workers in Laravel. When a job fails during processing, Laravel provides mechanisms to handle and retry failed jobs automatically. In this section, we'll explore how to manage failed jobs and configure retries.

Understanding Failed Jobs

When a job encounters an exception or error during processing, it is considered a failed job. Failed jobs are essential to monitor and handle, as they can indicate issues that need attention, such as network problems, API errors, or misconfigurations.

By default, Laravel will retry a failed job three times before marking it as permanently failed. You can customize the number of retries and other aspects of failed job handling based on your application's requirements.

Define the 'failed' Method in the Job Class

To handle what happens when a job fails, you can define a 'failed' method in your job class. This method will be called when a job fails, and you can implement custom logic to handle the failure.

For example, let's modify the 'SendWelcomeEmail' job class to handle failed email sending:

```
namespace App\Jobs;
use Illuminate\Bus\Queueable;
use Illuminate\Contracts\Queue\ShouldQueue;
use Illuminate\Foundation\Bus\Dispatchable;
use Illuminate\Queue\InteractsWithQueue;
use Illuminate\Queue\SerializesModels;
use Mail;
class SendWelcomeEmail implements ShouldQueue
{
    use Dispatchable, InteractsWithQueue, Queueable, SerializesModels;
    protected $user;
    public function __construct($user)
    {
        $this->user = $user;
    }
    public function handle()
```

```
    {
        // Logic to send the welcome email to $this->user
        Mail::to($this->user->email)->send(new WelcomeEmail($this->user));
    }
    public function failed(\Exception $exception)
    {
        // Logic to handle the failed job
        // For example, log the error or notify the administrators
        \Log::error('Failed to send welcome email to user: ' .
        $this->user->id);
    }
}
```

In this example, the 'failed' method logs the error using Laravel's 'Log' facade, but you can customize the handling based on your requirements, such as sending notifications or storing error details in the database.

Customizing Retries

You can also customize the number of times a job should be retried and the delay between retries. By default, Laravel will retry a failed job three times with a delay of a few seconds between each retry.

To customize the number of retries for a specific job, add a 'public $tries' property to your job class:

```
public $tries = 5;
```

In this example, the job will be retried up to five times before it's marked as permanently failed.

You can also specify the delay between retries using the 'public $retryAfter' property:

```
public $retryAfter = 60; // 60 seconds (1 minute) delay between retries
```

Retry Delay Strategies

By default, Laravel uses an exponential backoff delay strategy between retries, meaning that each retry will wait longer than the previous one. You can implement a custom retry delay strategy by defining a 'retryUntil' method in your job class:

```
public function retryUntil()
{
    // Define the time until the job should not be retried anymore
    return now()->addMinutes(30); // Retry for up to 30 minutes from the
    first failure.
}
```

In this example, the job will be retried 30 minutes after the first failure. After this time, the job will be marked as permanently failed.

Manually Retry Failed Jobs

Laravel provides an Artisan command to manually retry failed jobs:

```
php artisan queue:retry [job_id]
```

You need to provide the ID of the failed job as an argument. Laravel will then move the job back to the queue for processing.

Monitor Failed Jobs

Laravel stores information about failed jobs in the 'failed_jobs' table (created during the 'queue:table' migration). You can use this table to monitor failed jobs and investigate any recurring issues.

Additionally, you can set up logging or notifications to be alerted when a job fails, allowing you to take appropriate actions and ensure the smooth functioning of your application.

By managing failed jobs and retries effectively, you can ensure the reliability and fault tolerance of your application's background job processing.

Scheduling Jobs with Laravel's Task Scheduler

Laravel's task scheduler allows you to schedule jobs to run at specified intervals without the need for a separate queue or worker setup. This feature is useful for automating tasks that need to be executed periodically, such as sending reminder emails, generating reports, or performing regular maintenance tasks. In this section, we'll explore how to schedule jobs using Laravel's task scheduler.

Define the Scheduled Jobs in Kernel.php

To schedule jobs, you need to define them in the 'app/Console/Kernel.php' file. This file contains the 'schedule' method, where you can define your scheduled jobs. A closure or a command represents each scheduled job and executes it at the specified intervals.

Here's an example of scheduling a job to send a reminder email every day at 8:00 a.m.:

```
// app/Console/Kernel.php
protected function schedule(Schedule $schedule)
{
    $schedule->call(function () {
        // Logic to send reminder emails...
    })->dailyAt('08:00');
}
```

In this example, we use the 'dailyAt' method to schedule the job to run every day at 8:00 a.m. You can use various other scheduling methods provided by Laravel, such as 'hourly', 'twiceDaily', 'weekly', 'monthly', 'dailyAt', 'cron', etc., depending on your desired schedule.

Scheduling Artisan Commands

If you want to schedule an Artisan command instead of a closure, you can use the 'command' method in the 'schedule' method:

```
// app/Console/Kernel.php
protected function schedule(Schedule $schedule)
{
    $schedule->command('email:send-reminders')->dailyAt('08:00');
}
```

In this example, we schedule the 'email:send-reminders' Artisan command to run every day at 8:00 a.m.

Using Cron Expressions

For more complex scheduling requirements, you can use Cron expressions instead of the predefined scheduling methods. Cron expressions allow you to specify the exact times and dates when the job should run.

Here's an example of using a Cron expression to schedule a job to run every weekday at 6:00 p.m.:

```
// app/Console/Kernel.php
protected function schedule(Schedule $schedule)
{
    $schedule->call(function () {
        // Logic to perform the task...
    })->cron('0 18 * * 1-5');
}
```

In this example, the Cron expression "0 18 * * 1-5" corresponds to the following schedule:

'0': Minute (0–59)

'18': Hour (0–23)

'*': Day of the month (1–31)

'*': Month (1–12)

'1-5': Day of the week (0–7, where both 0 and 7 represent Sunday)

The Cron expression means the job will run at 6:00 p.m. (18:00) on any day of the month from Monday to Friday.

Register the Scheduler in Cron

To execute the scheduled jobs automatically, you need to add an entry to your server's crontab file. The crontab entry should call the 'schedule:run' Artisan command, which will check the defined schedule and execute the jobs accordingly:

```
* * * * * cd /path-to-your-project && php artisan schedule:run >> /dev/
null 2>&1
```

This entry will run the scheduler every minute, and Laravel will take care of executing the scheduled jobs at their specified intervals.

Remember to replace '/path-to-your-project' with the actual path to your Laravel project.

With the Laravel task scheduler, you can easily automate and manage repetitive tasks, improving the efficiency and maintenance of your application. By using the scheduling methods and Cron expressions, you can set up a variety of job schedules to suit your application's needs.

Summary

This chapter focused on the strong capabilities of queues and job scheduling in Laravel. You learned how to enhance application performance and scalability through the use of background queues to offload time-consuming operations and how to set up and configure queues to process tasks asynchronously, resulting in better user response times. The chapter explained how to create jobs to encapsulate specific tasks and how to dispatch jobs to the queue for processing. You also learned about work prioritizing, retrying failed jobs, and dealing with task delays.

In the next chapter, we will dig into advanced package development.

CHAPTER 11

Advanced Package Development

In the previous chapter, we delved into the powerful world of queues and job scheduling in Laravel, enabling us to optimize the performance and scalability of our applications through background processing. As our exploration of Laravel's capabilities continues, we now turn our attention to advanced package development—a crucial aspect of modular and reusable code in Laravel.

Introduction to Package Development in Laravel

In this section, we will gain insight into the significance of package development in Laravel. Packages allow us to encapsulate and distribute reusable functionality, promoting code organization and modularity. We will understand the benefits of package development and how it contributes to building maintainable and extensible applications.

Creating Custom Service Providers

Service providers are the backbone of package development in Laravel, facilitating the registration of package services, configurations, and bindings. We will explore how to create custom service providers, enabling seamless integration of our packages into Laravel applications.

Publishing Configuration and Assets

Laravel's publishing system allows us to expose configuration files, assets, and other resources from our packages to the hosting application. We will learn how to publish our package's configuration and assets, providing users with the flexibility to customize the package's behavior according to their needs.

Testing and Versioning Packages

Testing is crucial to ensuring the quality and reliability of our packages. In this section, we will discover how to write tests for our packages using Laravel's testing framework. Additionally, we will explore versioning our packages, enabling us to manage changes and provide backward compatibility to our users.

© Sivaraj Selvaraj 2024

S. Selvaraj, *Building Real-Time Marvels with Laravel*, https://doi.org/10.1007/978-1-4842-9789-6_11

Packaging and Distributing Laravel Packages

Packaging and distributing our packages are the final steps in making our creations accessible to the Laravel community. We will explore the process of packaging our packages for distribution, making them available through version control systems like GitHub and the Packagist repository.

Throughout this chapter, we will immerse ourselves in the world of advanced package development in Laravel. By creating reusable packages with proper testing, versioning, and distribution, we can contribute valuable tools and functionalities to the Laravel ecosystem. So let's embark on this journey of advanced package development and empower the Laravel community with our innovative solutions!

Introduction to Package Development in Laravel

Laravel's extensibility through packages has revolutionized the way developers build web applications. Packages are standalone components or libraries that seamlessly integrate into Laravel, offering additional functionality and simplifying complex tasks. This introduction to package development in Laravel will delve into the essential concepts and practices, empowering developers to create and distribute packages, foster code reusability, and contribute to the thriving Laravel ecosystem. By embracing package development, Laravel developers can streamline their workflows and deliver high-quality applications with ease. Let's explore the exciting world of package development in Laravel!

Creating a package in Laravel involves a few essential steps, which I will outline in the following.

Setting Up the Package Structure

Create a new directory for your package within the 'packages' directory in your Laravel project's root.

Inside the package directory, create the necessary subdirectories and files to structure your package. This typically includes directories like 'src' for source code and 'tests' for testing.

Defining the Composer Package

In the root of your package directory, create a 'composer.json' file. This file specifies the package's dependencies, autoloading configuration, and other metadata.

Define the package name, version, description, author information, and any required dependencies.

Specify the autoloading rules for your package's classes using the PSR-4 autoloading standard.

Implementing the Package Functionality

Write the actual code for your package inside the 'src' directory.

Structure your package code using classes, interfaces, traits, and other Laravel conventions.

Implement the desired functionality, such as adding new routes, providing custom commands, extending existing Laravel functionality, or introducing new features.

Testing the Package

Write unit tests and feature tests for your package inside the 'tests' directory.

Ensure that your tests cover the various aspects and use cases of your package's functionality.

Run the tests to verify that your package behaves as expected and to catch any issues.

Publishing the Package

Once your package is ready, you can publish it to a package repository like Packagist (https://packagist.org).

Create an account on Packagist and follow the guidelines to publish your package.

After publishing, other developers can include your package in their Laravel projects by adding it as a dependency in their 'composer.json' files.

Consuming the Package

To use a package in a Laravel project, include it as a dependency in the project's 'composer.json' file.

Run 'composer update' or 'composer install' to download the package and update the project's autoloader.

Use the package's functionality by referencing its classes, methods, or configuration options in your Laravel application's code.

By following these steps, you can create and distribute your own Laravel packages, making it easier to share code, collaborate with others, and extend the functionality of Laravel applications.

Creating Custom Service Providers

In Laravel, service providers play a crucial role in the application's bootstrapping process. They are responsible for binding classes, registering services, and performing any necessary setup tasks. By creating custom service providers, you can encapsulate the initialization logic for your package and integrate it seamlessly into Laravel applications. Here's how you can create custom service providers in Laravel.

Create the Service Provider Class

In your package's 'src' directory, create a new PHP class that extends the 'Illuminate\ Support\ServiceProvider' class.

The class name should reflect the purpose or functionality of your service provider.

Override the 'register()' method to define the bindings and services that your package provides.

Optionally, override the 'boot()' method to perform any additional setup or configuration tasks.

Register Bindings and Services

In the 'register()' method of your service provider, use the '$this->app' instance to register bindings and services.

You can use the 'bind()' method to bind an interface or abstract class to a concrete implementation.

Alternatively, you can use the 'singleton()' method to bind a class as a singleton, ensuring that only one instance is created throughout the application's lifecycle.

Use the 'app->bind()' or 'app->singleton()' method to register bindings if you prefer to use the container instance directly.

Load the Service Provider

To load your custom service provider, add it to the 'providers' array in the 'config/app. php' configuration file of your Laravel application.

If you're developing a package, you can also register the service provider automatically using the 'register()' method in the 'composer.json' file of your package.

Additional Configuration (if Required)

If your package requires additional configuration options, you can provide a configuration file.

In your service provider's 'boot()' method or in a separate method, you can use the 'publishes()' method to publish your package's configuration file to the Laravel application's configuration directory.

Optionally, you can also use the 'mergeConfigFrom()' method in the 'register()' method to merge your package's configuration with the application's existing configuration.

Using the Package's Functionality

Once you register your service provider, your Laravel application can access the functionality provided by your package.

Use dependency injection to resolve and use the classes or services bound to your service provider.

You can also use the 'app()' function or the Laravel container to resolve dependencies manually.

By creating custom service providers, you can encapsulate the initialization and configuration logic of your package, making it easy for users to integrate and utilize your package's functionality within their Laravel applications.

Publishing Configuration and Assets

Publishing configuration and assets is an important aspect of package development in Laravel. It allows users of your package to customize configuration options and access any published assets, such as CSS or JavaScript files. Here's how you can publish configuration and assets from your package.

Publishing Configuration

To publish the configuration file from your package, you need to define the publishing behavior in your service provider's 'boot()' method. Here's an example of how you can publish the configuration file:

```
/**
 * Bootstrap any application services.
 *
 * @return void
 */
public function boot()
{
    // Publish the configuration file
    $this->publishes([
        __DIR__.'/../config/yourpackage.php' => config_
path('yourpackage.php'),
    ], 'config');
}
```

In this example, we assume that your package's configuration file is named 'yourpackage.php' and that it resides in the 'config' directory of your package.

The 'publishes()' method is used to define the publishing behavior. It takes an array as its first argument, where the keys represent the source file path and the values represent the destination file path. In this case, we specify the source path of your package's configuration file and the destination path in the Laravel application's 'config' directory.

The second argument, "config", is a tag that allows users to selectively publish the configuration file. It provides flexibility for users to publish only the configuration file associated with your package instead of all the files from all packages.

To publish the configuration file, users can run the following command:

```
php artisan vendor:publish --tag=config
```

This command will publish the configuration file from your package to the Laravel application's 'config' directory. Users can then modify the configuration values according to their needs.

Publishing Assets

To publish assets from your package, such as CSS files, JavaScript files, or images, you can define the publishing behavior in your service provider's 'boot()' method. Here's an example of how you can publish assets:

```
/**
 * Bootstrap any application services.
 *
 * @return void
 */
public function boot()
{
    // Publish the assets
    $this->publishes([
        __DIR__.'/../resources/assets' => public_path('yourpackage'),
    ], 'public');
}
```

In this example, we assume that your package's assets are located in the 'resources/assets' directory of your package. We publish them to the Laravel application's 'public/yourpackage' directory.

The 'publishes()' method is used to define the publishing behavior. It takes an array as its first argument, where the keys represent the source directory or file path and the values represent the destination directory or file path. In this case, we specify the source path of your package's assets and the destination path in the Laravel application's 'public' directory.

The second argument, 'public', is a tag that allows users to selectively publish the assets. It provides flexibility for users to publish only the assets associated with your package instead of all the assets from all packages.

To publish the assets, users can run the following command:

```
php artisan vendor:publish --tag=public
```

This command will publish the assets from your package to the Laravel application's 'public/yourpackage' directory. Users can then access and use these assets in their views or include them in their asset pipelines.

Registering the Assets

To make the published assets accessible in the Laravel application's asset management system, you can register them with your package's service provider. Here's an example of how you can register the assets:

```
/**
 * Register any application services.
 *
 * @return void
 */
public function register()
{
    // Register package assets
    $this->app->bind('yourpackage.assets', function () {
        return public_path('yourpackage');
    });
}
```

In this example, we register the path to the published assets with the key "yourpackage.assets".

Inside the 'register()' method of your service provider, we use the 'bind()' method of the application container ('$this->app') to register the assets. The key "yourpackage.assets" serves as the unique identifier for the assets.

The closure passed to the 'bind()' method returns the path to the published assets using the 'public_path()' helper function. You need to specify the directory path where the assets are published.

Once the assets are registered, you or other developers can access them using the registered key "yourpackage.assets". For example, you can use the 'asset()' helper function to generate the URL to an asset file:

```
$assetUrl = asset('yourpackage/css/style.css');
```

In this example, we assume that you have a CSS file named 'style.css' in the 'yourpackage' directory of the published assets.

Make sure to update the key and asset paths according to your package's structure and naming conventions.

By registering the assets, you provide a convenient way for users of your package to reference and utilize the published assets in their views or asset pipelines.

By publishing configuration files and assets, you provide users of your package with the flexibility to customize settings and utilize any public assets that your package may provide. Remember to update the paths, tags, and keys according to your package's file structure and naming conventions.

Testing and Versioning Packages

Testing and versioning are crucial aspects of package development in Laravel. They ensure the quality and stability of your package and allow for proper version management. Let's explore testing and versioning packages in Laravel.

Testing Packages

Testing packages is a crucial aspect of package development in Laravel. It helps ensure the reliability and functionality of your package. Here's an overview of how you can test your Laravel package:

Set up the Testing Environment

Laravel provides a dedicated directory for tests within your package. Make sure you have a 'tests' directory in your package's root directory. Additionally, you can define any necessary testing dependencies in your package's 'composer.json' file. For example, you can require 'phpunit/phpunit' as a development dependency to use PHPUnit for testing.

Write Tests

Write test cases to cover different aspects of your package's functionality. Laravel supports both unit tests and feature tests.

1. *Unit tests*

Unit tests focus on testing individual units of code in isolation. These units can be methods, classes, or any small piece of code. Unit tests ensure that each unit behaves as expected. For example, let's say you have a class called Calculator with a method called 'add()' that adds two numbers. You can write a unit test to verify that the 'add()' method correctly adds two numbers:

```php
<?php
use YourPackage\Calculator;
use PHPUnit\Framework\TestCase;
class CalculatorTest extends TestCase
{
    public function testAdd()
    {
        $calculator = new Calculator();
        $result = $calculator->add(2, 3);
        $this->assertEquals(5, $result);
    }
}
```

2. *Feature tests*

Feature tests simulate end-to-end scenarios and test the behavior of multiple components working together. They ensure that different parts of your package interact correctly. For example, let's say you have a package that provides a user management system. You can write a feature test to simulate user registration and ensure that the registration process works as expected:

```php
<?php
use YourPackage\User;
use Illuminate\Foundation\Testing\DatabaseTransactions;
use Tests\TestCase;
class UserRegistrationTest extends TestCase
{
    use DatabaseTransactions;
    public function testUserRegistration()
    {
        $response = $this->post('/register', [
            'name' => 'John Doe',
            'email' => 'johndoe@example.com',
            'password' => 'password',
        ]);
        $response->assertRedirect('/dashboard');
        $this->assertDatabaseHas('users', ['email' =>
        'johndoe@example.com']);
    }
}
```

Use Laravel Testing Tools

Laravel provides a comprehensive testing framework with useful tools and assertions. Utilize these tools to simplify the testing process. For example, Laravel's testing tools include various assertion methods like 'assertTrue', 'assertEquals', 'assertJson', and 'assertDatabaseHas'. These assertions help you verify expected outcomes:

```php
$this->assertTrue($condition);
$this->assertEquals($expected, $actual);
$this->assertJson($response->getContent());
$this->assertDatabaseHas('users', ['email' => 'johndoe@example.com']);
```

Laravel's testing tools also include HTTP testing utilities for simulating requests, handling sessions, and making assertions on responses. You can use these utilities to simulate various HTTP methods like 'get()', 'post()', 'put()', and 'delete()':

```
$response = $this->get('/users');
$response->assertStatus(200);
$response->assertJson(['name' => 'John Doe']);
```

Organize and Run Tests

Organize your tests into relevant directories and files within the 'tests' directory. You can create subdirectories based on functionality or features to keep your tests organized. To run your tests, use the 'php artisan test' command. By default, it runs all the tests within the 'tests' directory. You can use the '--group' option to run specific test groups or the '--filter' option to run specific tests based on their names:

```
php artisan test
php artisan test --group=unit
php artisan test --filter=CalculatorTest
```

Test Database Interactions

If your package interacts with the database, you can use Laravel's testing utilities to handle database transactions and migrations. Laravel provides traits like 'RefreshDatabase' and 'DatabaseTransactions' to ensure a clean database state for each test and roll back changes after the test. For example, you can use the 'DatabaseTransactions' trait to automatically wrap each test in a database transaction and roll it back at the end:

```php
<?php
use Illuminate\Foundation\Testing\DatabaseTransactions;
use Tests\TestCase;
class UserTest extends TestCase
{
    use DatabaseTransactions;
```

```
    public function testUserCreation()
    {
        // Test user creation and database interactions
    }
}
```

Mocking and Dependency Injection

When testing, you may need to mock dependencies or modify the container's bindings to isolate the code under test. Laravel's container allows you to easily swap out real dependencies with mock or fake objects using the 'bind' method or the 'instance' method. This helps you isolate the behavior of individual components during testing:

```
$this->app->bind(YourDependency::class, function () {
    return new MockYourDependency();
});
$this->app->instance(YourDependency::class, new FakeYourDependency());
```

Continuous Integration (CI)

Consider setting up a continuous integration (CI) system to automatically run tests whenever changes are pushed to your package's repository.

Popular CI tools like GitHub Actions, Travis CI, and CircleCI allow you to configure workflows that run the appropriate testing commands for your package.

This helps ensure that your package's tests are regularly executed, catching potential issues early on.

Versioning Packages

Versioning your package is essential to tracking changes, providing backward compatibility, and managing dependencies effectively. Laravel package versioning typically follows the Semantic Versioning (SemVer) convention.

Semantic Versioning (SemVer)

Semantic Versioning is a widely adopted versioning convention that provides a clear and predictable way to indicate changes in your package.

It consists of three parts: 'MAJOR.MINOR.PATCH'

'MAJOR' version should be incremented for backward-incompatible changes or major updates. This means that existing functionality may break when users upgrade to a new major version.

'MINOR' version should be incremented for backward-compatible feature additions or significant updates. This indicates that new features have been added without breaking existing functionality.

'PATCH' version should be incremented for backward-compatible bug fixes or minor updates. These updates don't introduce new features but address issues in the existing codebase.

Following SemVer helps users understand the impact of new versions and allows them to manage dependencies effectively.

Update composer.json

In your package's 'composer.json' file, update the 'version' field to reflect the current version of your package, for example:

```
{
    "name": "your/package",
    "version": "1.0.0",
    ...
}
```

Whenever you release a new version, update the 'version' field accordingly.

Git Tagging

Tagging your package's repository with the corresponding version number is a common practice when releasing a new version. Git tags serve as markers to indicate specific points in your codebase that represent a version release. You can use lightweight tags or annotated tags.

To create a lightweight tag:

```
git tag 1.0.0
```

To create an annotated tag with additional information:

```
git tag -a 1.0.0 -m "Release version 1.0.0"
```

After creating the tag, push it to the remote repository:

```
git push --tags
```

This makes the tag available for other users and systems to reference.

Release Notes

Maintaining release notes or a changelog is beneficial for communicating changes between different versions. It provides a summary of what has been added, fixed, or changed in each release. This helps users understand the updates and make necessary adjustments.

For example, you can create a 'CHANGELOG.md' file in your package's root directory and follow a consistent format to document the changes. Here's an example entry:

```
[1.0.0] - 2023-07-13
Added new feature XYZ
Fixed issue ABC
Improved performance in module DEF
```

Including a release date and a list of changes helps users track the evolution of your package.

Publishing to the Package Repository

To make your package easily installable via Composer, publish it to a package repository like Packagist. Register your package with the appropriate version number. Users can then include it in their Laravel applications by referencing the version.

For example, when publishing your package with version '1.0.0', users can install it using Composer:

```
composer require your/package:^1.0.0
```

This ensures that users get the specific version they require and allows Composer to manage dependencies effectively.

Version Constraints

When including your package in other projects, users can specify version constraints in their 'composer.json' file. Version constraints define which versions of your package are acceptable for their project.

Here's an example of a version constraint that allows any '1.x' version of your package:

```
{
    "require": {
        "your/package": "^1.0"
    }
}
```

This constraint allows Composer to install any '1.x' version, including '1.0.0', '1.1.0', or '1.2.3', but excludes '2.0.0'.

Version constraints give users flexibility in managing their dependencies and ensure compatibility with their Laravel application.

Communication and Backward Compatibility

When releasing new versions, it's important to consider backward compatibility. Backward-incompatible changes introduced in a new major version can break existing functionality. It's crucial to communicate these changes to users and provide migration guides or documentation to help them upgrade smoothly.

For example, you can document breaking changes and provide instructions on how to update the code to be compatible with the new version. This minimizes disruptions and allows users to transition to the latest version with ease.

Following these versioning practices, you can effectively manage changes, communicate updates, and maintain compatibility for your Laravel package. Proper versioning allows users to understand the impact of updates, manage dependencies, and ensure a smooth upgrade process.

Testing and versioning are critical aspects of package development. Thorough testing assures the quality of your package, while proper versioning allows users to manage dependencies effectively.

Together, they contribute to the stability, reliability, and maintainability of your Laravel package.

Packaging and Distributing Laravel Packages

Packaging and distributing your Laravel package allows others to easily install and use it in their projects. Here are the steps to package and distribute your Laravel package.

Package Structure

Ensure your package follows a well-defined structure. Typically, a Laravel package consists of the following directories:

> 'src/': Contains the source code of your package, including classes, interfaces, and other necessary files

> 'config/': Contains configuration files for your package, if applicable

> 'resources/': Holds any additional resources like views, assets, or language files

'tests/': Contains test cases to ensure the quality of your package

'composer.json': Defines the package metadata, dependencies, and autoloading configuration

Create a Composer Package

Laravel packages are distributed using Composer, a dependency management tool for PHP. To make your package compatible with Composer, you need to create a 'composer.json' file in the root directory of your package.

The 'composer.json' file should include information about your package, such as its name, version, description, author, and license. You should also define any dependencies your package relies on.

Here's an example 'composer.json' file for a Laravel package:

```
{
    "name": "your/package",
    "version": "1.0.0",
    "description": "Your Laravel package description",
    "authors": [
        {
            "name": "Your Name",
            "email": "your@email.com"
        }
    ],
    "require": {
        "php": "^7.4",
        "illuminate/support": "^8.0"
    },
    "autoload": {
        "psr-4": {
            "Your\\Namespace\\": "src/"
        }
    }
}
```

Make sure to replace 'your/package', 'Your Name', 'your@email.com', and 'Your\\ Namespace' with your package-specific details.

Publish Your Package

Publish your package to a version control system (such as GitHub or GitLab) to make it accessible to others. Ensure that your package's repository includes all the necessary files and directories.

Register Your Package

Register your package with a package repository, such as Packagist, to make it easily installable via Composer. Create an account on Packagist, navigate to your account's dashboard, and add your package's repository URL. Packagist will automatically detect updates and make them available to users.

Versioning and Tagging

Follow the versioning conventions discussed earlier (Semantic Versioning) and create Git tags to mark specific versions of your package. Tagging helps users reference specific releases of your package.

To create a lightweight tag in Git:

```
git tag 1.0.0
```

To create an annotated tag with additional information:

```
git tag -a 1.0.0 -m "Release version 1.0.0"
```

After creating the tag, push it to the remote repository:

```
git push --tags
```

Installation via Composer

Users can include your package in their Laravel applications by adding it as a dependency in their 'composer.json' file. They need to specify the package name and version constraint.

For example, to require version 1.0 of your package, they would add the following line to their 'composer.json':

```
{
    "require": {
        "your/package": "^1.0"
    }
}
```

Users can then run 'composer install' or 'composer update' to install or update the package and its dependencies.

Documentation

Provide documentation to guide users on how to use your package effectively. This can include a README file in your package's repository, a dedicated documentation website, or inline code comments.

Document essential package features, usage examples, configuration options, and any necessary installation or setup instructions. Clear documentation helps users understand how to integrate and utilize your package.

By packaging and distributing your Laravel package, you make it easily accessible and installable for other developers. Following these steps ensures that your package is properly structured, compatible with Composer, and available through package repositories. Clear documentation assists users in effectively using your package in their Laravel projects.

Summary

In this chapter, we delved into the complexities of advanced package development in the Laravel framework, with a focus on generating reusable and extendable packages that can be easily integrated into Laravel apps or shared with the community. The package development workflow was explained, covering package structure, versioning, and dependency management. We discussed how to implement service providers, facades, and configuration options to give users a seamless integration experience, as well as publishing packages and maintaining package assets. You also learned about testing and debugging approaches related to package development.

The next chapter will cover performance monitoring and debugging.

CHAPTER 12

Performance Monitoring and Debugging

In the previous chapter, we explored the art of advanced package development in Laravel, creating modular and reusable components to enhance our application's functionality. As we continue our journey through Laravel's advanced features, we now delve into the realm of performance monitoring and debugging—vital aspects of ensuring our applications run smoothly and efficiently.

Profiling Laravel Applications

In this section, we will discover the significance of profiling Laravel applications to gain insights into their performance. Profiling allows us to measure and analyze various aspects of our applications, identifying potential bottlenecks and areas for optimization.

Debugging Techniques and Tools

Effective debugging is a skill every developer must master. Here, we will explore various debugging techniques and tools available in Laravel to pinpoint and resolve issues in our code, ensuring the reliability and correctness of our applications.

Performance Monitoring with Laravel Telescope

Laravel Telescope is a powerful tool that provides real-time insights into the performance of our applications. We will learn how to leverage Laravel Telescope to monitor key metrics, such as database queries, HTTP requests, and more, enabling us to identify and address performance-related problems.

Identifying and Resolving Performance Bottlenecks

Performance bottlenecks can hinder the responsiveness and scalability of our applications. We will delve into the process of identifying and resolving common performance bottlenecks, using profiling, debugging, and monitoring techniques to optimize the overall performance of our applications.

© Sivaraj Selvaraj 2024
S. Selvaraj, *Building Real-Time Marvels with Laravel*, https://doi.org/10.1007/978-1-4842-9789-6_12

Monitoring and Optimizing Application Security

In this final section, we will explore the crucial aspect of monitoring and optimizing application security. We will learn how to use security monitoring tools and techniques to identify and mitigate potential security vulnerabilities, ensuring the safety and integrity of our applications and user data.

Throughout this chapter, we will immerse ourselves in the world of performance monitoring and debugging in Laravel, equipping ourselves with the skills and tools to optimize the efficiency and reliability of our applications. By adopting effective debugging and monitoring practices, we can create high-performing and secure applications that deliver exceptional user experiences. So let's embark on this journey of performance monitoring and debugging to take our Laravel development to new heights!

Profiling Laravel Applications

Profiling is a crucial process in the world of software development, especially when it comes to optimizing performance and identifying potential bottlenecks. In Laravel applications, profiling enables developers to gain valuable insights into how the application behaves during runtime, helping them pinpoint areas that need improvement for enhanced efficiency.

In this guide, we will explore the various techniques and tools available for profiling Laravel applications. From utilizing built-in Laravel features to using third-party profiling tools, we will delve into the methods that allow developers to measure execution times, query performance, memory usage, and more.

By effectively profiling Laravel applications, developers can fine-tune their code, optimize database queries, and deliver a faster and more responsive user experience. Additionally, profiling aids in the identification of memory leaks and other performance-related issues, leading to more stable and reliable applications.

Whether you are a seasoned Laravel developer seeking to improve the performance of your existing applications or a newcomer looking to learn about the importance of profiling, this guide aims to equip you with the knowledge and tools needed to become proficient in profiling Laravel applications. Let's embark on this journey to unlock the full potential of your Laravel projects through effective profiling techniques.

Laravel Debugbar

Laravel Debugbar is a development package for Laravel that provides a powerful debugging and profiling toolbar for your application. It offers a range of features and insights to help you monitor and analyze the performance of your Laravel application during development. Here's an overview of how to install and use Laravel Debugbar.

Installation

You can install Laravel Debugbar via Composer by running the following command in your project directory:

```
composer require barryvdh/laravel-debugbar --dev
```

The '--dev' flag ensures that the package is installed as a development dependency.

Configuration

After installation, open your Laravel application's configuration file located at 'config/app.php' and add the following line to the 'providers' array:

```
Barryvdh\Debugbar\ServiceProvider::class,
```

This registers the Debugbar service provider.

Next, you need to publish the configuration file. Run the following command:

```
php artisan vendor:publish --provider="Barryvdh\Debugbar\ServiceProvider"
```

This command will create a 'debugbar.php' file in your 'config' directory, allowing you to customize the Debugbar's behavior.

Enabling the Debugbar

By default, the Debugbar is only enabled in the local environment. If you want to enable it in other environments, open the 'debugbar.php' file and modify the "enabled" option as per your requirements.

You can also enable or disable specific collectors to control the information displayed by the Debugbar. The collectors are responsible for gathering and displaying different types of data, such as queries, views, routes, memory usage, and more.

Usage

Once you have enabled the Debugbar, you can start using it in your application. By default, the Debugbar is displayed at the top of your web pages. Clicking the toolbar expands it to reveal detailed information about your application's execution.

The Debugbar provides various tabs, including "Queries", "Timeline", "Views", "Route", "Logs", and more. Each tab offers specific insights into different aspects of your application's performance and behavior.

For example, the "Queries" tab displays all executed database queries, their execution time, and the number of rows returned. This information can help you identify slow or redundant queries.

The "Timeline" tab provides a visual representation of the application's execution flow, allowing you to analyze the time spent in different parts of your code. This can help identify areas where optimization is needed.

Additionally, the Debugbar integrates with Laravel's logging system, allowing you to view application logs directly from the toolbar.

You can also use Debugbar's API to collect and display custom data and measurements specific to your application.

Remember to disable or remove the Debugbar from your production environment to prevent unauthorized access to sensitive information and unnecessary performance overhead.

Laravel Debugbar is a valuable tool for profiling and debugging Laravel applications. It helps you gain insights into your application's performance and behavior, making it easier to optimize and troubleshoot issues during development.

Xdebug

Xdebug is a powerful PHP extension that provides debugging and profiling capabilities for PHP applications, including Laravel. It offers features like stack traces, profiling information, code coverage analysis, and remote debugging. Developers widely use Xdebug to enhance their development and debugging experiences. Here's an overview of how to install and use Xdebug with Laravel.

Installation

Before using Xdebug, you need to install the extension on your system. The installation process may vary depending on your operating system. Here are some general steps:

    a.   Check if Xdebug is already installed: Run the 'php -m' command in your terminal or command prompt to see if Xdebug is listed. If not, you'll need to install it.

    b.   Install Xdebug: Use the package manager specific to your operating system to install Xdebug. For example, on Ubuntu, you can run 'sudo apt install php-xdebug'.

    c.   Verify installation: After installing, run the 'php -m' command again to ensure that Xdebug is now listed.

Configuration

Once Xdebug is installed, you need to configure it to work with Laravel. The configuration involves modifying your PHP settings. Locate the 'php.ini' file used by your PHP installation (you can find its location by running 'php --ini' in the terminal) and make the following changes:

```
-----------------------------------------------------------------------
[Xdebug]
zend_extension=path/to/xdebug.so
xdebug.mode=debug
xdebug.client_host=127.0.0.1
xdebug.client_port=9000
-----------------------------------------------------------------------
```

Replace 'path/to/xdebug.so' with the actual path to the Xdebug extension file on your system. The 'xdebug.client_host' and 'xdebug.client_port' settings specify the host and port where the remote debugger will connect. Set these values according to your debugging environment.

Remote Debugging

To use Xdebug for remote debugging in Laravel, follow these steps:

a. Configure your IDE: Enable Xdebug support in your integrated development environment (IDE) and configure the debugger settings. Refer to your IDE's documentation for specific instructions.

b. Start the debugging session: In your IDE, set a breakpoint in the code where you want to start debugging. Then, trigger the code execution in your Laravel application, either by accessing it through a web browser or running a command.

c. IDE connection: Your IDE should listen for incoming debugging connections on the specified host and port. When the code execution hits the breakpoint, the IDE will stop and allow you to inspect variables, step through code, and analyze the application's state.

Profiling

Xdebug also provides profiling capabilities to analyze the performance of your Laravel application. To enable profiling, modify the 'php.ini' file as follows:

```
----------------------------------------------------------------------
[Xdebug]
zend_extension=path/to/xdebug.so
xdebug.mode=profile
xdebug.output_dir=/path/to/profiles/directory
----------------------------------------------------------------------
```

Replace '/path/to/profiles/directory' with the directory where you want to store the profiling files generated by Xdebug.

With profiling enabled, Xdebug will generate profiling files during the execution of your Laravel application. You can then analyze these files using tools like KCachegrind or QCacheGrind to gain insights into the application's performance, identify bottlenecks, and optimize your code.

Xdebug is a valuable tool for debugging and profiling Laravel applications. It helps you identify and resolve issues efficiently, making the development process smoother and more productive.

Blackfire

Blackfire is a commercial profiling and performance management platform that helps developers optimize the performance of their applications. It provides in-depth insights into your application's performance, identifies performance bottlenecks, and suggests optimizations. Blackfire supports various frameworks and languages, including Laravel.

Here's an overview of how to use Blackfire with Laravel.

Sign Up and Obtain an Authentication Token

Visit the Blackfire website (https://blackfire.io/) and sign up for an account. Once you have an account, you will receive an authentication token. This token will be used to configure Blackfire in your Laravel application.

Install the Blackfire Probe

Blackfire uses a PHP extension called the Blackfire Probe to collect profiling data from your application. To install the probe, follow the instructions provided in the Blackfire documentation (https://blackfire.io/docs/up-and-running/installation) specific to your operating system and PHP version.

Configure Blackfire in Laravel

Open your Laravel application's '.env' file and add the following lines:

```
BLACKFIRE_SERVER_ID=your_server_id
BLACKFIRE_SERVER_TOKEN=your_server_token
```

Replace 'your_server_id' and 'your_server_token' with the values provided by Blackfire during your account setup.

Profile Your Application

Once Blackfire is configured, you can start profiling your Laravel application. To profile a specific code path, you can use the 'blackfire()' helper function in your code, for example:

```
Route::get('/profile', function () {
 blackfire()->profile();
 // Your code to profile
});
```

When the code execution reaches the 'blackfire()->profile()' line, Blackfire will start collecting profiling data.

Analyze the Results

After profiling, you can view and analyze the results on the Blackfire website. The Blackfire UI provides detailed information about the execution flow, including function calls, queries, HTTP requests, and more. It highlights performance bottlenecks and suggests improvements to optimize your application.

Blackfire also offers various features such as comparisons, flame graphs, performance metrics, and integrations with popular tools like IDEs and continuous integration platforms. Refer to the Blackfire documentation for detailed information on utilizing these features.

It's worth noting that while Blackfire offers a free tier with limited features, some advanced functionalities may require a subscription. The pricing details and available plans can be found on the Blackfire website.

Using Blackfire with Laravel allows you to gain deep insights into your application's performance and optimize it for better speed and efficiency. By profiling your code and identifying bottlenecks, you can make informed decisions on where to focus your optimization efforts.

Profiling Laravel applications helps you identify performance bottlenecks, optimize critical parts of your code, and ensure your application delivers the best possible performance. Whether you choose to use Laravel Debugbar, Xdebug, Blackfire, or a combination of these tools, profiling should be an integral part of your development and optimization workflow.

Debugging Techniques and Tools

Debugging is an essential skill for developers, and having the right techniques and tools can greatly simplify the process of identifying and resolving issues in your code. In this section, we will explore some commonly used debugging techniques and tools that can help you debug your Laravel applications effectively.

Logging

Logging is a fundamental technique for debugging and monitoring applications. It involves recording messages or events at various points in your code to track the flow and state of your application during execution. The Monolog library in Laravel handles logging, offering a flexible and powerful logging system. Here's an overview of how to use logging in Laravel.

Logging Levels

Laravel supports various logging levels that indicate the severity or importance of log messages. The available logging levels in Laravel, in increasing order of severity, are

'emergency': The system is unusable.

'alert': Action must be taken immediately.

'critical': Critical conditions.

'error': Runtime errors that do not require immediate action.

'warning': Exceptional occurrences that are not errors.

'notice': Normal but significant events.

'info': Interesting events or information.

'debug': Detailed debug information.

By using the appropriate logging level, you can categorize log messages based on their significance and easily filter them during debugging or production.

Logging Syntax

In Laravel, you can use the 'Log' facade to write log messages. The 'Log' facade provides static methods for logging messages at different levels. The basic syntax for logging is as follows:

```
use Illuminate\Support\Facades\Log;
Log::level('Log message');
```

Replace 'level' with the desired logging level, such as 'debug', 'info', 'warning', 'error', etc. The log message can be a string or an array containing additional context data.

Logging Context

Logging context provides additional information along with the log message. It can include data such as request information, user details, timestamps, or any other relevant information that helps in troubleshooting. You can pass the context as an associative array as the second argument to the logging methods, for example:

```
Log::info('User login successful', ['user_id' => $user->id, 'ip' =>
$request->ip()]);
```

The context data will be included in the log message and can be used for additional analysis or filtering.

Logging Channels

Laravel supports multiple logging channels, allowing you to direct log messages to different destinations or channels. The default channel is configured in the 'config/logging. php' file. Laravel provides various built-in channels like 'stack', 'single', 'daily', 'syslog', 'errorlog', etc. You can also create custom channels to suit your specific logging needs.

Log Files and Locations

By default, Laravel logs messages to a file specified in the logging configuration file ('config/logging.php'). The log files are stored in the 'storage/logs' directory. Laravel rotates log files automatically, ensuring that log files do not grow excessively.

Additional Configuration

Laravel's logging system offers extensive configuration options. You can customize the logging behavior, define log channels, specify the log file format, configure log levels, and more. The logging configuration file ('config/logging.php') provides detailed information and options to fine-tune the logging system.

Viewing Logs

To view log messages, you can access the log files directly in the 'storage/logs' directory. However, Laravel also provides an artisan command to read and display log files conveniently. Use the following command in your terminal:

```
php artisan log:tail
```

This command will stream the latest log entries to your console, allowing you to monitor the logs in real time during development or troubleshooting.

Logging is a powerful tool for tracking behavior and identifying issues in your Laravel applications. By strategically placing log statements and using the appropriate logging levels, you can gain valuable insights into the execution flow, variable values, and potential errors, helping you debug and maintain your application effectively.

Dumping and Die Statements

Dumping and die statements are debugging techniques used to inspect the values of variables and halt the execution of code at a specific point. In Laravel, you can use the 'dump' and 'dd' functions to perform these actions. Here's an overview of how to use dumping and die statements in Laravel.

Dumping Variables with 'dump'

The 'dump' function is used to display the contents of variables or other data structures. It is non-destructive, meaning that it does not halt the execution of code and allows the program to continue running after the dump. The output of the 'dump' function is displayed in the browser's console or terminal, depending on the context in which the code is executed.

Here's an example of using 'dump' in Laravel:

```
$name = 'John Doe';
$age = 25;
$data = ['name' => $name, 'age' => $age];
dump($name);
dump($age);
dump($data);
```

The 'dump' function will display the values of the variables '$name', '$age', and '$data' along with their data types.

Dumping and Halting Execution with 'dd'

The 'dd' function, which stands for "dump and die," is used to display the contents of variables and immediately halt the execution of code. This is useful when you want to inspect the value of a variable at a specific point and prevent further code execution.

Here's an example of using 'dd' in Laravel:

```
$name = 'John Doe';
$age = 25;
$data = ['name' => $name, 'age' => $age];
dd($name);
dd($age);
dd($data);
```

When 'dd' is called, it will output the value of the variable and terminate the script execution, preventing any code that follows it from running.

The 'dd' function also provides a convenient way to examine the call stack and trace the execution flow at the point of termination.

Dumping and die statements are helpful when you want to inspect the values of variables, objects, or arrays during the execution of your Laravel application. They provide a quick way to debug and understand the state of your code at a specific point, allowing you to identify issues and verify the correctness of your data. However, remember to remove or disable these statements from production code, as they can impact performance and expose sensitive information.

Exception Handling

Exception handling is a critical aspect of error management in any application, including Laravel. Exceptions are errors or exceptional conditions that occur during the execution of your code and can disrupt the normal flow of your application. Laravel provides a robust exception handling mechanism that allows you to catch, handle, and respond to exceptions gracefully. Here's an overview of exception handling in Laravel.

Understanding Exceptions

Exceptions in PHP are represented by special classes that extend the base 'Exception' class or its subclasses. Laravel uses exceptions extensively to handle various types of errors, such as database connection failures, file not found errors, validation failures, and more.

Exception Handling in Laravel

Laravel's exception handling is centralized in the 'App\Exceptions\Handler' class. This class contains methods for handling various types of exceptions and customizing the way they are reported or responded to. By default, Laravel's exception handler is responsible for catching and responding to exceptions thrown by your application.

Handling Exceptions

In Laravel, you can handle exceptions in multiple ways:

a. Catching exceptions: To catch and handle a specific type of exception, you can use a 'try-catch' block. Inside the 'catch' block, you can define the actions to be taken when the exception occurs, for example:

```
try {
 // Code that may throw an exception
} catch (ExceptionType $e) {
 // Exception handling code
}
```

In the catch block, you can log the exception, display a user-friendly error message, redirect the user to an error page, or perform any other necessary actions.

b. Custom exception handlers: Laravel allows you to define custom exception handlers to handle specific types of exceptions. You can override the 'render' method in the 'App\Exceptions\Handler' class to customize the response for specific exceptions, for example:

```
public function render($request, Exception $exception)
{
 if ($exception instanceof \App\Exceptions\
 CustomException) {
  // Handle specific exception
  return response()->view('errors.custom', [], 500);
 }
 return parent::render($request, $exception);
}
```

In this example, when a 'CustomException' occurs, the 'render' method returns a custom error view with an HTTP status code of 500 (Internal Server Error).

Logging Exceptions

Logging exceptions is essential for debugging and error monitoring. Laravel's exception handling automatically logs exceptions to the default log channel specified in the 'config/logging.php' file. You can also customize the logging behavior by overriding the 'report' method in the 'App\Exceptions\Handler' class.

By logging exceptions, you can review error details, stack traces, and associated information to identify the root cause of the issue and make necessary improvements to your code.

Displaying Debug Information

During development, Laravel provides a detailed error page for exceptions. This page includes information such as the exception message, stack trace, and relevant request details. By default, Laravel shows the error page when the 'APP_DEBUG' configuration in the '.env' file is set to 'true'. However, it's crucial to disable this feature in production to prevent sensitive information from being exposed.

Exception handling is an essential aspect of ensuring the stability and resilience of your Laravel applications. By catching and handling exceptions, you can gracefully handle errors, provide appropriate responses to users, and maintain the overall integrity of your application.

IDE Debugging Tools

Modern integrated development environments (IDEs) offer powerful debugging tools that can greatly enhance your debugging experience. IDEs like PhpStorm, Visual Studio Code, and Eclipse provide features like breakpoints, step-by-step execution, variable inspection, and call stack analysis.

By setting breakpoints at specific lines of code, you can pause the execution of your Laravel application and examine the values of variables, trace the execution flow, and identify issues. IDEs also allow you to step through your code line by line, enabling you to understand the behavior of your application in detail.

To utilize the debugging features of your IDE with Laravel, you must configure the necessary settings and set up the debugger according to your IDE's documentation.

Chrome DevTools

Chrome DevTools is a set of web development and debugging tools built into the Google Chrome browser. It offers a range of features that can be utilized for debugging Laravel applications, especially on the client side.

With Chrome DevTools, you can inspect the network traffic, analyze JavaScript execution, examine HTML and CSS, debug AJAX requests, and much more. It provides a powerful interface to monitor and debug the frontend components of your Laravel application.

To open Chrome DevTools, right-click a web page in Chrome and select "Inspect" or press F12 on Windows or Command+Option+I on macOS. Refer to the Chrome DevTools documentation for detailed information on how to use its features effectively.

Debugging is an iterative process, and different techniques and tools may be suitable for different scenarios. By combining logging, dumping statements, exception handling, IDE debugging tools, and Chrome DevTools, you can efficiently identify and resolve issues in your Laravel applications.

Performance Monitoring with Laravel Telescope

Laravel Telescope is a performance monitoring and debugging tool provided by Laravel. It offers real-time insights into requests, database queries, exceptions, and more, helping you analyze and optimize the performance of your Laravel applications. Here's an overview of how to use Laravel Telescope for performance monitoring.

Installation

To install Laravel Telescope, you can use Composer. Open your terminal or command prompt and run the following command in your Laravel project directory:

```
composer require laravel/telescope --dev
```

The '--dev' flag ensures that Telescope is installed as a development dependency.

Configuration

After installing Telescope, you need to run the setup command to publish its configuration file and assets. Run the following command in your terminal:

```
php artisan telescope:install
```

This command will create a 'telescope.php' configuration file in your 'config' directory.

Database Setup

To set up the database for Laravel Telescope, follow these steps.

Run Migrations

Laravel Telescope uses a database to store its monitoring data. To create the necessary tables, run the following command in your terminal:

```
php artisan migrate
```

This command will execute the Telescope migrations and create the required tables in your database. By default, the migrations are located in the 'vendor/laravel/telescope/database/migrations' directory.

Run the Telescope Prune Command (Optional)

Telescope records a lot of data over time, and it can accumulate and occupy significant storage space in your database. To prune (clean up) the old data and limit the size of the Telescope database tables, you can run the Telescope prune command.

```
php artisan telescope:prune
```

This command will delete old entries from the Telescope database tables, keeping the size under control. You can schedule this command to run periodically using Laravel's task scheduler ('app/Console/Kernel.php') to automate the data pruning process.

Database Connection Configuration

Laravel Telescope uses the same database connection as your main Laravel application. Ensure that your Laravel application's database connection configuration (specified in the '.env' file) is correctly set up, allowing Laravel to connect to the database.

Verify the following database connection details in your '.env' file:

'DB_CONNECTION': The database connection driver (e.g., mysql, sqlite, pgsql)

'DB_HOST': The host where your database server is running

'DB_PORT': The port number to connect to the database server

'DB_DATABASE': The name of the database that will store Telescope's monitoring data

'DB_USERNAME': The username to authenticate with the database server

'DB_PASSWORD': The password to authenticate with the database server

Update these values as per your database setup.

Verify the Database Connection

After configuring the database connection details in the '.env' file, you can verify the connection by running the following command in your terminal:

```
php artisan telescope:check-connection
```

This command will check the connection to the configured database and display a success message if the connection is established.

With these steps, you should have the database set up for Laravel Telescope. It will use the same database connection as your Laravel application, and the necessary tables will be created to store Telescope's monitoring data. You can now start using Telescope to monitor and debug your Laravel application's performance.

Enabling Telescope

By default, Telescope is enabled in the local development environment. If you want to enable it in other environments, open the 'telescope.php' configuration file and modify the "enabled" option as per your requirements.

Accessing Telescope

Once Telescope is installed and enabled, you can access it via a web browser. In your local development environment, visit 'http://your-app-url/telescope' to access the Telescope dashboard. Here, you will find various tabs providing real-time insights into your application's performance and behavior.

Telescope Features

Laravel Telescope offers several features to monitor and analyze your application's performance. Here are some key features:

Requests: Telescope captures detailed information about each incoming HTTP request, including route information, request parameters, headers, response status, and more.

Queries: It logs all executed database queries, allowing you to review the query statements, their execution time, and the number of rows returned. This helps you identify and optimize slow queries.

Exceptions: Telescope records information about any exceptions thrown during the execution of your application. You can view the exception details and stack trace and analyze the occurrence frequency to pinpoint and resolve issues.

Mail: It tracks the emails sent by your application, providing insights into the recipients, subject, and contents of each email.

Jobs: Telescope monitors queued jobs, allowing you to analyze their status, payload, and execution time.

Notifications: It captures information about the notifications sent by your application, helping you track and debug notification-related issues.

Logs: Telescope integrates with Laravel's logging system, providing a streamlined view of your application's log entries.

These features, along with others, offer comprehensive monitoring capabilities for your Laravel application, making it easier to identify performance bottlenecks and troubleshoot issues.

Telescope is a powerful tool for performance monitoring and debugging in Laravel. By utilizing its real-time insights and detailed information about requests, queries, exceptions, and more, you can optimize your application's performance, improve the user experience, and resolve issues efficiently.

Identifying and Resolving Performance Bottlenecks

Identifying and resolving performance bottlenecks is an important task in optimizing the performance of your Laravel application. Here are some steps you can follow to identify and address performance issues.

Monitoring and Profiling

Use monitoring and profiling tools like Laravel Telescope, Xdebug, or Blackfire to gather data about your application's performance. These tools provide insights into database queries, request timings, memory usage, and other metrics. By monitoring and profiling your application, you can identify areas that need optimization.

Identify Bottlenecks

Look for areas where your application is experiencing slowness or resource-intensive operations. Some common areas to investigate include

Database queries: Identify slow-running queries or queries that are executed multiple times unnecessarily. Optimize database queries by indexing tables, using eager loading or lazy loading where appropriate, and avoiding the N+1 query problem.

Code execution: Look for sections of code that are causing performance issues. This could include heavy computations, inefficient algorithms, or excessive loops. Refactor or optimize these sections to improve performance.

External requests: Evaluate any external API calls or third-party integrations. Identify any delays or bottlenecks in these interactions and optimize them where possible.

Resource usage: Monitor CPU and memory usage to identify any resource-intensive operations. Look for opportunities to optimize code or utilize caching mechanisms to reduce resource consumption.

Query Optimization

Use Laravel's query builder or ORM (Eloquent) to optimize database queries. Ensure that you're only retrieving the required data and avoiding retrieving unnecessary data from the database. Utilize query constraints, eager loading, and database indexes to improve query performance.

Caching

Implement caching mechanisms to store frequently accessed or computationally expensive data. Use Laravel's caching features like the Cache facade, Redis caching, or Laravel cache tags to cache data and reduce the need for repeated computations.

Code Optimization

Review your code for any inefficiencies or performance bottlenecks. Look for areas where you can optimize code execution, reduce unnecessary loops or iterations, and improve algorithmic efficiency. Consider using Laravel's collection methods, optimizing loops, and avoiding redundant calculations.

Use Queues for Background Processing

Offload time-consuming tasks to background queues using Laravel's built-in queue system. By moving non-critical tasks to queues, you can free up the main application thread and improve the responsiveness and performance of your application.

Profiling and Benchmarking

Utilize profiling and benchmarking tools to measure the impact of optimizations. Tools like Xdebug, Blackfire, or Laravel Telescope can help you identify performance improvements and validate their effectiveness.

Load Testing

Perform load testing to simulate high-traffic scenarios and identify how your application performs under heavy load. Use tools like Apache JMeter or Artillery to stress-test your application and analyze its performance. Load testing helps uncover bottlenecks and ensures your application can handle increased traffic.

Optimize Asset Delivery

Optimize the delivery of static assets like CSS, JavaScript, and images. Use techniques such as asset minification, compression, caching, and CDNs (Content Delivery Networks) to reduce the file sizes and improve their delivery speed to end users.

Scalability and Infrastructure

Consider the scalability of your infrastructure. Ensure your servers or hosting environment can handle the anticipated load. If needed, scale horizontally by adding more servers or vertically by upgrading hardware specifications.

By following these steps, you can identify and address performance bottlenecks in your Laravel application, leading to improved responsiveness, faster execution, and a better user experience. Continuous monitoring and optimization are key to maintaining optimal performance as your application evolves.

Monitoring and Optimizing Application Security

Monitoring and optimizing application security is crucial to protecting your Laravel application from potential vulnerabilities and attacks. By implementing appropriate security measures and following best practices, you can minimize the risk of security breaches. Here are some key steps for monitoring and optimizing application security in Laravel.

Keep Dependencies Up to Date

Regularly update your Laravel framework and all third-party dependencies to their latest versions. Updates often include security patches that address known vulnerabilities. Stay informed about security advisories and announcements from Laravel and the packages you use, and promptly apply any necessary updates.

Implement Secure Authentication

Ensure that your application's authentication system is properly implemented and follows security best practices. Use Laravel's built-in authentication features, such as the 'make:auth' Artisan command, to create a secure authentication system. Utilize features like password hashing, remember me functionality, and two-factor authentication (2FA) to enhance security.

Protect Routes and Sensitive Data

Apply appropriate access controls and authorization mechanisms to protect your application's routes and sensitive data. Use Laravel's middleware, such as 'auth' and 'can', to control access to routes and actions. Implement role-based access control (RBAC) or permissions systems to restrict access to specific resources.

Sanitize and Validate User Input

Protect your application from common security vulnerabilities like SQL injection and Cross-Site Scripting (XSS) attacks by sanitizing and validating user input. Use Laravel's built-in validation features, such as form requests and validation rules, to ensure that user input is validated and sanitized before processing.

Implement CSRF Protection

Enable Laravel's built-in Cross-Site Request Forgery (CSRF) protection mechanism to guard against CSRF attacks. Laravel automatically generates CSRF tokens for forms and verifies them during form submissions. Ensure that CSRF protection is applied to all forms in your application.

Secure Database Access

Protect your database credentials and ensure that your database connection is properly configured. Store database credentials securely, away from public access. Use environment variables or Laravel's configuration files to manage sensitive information. Consider encrypting sensitive data stored in the database or using database encryption features where available.

Implement Content Security Policies (CSPs)

Content Security Policies help prevent various types of attacks, including Cross-Site Scripting (XSS) and code injection attacks. Implement a CSP that restricts the types of content that can be loaded on your application's pages. Configure CSP directives to allow only trusted sources for scripts, stylesheets, images, and other resources.

Protect Against Cross-Site Scripting (XSS)

Prevent Cross-Site Scripting attacks by properly escaping user-generated content when rendering it in your views. Use Laravel's '{{ }}' syntax or the '@{{ }}' Blade directive to automatically escape content to protect against XSS vulnerabilities. Avoid using '{!! !!}' or '@{!! !!}' to render unescaped content unless absolutely necessary.

Log and Monitor Security Events

Configure comprehensive logging to capture security-related events, errors, and unauthorized access attempts. Laravel provides a robust logging system that allows you to log security-related information, including failed login attempts, authorization failures, and suspicious activities. Regularly monitor your application's logs and set up alerts to detect potential security breaches.

Perform Security Audits and Penetration Testing

Conduct regular security audits and penetration testing to identify vulnerabilities in your application. Engage security professionals or use automated security scanning tools to assess your application's security posture. Address any vulnerabilities or weaknesses discovered during the audit or testing process.

Educate Developers and Users

Promote security awareness and provide training to developers and users on secure coding practices and potential security risks. Encourage developers to follow security best practices and provide guidelines for handling sensitive data. Educate users about common security threats, such as phishing attempts and password security, and encourage them to use strong and unique passwords.

Stay Updated with Security Practices

Stay informed about the latest security best practices, vulnerabilities, and attack techniques. Regularly review Laravel's security documentation, security blogs, and other reliable sources to stay up to date with emerging threats and security recommendations. Implement security practices that are specific to your application's requirements and the evolving security landscape.

By following these steps, you can proactively monitor and optimize the security of your Laravel application, reducing the risk of security breaches and protecting sensitive data. Remember that security is an ongoing effort, and staying vigilant and proactive is key to maintaining a secure application environment.

Summary

In this chapter, we covered performance monitoring and debugging strategies in the context of Laravel web development. We focused on how to optimize web application performance as well as how to recognize and resolve potential difficulties. Numerous tools and approaches for monitoring application performance were demonstrated, such as Laravel Telescope and third-party services such as New Relic. We also discussed code profiling, finding bottlenecks, and optimizing database queries. You learned about error logging and debugging methodologies to successfully troubleshoot and resolve application difficulties. Furthermore, the chapter delved into best practices for handling exceptions and recording problems.

The next chapter will focus on scaling Laravel applications.

CHAPTER 13

Scaling Laravel Applications

In the previous chapter, we delved into the essential aspects of performance monitoring and debugging in Laravel, ensuring the efficiency and reliability of our applications. As our exploration of Laravel's advanced features continues, we now shift our focus to a critical aspect of building high-performance applications—scaling.

Scaling Strategies and Considerations

In this section, we will gain insights into the importance of scaling applications to accommodate increasing demands and user traffic. We will explore various scaling strategies and considerations, understanding when and how to scale our applications effectively.

Load Balancing and Horizontal Scaling

Load balancing and horizontal scaling are essential techniques to distribute traffic evenly across multiple servers, ensuring optimal performance and resource utilization. We will learn how to implement load balancing and horizontal scaling to handle increased user requests and maintain application responsiveness.

Database Scaling Techniques

As user data and application usage grow, database scaling becomes a crucial consideration. In this section, we will explore various database scaling techniques, such as sharding, read replicas, and database partitioning, to handle large amounts of data and maintain database performance.

Caching and Content Delivery Networks (CDNs)

Caching and Content Delivery Networks (CDNs) play a significant role in scaling applications by reducing the load on servers and improving content delivery speed. We will discover how to implement caching mechanisms and leverage CDNs to optimize the performance and availability of our applications.

© Sivaraj Selvaraj 2024
S. Selvaraj, *Building Real-Time Marvels with Laravel*, https://doi.org/10.1007/978-1-4842-9789-6_13

Implementing Queue Workers for High Traffic

Queue workers are essential components of scaling applications to handle high-traffic scenarios. We will learn how to implement and configure queue workers to offload time-consuming tasks, ensuring seamless processing even during peak loads.

Throughout this chapter, we will immerse ourselves in the world of scaling Laravel applications, equipping ourselves with the knowledge and techniques to handle increased user traffic and maintain high performance. By adopting effective scaling strategies and optimizing our applications for growth, we can build robust and scalable solutions that cater to the needs of a growing user base. So let's embark on this journey of scaling Laravel applications to take our development expertise to new heights!

Scaling Strategies and Considerations

In the fast-paced world of software development, scalability is a critical factor that determines the success of an application. As user bases grow and workloads increase, applications must adapt and perform reliably to meet rising demands. Scaling strategies play a vital role in ensuring that applications can handle the increasing load without compromising performance.

This guide will explore various scaling strategies and considerations for designing and maintaining scalable applications. From horizontal and vertical scaling techniques to leveraging cloud computing platforms and optimizing code efficiency, we will delve into the essential aspects of building robust and scalable software solutions. Whether you are a developer planning for future growth or managing high-traffic applications, understanding scaling strategies is paramount in today's competitive digital landscape. Let's dive into the world of scaling and unlock the potential to create high-performance applications.

Caching

Caching is a crucial strategy for improving the performance of Laravel applications. By caching frequently accessed data, you can reduce the load on your servers and decrease response times. Laravel provides built-in support for popular caching systems like Redis and Memcached.

For Illustration, refer to the following snippet.

Let's say you have a Laravel application that fetches a list of blog posts from the database. Instead of querying the database every time a user requests a list of posts, you can cache the result for a specific duration. Here's an Illustration using Laravel's caching syntax:

```
use Illuminate\Support\Facades\Cache;
$posts = Cache::remember('posts', 60, function () {
    return DB::table('posts')->get();
});
```

In this Illustration, the 'remember' method tries to fetch the "posts" key from the cache. If it exists, it returns the cached value; otherwise, it executes the closure and stores the result in the cache for 60 seconds.

Database Optimization

Optimizing your database queries is essential for scaling Laravel applications. By utilizing proper indexes, avoiding N+1 query issues, and eager-loading relationships, you can improve the efficiency of your database operations.

The following is an illustration of this feature.

Suppose you have a Laravel application with a 'User' model that has a one-to-many relationship with a 'Post' model. Instead of fetching posts for each user individually (leading to an N+1 query problem), you can use eager loading to fetch all the posts for a set of users in a single query:

```
$users = User::with('posts')->get();
foreach ($users as $user) {
    foreach ($user->posts as $post) {
        // Access the posts
    }
}
```

In this Illustration, the 'with('posts')' method eagerly loads the posts relationship for all the users in a single query, significantly reducing the number of database queries executed.

Queue System

Implementing a queue system can offload time-consuming tasks to background workers, improving response times for user requests. Laravel provides a built-in queue system, and tools like RabbitMQ or Beanstalkd can also be integrated.

Let's see the following for illustration.

Suppose you have a Laravel application that sends email notifications. Instead of sending emails synchronously, you can push them to a queue and process them asynchronously. Here's an Illustration using Laravel's built-in queue:

```
use Illuminate\Support\Facades\Mail;
use App\Mail\NotificationEmail;
Mail::to($user->email)->queue(new NotificationEmail($user));
```

In this Illustration, the 'queue' method adds the email to the Laravel queue. You can then configure a worker to process the queued jobs.

Monitoring and Scaling Metrics

Implementing monitoring tools and gathering relevant metrics is essential for identifying bottlenecks and determining when to scale your infrastructure. Monitoring response times, CPU and memory usage, database queries per second, and error rates can provide valuable insights into your application's performance.

The following is an illustration of this feature.

Let's say you have a Laravel application deployed on a cloud platform like AWS. You can use AWS CloudWatch to monitor key metrics. For Illustration, you can set up alarms to trigger when CPU utilization exceeds a certain threshold, indicating the need for scaling. Here's an Illustration of monitoring CPU utilization with CloudWatch:

```
aws cloudwatch put-metric-alarm \
    --alarm-name "CPUUtilizationAlarm" \
    --metric-name "CPUUtilization" \
    --namespace "AWS/EC2" \
    --statistic "Average" \
    --period 300 \
    --threshold 80 \
    --comparison-operator "GreaterThanOrEqualToThreshold" \
    --evaluation-periods 2 \
    --alarm-description "Scale up if CPU utilization is above 80%" \
    --dimensions "Name=AutoScalingGroupName,Value=my-auto-scaling-group"
```

In this Illustration, the alarm triggers when the average CPU utilization of your auto-scaling group exceeds 80% for two consecutive evaluation periods.

Auto-scaling

Implementing auto-scaling mechanisms allows your infrastructure to dynamically add or remove servers based on predefined thresholds or metrics. Cloud providers like AWS, Google Cloud, or Azure offer auto-scaling features that can automatically adjust the number of instances based on your application's demand.

The following is an illustration of this feature.

Assume you have a Laravel application running on AWS Elastic Beanstalk. You can configure auto-scaling rules to scale the number of instances based on CPU utilization. Here's an Illustration of scaling based on CPU utilization with Elastic Beanstalk:

```
Resources:
  AWSEBAutoScalingGroup:
    Type: "AWS::AutoScaling::AutoScalingGroup"
    Properties:
      AutoScalingGroupName: {"Ref": "AWSEBAutoScalingGroupName"}
      MinSize: "2"
      MaxSize: "10"
```

```
MetricsCollection:
  - Granularity: "1Minute"
ScalingTrigger:
  UpperThreshold: "75"
  LowerThreshold: "25"
  MeasureName: "CPUUtilization"
  Namespace: "AWS/EC2"
ScalingAdjustment: "1"
Cooldown: "60"
```

In this Illustration, the auto-scaling group scales up or down based on CPU utilization thresholds. If the CPU utilization exceeds 75%, it scales up by one instance, and if it falls below 25%, it scales down by one instance.

Caching HTTP Responses

Implementing HTTP response caching can significantly improve the performance of static or relatively static content by caching the entire response of frequently accessed pages. This reduces the load on your application servers and improves response times for users.

The following is an illustration of this feature.

Let's say you have a Laravel application that serves static pages. By utilizing HTTP response caching, you can cache the entire response for a specific duration. Here's an Illustration using Laravel's caching syntax:

```
use Illuminate\Support\Facades\Cache;
use Illuminate\Support\Facades\Request;
use Illuminate\Support\Facades\Response;
Route::get('/home', function () {
    return Cache::remember(Request::fullUrl(), 3600, function () {
        // Generate the dynamic content
        return Response::view('home');
    });
});
```

In this Illustration, the 'remember' method caches the entire response of the '/home' route for one hour. Subsequent requests to the same URL within the caching duration will be served from the cache, reducing the load on your application servers.

Code Optimization

Regularly optimizing and profiling your code is crucial for identifying performance bottlenecks. Laravel provides built-in debugging tools, and additional profiling tools like Blackfire can help analyze your application's performance and optimize resource-intensive areas.

The following is an illustration of this feature.

Assume you have a Laravel application with a slow-running endpoint. You can use Laravel's built-in debugging tools, like the Telescope package, to identify performance issues. Here's an Illustration of using Telescope to profile an endpoint:

```
-----------------------------------------------------------------------
php artisan telescope:enable
Perform actions on your application that hit the slow endpoint
php artisan telescope:dump
-----------------------------------------------------------------------
```

In this Illustration, enabling Telescope allows you to monitor and record various performance metrics during the actions performed on your application. The 'dump' command generates a report that provides insights into the slow endpoint and helps identify areas that require optimization.

By implementing these strategies and considerations, you can effectively scale your Laravel application to handle increasing traffic and user demands while maintaining optimal performance. Remember to continually monitor and optimize your application as it grows to ensure smooth operation.

Load Balancing and Horizontal Scaling

Load balancing and horizontal scaling are two key strategies for scaling Laravel applications to handle increased traffic and user load. In this section, we will explore these strategies in more detail and provide illustrations of how to implement them effectively.

Load Balancing

Load balancing involves distributing incoming traffic across multiple servers to ensure efficient utilization of resources and prevent any single server from becoming overwhelmed. By evenly distributing the requests, load balancing helps improve application performance, scalability, and availability.

There are various load balancing techniques, and popular tools like Nginx and HAProxy can be used to implement them. These tools act as reverse proxies, receiving incoming requests and forwarding them to the appropriate backend servers based on predefined rules.

The following is an illustration of this feature.

Let's say you have a Laravel application running on multiple servers and want to implement load balancing using Nginx. Here's an Illustration of an Nginx configuration file:

```
http {
    upstream laravel {
        server app1.Illustration.com;
        server app2.Illustration.com;
        server app3.Illustration.com;
    }
    server {
        listen 80;
        server_name Illustration.com;
        location / {
            proxy_pass http://laravel;
            proxy_set_header Host $host;
            proxy_set_header X-Real-IP $remote_addr;
        }
    }
}
```

In this Illustration, the 'upstream' directive defines a group of backend servers hosting your Laravel application. The 'proxy_pass' directive forwards the incoming requests to the 'laravel' upstream group. Requests are evenly distributed among the servers, balancing the load across them.

Horizontal Scaling

Horizontal scaling involves adding more servers or instances to your infrastructure to handle increased workload and traffic. Instead of increasing the resources of a single server, you add more servers to distribute the load and improve overall performance and scalability.

Containerization and orchestration technologies like Docker and Kubernetes can simplify the process of managing multiple instances and scaling horizontally.

The following is an illustration of this feature.

Assume you have a Laravel application running in Docker containers. With Docker and Docker Compose, you can easily scale your application horizontally by adding more instances. Here's an Illustration of a 'docker-compose.yml' file:

```
version: '3'
services:
  app:
    build:
      context: .
      dockerfile: Dockerfile
    ports:
      - 80:80
    Other configurations...
  app2:
    build:
      context: .
      dockerfile: Dockerfile
    ports:
      - 81:80
    Other configurations...
```

```
app3:
  build:
    context: .
    dockerfile: Dockerfile
  ports:
    - 82:80
  Other configurations...
```

In this Illustration, you define multiple services ('app', 'app2', 'app3') representing different instances of your Laravel application. By running 'docker-compose up --scale app=3', you can start three instances of your application, each running on a separate port.

When combined with load balancing, horizontal scaling allows you to handle a higher volume of traffic by distributing it across multiple instances. As the demand increases, you can add more instances to the pool, ensuring optimal performance and availability.

It's important to note that load balancing and horizontal scaling often go hand in hand. Load balancing enables efficient distribution of traffic among multiple instances, while horizontal scaling provides the ability to add or remove instances dynamically based on the workload.

By implementing load balancing and horizontal scaling strategies, you can ensure your Laravel application can handle increased traffic, maintain high availability, and provide an optimal user experience.

Database Scaling Techniques

Scaling the database is a crucial aspect of scaling Laravel applications to ensure optimal performance, handle increased traffic, and maintain data integrity. In this section, we will explore various database scaling techniques that can be employed to achieve these goals.

Vertical Scaling

Vertical scaling involves increasing the resources of a single database server to handle increased workload. This can be done by upgrading the hardware components, such as CPU, memory, or storage, of the database server. Vertical scaling is relatively straightforward but has limits to how much it can scale before reaching the hardware's maximum capacity.

The following is an illustration of this feature.

If you have a Laravel application with a MySQL database running on a single server, you can vertically scale by upgrading the server's resources. For instance, you can increase the server's RAM or CPU cores or switch to faster storage devices like SSDs. These enhancements allow the database server to handle more concurrent connections and process queries faster.

Database Replication

Database replication involves creating multiple copies of the database to distribute the workload and improve read scalability. In a replication setup, there is a master database that handles write operations, and one or more replica databases handle read operations. Replication ensures data consistency across all replicas by synchronizing changes from the master to the replicas.

The following is an illustration of this feature.

Let's say you have a Laravel application with a PostgreSQL database. To implement database replication, you can set up a master-slave replication configuration. The master database handles write operations, while the slave database(s) handle(s) read operations. Here's an Illustration using PostgreSQL's streaming replication:

```
-----------------------------------------------------------------------
On the master database server
wal_level = replica
max_wal_senders = 10
wal_keep_segments = 32
On the slave database server(s)
hot_standby = on
-----------------------------------------------------------------------
```

In this Illustration, the master database is configured to stream the write-ahead logs (WAL) to the slave databases, enabling them to stay up to date with the changes happening on the master. The slave databases can handle read operations, offloading the read workload from the master.

Database Sharding

Database sharding involves horizontally partitioning data across multiple database servers or shards. Each shard contains a subset of the data based on a specific rule, such as hashing, range-based partitioning, or consistent hashing. Sharding allows the database to distribute the workload across multiple servers, improving both read and write scalability.

The following is an illustration of this feature.

Suppose you have a Laravel application with a MySQL database, and you decide to shard the data based on a consistent hashing algorithm. You can use a sharding library or framework like Laravel Shard to handle the sharding logic. Here's an Illustration of configuring Laravel Shard for sharding:

```
'mysql' => [
    'driver' => 'mysql',
    'shard' => [
        'type' => 'consistent',
        'size' => 4,
    ],
    'shards' => [
        'shard1' => [
            'host' => 'shard1.Illustration.com',
            'database' => 'shard1',
            // Other configurations...
        ],
        'shard2' => [
            'host' => 'shard2.Illustration.com',
            'database' => 'shard2',
            // Other configurations...
        ],
```

```
    // Add more shards...
    ],
],
```

In this Illustration, the 'shard' configuration specifies that the sharding strategy is based on consistent hashing, and there are four shards ('shard1', 'shard2', etc.). Laravel Shard handles routing queries to the appropriate shard based on the configured rules, distributing the workload across the shards.

Database Partitioning

Database partitioning involves dividing a large table into smaller, more manageable partitions based on specific criteria such as a range of values, a list of values, or a hash value. Each partition is stored separately and can be managed and accessed independently, leading to improved query performance and easier data maintenance.

The following is an illustration of this feature.

Suppose you have a Laravel application with a large table that stores user data, and you decide to partition the table based on a range of values, such as date ranges. Here's an Illustration of creating a partitioned table in MySQL:

```
CREATE TABLE users (
    id INT NOT NULL AUTO_INCREMENT,
    name VARCHAR(100) NOT NULL,
    created_at DATE NOT NULL,
    PRIMARY KEY (id, created_at)
)
PARTITION BY RANGE (YEAR(created_at)) (
    PARTITION p0 VALUES LESS THAN (2022),
    PARTITION p1 VALUES LESS THAN (2023),
    PARTITION p2 VALUES LESS THAN (2024),
    PARTITION p3 VALUES LESS THAN MAXVALUE
);
```

In this Illustration, the 'users' table is partitioned based on the 'created_at' column, with each partition representing a range of years. This allows for efficient pruning of partitions during query execution, reducing the amount of data that needs to be scanned.

Database Caching

Database caching involves caching frequently accessed data or query results to reduce the load on the database server and improve response times. By caching data in memory using tools like Redis or Memcached, subsequent requests can be served directly from the cache, eliminating the need to query the database.

The following is an illustration of this feature.

In a Laravel application, you can use the built-in caching mechanisms to cache query results. Here's an Illustration of caching a database query using Laravel's caching syntax:

```
use Illuminate\Support\Facades\Cache;
$users = Cache::remember('users', 3600, function () {
    return DB::table('users')->get();
});
```

In this Illustration, the 'remember' method caches the result of the 'users' query for one hour. Subsequent requests within the caching duration will be served directly from the cache, reducing the load on the database server.

Implementing one or a combination of these database scaling techniques can significantly improve the scalability and performance of your Laravel application. The choice of technique depends on factors such as the application's specific requirements, anticipated growth, and the database system being used. It's essential to carefully analyze your application's needs and consider the trade-offs of each technique before implementing a scaling solution.

Caching and Content Delivery Networks (CDNs)

Caching and Content Delivery Networks (CDNs) are essential components in scaling Laravel applications. They help improve performance, reduce server load, and enhance the user experience by delivering content quickly and efficiently. In this section, we will explore caching strategies and the use of CDNs in Laravel applications.

Caching

Caching involves storing frequently accessed data in memory or a fast storage system to avoid repetitive processing and reduce the load on the server. Laravel provides powerful caching mechanisms that can be used to cache various types of data, such as database query results, rendered views, or API responses.

Database Query Caching

Caching database query results can significantly improve the performance of Laravel applications. Instead of executing the same query multiple times, you can cache the result and serve it directly from the cache.

The following is an illustration of this feature.

In Laravel, you can use the 'cache()' helper function to cache query results. Here's an Illustration of caching a database query result for five minutes:

```
$users = cache()->remember('users', 300, function () {
    return DB::table('users')->get();
});
```

In this Illustration, the 'remember()' method caches the result of the database query for five minutes. Subsequent requests within the caching duration will be served directly from the cache, reducing the load on the database server.

View Caching

Caching rendered views can improve the response time of pages that don't frequently change. By caching the HTML output of a view, you can avoid rendering the view on each request, resulting in faster response times.

The following is an illustration of this feature.

To cache a view in Laravel, you can use the '@cache' directive in your Blade templates. Here's an Illustration:

```
@cache('homepage', 1440) // Cache for 24 hours
    <!-- Your view content here -->
@endcache
```

In this Illustration, the content within the '@cache' directive will be cached for 24 hours. Subsequent requests for the same view will be served from the cache, eliminating the need to re-render the view.

Content Delivery Networks (CDNs)

CDNs are geographically distributed networks of servers that cache and deliver static content, such as images, CSS files, and JavaScript files, closer to the end users. By serving content from servers located closer to the users, CDNs help reduce latency, improve page load times, and reduce the load on the origin server.

Laravel integrates seamlessly with CDNs, allowing you to leverage their caching and content delivery capabilities.

The following is an illustration of this feature.

Cloudflare CDN Integration with Laravel

Sign up for a Cloudflare account.

Visit the Cloudflare website (www.cloudflare.com/) and sign up for a free or paid account.

Configure your domain.

Once you have signed up, add your domain to Cloudflare and update your domain's DNS settings to point to Cloudflare's nameservers.

Install the Cloudflare package for Laravel.

Install the 'cloudflare' package for Laravel using Composer:

```
composer require spatie/laravel-cloudflare
```

Configure Cloudflare settings.

In your Laravel configuration file ('config/cloudflare.php'), add your Cloudflare API key and email:

```
return [
    'api_key' => env('CLOUDFLARE_API_KEY'),
    'email' => env('CLOUDFLARE_EMAIL'),
];
```

Cache assets using Cloudflare CDN.

In your views or Blade templates, use the 'asset()' helper function to generate URLs for your static assets:

```
<link rel="stylesheet" href="{{ asset('css/style.css') }}">
<script src="{{ asset('js/app.js') }}"></script>
```

When your application is deployed, Cloudflare will cache these assets and serve them from their global edge locations, reducing the load on your server and improving page load times for users.

Amazon CloudFront CDN Integration with Laravel

Set up Amazon CloudFront distribution.

Sign into your AWS account and create a new CloudFront distribution. Configure the origin settings to point to your Laravel application's origin server (e.g., your application's load balancer or server IP address).

Create a CloudFront key pair (optional).

If you want to use private content with CloudFront, you can create a CloudFront key pair in the AWS Management Console. This step is optional for public content.

Install the AWS SDK for Laravel.

Install the AWS SDK for Laravel using Composer:

```
composer require aws/aws-sdk-php-laravel
```

Configure CloudFront CDN in Laravel.

In your Laravel configuration file ('config/filesystems.php'), add the CloudFront CDN configuration to the 'cloud' disk:

```
'cloudfront' => [
    'driver' => 'cloudfront',
    'key' => env('AWS_CLOUDFRONT_KEY'),
    'secret' => env('AWS_CLOUDFRONT_SECRET'),
    'distribution' => env('AWS_CLOUDFRONT_DISTRIBUTION'),
],
```

Use CloudFront URLs for assets.

In your views or Blade templates, use the 'cloudfront()' helper function to generate URLs for your static assets:

```
<link rel="stylesheet" href="{{ cloudfront('css/style.css') }}">
<script src="{{ cloudfront('js/app.js') }}"></script>
```

When your application is deployed, Laravel will generate CloudFront URLs for your assets, and Amazon CloudFront will serve them from its edge locations, reducing latency and improving performance.

Note   In both examples, the CDN configuration should be set up according to your specific CDN provider's settings. Also, make sure to handle caching and cache invalidation appropriately based on your application's requirements.

By integrating CDNs like Cloudflare or Amazon CloudFront with Laravel, you can effectively optimize the delivery of static assets, improve performance, and provide a better experience for users accessing your web application from around the world.

Caching and CDNs play a vital role in scaling Laravel applications. By effectively utilizing caching mechanisms and leveraging the distribution capabilities of CDNs, you can significantly enhance the performance and scalability of your application while improving the user experience.

Implementing Queue Workers for High Traffic

As traffic increases in a Laravel application, handling time-consuming tasks synchronously can impact response times and the user experience. Implementing queue workers allows you to offload these tasks to background processes, improving performance and scalability. In this section, we will explore how to implement queue workers in Laravel for handling high-traffic scenarios.

Laravel provides a robust queue system that supports various queue drivers like Redis, Beanstalkd, and Amazon SQS. The queue system allows you to define jobs and dispatch them to be processed asynchronously by workers. Here's how you can implement queue workers in Laravel.

Set Up the Queue Connection

First, configure the queue connection in your Laravel application's '.env' file. You can choose from various queue drivers based on your requirements and infrastructure setup.

Here's an Illustration using the Redis queue driver:

```
QUEUE_CONNECTION=redis
```

Create a job.

Next, create a job class that represents the task you want to process asynchronously. Jobs can be generated using Laravel's Artisan command:

```
php artisan make:job ProcessData
```

This command will create a 'ProcessData' job class under the 'app/Jobs' directory. Implement the 'handle' method within the job class to define the logic of the task to be performed asynchronously:

```
<?php
namespace App\Jobs;
class ProcessData
```

```
{
    public function handle()
    {
        // Logic to process the task
    }
}
```

You can also pass data to the job's constructor to provide context for the task being performed.

Dispatch jobs.

To dispatch jobs for asynchronous processing, you can use Laravel's 'dispatch' helper function. It allows you to enqueue a job onto the specified queue:

```
use App\Jobs\ProcessData;
dispatch(new ProcessData());
```

In this Illustration, the 'ProcessData' job is dispatched to the default queue for asynchronous processing.

Start queue workers.

To process the queued jobs, you need to start the queue workers. Laravel provides an Artisan command for this purpose:

```
php artisan queue:work
```

This command starts the worker process that continuously listens to the queue and processes jobs as they arrive. By default, the worker runs in the foreground, but you can use options like '--daemon' or '--queue' to customize the worker's behavior:

```
php artisan queue:work --queue=high_priority_queue --tries=3
```

In this Illustration, the worker listens to the 'high_priority_queue' and attempts each job up to three times before marking it as failed.

Scale queue workers.

As traffic increases, you may need to scale the number of queue workers to handle the workload efficiently. You can start multiple worker processes simultaneously to process jobs in parallel. Containerization and orchestration tools like Docker and Kubernetes can help manage the scaling of queue workers.

Using Docker Compose

Docker Compose is a tool that allows you to define and manage multi-container Docker applications. It provides a way to specify the services, networks, and volumes required for your application in a simple YAML file, making it easier to set up and deploy complex applications with multiple interconnected containers.

With Docker Compose, you can define all the services your application needs, their configurations, and how they should interact with each other. This is particularly useful when your application relies on multiple services like web servers, databases, cache systems, message queues, and more.

Key Features and Benefits of Docker Compose

Simplified container orchestration: Docker Compose abstracts away the complexity of managing individual containers and their configurations. It allows you to define your entire application stack in a single file, making it easier to set up and maintain your development and production environments.

Reproducible environments: With Docker Compose, you can create consistent and reproducible environments for your application, ensuring that the development, testing, and production environments are identical.

Scalability and flexibility: Docker Compose supports scaling services, enabling you to replicate containers to handle increased traffic or demand. This makes it easy to scale your application horizontally when required.

Environment variables and secrets: Docker Compose allows you to manage environment variables and secrets securely. You can store sensitive information, such as database passwords or API keys, in environment files or in external secret management systems.

Easy networking: Docker Compose automatically creates and manages networks for your application, enabling seamless communication between services without the need to expose unnecessary ports to the outside world.

Volume management: Docker Compose simplifies the management of data volumes, ensuring that data persists across container restarts or when containers are recreated.

Portability: Since Docker Compose uses a declarative YAML file, it is highly portable across different environments and platforms. You can easily share the same Docker Compose configuration between team members or deploy it to various cloud providers.

Example Docker Compose File

The following is an example of a simple Docker Compose configuration for a web application that requires a web server (nginx) and a PHP application server (php-fpm) using the official nginx and php-fpm Docker images:

```
version: '3'
services:
  web:
    image: nginx:latest
    ports:
      - "80:80"
    volumes:
      - ./app:/var/www/html
  app:
    image: php:latest
    volumes:
      - ./app:/var/www/html
```

In this example, the 'web' service uses the official nginx image and exposes port 80 for web traffic. It also mounts the './app' directory on the host machine into the '/var/www/html' directory inside the container. Similarly, the 'app' service uses the official PHP image and mounts the same './app' directory.

To start the application using Docker Compose, save the preceding configuration in a file named 'docker-compose.yml', navigate to the directory containing the file, and run

```
docker-compose up -d
```

This command will create and start the containers defined in the Docker Compose file in detached mode (in the background).

Docker Compose is a powerful tool for simplifying the management and deployment of complex multi-container applications. It is widely used in modern development workflows to ensure consistency and efficiency across different environments.

By scaling the number of queue workers, you can distribute the processing load and handle high-traffic scenarios effectively.

Implementing queue workers in Laravel allows you to handle time-consuming tasks asynchronously, improving the responsiveness and scalability of your application. By offloading these tasks to background workers, you can maintain optimal performance even under high-traffic conditions.

Summary

In this chapter, we explored ideas and tactics for scaling Laravel apps to manage rising traffic and expanding user demands. The chapter underlined the significance of building applications from the start with scalability in mind. You learned about horizontal and vertical scaling methodologies, as well as when to use each strategy based on the needs of your application. We also discussed load balancing, caching, and database scalability in order to properly allocate resources and improve application performance. We also delved into microservices and how to use them to develop scalable and maintainable systems and addressed cloud-based options for auto-scaling and resource management, such as AWS and Azure.

In the next chapter, we will cover advanced error handling and exception management.

CHAPTER 14

Advanced Error Handling and Exception Management

In the previous chapter, we explored the critical aspect of scaling Laravel applications, ensuring that our software can handle increased demands and traffic effectively. As our journey through Laravel's advanced features continues, we now shift our focus to advanced error handling and exception management—essential components of building robust and resilient applications.

Customizing Error Pages and Handling Exceptions

In this section, we will delve into customizing error pages and handling exceptions in Laravel. We will learn how to create personalized error pages that provide meaningful feedback to users when errors occur. Additionally, we will explore how to gracefully handle exceptions, prevent unexpected crashes, and maintain a positive user experience.

Logging and Monitoring Application Errors

Effective error management involves proper logging and monitoring of application errors. We will explore how to set up error logging to capture valuable information about errors, exceptions, and application behavior for debugging and analysis.

Implementing Error Reporting and Alerting Systems

Timely error reporting is crucial for addressing issues promptly and ensuring application stability. Here, we will learn how to implement error reporting and alerting systems, enabling us to receive real-time notifications when critical errors occur.

© Sivaraj Selvaraj 2024
S. Selvaraj, *Building Real-Time Marvels with Laravel*, https://doi.org/10.1007/978-1-4842-9789-6_14

Debugging Production Errors with Remote Logging and Tracing

Debugging errors in production environments can be challenging. We will discover how to use remote logging and tracing tools to investigate and resolve production errors efficiently, ensuring seamless operations of our applications.

Error Recovery and Graceful Degradation Strategies

In this final section, we will explore error recovery and graceful degradation strategies. We will learn how to build fallback mechanisms and alternative routes to ensure that our applications continue to function even in the presence of errors or service interruptions.

Throughout this chapter, we will immerse ourselves in the world of advanced error handling and exception management in Laravel. By mastering the art of custom error handling, effective logging, and timely reporting, we can build applications that are resilient, stable, and user-friendly. So let's embark on this journey of advanced error handling and exception management to elevate the reliability and robustness of our Laravel applications!

Customizing Error Pages and Handling Exceptions
Error Handling and Exception Management

Error handling and exception management are critical aspects of web application development that play a crucial role in enhancing the user experience and ensuring application stability. Let's delve deeper into the significance of robust error handling in web applications.

Importance of Robust Error Handling

Better user experience: Error handling directly impacts the user experience. When users encounter errors, such as a broken page or unexpected behavior, it can be frustrating and may lead to them abandoning the application. A well-implemented error handling system provides user-friendly error messages, clear instructions, and graceful fallbacks, helping users understand and resolve the issue quickly.

Application stability: Robust error handling ensures that the application remains stable even in the face of unexpected issues or exceptional situations. By handling errors gracefully, developers can prevent application crashes and mitigate the risk of data loss or corruption.

Bug identification and debugging: Effective error handling helps developers identify and diagnose bugs and issues in the application. Error logs with detailed information about the error, including stack traces and context data, are invaluable for understanding the root cause of problems and speeding up the debugging process.

Security considerations: Proper error handling is crucial for maintaining application security. Displaying detailed error messages to end users could potentially expose sensitive information or provide attackers with valuable insights into the application's architecture. By handling errors carefully, developers can minimize security risks.

Business reputation: A reliable and well-handled application instills confidence in users and builds a positive reputation for the business or organization. Users are more likely to trust and continue using an application that rarely encounters errors and provides a seamless experience.

Monitoring and performance insights: Implementing error tracking and monitoring mechanisms allows developers to proactively identify patterns of errors, measure application performance, and prioritize improvements or bug fixes based on their impact.

In summary, robust error handling and exception management are essential for maintaining application stability, improving the user experience, and ensuring the security and reliability of web applications. By investing in error handling practices, developers can build more resilient and user-friendly applications, leading to increased user satisfaction and business success.

Overview of PHP Exceptions and Laravel's Exception Handling Mechanism Using Try-Catch Blocks

Overview of PHP Exceptions

In PHP, exceptions are a powerful mechanism for handling errors and exceptional situations in code. An exception represents an abnormal condition that disrupts the normal flow of code execution. When an exceptional situation occurs, PHP throws an exception object, which contains information about the error, such as the type of exception and a descriptive message.

Exceptions are a part of object-oriented programming and follow a hierarchy of exception classes. The base exception class is 'Exception', and there are several built-in child classes that represent specific types of exceptions, such as 'InvalidArgumentException', 'RuntimeException', and 'PDOException'.

311

To handle exceptions in PHP, developers use try-catch blocks. The 'try' block encloses the code that may throw an exception, while the 'catch' block contains the code to handle the exception if it occurs. If an exception is thrown within the try block, PHP looks for an appropriate catch block to handle the exception based on the exception type.

Overview of Laravel's Exception Handling Mechanism

Laravel, being a PHP web application framework, leverages PHP's exception handling capabilities to provide a robust and structured way to handle errors. Laravel's exception handling mechanism builds on top of PHP's native exceptions and adds additional features to streamline error handling.

When an exception occurs in a Laravel application, it is automatically converted into an HTTP response with an appropriate status code, allowing for easy customization of error pages. Laravel provides a user-friendly and consistent way to present error information to users, making the application more approachable.

Key features of Laravel's exception handling mechanism include

Exception handling middleware: Laravel includes middleware that automatically catches exceptions and converts them into proper HTTP responses. The middleware ensures that all exceptions are appropriately handled before they reach the end user, preventing unintended error messages from being displayed.

Custom exception classes: Laravel encourages the use of custom exception classes. By extending Laravel's base 'Exception' class or its child classes, developers can create specific exception types for different error scenarios, making code more organized and readable.

Exception reporting: Laravel comes with built-in error reporting mechanisms that allow developers to log and monitor exceptions. Exception details are recorded in log files, making it easier to track errors and perform debugging.

Custom error pages: Laravel allows developers to customize error pages easily. By creating Blade templates for specific HTTP error codes, developers can tailor the appearance of error pages to match the application's design and provide helpful information to users.

Error rendering: Laravel provides a dedicated error rendering system, which allows developers to customize the error response format. This feature is especially useful when building APIs, as developers can define how errors are presented in JSON or other formats.

By leveraging PHP exceptions and enhancing them with Laravel's additional features, developers can implement robust error handling in their Laravel applications. This helps ensure a seamless user experience and better application stability by gracefully handling errors and exceptional situations.

Handling Exceptions in Laravel

Catching and Handling Exceptions in Laravel Controllers and Routes with Try-Catch Blocks

In Laravel, catching and handling exceptions in controllers and routes involves using try-catch blocks to encapsulate the code that may throw exceptions. By doing so, developers can gracefully handle exceptions, customize error responses, and prevent the application from crashing when unexpected errors occur. Let's explore how to do this step-by-step.

Catch exceptions in controllers.

In Laravel controllers, you can use try-catch blocks to catch and handle exceptions that may occur during the execution of controller methods. Here's a basic example:

```
-----------------------------------------------------------------
use App\Http\Controllers\Controller;
use Illuminate\Http\Request;
class MyController extends Controller
{
    public function myMethod(Request $request)
    {
        try {
            // Code that may throw an exception, e.g., accessing a non-
                existent property.
            $data = $request->nonExistentProperty;
        } catch (\Exception $e) {
            // Exception handling logic.
            // For example, you can log the exception, customize the error
                response, or redirect the user to an error page.
            return response()->json(['error' => 'Something went
            wrong.'], 500);
        }
```

313

```
        // Continue with the normal flow of the method if no
            exception occurs.
        return response()->json(['data' => $data]);
    }
}
```

In the preceding example, we use a try-catch block to wrap the code that may throw an exception, that is, accessing the '$request->nonExistentProperty'. If an exception occurs, it will be caught in the catch block, and we can then decide how to handle the exception. In this case, we return a JSON response with an error message and a 500 status code.

Catch exceptions in routes.

In Laravel routes, you can use the 'try' method to catch and handle exceptions that might occur while executing the route's callback. Here's how you can do it:

```
use Illuminate\Support\Facades\Route;
Route::get('/my-route', function () {
    try {
        // Code that may throw an exception.
        $data = SomeModel::findOrFail(123); // Assume the model with ID 123
        does not exist.
    } catch (\Exception $e) {
        // Exception handling logic.
        // For example, you can log the exception, customize the error
        response, or redirect the user to an error page.
        return response()->json(['error' => 'Resource not found.'], 404);
    }
    // Continue with the normal flow of the route if no exception occurs.
    return response()->json(['data' => $data]);
});
```

In this route example, we use the 'try' method to wrap the code that may throw an exception, that is, calling 'SomeModel::findOrFail(123)' to find a model with a non-existent ID. If an exception occurs, it will be caught in the catch block, and we can handle it by returning a JSON response with an error message and a 404 status code.

By catching and handling exceptions in controllers and routes with try-catch blocks, you can effectively manage errors and ensure a smoother user experience. Additionally, you have the flexibility to customize error responses, log exceptions for debugging, or take appropriate actions based on the specific error scenario.

Creating Custom Exception Classes and Throwing Exceptions to Manage Specific Error Scenarios Effectively

Creating custom exception classes in Laravel allows you to define specific exception types to manage different error scenarios effectively. By throwing custom exceptions, you can distinguish between various types of errors and handle them uniquely in your application. Here's how you can create custom exception classes and throw exceptions in Laravel.

Create a custom exception class.

To create a custom exception class, you need to extend Laravel's base 'Exception' class or one of its child classes. It's a good practice to define your custom exception classes in the 'app/Exceptions' directory. For example, let's create a custom exception for a resource not found error:

```
// app/Exceptions/ResourceNotFoundException.php
namespace App\Exceptions;
use Exception;
class ResourceNotFoundException extends Exception
{
    // Optionally, you can define custom properties or methods specific to
    this exception.
}
```

Throw custom exceptions.

In your application's code, you can throw the custom exception whenever a specific error scenario occurs. For example, if you want to throw the 'ResourceNotFoundException' when a record is not found in the database, you can do it like this:

```
use App\Models\User;
use App\Exceptions\ResourceNotFoundException;
public function getUserById($id)
{
    $user = User::find($id);
    if (!$user) {
        throw new ResourceNotFoundException("User with ID $id not found.");
    }
    return $user;
}
```

In the preceding example, we use the 'ResourceNotFoundException' custom exception to handle the scenario when a user with a specific ID is not found in the database. When the condition inside the if statement is met (i.e., '$user' is null), we throw the custom exception with a descriptive message.

Catch custom exceptions.

To catch and handle the custom exceptions, you can use try-catch blocks as shown in the previous examples. When an exception is thrown, PHP will look for the appropriate catch block based on the type of the thrown exception. In this case, since we have thrown a 'ResourceNotFoundException', we can catch it specifically and handle it accordingly:

```
try {
    $user = $this->getUserById(123);
} catch (ResourceNotFoundException $e) {
    // Exception handling logic for ResourceNotFoundException.
    // For example, return a custom error response or redirect to an
    error page.
    return response()->json(['error' => $e->getMessage()], 404);
}
```

By creating custom exception classes and throwing exceptions for specific error scenarios, you can effectively manage different types of errors in your Laravel application. This helps keep your code organized, improve error handling, and provide more informative error messages to users and developers. Custom exceptions also make it easier to understand and debug exceptional situations in your application.

Customizing Error Pages

Designing and Creating Custom Error Pages for Different HTTP Status Codes (e.g., 404, 500) Using Laravel's Blade Templates

Designing and creating custom error pages for different HTTP status codes (e.g., 404, 500) using Laravel's Blade templates is a straightforward process. Laravel allows you to customize error views for specific HTTP status codes, providing a more user-friendly and branded experience when users encounter errors. Here's how you can do it.

Create custom error views.

In the 'resources/views/errors' directory, create Blade templates for each error status code you want to customize. The filenames should match the HTTP status code followed by '.blade.php'. For example, to create a custom view for the 404 error, create a file named '404.blade.php':

```
// resources/views/errors/404.blade.php
@extends('layouts.app') // Assuming you have a base layout for your
application.
@section('content')
    <div class="error-page">
        <h1>404 Not Found</h1>
        <p>Sorry, the page you are looking for does not exist.</p>
    </div>
@endsection
```

You can repeat the preceding process to create custom views for other HTTP status codes, such as '500.blade.php', '403.blade.php', etc.

Customize the 'Exception' handler.

To tell Laravel to use your custom error views for specific HTTP status codes, you need to modify the 'render' method in the 'app/Exceptions/Handler.php' file. Open the file and add logic to check for specific HTTP status codes and return the corresponding custom views:

```php
// app/Exceptions/Handler.php
use Symfony\Component\HttpKernel\Exception\HttpException;
use Illuminate\Foundation\Exceptions\Handler as ExceptionHandler;
class Handler extends ExceptionHandler
{
    // Other code in the class...
    public function render($request, Throwable $exception)
    {
        if ($this->isHttpException($exception)) {
            $statusCode = $exception->getStatusCode();
            if (view()->exists("errors.$statusCode")) {
                return response()->view("errors.$statusCode", [],
                    $statusCode);
            }
        }
        return parent::render($request, $exception);
    }
}
```

In the preceding code, we check if the '$exception' is an instance of 'HttpException', which represents HTTP status code–related exceptions. If it is, we extract the status code using '$exception->getStatusCode()'. Then, we check if a custom view exists for that status code using 'view()->exists("errors.$statusCode")'. If it does, we return the custom view with the appropriate HTTP status code using 'response()->view("errors.$statusCode", [], $statusCode)'. If no custom view is found, Laravel will render its default error view.

Test the custom error pages.

Once you've created the custom error views and modified the 'Handler.php' file, you can test the custom error pages by triggering the corresponding HTTP status codes in your routes or controllers, for example:

```
use Illuminate\Support\Facades\Route;
Route::get('/test-404', function () {
    abort(404); // This will trigger the 404 error.
});
Route::get('/test-500', function () {
    // Custom logic that results in a server error.
    throw new Exception('Something went wrong.');
});
```

When you access '/test-404' and '/test-500' routes, you should see your custom error pages for the 404 and 500 status codes, respectively.

With these steps, you can design and create custom error pages for different HTTP status codes in your Laravel application using Blade templates. This allows you to provide a more personalized and branded error experience for your users and make your application more user-friendly.

Demonstrating User-Friendly Error Pages with Relevant Information and Helpful Instructions

To demonstrate user-friendly error pages with relevant information and helpful instructions in Laravel, we'll update the custom error views created earlier. These error pages will not only provide a clear indication of the encountered error but also offer guidance to the users on how to proceed. Let's continue from the previous example and improve the custom error pages.

Update custom error views.

Assuming we have already created the custom error views for 404 and 500 errors, let's improve them to display more relevant information and helpful instructions:

```
// resources/views/errors/404.blade.php
@extends('layouts.app')
@section('content')
    <div class="error-page">
        <h1>404 Not Found</h1>
        <p>Sorry, the page you are looking for does not exist.</p>
        <a href="{{ url('/') }}">Go back to the home page</a>
    </div>
@endsection
```

```
// resources/views/errors/500.blade.php
@extends('layouts.app')
@section('content')
    <div class="error-page">
        <h1>500 Internal Server Error</h1>
        <p>Oops! Something went wrong on our end. We are already working on
fixing it.</p>
        <p>Please try again later.</p>
        <a href="{{ url('/') }}">Go back to the home page</a>
    </div>
@endsection
```

In the updated error views, we added a brief error message along with a link to the home page, providing users with a way to navigate back to the main content of the application.

Customize the 'Exception' handler.

Ensure that the 'Handler.php' file in the 'app/Exceptions' directory is updated as shown earlier. It will automatically use the custom error views we just updated.

Test the user-friendly error pages.

You can test the user-friendly error pages by triggering the respective HTTP status codes using the defined routes or methods:

```
use Illuminate\Support\Facades\Route;
Route::get('/test-404', function () {
    abort(404); // This will trigger the 404 error.
});
Route::get('/test-500', function () {
    // Custom logic that results in a server error.
    throw new Exception('Something went wrong.');
});
```

When accessing '/test-404' and '/test-500' routes, you should now see the improved user-friendly error pages with relevant information and helpful instructions. For the 404 error, it displays a message indicating the page doesn't exist and provides a link to return to the home page. For the 500 error, it acknowledges the issue and assures the user that it's being worked on, recommending them to try again later.

By providing user-friendly error pages with relevant information and helpful instructions, you create a positive user experience even in the event of errors. This reduces user frustration, increases user trust in your application, and improves overall satisfaction with your web application.

Exception Logging and Reporting

Configuring Laravel's Logging Mechanism to Record Exceptions in Various Channels (e.g., File, Database, Syslog) for Effective Error Tracking

In Laravel, you can configure the logging mechanism to record exceptions in various channels, such as files, databases, or syslog. This allows you to effectively track errors and exceptions that occur in your application, making it easier to diagnose issues and improve application stability. Here's how you can configure Laravel's logging system to record exceptions in different channels.

Configure logging channels.

In Laravel, logging channels are defined in the 'config/logging.php' configuration file. Open the file and add or modify the channels to include the desired log drivers and configurations. For example, to enable logging to both the 'daily' file channel and the 'database' channel, you can set up the configuration like this:

```php
// config/logging.php
return [
    'default' => env('LOG_CHANNEL', 'stack'),
    'channels' => [
        'stack' => [
            'driver' => 'stack',
            'channels' => ['daily', 'database'],
        ],
        'daily' => [
            'driver' => 'daily',
            'path' => storage_path('logs/laravel.log'),
            'level' => 'debug',
            'days' => 14,
        ],
        'database' => [
            'driver' => 'database',
            'table' => 'logs', // Set the table name where logs will be
            stored in the database.
            'connection' => env('DB_CONNECTION', 'mysql'), // The database
            connection to use.
            'queue' => true, // Optionally, log the entries to the queue
            for better performance.
            'tap' => [App\Logging\LogDatabaseProcessor::class], // Optional:
            You can use a custom log processor for database logging.
        ],
        // Other channels...
    ],
    // Other logging configurations...
];
```

Create the database log table (if not already created).

If you are using the 'database' channel for logging exceptions, you need to create the database table to store the log entries. You can do this by running the following Artisan command:

```
php artisan migrate
```

This command will create the default 'logs' table specified in the 'database' channel configuration.

Log exceptions.

With the channels configured, Laravel will automatically log exceptions to the defined channels. To log an exception manually, you can use Laravel's built-in 'Log' façade, for example:

```
use Illuminate\Support\Facades\Log;
try {
    // Code that may throw an exception.
    // ...
} catch (\Exception $e) {
    // Log the exception using the 'error' method of the Log facade.
    Log::error('An exception occurred: ' . $e->getMessage(), ['exception'
    => $e]);
}
```

In the preceding code, we catch the exception and use the 'Log::error()' method to log the exception message and additional context data (the '$e' object) to the configured channels.

View logs.

You can view the logs in the respective channels, depending on the configuration, for example:

Daily file logs: Logs are stored in the 'storage/logs/laravel.log' file.

Database logs: Logs are stored in the 'logs' table in the database.

With this configuration, your Laravel application will effectively track and log exceptions in the specified channels, helping you monitor and troubleshoot errors in the application easily. Logging exceptions is an essential practice for maintaining a stable and reliable web application.

Best Practices for Logging Exceptions with Context-Specific Information and Timestamps

Logging exceptions with context-specific information and timestamps is essential for effective debugging and monitoring of your application. Properly formatted log entries help you understand the context in which an exception occurred and when it happened, enabling you to diagnose issues more efficiently. Here are some best practices for logging exceptions in Laravel:

Include context-specific information.

Log relevant information along with the exception, such as the user's ID, the route or URL being accessed, the request parameters, and any other data that may be helpful for understanding the cause of the exception.

Use Laravel's logging context to add this additional data to the log entry. The context allows you to include an array of extra data that will be appended to the log entry.

Log the exception stack trace.

The stack trace provides valuable information about the sequence of method calls leading to the exception. It can help pinpoint the exact location and sequence of events that triggered the error.

Laravel's logging system automatically includes the stack trace when logging exceptions, so you don't need to add it separately.

Use appropriate log levels.

Use the appropriate log level for exceptions. Generally, exceptions are logged at the "error" level, as they represent critical issues in the application.

For less critical information or debugging messages, use lower log levels like "info" or "debug."

Include timestamps.

Log entries should include timestamps to record when the exception occurred. Timestamps are crucial for tracking the sequence of events and identifying patterns in error occurrences.

Utilize Monolog processors.

Laravel uses the Monolog library for logging. Monolog provides processors that allow you to add context data automatically to all log entries.

Implement custom Monolog processors to add common context data, such as the current user's information, the request URL, or the server environment, to every log entry.

Centralize logs for monitoring.

Consider centralizing logs in a dedicated log management system (e.g., ELK stack, Loggly, Papertrail) for easier monitoring and analysis. Centralized logging enables you to search, filter, and analyze logs from multiple servers and applications in one place.

Implement log rotation.

Implement log rotation to prevent log files from becoming too large. Laravel's default log channel, 'daily', rotates logs daily, but you can customize this behavior as per your requirements.

Use log channels wisely.

Configure log channels carefully based on your application's needs and infrastructure. Different channels may have different purposes (e.g., file logs for local development, database logs for production).

Be cautious with sensitive data.

Be cautious about logging sensitive information like passwords or credit card numbers. Make sure you mask or omit such data from logs to maintain security and compliance.

By following these best practices, you can ensure that your exception logs provide valuable insights for debugging and monitoring your Laravel application. Well-formatted logs with context-specific information and timestamps will help you diagnose and resolve issues more effectively, leading to a more stable and reliable application.

Logging and Monitoring Application Errors
Logging in Laravel
Understanding the Laravel Logging System and Its Built-In Logging Channels and Drivers (e.g., Single, Daily, Slack)

The Laravel logging system is a powerful and flexible mechanism for recording and managing log messages in your application. It allows you to track various events, errors, and informational messages, helping you monitor the application's behavior, debug issues, and gain insights into its performance. Laravel provides several built-in logging channels and drivers that enable you to store log messages in different locations, such as files, databases, or external services like Slack. Let's explore some of the key aspects of the Laravel logging system and its logging channels and drivers.

Logging Channels

In Laravel, logging channels represent the destinations where log messages are sent. Each channel is associated with a specific driver that determines how the log messages are processed and stored. The default logging channel is typically named 'stack', and it defines a stack of multiple channels, allowing you to log to multiple destinations simultaneously.

Built-In Logging Drivers

Laravel provides several built-in logging drivers that you can use for different purposes:

Single channel

Driver: 'single'

The 'single' driver logs all messages to a single log file specified in the configuration. It is useful for local development or when you need a simple log file without log rotation.

Daily channel

Driver: 'daily'

The 'daily' driver logs messages to a new log file each day, ensuring that log files don't grow too large over time. It is commonly used for production environments to manage log files more effectively.

Syslog channel

Driver: 'syslog'

The 'syslog' driver sends log messages to the system's syslog service. This is useful when you want to centralize log management or integrate with third-party log management solutions.

ErrorLog channel

Driver: 'errorlog'

The 'errorlog' driver logs messages to the PHP error log, which is a system-specific error logging mechanism. It is useful for shared hosting environments or when you want to utilize the system's error logging capabilities.

Custom channel

Driver: Custom

You can create custom logging channels by defining your own driver, allowing you to log messages to any desired location or external service. Custom channels are often used to integrate with external logging services like Elasticsearch, Logstash, or external APIs.

Configure logging channels.

The configuration for logging channels is defined in the 'config/logging.php' configuration file. It allows you to specify the driver for each channel and set channel-specific configurations, for example:

```
// config/logging.php
return [
    'default' => env('LOG_CHANNEL', 'stack'),
    'channels' => [
        'stack' => [
            'driver' => 'stack',
            'channels' => ['single', 'daily'],
            'ignore_exceptions' => false,
        ],
        'single' => [
            'driver' => 'single',
            'path' => storage_path('logs/laravel.log'),
            'level' => 'debug',
        ],
        'daily' => [
            'driver' => 'daily',
            'path' => storage_path('logs/laravel.log'),
            'level' => 'debug',
            'days' => 14,
        ],
        // Other channels...
    ],
    // Other logging configurations...
];
```

In the preceding configuration, the 'stack' channel is the default logging channel, which includes both the 'single' and 'daily' channels. The 'single' channel logs messages to a single file, while the 'daily' channel logs messages to a new file each day.

Use logging in Laravel.

You can use Laravel's built-in logging methods to record log messages in your application:

```
use Illuminate\Support\Facades\Log;
// Example log messages
Log::debug('This is a debug message.');
Log::info('This is an informational message.');
Log::warning('This is a warning message.');
Log::error('This is an error message.');
```

The log messages will be processed and sent to the configured logging channels based on their severity level and the defined channel configurations.

By utilizing the Laravel logging system and its built-in logging channels and drivers, you can effectively manage log messages and gain valuable insights into your application's behavior, performance, and error occurrences. It also allows you to customize log storage locations and integrate with external log management services for more comprehensive monitoring and debugging.

Customizing Logging Configurations for Controlling Log Levels, Format, and Storage Location

Customizing logging configurations in Laravel allows you to have full control over log levels, log format, and storage location for your application's log messages. By adjusting these configurations, you can tailor the logging behavior to suit your specific needs and improve the effectiveness of your log management. Here's how you can customize logging configurations in Laravel.

Configure log channels and drivers.

In Laravel, logging channels and drivers are defined in the 'config/logging.php' configuration file. You can specify the log drivers for each channel and set other channel-specific configurations. For example, here's how to configure two logging channels—one for daily logs and another for a single log file:

```php
// config/logging.php
return [
    'default' => env('LOG_CHANNEL', 'stack'),
    'channels' => [
        'stack' => [
            'driver' => 'stack',
            'channels' => ['daily', 'single'],
            'ignore_exceptions' => false,
        ],
        'daily' => [
            'driver' => 'daily',
            'path' => storage_path('logs/laravel.log'),
            'level' => 'debug',
            'days' => 14,
        ],
        'single' => [
            'driver' => 'single',
            'path' => storage_path('logs/laravel_single.log'),
            'level' => 'info',
        ],
        // Other channels...
    ],
    // Other logging configurations...
];
```

In the preceding configuration, we have two channels: 'daily' and 'single'. The 'daily' channel logs messages to a new log file each day, while the 'single' channel logs messages to a single log file.

Set log levels.

Laravel supports various log levels that define the severity of log messages. You can customize the log level for each channel in the configuration. The available log levels, in descending order of severity, are 'emergency', 'alert', 'critical', 'error', 'warning', 'notice', 'info', and 'debug', for example:

```
'daily' => [
    'driver' => 'daily',
    'path' => storage_path('logs/laravel.log'),
    'level' => 'warning', // Set the log level to 'warning'.
    'days' => 14,
],
```

In this example, the 'daily' channel is set to log messages with a severity level of 'warning' or higher. Messages with a severity level of 'info' or 'debug' will not be logged.

Customize log format.

By default, Laravel uses the Monolog library for logging, which allows you to customize the log format. You can define custom log formats by creating a log processor class. The log processor modifies the log message before the logging system handles it. To define a custom log processor, create a new PHP class that implements the '__invoke' method and add it to the log channel configuration:

```
// app/Logging/CustomLogProcessor.php
namespace App\Logging;
class CustomLogProcessor
{
    public function __invoke(array $record)
    {
        // Customize the log format here.
        // Add or modify fields in the $record array.
        return $record;
    }
}
```

In the log channel configuration:

```
'daily' => [
    'driver' => 'daily',
    'path' => storage_path('logs/laravel.log'),
```

```
    'level' => 'debug',
    'days' => 14,
    'tap' => [App\Logging\CustomLogProcessor::class], // Add the custom log
    processor here.
],
```

In the preceding example, we added our custom log processor class 'CustomLogProcessor' to the 'daily' channel. The log processor allows you to add or modify fields in the log message.

There are additional logging configurations.

Laravel's logging system offers additional configurations that can be set in the 'config/logging.php' file. Some commonly used configurations include

'tap': This allows you to add additional log processors to a specific channel, providing more flexibility in log message processing.

'days': For channels with daily log rotation, this defines the number of days to keep log files before they are rotated.

'max_files': For channels with file log rotation, this defines the maximum number of log files to keep before older log files are deleted.

Using the Customized Logging Configurations

After customizing the logging configurations, you can use Laravel's built-in logging methods to log messages, for example:

```
use Illuminate\Support\Facades\Log;
Log::debug('This is a debug message.');
Log::info('This is an informational message.');
Log::warning('This is a warning message.');
Log::error('This is an error message.');
```

The log messages will be processed based on the defined log levels and channeled to the respective log drivers and storage locations according to your configurations.

By customizing logging configurations in Laravel, you can optimize your application's logging behavior to best suit your needs. This flexibility allows you to control the log levels, format, and storage locations effectively, making your logging system more efficient and adaptable to your application's requirements.

Centralized Logging with Laravel

Setting Up Centralized Logging Systems (e.g., ELK Stack: Elasticsearch, Logstash, Kibana) to Collect and Analyze Logs from Multiple Servers and Environments

Setting up a centralized logging system, such as the ELK (Elasticsearch, Logstash, and Kibana) stack, allows you to collect and analyze logs from multiple servers and environments in one centralized location. This enables easier monitoring, searching, and analysis of log data, leading to improved application troubleshooting, performance analysis, and error detection. Here's a step-by-step guide to setting up the ELK stack for centralized logging.

Install Elasticsearch.

Download and install Elasticsearch on a dedicated server or a server that will act as the central log repository.

Configure Elasticsearch by adjusting the 'elasticsearch.yml' configuration file. Pay attention to settings like cluster name, node name, network binding, and memory settings.

Start the Elasticsearch service and ensure it's running correctly.

Install Logstash.

Download and install Logstash on a separate server or the same server as Elasticsearch.

Configure Logstash by creating a Logstash configuration file (e.g., 'logstash.conf') that defines input sources, filters, and output destinations.

In the Logstash configuration file, specify the input sources to collect logs from multiple servers and environments. Common inputs include Filebeat (for log files) or Beats (for various data types).

Add filters (if needed) to parse, enrich, or modify log data before sending it to Elasticsearch.

Define the Elasticsearch output in the configuration to send processed log data to the Elasticsearch cluster.

Start the Logstash service and ensure it's running correctly.

Install Kibana.

Download and install Kibana on a separate server or the same server as Elasticsearch and Logstash.

Configure Kibana by adjusting the 'kibana.yml' configuration file. Specify the Elasticsearch URL to connect to the Elasticsearch cluster.

Start the Kibana service and ensure it's running correctly.

Ship logs to Logstash (optional).

If you want to ship logs from different servers to Logstash, you can use Beats (Filebeat, Metricbeat, Packetbeat, etc.) or other log shippers. Configure the Beats agents to send logs to the Logstash server. Beats can be installed on each server you want to collect logs from.

Visualize and analyze logs with Kibana.

Access Kibana's web interface (by default, it's available on port 5601).

Define the index pattern in Kibana to match the index pattern used by Elasticsearch to store log data.

Start exploring and analyzing logs using Kibana's powerful visualizations, dashboards, and search capabilities.

Monitor and manage the ELK stack.

To ensure the ELK stack's reliability and performance, monitor and manage each component:

Regularly check the health of Elasticsearch clusters and Logstash instances.

Tune Elasticsearch and Logstash configurations based on performance requirements.

Back up important Elasticsearch data regularly.

Secure access to Kibana and Elasticsearch by setting up authentication and access controls.

With the ELK stack set up for centralized logging, you can now collect and analyze logs from multiple servers and environments in one place. This allows you to gain valuable insights into your application's behavior, troubleshoot issues, detect errors, and make informed decisions for optimizing your application's performance and stability.

Benefits of Centralizing Logs for Easier Debugging and Monitoring

Centralizing logs offers numerous benefits for easier debugging and monitoring in a web application. Here are some key advantages of centralizing logs:

Simplified log management

With logs centralized in one location, you don't need to access individual servers or applications to review log files. This simplifies log management and reduces the effort required to analyze log data.

Comprehensive view of application behavior

Centralized logs provide a holistic view of the application's behavior across multiple servers and environments. You can see the entire log history in one place, making it easier to identify patterns, trends, and anomalies.

Faster issue detection and troubleshooting

Centralized logs enable faster issue detection and troubleshooting. Instead of searching through numerous log files, you can use the powerful search and filtering capabilities of the centralized logging system to pinpoint specific events and errors.

Simplified error tracking

With centralized logs, you can easily track and monitor errors across the entire application. This helps in identifying recurring issues and enables proactive problem-solving.

Improved application performance monitoring

Centralized logs allow you to monitor the performance of the application more effectively. You can analyze response times, resource consumption, and other performance metrics from a centralized dashboard.

Real-time monitoring and alerts

Centralized logging systems often provide real-time log monitoring and alerting capabilities. You can set up alerts for specific log events or error conditions, allowing you to respond promptly to critical issues.

Historical analysis and auditing

Centralized logs maintain historical data, enabling you to perform retrospective analysis and audits. You can review past events, track changes, and investigate incidents in detail.

Simplified compliance and security audits

Centralized logs ease compliance and security audits. Having all logs in one place facilitates demonstrating compliance with industry regulations and security standards.

Better resource utilization

Centralized logging can lead to better resource utilization on individual servers. Since logs are not stored locally, there's no need to allocate disk space on each server for log storage.

Scalability and redundancy

Centralized logging systems like the ELK stack can be scaled and distributed to handle large amounts of log data efficiently. This ensures redundancy and reliability in log storage.

Support for historical forensics

Centralized logs facilitate historical forensics, allowing you to investigate past incidents and understand the root causes of problems.

By centralizing logs, you can transform your application's logging into a powerful tool for debugging, monitoring, and improving overall performance. The ability to access and analyze logs from a single location streamlines the debugging process, reduces downtime, and enhances the stability and reliability of your web application.

Monitoring Application Errors

Integrating Error Monitoring Tools (e.g., BugSnag, Sentry) with Laravel Applications for Automatic Exception Tracking and Reporting

Integrating error monitoring tools like BugSnag or Sentry with Laravel applications allows for automatic exception tracking, reporting, and error monitoring. These tools help developers identify and diagnose errors, exceptions, and application issues in real time. The following are the steps to integrate BugSnag or Sentry with a Laravel application.

Create an account and obtain API keys.

Sign up for an account on the BugSnag or Sentry website, depending on the tool you choose. After creating an account, you will obtain the API keys or tokens required for integration.

Install the error monitoring package.

Both BugSnag and Sentry have official Laravel packages that make integration straightforward. You can install the package using Composer. For BugSnag, run

```
composer require bugsnag/bugsnag-laravel
```

For Sentry, run

```
composer require sentry/sentry-laravel
```

Configure.

After installation, configure the package by adding the API keys or tokens obtained from BugSnag or Sentry to the Laravel '.env' file.

For BugSnag:

```
BUGSNAG_API_KEY=your_bugsnag_api_key
```

For Sentry:

```
SENTRY_LARAVEL_DSN=your_sentry_dsn
```

Register the service provider.

In Laravel, you need to register the service provider for the error monitoring package. Open the 'config/app.php' file and add the following service provider in the 'providers' array.

For BugSnag:

```
Bugsnag\BugsnagLaravel\BugsnagServiceProvider::class,
```

For Sentry:

```
Sentry\Laravel\ServiceProvider::class,
```

Register middleware and exception handler.

Both BugSnag and Sentry provide middleware and exception handlers to automatically track exceptions and errors in the Laravel application. You need to register this middleware and exception handler to enable automatic exception tracking.

For BugSnag, add the middleware to the '$middleware' array in 'app/Http/Kernel.php':

```
protected $middleware = [
    // Other middleware...
    \Bugsnag\BugsnagLaravel\Middleware\ReportExceptions::class,
];
```

For Sentry, add the middleware to the '$middleware' array in 'app/Http/Kernel.php':

```
protected $middleware = [
    // Other middleware...
    \Sentry\Laravel\Tracing\Middleware\RecordTransaction::class,
];
```

Also, update the exception handler in 'app/Exceptions/Handler.php' to use the Sentry exception handler:

```
use Sentry\Laravel\Integration\SentryExceptionHandler;
```

And update the 'report' method:

```
public function report(Throwable $exception)
{
    if (app()->bound('sentry') && $this->shouldReport($exception)) {
        app('sentry')->captureException($exception);
    }
    parent::report($exception);
}
```

Test the integration.

With the integration completed, the error monitoring tool will automatically track and report exceptions that occur in your Laravel application. You can test it by intentionally throwing an exception, and it should appear in your BugSnag or Sentry dashboard.

Integrating error monitoring tools with your Laravel application ensures that exceptions and errors are promptly detected, logged, and reported to the monitoring platform. This allows developers to stay informed about application issues and respond quickly to fix problems, leading to a more reliable and stable web application.

Configuring Real-Time Alerts to Notify Developers or System Administrators During Critical Errors

Configuring real-time alerts is crucial to promptly notify developers or system administrators of critical errors in a web application. Real-time alerts ensure that the right people are informed immediately when critical issues occur, enabling rapid response and reducing downtime. To achieve this in Laravel, you can integrate error monitoring tools like BugSnag or Sentry, as mentioned earlier, or use other notification mechanisms. Here's a general approach to configuring real-time alerts for critical errors.

Choose a notification method.

Decide on the notification method that suits your team's workflow and preferences. Common notification methods include

> Email: Send alert emails to developers or administrators.

> Slack: Notify relevant channels or users through Slack messages.

> SMS: Send text messages to designated phone numbers.

> Webhooks: Trigger external services or custom scripts via HTTP requests.

Customize alert conditions.

Determine the criteria that define a critical error or exception in your application. For example, you may want to trigger alerts for errors with a specific log level (e.g., "error" or "critical") or for specific exception types (e.g., "PDOException" or "HttpException").

Integrate with Laravel's logging system.

BugSnag or Sentry already handles integration with Laravel's logging system if you're using their respective packages. If you prefer a custom notification method, you can manually configure Laravel's logging system to send alerts when critical errors occur. Update the 'report' method in the 'app/Exceptions/Handler.php' file to include your custom notification logic.

For example, here's how to send an email notification when a critical error occurs:

```
use Illuminate\Support\Facades\Mail;
public function report(Throwable $exception)
{
    if ($this->shouldReport($exception)) {
        // Custom logic to check if the exception is critical.
        $isCriticalError = $this->isCriticalError($exception);
        if ($isCriticalError) {
            // Send email notification to developers or administrators.
            Mail::raw('A critical error occurred in the application.',
            function ($message) {
                $message->to('developer@example.com')->subject('Critical
                Error Alert');
            });
        }
        // Log the exception.
        parent::report($exception);
    }
}
private function isCriticalError(Throwable $exception)
{
    // Custom logic to determine if the exception is critical.
    return $exception->getCode() >= 500; // Example: Consider any 500+ HTTP
    status code as critical.
}
```

Test and monitor alerts.

Test the alerts to ensure they are triggered correctly for critical errors. Monitor the alerts and verify that they reach the intended recipients promptly.

Set up monitoring and alerting services (optional).

For more sophisticated alerting capabilities, you can use monitoring and alerting services like Prometheus, Grafana, or other cloud-based solutions. These services allow you to set up more advanced alerting rules and conditions based on various metrics and performance indicators.

By configuring real-time alerts, you can ensure that your team is promptly notified of critical errors, allowing them to respond quickly and address issues before they escalate. This proactive approach to error management significantly contributes to maintaining a reliable and robust web application.

Implementing Error Reporting and Alerting Systems

Error Reporting with Notifications

Configuring Notifications to Alert Developers or Administrators When Exceptions Occur in the Application

Configuring notifications for error reporting is crucial for promptly alerting developers or administrators when exceptions occur in a web application. This enables the development team to be immediately informed about critical issues, allowing them to take swift action and resolve problems efficiently. In Laravel, you can set up notifications to be delivered through various channels such as email, Slack, SMS, or any custom method. Here's how you can configure notifications for error reporting in Laravel.

Choose a notification channel.

Start by deciding on the notification channel through which you want to send alerts. Laravel supports various notification channels out of the box, including email, Slack, SMS, database, and more. Additionally, you can create custom notification channels to suit your specific requirements.

Create a custom notification.

If you are using a custom notification channel or need to customize the content and format of the error notification, create a custom notification class. Run the following Artisan command to generate a new notification:

```
php artisan make:notification ErrorOccurred
```

This will create a new notification class in the `app/Notifications` directory.

Define the notification content.

Customize the notification content in the newly created `ErrorOccurred` notification class. You can define the notification message, subject, and any additional information you want to include, for example:

```php
// app/Notifications/ErrorOccurred.php
use Illuminate\Notifications\Notification;
use Illuminate\Notifications\Messages\MailMessage;
use Illuminate\Notifications\Messages\SlackMessage;
class ErrorOccurred extends Notification
{
    public function toMail($notifiable)
    {
        return (new MailMessage)
            ->subject('Critical Error Alert')
            ->line('An exception occurred in the application.')
            ->line('Exception message: '.$this->exception->getMessage())
            ->action('View Error', $this->url);
    }
    public function toSlack($notifiable)
    {
        return (new SlackMessage)
            ->content('An exception occurred in the application.')
            ->attachment(function ($attachment) {
                $attachment->title('Error Information')
                        ->content('Exception message: '.$this-
                        >exception->getMessage())
```

341

```
                    ->action('View Error', $this->url);
        });
    }
}
```

Send the notification when an exception occurs.

In the Laravel exception handler (`app/Exceptions/Handler.php`), add logic to send the notification when an exception occurs. You can do this in the `report` method:

```
use App\Notifications\ErrorOccurred;
public function report(Throwable $exception)
{
    if ($this->shouldReport($exception)) {
        // Customize the list of recipients to whom the notification should
        be sent.
        $recipients = ['developer@example.com', 'admin@example.com'];
        // Send the notification to each recipient.
        foreach ($recipients as $recipient) {
            $user = User::where('email', $recipient)->first();
            if ($user) {
                $user->notify(new ErrorOccurred($exception, $this->getUrl()));
            }
        }
        // Log the exception.
        parent::report($exception);
    }
}
protected function getUrl()
{
    // Customize this method to generate the URL for viewing the error or
    the relevant log in your application.
    return 'https://your-app-url/errors';
}
```

Test the notification.

Test the notification by intentionally throwing an exception in your application. Ensure that the notifications are being delivered to the specified recipients through the chosen notification channel.

By configuring error notifications in this manner, you can keep your development team informed about critical issues, enabling them to respond swiftly and resolve problems efficiently. This proactive approach to error reporting contributes significantly to maintaining a reliable and robust web application.

Customizing Notification Channels (e.g., Email, Slack, SMS) Based on Team Preferences and Urgency Levels

Customizing notification channels based on team preferences and urgency levels allows you to ensure that the right team members receive notifications in the most appropriate format for critical issues. Different team members or roles may have distinct preferences for receiving alerts, and some notifications may require immediate attention, while others can be less urgent. In Laravel, you can achieve this by using Laravel's built-in notification channels and customizing their behavior based on the urgency level of the notification. Here's how you can customize notification channels.

Define notification channels.

Start by defining the notification channels you want to use in your application. For example, you may have email, Slack, SMS, and database channels. You can configure these channels in the `config/services.php` configuration file:

```
return [
    // Other service configurations...
    'slack' => [
        'webhook_url' => env('SLACK_WEBHOOK_URL'),
    ],
    'nexmo' => [
        'sms_from' => 'YourApp',
    ],
];
```

Customize the notification content.

Customize the notification content for each channel based on team preferences. Create a custom notification class for each notification type. Here's an example of customizing the content for email and Slack channels:

```php
// app/Notifications/CriticalErrorOccurred.php
use Illuminate\Notifications\Notification;
use Illuminate\Notifications\Messages\MailMessage;
use Illuminate\Notifications\Messages\SlackMessage;
class CriticalErrorOccurred extends Notification
{
    public function toMail($notifiable)
    {
        return (new MailMessage)
            ->subject('Critical Error Alert')
            ->line('An exception occurred in the application.')
            ->line('Exception message: '.$this->exception->getMessage())
            ->action('View Error', $this->getUrl());
    }
    public function toSlack($notifiable)
    {
        return (new SlackMessage)
            ->content('An exception occurred in the application.')
            ->attachment(function ($attachment) {
                $attachment->title('Error Information')
                        ->content('Exception message: '.$this-
                        >exception->getMessage())
                        ->action('View Error', $this->getUrl());
            });
    }
}
```

Customize recipients and channels in the exception handler.

In the Laravel exception handler (`app/Exceptions/Handler.php`), customize the recipients and channels for each notification based on the urgency level of the error, for example:

```
-------------------------------------------------------------------------
use App\Notifications\CriticalErrorOccurred;
public function report(Throwable $exception)
{
    if ($this->shouldReport($exception)) {
        // Customize the list of recipients and channels based on
        urgency level.
        $recipients = [];
        $channels = [];
        if ($this->isCriticalError($exception)) {
            // Critical error requires immediate attention.
            $recipients = ['admin@example.com'];
            $channels = ['slack', 'email'];
        } else {
            // Non-critical error can be sent to developers for monitoring.
            $recipients = ['developer@example.com'];
            $channels = ['slack', 'database'];
        }
        // Send the notification to each recipient and channel.
        foreach ($recipients as $recipient) {
            $user = User::where('email', $recipient)->first();
            if ($user) {
                $user->notify(new CriticalErrorOccurred($exception,
                $this->getUrl()));
            }
        }
        // Log the exception.
        parent::report($exception);
    }
}
```

```
protected function isCriticalError(Throwable $exception)
{
    // Customize this method to determine if the exception is critical
based on your application's logic.
    // For example, you can check for specific HTTP status codes or
exception types.
    return $exception->getCode() >= 500;
}
```

Test the notifications.

Test the notifications by intentionally triggering errors with different urgency levels. Verify that notifications are being sent to the appropriate recipients through the specified channels.

By customizing notification channels based on team preferences and urgency levels, you can ensure that critical issues are brought to the attention of the right team members in the most suitable format. This flexibility in notification configuration allows for better incident response and helps maintain a well-coordinated and efficient development process.

Real-Time Error Reporting with WebSockets

Integrating WebSockets into Laravel for Real-Time Error Reporting and Application Monitoring

Integrating WebSockets into Laravel allows for real-time error reporting and application monitoring, enabling developers and administrators to receive live updates on errors, exceptions, and other critical events as they happen. WebSockets provide a bidirectional communication channel between the client and server, allowing the server to push data to the client instantly. In Laravel, you can achieve this by using the Laravel Echo and Laravel WebSockets packages.

Here's how you can set up real-time error reporting with WebSockets in Laravel:

Install the required packages.

Install the required packages for WebSocket support in Laravel:

```
composer require beyondcode/laravel-websockets
php artisan vendor:publish --provider="BeyondCode\LaravelWebSockets\
WebSocketsServiceProvider" --tag="migrations"
php artisan migrate
```

```
npm install laravel-echo pusher-js
```

Configure WebSockets.

Configure the WebSocket server and broadcasting settings in `config/websockets.php`:

```php
// config/websockets.php
return [
    'apps' => [
        [
            'id' => env('PUSHER_APP_ID'),
            'key' => env('PUSHER_APP_KEY'),
            'secret' => env('PUSHER_APP_SECRET'),
            'enable_client_messages' => false,
            'enable_statistics' => true,
        ],
    ],
    'ssl' => [
        'local_cert' => null,
        'local_pk' => null,
        'passphrase' => null,
    ],
    'protocol' => 'https',
    'host' => '0.0.0.0',
```

```
        'port' => env('WS_PORT', 6001),
        'path' => 'ws',
        'debug' => false,
];
```

Set up broadcasting.

Configure broadcasting settings in `config/broadcasting.php` to use the WebSocket driver:

```
// config/broadcasting.php
return [
    'default' => 'ws',
    'connections' => [
        'ws' => [
            'driver' => 'pusher',
            'key' => env('PUSHER_APP_KEY'),
            'secret' => env('PUSHER_APP_SECRET'),
            'app_id' => env('PUSHER_APP_ID'),
            'options' => [
                'cluster' => env('PUSHER_APP_CLUSTER'),
                'useTLS' => true,
            ],
        ],
    ],
];
```

Set up event broadcasting.

Define an event that will broadcast the error information to the WebSocket channel:

```
// app/Events/ErrorOccurredEvent.php
namespace App\Events;
use Illuminate\Broadcasting\Channel;
use Illuminate\Broadcasting\InteractsWithSockets;
```

```php
use Illuminate\Broadcasting\PresenceChannel;
use Illuminate\Broadcasting\PrivateChannel;
use Illuminate\Contracts\Broadcasting\ShouldBroadcast;
use Illuminate\Foundation\Events\Dispatchable;
use Illuminate\Queue\SerializesModels;
class ErrorOccurredEvent implements ShouldBroadcast
{
    use Dispatchable, InteractsWithSockets, SerializesModels;
    public $errorMessage;
    public function __construct($errorMessage)
    {
        $this->errorMessage = $errorMessage;
    }
    public function broadcastOn()
    {
        return new Channel('error-channel');
    }
    public function broadcastAs()
    {
        return 'error-occurred';
    }
}
```

Broadcast error events.

In the Laravel exception handler (`app/Exceptions/Handler.php`), broadcast the error event whenever a critical error occurs:

```php
use App\Events\ErrorOccurredEvent;
public function report(Throwable $exception)
{
    if ($this->shouldReport($exception)) {
        if ($this->isCriticalError($exception)) {
            event(new ErrorOccurredEvent($exception->getMessage()));
        }
```

```
        // Log the exception.
        parent::report($exception);
    }
}
```

Set up JavaScript frontend.

On the frontend, use Laravel Echo to listen for error events and update the user
interface accordingly—for example, in a Vue component:

```
// resources/js/components/Errors.vue
import Echo from 'laravel-echo';
export default {
    data() {
        return {
            errors: [],
        };
    },
    created() {
        this.listenForErrors();
    },
    methods: {
        listenForErrors() {
            Echo.channel('error-channel')
                .listen('.error-occurred', (error) => {
                    this.errors.push(error.errorMessage);
                });
        },
    },
};
```

Start the WebSocket server.

Start the WebSocket server to handle real-time events:

```
php artisan websockets:serve
```

Test the real-time error reporting.

Test the real-time error reporting by intentionally triggering critical errors in your application. The errors should be instantly reported and displayed in the user interface.

By integrating WebSockets into Laravel for real-time error reporting, developers and administrators can receive live updates on critical events, enabling them to respond quickly and address issues proactively. This enhanced monitoring capability contributes to a more reliable and responsive web application.

Building a Live Dashboard to Display Error Data As It Occurs to Facilitate Quick Response and Debugging

To build a live dashboard that displays error data as it occurs, facilitating quick response and debugging, you can leverage Laravel for the backend and a JavaScript framework like Vue.js for the frontend. The live dashboard will receive real-time error data through WebSockets and update the user interface accordingly. Here's a step-by-step guide to building the live dashboard.

Set up WebSockets (already covered in the previous section).

As mentioned earlier, set up WebSockets in Laravel using the Laravel Echo and Laravel WebSockets packages. Configure the WebSocket server and broadcasting settings as described in the previous section.

Create a live dashboard component.

In the Vue.js frontend, create a live dashboard component that will display the real-time error data, for example:

```
<!-- resources/js/components/LiveDashboard.vue -->
<template>
  <div>
    <h2>Live Dashboard</h2>
    <ul>
      <li v-for="error in errors" :key="error.id">
```

```
        {{ error.message }}
      </li>
    </ul>
  </div>
</template>
<script>
import Echo from 'laravel-echo';
export default {
  data() {
    return {
      errors: [],
    };
  },
  created() {
    this.listenForErrors();
  },
  methods: {
    listenForErrors() {
      Echo.channel('error-channel').listen('.error-occurred', (error) => {
        this.errors.push(error.errorMessage);
      });
    },
  },
};
</script>
```

Include the live dashboard component.

Include the `LiveDashboard` component in your main application layout or any page where you want to display the live error data:

```
<!-- resources/js/app.js -->
import Vue from 'vue';
import LiveDashboard from './components/LiveDashboard.vue';
new Vue({
```

```
  components: {
    LiveDashboard,
  },
}).$mount('#app');
```

```
<!-- resources/views/layouts/app.blade.php -->
<!DOCTYPE html>
<html>
<head>
  <!-- Other meta tags, stylesheets, etc. -->
  <!-- Include the JavaScript files -->
  <script src="{{ mix('js/app.js') }}" defer></script>
</head>
<body>
  <div id="app">
    <!-- Include the LiveDashboard component -->
    <live-dashboard></live-dashboard>
  </div>
</body>
</html>
```

Test the live dashboard.

Start the WebSocket server using the command `php artisan websockets:serve`.
Load your application in the browser and trigger some critical errors. The live dashboard
should display the errors as they occur, updating the user interface in real time.

There are also enhancements (optional).

You can further enhance the live dashboard by

> Adding more details to the error data, such as timestamps, stack
> traces, and error levels.

> Implementing error filtering and searching capabilities for better
> navigation through the error data.

Styling the live dashboard to make it visually appealing and user-friendly.

Using charts or graphs to visualize error trends over time.

By building a live dashboard that displays error data in real time, developers and administrators can quickly respond to critical issues, enabling them to debug and resolve problems promptly. This enhanced monitoring and debugging capability contributes to better application stability and reliability.

Debugging Production Errors with Remote Logging and Tracing

Debugging production errors can be challenging, especially when issues occur in a live environment. Remote logging and tracing techniques provide valuable insights into the behavior of your application, allowing you to diagnose and resolve production errors effectively. Here's an overview of debugging production errors with remote logging and tracing.

Remote Logging

Remote logging allows you to capture and transmit log data from your production environment to a centralized location for analysis. This enables you to monitor and inspect logs without direct access to the production servers. Here's how you can implement remote logging:

Configure a centralized logging system.

Set up a centralized logging system that aggregates logs from various production instances. The ELK (Elasticsearch, Logstash, and Kibana) stack is a popular choice for centralized logging. Alternatively, you can use cloud-based logging services like AWS CloudWatch Logs or Google Cloud Logging.

Configure log forwarding.

Configure your application's logging framework to send logs to the centralized logging system. For example, if you're using Log4j as your logging framework, you can configure it to send logs to Logstash. Here's an example Log4j configuration ('log4j2. xml') for Logstash:

```xml
<?xml version="1.0" encoding="UTF-8"?>
<Configuration>
    <Appenders>
        <Socket name="logstash" host="logstash.example.com" port="5000">
            <JsonLayout properties="true" />
        </Socket>
    </Appenders>
    <Loggers>
        <Root level="info">
            <AppenderRef ref="logstash" />
        </Root>
    </Loggers>
</Configuration>
```

Filter and search logs.

Utilize the capabilities of the centralized logging system to filter and search log data based on criteria like time range, log levels, specific error messages, or other relevant keywords. This helps narrow down and focus on the logs related to the specific error.

Distributed Tracing

Distributed tracing helps trace the flow of a request across various components and services in your application. It assists in identifying performance bottlenecks, dependencies, and errors occurring across different parts of your system. Here's how you can implement distributed tracing:

Instrumentation

Integrate a distributed tracing framework or library into your application's codebase. OpenTelemetry is a popular framework that provides APIs and instrumentation agents for tracing. Here's an example of how you can instrument your Java application with OpenTelemetry using the Java Agent:

```
java -javaagent:/path/to/opentelemetry-javaagent.jar \
    -Dotel.exporter=jaeger \
    -Dotel.exporter.jaeger.service.name=my-application \
    -jar my-application.jar
```

Tracing context propagation

Ensure that tracing context is propagated across services and components. This allows the tracing system to link requests and correlate logs or errors across distributed systems. The tracing context typically includes trace IDs and span IDs. The specific implementation depends on the tracing framework you're using.

Trace analysis

Analyze traces to identify patterns, bottlenecks, or errors occurring during request processing. Focus on spans associated with errors or exceptions to understand the sequence of operations leading to the error. Distributed tracing tools like Jaeger or Zipkin provide visualization and analysis capabilities for exploring traces.

Error Alerting and Monitoring

Configure error alerts and monitoring to be notified promptly when critical errors occur in the production environment. Set up threshold-based alerts based on error severity, occurrence frequency, or other relevant criteria. This enables you to take immediate action when errors of significance arise. Here's an example using AWS CloudWatch Alarms to trigger an alert for a specific error count threshold:

```
import boto3
client = boto3.client('cloudwatch')
def create_error_alarm():
    response = client.put_metric_alarm(
        AlarmName='ErrorCountThreshold',
        AlarmDescription='Triggered when error count exceeds threshold',
        MetricName='ErrorCount',
        Namespace='MyAppMetrics',
        Statistic='SampleCount',
        Period=60,
```

```
EvaluationPeriods=5,
Threshold=10,
ComparisonOperator='GreaterThanOrEqualToThreshold',
AlarmActions=['arn:aws:sns:us-east-1:123456789012:MyErrorTopic'],
Dimensions=[
    {
        'Name': 'Environment',
        'Value': 'Production'
    }
]
)
```

Live Debugging Tools

Consider using live debugging tools or techniques that allow you to inspect and analyze your application's behavior in a production environment. Remote debugging tools like Java's remote debugging or remote PowerShell debugging in .NET can help investigate and troubleshoot issues directly on live instances. Here's an example of remote debugging in Java.

Start the application with remote debugging enabled:

```
java -agentlib:jdwp=transport=dt_socket,server=y,suspend=n,
address=*:5005 -jar my-application.jar
```

Connect the debugger from your development environment (e.g., IntelliJ IDEA or Eclipse) to the remote debugging port (5005 in this example). This allows you to set breakpoints, inspect variables, and step through the code in the live production environment.

Log Analysis and Error Investigation

Analyze logs, distributed traces, and other diagnostic information to understand the root cause of production errors. Look for patterns, examine error stacks, and identify relevant contextual information. Leverage the aggregated logs and traces to reproduce and debug the error in a controlled development or test environment.

Postmortem Analysis and Resolution

Conduct a postmortem analysis of production errors to identify their impact, root causes, and preventive measures. Collaborate with the development team to resolve the errors, address any underlying issues, and improve the resilience of your application. Use the insights gained from remote logging, distributed tracing, and error monitoring to make informed decisions for bug fixes, performance optimizations, or system enhancements.

By leveraging remote logging and tracing techniques, you gain valuable insights into the behavior of your production application, allowing for effective debugging, troubleshooting, and resolution of errors. These practices enhance your ability to maintain the stability, performance, and reliability of your software in live environments.

Error Recovery and Graceful Degradation Strategies

Graceful Degradation

Strategies for Gracefully Handling Errors and Providing Fallback Mechanisms When Critical Services or Functionalities Are Unavailable

Graceful degradation is a design principle used in software development to ensure that an application can continue to function and provide a satisfactory user experience even when certain critical services or functionalities become unavailable. The goal is to maintain basic functionality and user access instead of experiencing complete failure. Here are some strategies for gracefully handling errors and implementing fallback mechanisms:

Fail silently or provide user-friendly errors: For non-critical features or services, consider failing silently and presenting a user-friendly error message to the user. This way, users are aware that something is not working, but they are not overwhelmed with technical details. For example, if a non-essential widget on a website fails to load, it's better to hide it or display an error message gracefully.

Use default values or cached data: In case a service or data source is unavailable, consider using default values or cached data as a fallback. This ensures that users can still access the necessary information or functionality even if the real-time data is temporarily unavailable.

Load external scripts asynchronously: When integrating external scripts or resources from third-party services, load them asynchronously. If the external service becomes unavailable, it won't block the entire page from loading. Instead, the application can continue working without the external resource.

Retry mechanisms: Implement retry mechanisms for essential operations or services that might experience temporary unavailability. Retrying a failed request after a short delay can often result in success if the issue was temporary.

Graceful UI degradation: For complex applications or components, design the user interface in a way that gracefully degrades when essential features are unavailable. Simplify the UI or disable non-essential features to focus on core functionality.

Fallback APIs: If a primary API or service becomes unavailable, have a fallback API or service that provides basic functionality. This can be a less feature-rich version or a backup system that can handle a subset of operations.

Monitoring and alerting: Implement monitoring and alerting systems to be notified when critical services go down. This enables your team to respond quickly and either fix the issue or implement the appropriate fallback mechanisms.

Feature toggling: Use feature toggles or feature flags to enable or disable certain functionalities at runtime. This allows you to toggle off critical features if they are causing issues and switch to fallback options.

Circuit breaker pattern: Implement the circuit breaker pattern to detect when a service is consistently failing and temporarily stop calling that service. Instead, the application can provide a fallback response while periodically checking if the service is back up.

User communication: Inform users about the degraded state of the application and provide instructions on what to do or how to proceed. Transparency and clear communication are essential during times of service degradation.

By employing these strategies, you can ensure that your application continues to provide essential functionality and a positive user experience even during temporary service unavailability or degraded states. Graceful degradation promotes application stability and reliability in the face of unpredictable situations and is an important aspect of building robust systems.

Techniques for Displaying User-Friendly Error Messages and Alternative Content During Degraded Conditions

Displaying user-friendly error messages and alternative content during degraded conditions is crucial for maintaining a positive user experience when critical services or functionalities are unavailable. Here are some techniques to achieve this:

Custom error pages: Create custom error pages for different HTTP status codes (e.g., 404, 500). These pages can provide clear and user-friendly messages, guiding users back to the main navigation or offering alternative content.

Friendly error messages: Use clear and concise error messages that inform users about the issue in simple language. Avoid technical jargon and provide instructions on what actions users can take to resolve the problem.

Gracious UI degradation: Design the user interface to gracefully degrade when essential features are unavailable. Hide or disable non-critical elements, focus on core functionality, and avoid overwhelming users with irrelevant information.

Fallback content: Offer fallback content for unavailable or dynamic data. For example, if real-time weather information is unavailable, display a default weather status or use cached data until the service is restored.

Caching and offline mode: Implement caching mechanisms to store previously accessed data, allowing the application to display cached content during degraded conditions or when the Internet connection is lost.

Asynchronous loading of resources: Load external resources or third-party scripts asynchronously. This prevents the entire page from being blocked if the resource is unavailable, allowing users to access the rest of the content.

Feature toggling: Use feature toggles or feature flags to enable or disable specific functionalities at runtime. This allows you to switch off critical features temporarily and display alternative content if necessary.

User notifications: Inform users about the degraded conditions through nonintrusive notifications or banners. Let users know that certain features may be limited and provide context for the issue.

Offline mode design: If your application relies heavily on real-time data or services, consider designing an offline mode that provides core functionalities even when the Internet connection is unavailable.

User assistance and support: Offer support options, such as a help center or a contact form, to assist users in resolving issues or getting further assistance during degraded conditions.

Fallback APIs or services: When essential APIs or services are down, use fallback APIs or services to provide basic functionality or data. This ensures that the application can still serve critical content.

Retry mechanisms: Implement retry mechanisms for essential operations or services that might experience temporary unavailability. Retry the operation after a short delay to give the service a chance to recover.

Remember that transparency and communication are vital in degraded conditions. Clearly communicate the issue to users and keep them informed about any updates or improvements. The goal is to make the user experience as smooth as possible, even in less-than-ideal conditions, and to provide alternative options whenever feasible.

Implementing Retry Mechanisms

Building Robust Retry Logic for Failed Operations (e.g., API Requests, Database Transactions) to Improve Application Resilience and Reliability

Implementing retry mechanisms is essential for building a resilient and reliable application. Retry logic allows the application to automatically attempt failed operations, such as API requests or database transactions, a certain number of times before raising an error or taking alternative actions. Here are steps to implement robust retry mechanisms in your application.

Identify retriable operations.

Identify the operations that can benefit from retrying in the event of failure. Examples include API calls, database transactions, file uploads, or any external service interactions.

Define retry configuration.

Define a retry configuration that includes parameters such as the maximum number of retries, the time delay between retries (backoff strategy), and any additional conditions that should trigger a retry:

```
// Retry configuration example
$maxRetries = 3;
$retryDelayMs = 1000; // 1 second
```

Implement retry logic.

Wrap the retriable operation in a retry loop that will attempt the operation the specified number of times:

```
function retryableOperation($maxRetries, $retryDelayMs)
{
    $retries = 0;
    while ($retries < $maxRetries) {
        try {
            // Perform the operation here (e.g., API call, database
            transaction)
            $result = performOperation();
            // Operation succeeded, return the result
            return $result;
        } catch (Exception $e) {
            // Operation failed, increment retry count
            $retries++;
            // Add optional logging here to record the failure
            // Wait before retrying (implement a backoff strategy)
            usleep($retryDelayMs * 1000); // Convert milliseconds to
            microseconds
        }
    }
    // If the maximum retries are exceeded, throw an exception or take
    alternative actions
    throw new Exception('Operation failed after maximum retries.');
}
```

Implementing a Backoff Strategy

Implement a backoff strategy to prevent overwhelming the service or causing additional issues in high-load scenarios. Common backoff strategies include fixed delay, exponential backoff, and jitter.

Fixed delay

Use a constant delay between retries.

Exponential backoff

Gradually increase the delay between retries to give the service more time to recover.

Jitter

Add random variation to the delay to prevent synchronized retry attempts from multiple clients.

Handle exception and failure cases.

Catch any exceptions raised by the retriable operation and decide whether to retry or take alternative actions, such as logging the failure or notifying administrators:

```
try {
    $result = retryableOperation($maxRetries, $retryDelayMs);
    // Use the result here
} catch (Exception $e) {
    // Handle the failure or take alternative actions
    // Log the failure or notify administrators
}
```

By implementing robust retry mechanisms, your application can automatically recover from transient failures, network issues, or the temporary unavailability of external services. This enhances application resilience and reliability, ensuring a smoother user experience and reducing the impact of temporary service disruptions. However, be cautious with retrying, as it may not be suitable for all types of operations, especially if the operation is prone to causing side effects or data inconsistencies. Consider the nature of the operation and the potential impact of retrying before implementing this approach.

Leveraging Laravel's Job Retries and Backoff Strategies to Handle Transient Failures Effectively

In Laravel, you can leverage the built-in job retries and backoff strategies to handle transient failures effectively, especially when dealing with queueable jobs. Laravel provides a clean and straightforward way to automatically retry failed jobs, along with different backoff strategies to control the delay between retry attempts. Here's how you can use these features:

Define the job.

Create a job class that implements the `Illuminate\Contracts\Queue\ShouldQueue`
interface. This interface indicates that the job should be queued and processed by a
queue worker:

```
namespace App\Jobs;
use Illuminate\Contracts\Queue\ShouldQueue;
use Illuminate\Foundation\Bus\Dispatchable;
use Illuminate\Queue\InteractsWithQueue;
use Illuminate\Queue\SerializesModels;
class MyJob implements ShouldQueue
{
    use Dispatchable, InteractsWithQueue, SerializesModels;
    /
     * Execute the job.
     *
     * @return void
     */
    public function handle()
    {
        // Your job logic here
    }
}
```

Set the number of retries.

By default, Laravel will retry a failed job three times. If you want to customize the
number of retries, you can define a `tries` property in your job class:

```
namespace App\Jobs;
use Illuminate\Contracts\Queue\ShouldQueue;
use Illuminate\Foundation\Bus\Dispatchable;
use Illuminate\Queue\InteractsWithQueue;
use Illuminate\Queue\SerializesModels;
class MyJob implements ShouldQueue
```

```
{
    use Dispatchable, InteractsWithQueue, SerializesModels;
    /
     * The number of times the job may be attempted.
     *
     * @var int
     */
    public $tries = 5;
    /
     * Execute the job.
     *
     * @return void
     */
    public function handle()
    {
        // Your job logic here
    }
}
```

Implement backoff strategies.

Laravel supports different backoff strategies that control the delay between retry attempts. By default, Laravel uses an exponential backoff strategy, but you can customize this by defining a `backoff` property in your job class:

```
namespace App\Jobs;
use Illuminate\Contracts\Queue\ShouldQueue;
use Illuminate\Foundation\Bus\Dispatchable;
use Illuminate\Queue\InteractsWithQueue;
use Illuminate\Queue\SerializesModels;
class MyJob implements ShouldQueue
{
    use Dispatchable, InteractsWithQueue, SerializesModels;
    /
     * The number of times the job may be attempted.
```

```
    *
    * @var int
    */
  public $tries = 5;
  /
    * The number of seconds to wait before retrying the job.
    *
    * @var int
    */
  public $backoff = 10;
  /
    * Execute the job.
    *
    * @return void
    */
  public function handle()
  {
      // Your job logic here
  }
}
```

In this example, the job will be retried five times, and there will be a ten-second delay between each retry attempt. The backoff property can be defined as a constant value or an array of values to specify different backoff times for each retry.

Handle failed jobs.

Laravel automatically handles failed jobs by logging them. You can view the failed jobs using the `php artisan queue:failed` command. If a job exceeds the maximum number of retries, it will be marked as failed, and you can investigate and take appropriate actions based on the failure reasons.

By leveraging Laravel's job retries and backoff strategies, you can effectively handle transient failures and improve the robustness of your application. Retry mechanisms are particularly useful when dealing with external services, API requests, or any operation that may experience temporary issues. With the built-in features provided by Laravel, you can easily implement reliable and resilient job processing in your application.

Circuit Breaker Pattern

Understanding the Circuit Breaker Pattern and Its Application in Laravel Applications

The circuit breaker pattern is a design pattern used to improve the resilience of applications by preventing cascading failures and reducing the load on failing services. It is commonly applied in distributed systems, microservices architectures, and any situation where services or external dependencies may experience temporary failures or become unavailable.

The circuit breaker pattern operates similarly to an electrical circuit breaker. When a service or dependency is functioning correctly, the circuit remains closed, and requests can pass through. However, when the service starts to fail, the circuit is "tripped", and further requests are stopped from reaching the failing service. Instead, the circuit breaker pattern provides an alternative behavior, such as using cached data, returning a default value, or returning a predefined fallback response.

Here are key components of the circuit breaker pattern:

Closed state: In the closed state, the circuit is operating normally, and requests are allowed to pass through to the service or dependency.

Open state: When the circuit is tripped due to repeated failures, it transitions to the open state. In this state, any requests to the failing service are immediately redirected to the fallback behavior.

Half-open state: After a specified time, the circuit enters the half-open state. In this state, a limited number of requests are allowed to pass through to the service to check if it has recovered. If these requests succeed, the circuit is closed again; otherwise, it reverts to the open state.

Here's how to apply the circuit breaker pattern in Laravel.

In Laravel applications, you can implement the circuit breaker pattern to handle failures when interacting with external services, APIs, or any other dependency that may be prone to transient issues. The pattern can be applied in different ways, such as in API calls, database queries, or remote service interactions.

Identify circuit breaker points: Identify the points in your application where external dependencies or services are being used. These points can be API requests, database queries, or any remote service interactions.

Wrap dependency calls: Wrap the calls to external dependencies or services in a circuit breaker class or middleware. This class will handle state transitions and circuit tripping logic.

Set thresholds and timeouts: Determine the number of failures and time window after which the circuit should be tripped. For example, if three consecutive failures occur within a five-second window, the circuit will trip.

Implement fallback behavior: Define the fallback behavior or response that should be provided when the circuit is open. This can be a default value, cached data, or a predefined error message.

State management: Track the state of the circuit (open, closed, or half-open) and ensure proper state transitions based on the failure count and time thresholds.

Monitoring and alerting: Implement monitoring and alerting mechanisms to be notified when the circuit trips and when it transitions back to the closed state.

By applying the circuit breaker pattern in Laravel, your application can gracefully handle failures and mitigate the impact of transient issues in external services or dependencies. This promotes better resilience, reduces the risk of cascading failures, and improves the overall reliability of your application.

Implementing the Circuit Breaker Pattern to Protect Against Cascading Failures and Reduce Downtime During Critical Errors

Implementing the circuit breaker pattern in Laravel can help protect against cascading failures and reduce downtime during critical errors in your application. Here's how you can do it step-by-step:

Create the circuit breaker class.

Start by creating a circuit breaker class that will manage the state transitions and handle requests to external services or dependencies. This class will be responsible for deciding whether to allow requests to pass through or trigger fallback behavior:

```
namespace App\Services;
use Carbon\Carbon;
class CircuitBreaker
{
    protected $state;
    protected $failureCount;
```

```php
protected $lastFailureTime;
protected $timeoutDuration;
public function __construct(int $failureThreshold, int
$timeoutDuration)
{
    $this->state = 'closed';
    $this->failureCount = 0;
    $this->timeoutDuration = $timeoutDuration;
    $this->failureThreshold = $failureThreshold;
}
public function allowRequest(): bool
{
    if ($this->state === 'open' && $this->isTimeoutExpired()) {
        $this->state = 'half-open';
        return true;
    }
    return $this->state === 'closed';
}
public function reportFailure()
{
    if ($this->state === 'half-open') {
        $this->state = 'open';
    } else {
        $this->failureCount++;
        $this->lastFailureTime = Carbon::now();
        if ($this->failureCount >= $this->failureThreshold) {
            $this->state = 'open';
        }
    }
}
public function reportSuccess()
{
    $this->reset();
}
```

```php
    protected function isTimeoutExpired(): bool
    {
        return Carbon::now()->diffInSeconds($this->lastFailureTime) >=
        $this->timeoutDuration;
    }
    protected function reset()
    {
        $this->state = 'closed';
        $this->failureCount = 0;
        $this->lastFailureTime = null;
    }
}
```

Implement the circuit breaker in API requests.

Use the circuit breaker class to wrap API requests or other external service calls in your Laravel application. Check whether the circuit breaker allows the request to proceed or triggers the fallback behavior:

```php
use App\Services\CircuitBreaker;
use Illuminate\Support\Facades\Http;
class MyController extends Controller
{
    public function makeApiRequest()
    {
        $circuitBreaker = new CircuitBreaker(3, 30); // Allow 3 failures
        within 30 seconds before tripping
        if ($circuitBreaker->allowRequest()) {
            try {
                $response = Http::get('https://api.example.com');
                // Process the API response
                $circuitBreaker->reportSuccess();
            } catch (\Exception $e) {
                // Handle API request failure
                $circuitBreaker->reportFailure();
            }
```

```
        } else {
            // Fallback behavior (e.g., return cached data or default
            response)
        }
    }
}
```

Implement monitoring and logging.

Implement monitoring and logging for the circuit breaker to track state transitions, failures, and fallback events. This will help you identify issues and understand the circuit breaker's behavior in production.

Test and tune.

Test the circuit breaker thoroughly and tune the failure threshold and timeout duration based on the characteristics of the external services and the expected frequency of failures.

By implementing the circuit breaker pattern, your Laravel application can protect against cascading failures, reduce downtime during critical errors, and gracefully handle external service failures. The circuit breaker prevents your application from continuously sending requests to failing services, giving them time to recover and reducing the overall impact on your application's stability and performance.

Summary

This chapter explored advanced error handling and exception management in Laravel. It explained why robust error handling is needed to increase application stability and enhance user experience. You learned custom error pages, exception handling, and logging techniques to gracefully manage unanticipated situations and deliver useful error messages to users. We also discussed global exception handling as well as how to modify error answers for various contexts. We explored the use of third-party services like BugSnag and Sentry to implement error tracking and reporting.

The next chapter will show how Laravel can be used to build internationalized applications.

CHAPTER 15

Building Internationalized Applications with Laravel

In the previous chapter, we explored the critical aspects of advanced error handling and exception management in Laravel, ensuring that our applications can gracefully recover from errors and provide a seamless user experience. As our journey through Laravel's advanced features continues, we now focus on building internationalized applications—a key aspect of catering to a global audience with diverse language and cultural preferences.

Introduction to Internationalization (i18n) and Localization (l10n)

In this section, we will delve into the concepts of internationalization and localization in Laravel. Internationalization (i18n) is the process of designing applications to support multiple languages and regions, while localization (l10n) involves adapting the application to specific languages and cultural preferences. We will understand the importance of i18n and l10n and the benefits they offer for reaching a broader audience.

Configuring Language Files and Translation Strings

Laravel provides robust support for managing language files and translation strings. We will explore how to configure and utilize language files to store translation strings, allowing us to easily translate our application's content into multiple languages.

Translating Database Content and User Input

In this section, we will learn how to translate database content and user input, ensuring that our applications can handle and display data in different languages. We will explore techniques to store and retrieve multilingual data from the database and handle user input in diverse languages.

© Sivaraj Selvaraj 2024

S. Selvaraj, *Building Real-Time Marvels with Laravel*, https://doi.org/10.1007/978-1-4842-9789-6_15

Managing Locale-Specific Views and Assets

Locale-specific views and assets are essential for delivering a tailored user experience. We will discover how to organize and manage views and assets for different locales, presenting the most relevant content and visuals to users based on their language and region.

Implementing Multilingual URLs and URL Routing

Building multilingual URLs and handling URL routing for various locales is crucial for SEO and user navigation. We will explore how to implement multilingual URLs and manage URL routing to ensure users are directed to the appropriate language-specific pages.

Throughout this chapter, we will immerse ourselves in the world of building internationalized applications with Laravel. By adopting internationalization and localization practices, we can create user-friendly and culturally relevant applications that resonate with a diverse global audience. So let's embark on this journey of building internationalized applications to expand the reach and impact of our Laravel projects!

Introduction to Internationalization (i18n) and Localization (l10n)

Internationalization (i18n) and localization (l10n) are essential concepts to understand when developing applications that can cater to users from various regions and cultures. Laravel provides robust internationalization and localization support, making it simple to build applications that can be easily translated into multiple languages and adapted to different locales.

Internationalization (i18n)

Internationalization is the process of designing an application so that it can be easily adapted for different languages and regions without requiring code changes. The goal of internationalization is to make the application adaptable to text expansion, different date and time formats, currency symbols, and other regional differences. Developers can lay the groundwork for a multilingual application by implementing internationalization.

Localization (l10n)

Localization, on the other hand, refers to the process of tailoring an application to a specific locale or language. It entails translating user interface (UI) elements into the target language, such as text labels, messages, and error messages. Localization also includes handling date and time formats, numeric formats, and other region-specific settings to provide users with a consistent experience in their preferred language and culture.

Key Components of Internationalization and Localization in Laravel

Language files

Laravel uses language files ('.php' or '.json') to store translations for different languages. These files contain arrays with key-value pairs, where the keys represent the original text in the application (in the default language) and the values represent the translated text in other languages.

Localization helpers

Laravel provides localization helpers like 'trans ()' and '__ ()' that allow you to access translated strings in your application. These helpers fetch the appropriate translation based on the user's selected locale or the default fallback locale.

Locale detection

Laravel can automatically detect the user's preferred locale based on the HTTP request's language headers. It can also allow users to manually set their preferred language through the application's settings.

Pluralization and language variants

Laravel supports pluralization rules and language variants, allowing you to handle singular and plural forms of words and apply language-specific rules to formatting text.

Date and time localization

Laravel provides built-in support for localizing date and time formats, allowing you to display dates and times according to the user's preferred locale.

With Laravel's built-in features for internationalization and localization, developers can create applications that can serve users from various regions with different language preferences. This ensures that the application's user interface is accessible and user-friendly for a diverse global audience. Throughout this chapter, we will explore how to implement internationalization and localization in Laravel applications, enabling developers to build truly inclusive and multilingual web applications.

Configuring Language Files and Translation Strings
Understanding Language Files

In Laravel, language files play a crucial role in the internationalization process. They act as repositories for translation strings, allowing developers to organize and store user-facing content separately from the application code. This separation is essential as it enables the application to be easily adapted to different languages and regions without having to modify the core application logic.

Language files are typically stored in the 'resources/lang' directory of a Laravel project. Each language file corresponds to a specific locale, such as 'en' for English, 'es' for Spanish, 'fr' for French, and so on. This organizational structure makes it convenient to manage translations for different languages in an efficient and systematic manner.

Creating Language Files

To create a language file, developers can take advantage of Laravel's built-in Artisan command-line tool. By running the following command, Laravel will generate a new language file for the desired locale:

```
php artisan lang:publish {locale}
```

For example, to create a language file for the Spanish (ES) locale, the command would be

```
php artisan lang:publish es
```

Once the language file is generated, it will be stored in the 'resources/lang/{locale}' directory. Let's take a look at an example of how a language file for English and Spanish might look:

```
// English (en) language file: resources/lang/en/messages.php
return [
    'welcome' => 'Welcome to our application!',
    'hello' => 'Hello, :name!',
    'greetings' => 'Greetings!',
];
```

```
// Spanish (es) language file: resources/lang/es/messages.php
return [
    'welcome' => '¡Bienvenido a nuestra aplicación!',
    'hello' => '¡Hola, :name!',
    'greetings' => '¡Saludos!',
];
```

Writing Translation Strings

Translation strings in Laravel follow a simple key-value pair structure. The keys represent the original language, typically English, and the values store the corresponding translations in other languages. For example, the "welcome" key has a translation of "Welcome to our application!" in English and *"¡Bienvenido a nuestra aplicación!"* in Spanish.

To retrieve a translation string in your application, Laravel provides two primary helper functions.

Using the 'trans()' function:

```
echo trans('messages.welcome'); // Output: "Welcome to our application!"
```

Using the '__()' function (double underscore):

```
echo __('messages.welcome'); // Output: "Welcome to our application!"
```

Both of these methods will output the appropriate translation based on the user's locale. If the user's locale is set to Spanish, the 'trans()' or '__()' function will fetch the corresponding translation from the 'resources/lang/es/messages.php' file.

You can also include placeholders in your translation strings to dynamically insert values, for example:

```
// English (en) language file: resources/lang/en/messages.php
return [
    'greet_user' => 'Hello, :name! Welcome to our application.',
];
```

```
// Spanish (es) language file: resources/lang/es/messages.php
return [
    'greet_user' => '¡Hola, :name! Bienvenido a nuestra aplicación.',
];
```

Now, when you use the 'trans()' or '__()' function and pass the 'name' parameter, it will be dynamically inserted into the translation:

```
$name = 'Divya';
echo trans('messages.greet_user', ['name' => $name]);
// Output (English): "Hello, Divya! Welcome to our application."
// Output (Spanish): "¡Hola, Divya! Bienvenido a nuestra aplicación."
```

Overriding Package Translations

Laravel packages often come with their own translations. However, there may be instances where you need to customize these translations to better suit your application's context or to correct any inaccuracies.

Instead of modifying the package's language files directly, Laravel provides a safe way to customize the translations. You can publish the package's language files to your project, allowing you to edit the published files without affecting the original package files.

To publish a package's language files, use the following Artisan command:

```
php artisan vendor:publish --tag=lang --provider=Vendor\\Package\\
ServiceProvider
```

For example, if you have a package named 'example/package', the command would be

```
php artisan vendor:publish --tag=lang --provider=Example\\Package\\
ServiceProvider
```

After running this command, the package's language files will be available in the 'resources/lang/vendor/{locale}' directory, where you can make the necessary adjustments to fit your application's requirements.

Translating Database Content and User Input

Translating Database Content

When building internationalized applications, it is common to have dynamic content that needs to be translated into multiple languages. Content such as user-generated posts, product descriptions, or any other data stored in the database may require translation to cater to users from different language backgrounds.

To handle content translations efficiently, Laravel provides a convenient approach using translation models. The idea is to store the translations of each piece of content in a separate table, associated with the primary table storing the original content. This allows for easy retrieval and management of translations for various languages.

Let's go through the step-by-step process of translating database content in a Laravel application.

Create a Migration for the Translation Table

First, let's create a migration to generate the table that will store the translations. For example, if we have a 'posts' table that stores blog posts in the application, we'll create a corresponding 'post_translations' table to hold the translated versions of each post:

```
php artisan make:migration create_post_translations_table --create=post_
translations
```

In the migration file, define the table structure for storing translations:

```php
// database/migrations/yyyy_mm_dd_create_post_translations_table.php
use Illuminate\Database\Migrations\Migration;
use Illuminate\Database\Schema\Blueprint;
use Illuminate\Support\Facades\Schema;
class CreatePostTranslationsTable extends Migration
{
    public function up()
    {
        Schema::create('post_translations', function (Blueprint $table) {
            $table->id();
            $table->unsignedBigInteger('post_id');
            $table->string('locale');
            $table->string('title');
            $table->text('content');
            $table->timestamps();
        });
    }
    public function down()
    {
        Schema::dropIfExists('post_translations');
    }
}
```

Run the migration.

Execute the migration to create the 'post_translations' table in the database:

```
php artisan migrate
```

Define relationships in Eloquent models.

Next, update the 'Post' model to define the relationship with the 'post_translations' table:

```php
// app/Models/Post.php
use Illuminate\Database\Eloquent\Model;
class Post extends Model
{
    // Your existing model code...
    public function translations()
    {
        return $this->hasMany(PostTranslation::class);
    }
}
```

Similarly, create a 'PostTranslation' model to interact with the 'post_translations' table:

```
php artisan make:model PostTranslation
```

Define the relationship between the 'PostTranslation' and 'Post' models:

```php
// app/Models/PostTranslation.php
use Illuminate\Database\Eloquent\Model;
class PostTranslation extends Model
{
    public function post()
```

```
    {
        return $this->belongsTo(Post::class);
    }
}
```

Store and retrieve translations.

With the translation models set up, you can now store and retrieve translations for each post:

```
use App\Models\Post;
use App\Models\PostTranslation;
// Creating a new post with translations
$post = new Post();
$post->save();
$post->translations()->create([
    'locale' => 'en',
    'title' => 'Hello World!',
    'content' => 'This is the English version of the post.',
]);
$post->translations()->create([
    'locale' => 'es',
    'title' => '¡Hola Mundo!',
    'content' => 'Esta es la versión en español del post.',
]);
// Retrieving translations for a post
$englishPost = $post->translations()->where('locale', 'en')->first();
$spanishPost = $post->translations()->where('locale', 'es')->first();
echo $englishPost->title; // Output: "Hello World!"
echo $spanishPost->title; // Output: "¡Hola Mundo!"
```

Handling User Input in Different Languages

To create a user-friendly experience, your application should support multilingual input for forms and validation messages. This allows users to interact with the application in their preferred language.

Set the application locale.

Laravel allows you to set the application locale dynamically based on user preferences or other criteria. One common approach is to use middleware to detect the user's preferred language and set the application locale accordingly:

```
// app/Http/Middleware/SetLocale.php
namespace App\Http\Middleware;
use Closure;
use Illuminate\Http\Request;
class SetLocale
{
    public function handle(Request $request, Closure $next)
    {
        $locale = $request->getPreferredLanguage(['en', 'es']);
        app()->setLocale($locale);
        return $next($request);
    }
}
```

Don't forget to register the middleware in the 'Kernel.php' file:

```
// app/Http/Kernel.php
protected $middleware = [
    // Other middleware entries...
    \App\Http\Middleware\SetLocale::class,
];
```

Handle multilingual validation.

When validating user input, it's important to show validation error messages in the user's selected language. Laravel provides localization for validation messages, allowing you to define error messages in various languages.

Create a new language file for validation messages:

```
php artisan lang:publish en
```

In the 'resources/lang/en' directory, you'll find a 'validation.php' file where you can customize validation messages:

```
// resources/lang/en/validation.php
return [
    'required' => 'The :attribute field is required.',
    'email' => 'The :attribute must be a valid email address.',
    // Additional validation messages...
];
```

Now, Laravel will automatically use the appropriate validation message based on the user's selected language.

Managing Locale-Specific Views and Assets

When building internationalized applications with Laravel, it's essential to handle locale-specific views and assets. Different languages might require different layouts, images, stylesheets, and other resources to provide an optimized user experience.

In this section, we'll explore how to manage these locale-specific views and assets.

Organizing Locale-Specific Views

To organize locale-specific views, you can create separate directories for each language under the 'resources/views' folder. For example, if you have English and Spanish versions of your views, you can create two folders: 'resources/views/en' and 'resources/views/es'.

Let's say you have a view called 'welcome.blade.php' for the English version and another one for the Spanish version. Place the English version in 'resources/views/en/welcome.blade.php' and the Spanish version in 'resources/views/es/welcome.blade.php'.

To render the appropriate view based on the user's selected locale, you can use the 'view()' function with the locale as a parameter, for example:

```
public function welcome()
{
    return view(app()->getLocale() . '.welcome');
}
```

If the user's locale is set to English, this code will load 'resources/views/en/welcome.blade.php'. If it's set to Spanish, it will load 'resources/views/es/welcome.blade.php'.

Handling Locale-Specific Assets

Assets such as images, CSS files, and JavaScript files may also differ between languages. To handle locale-specific assets, you can create separate directories for each language under the 'public' folder.

For example, create two directories: 'public/en' and 'public/es'. Place the assets specific to the English version in the 'public/en' directory and the assets for the Spanish version in the 'public/es' directory.

When linking to these assets in your views, you can use the 'asset()' helper function and specify the locale in the path, for instance:

```
<!-- Link to the CSS file for English -->
<link href="{{ asset(app()->getLocale() . '/css/styles.css') }}"
rel="stylesheet">
<!-- Link to the CSS file for Spanish -->
<link href="{{ asset(app()->getLocale() . '/css/styles.css') }}"
rel="stylesheet">
```

This will generate the appropriate URLs for the CSS file based on the user's selected locale.

Localization of Asset URLs

In some cases, you may have assets or URLs that need to be fully localized, such as links to external websites or API endpoints specific to a language or region. For this, you can create a language-specific configuration file.

Create a new language-specific configuration file in the 'config' directory. For example, create 'config/en/urls.php' and 'config/es/urls.php'.

Define the URLs specific to each language in the respective configuration files:

```php
// config/en/urls.php
return [
    'api' => 'https://api.example.com/en',
    'website' => 'https://www.example.com/en',
];
// config/es/urls.php
return [
    'api' => 'https://api.example.com/es',
    'website' => 'https://www.example.com/es',
];
```

Use the 'config()' helper function to retrieve the appropriate URL in your application:

```php
// In a controller or view
$apiUrl = config(app()->getLocale() . '.urls.api');
$websiteUrl = config(app()->getLocale() . '.urls.website');
```

Now, '$apiUrl' and '$websiteUrl' will contain the correct URLs based on the user's selected language.

Managing locale-specific views and assets in Laravel involves organizing your view files and assets based on different locales to provide a localized user interface and deliver language-specific assets. By following these practices, you can create a fully internationalized application that caters to users from different language backgrounds, providing a seamless and localized experience.

Implementing Multilingual URLs and URL Routing

Multilingual URLs and URL routing are essential aspects of building internationalized applications with Laravel. They enable users to access language-specific routes and content based on their preferred language. In this section, we'll explore how to implement multilingual URLs and URL routing in a Laravel application.

Setting Up Multilingual Routes

To begin, we need to define language-specific routes in the Laravel application. Instead of manually adding language prefixes to each route, we can use route grouping and parameter binding to achieve this dynamically.

First, define the supported locales and their corresponding language codes in the 'config/app.php' configuration file:

```
// config/app.php
return [
    'locales' => ['en', 'es'],
];
```

Next, create a route group that handles the multilingual routes in the 'routes/web. php' file:

```
// routes/web.php
use Illuminate\Support\Facades\Route;
// Define a route group for multilingual routes
Route::group(['prefix' => '{locale}', 'middleware' => 'locale'],
function () {
    Route::get('/', 'HomeController@index')->name('home');
    Route::get('/about', 'AboutController@index')->name('about');
    // Define more language-specific routes here...
});
```

Create a custom middleware named 'locale' that will handle setting the application locale based on the URL parameter:

```
php artisan make:middleware LocaleMiddleware
```

In the 'LocaleMiddleware' class, handle the application locale based on the URL parameter:

```php
// app/Http/Middleware/LocaleMiddleware.php
namespace App\Http\Middleware;
use Closure;
use Illuminate\Http\Request;
class LocaleMiddleware
{
    public function handle(Request $request, Closure $next)
    {
        $locale = $request->segment(1);
        if (in_array($locale, config('app.locales'))) {
            app()->setLocale($locale);
        } else {
            app()->setLocale(config('app.fallback_locale'));
        }
        return $next($request);
    }
}
```

Register the 'LocaleMiddleware' in the 'Kernel.php' file:

```php
// app/Http/Kernel.php
protected $routeMiddleware = [
    // Other middleware entries...
    'locale' => \App\Http\Middleware\LocaleMiddleware::class,
];
```

Now, when a user accesses a URL like '/en' or '/es', the 'LocaleMiddleware' will set the application locale accordingly, and the route group will handle the request to the appropriate controller.

Generating Multilingual URLs

To generate multilingual URLs in your application, you can use the 'route()' and 'url()' helper functions provided by Laravel:

```
// In a controller or view
// Generating URLs for language-specific routes
$englishUrl = route('home', ['locale' => 'en']);
$spanishUrl = route('home', ['locale' => 'es']);
// Generating absolute URLs for language-specific routes
$englishFullUrl = url('en');
$spanishFullUrl = url('es');
```

By passing the 'locale' parameter in the route function, Laravel will generate URLs with the appropriate language prefix.

Language Switching

To allow users to switch between different language versions of the application, you can create language switcher links in your views:

```
<!-- Language Switcher Links -->
<a href="{{ route('home', ['locale' => 'en']) }}">English</a>
<a href="{{ route('home', ['locale' => 'es']) }}">Español</a>
```

Clicking these links will take the user to the corresponding language-specific routes, and the 'LocaleMiddleware' will handle the application locale accordingly.

With the completion of this chapter, you now have a comprehensive understanding of building internationalized applications with Laravel. You have learned about internationalization, localization, configuring language files, translating content, managing locale-specific views and assets, and implementing multilingual URLs and URL routing.

Summary

In this chapter, you learned how to create internationalized applications using Laravel. The chapter explained how to develop web apps that cater to a global audience by adapting to diverse languages, geographies, and cultures. We also covered Laravel's built-in localization features, as well as how to integrate multi-language support into your apps. We discussed how to translate text, dates, and numbers, as well as how to deal with pluralization and language-specific content. Additionally, you learned how to manage language files, detect user locales, and dynamically swap between multiple translations and best practices for building user interfaces with internationalization in mind.

The next chapter's focus will be using Laravel for advanced frontend development.

CHAPTER 16

Advanced Frontend Development with Laravel

In the previous chapter, we explored the exciting realm of building internationalized applications with Laravel, enabling us to cater to a diverse global audience with multilingual and culturally relevant experiences. As our journey through Laravel's advanced features continues, we now shift our focus to advanced frontend development—a crucial aspect of crafting modern and interactive user interfaces.

Integrating Laravel with Modern Frontend Frameworks

In this section, we will delve into the seamless integration of Laravel with modern frontend frameworks like React, Angular, or Vue.js. We will learn how to set up and configure Laravel to work harmoniously with these frameworks, allowing us to leverage their capabilities to build powerful and responsive user interfaces.

Building Single-Page Applications (SPAs) with Laravel and JavaScript

Single-page applications (SPAs) offer a smooth and dynamic user experience by loading only the necessary content without full page reloads. We will explore how to build SPAs using Laravel and JavaScript, allowing users to navigate and interact with the application seamlessly.

Enhancing User Experience with AJAX and Vue.js Components

AJAX enables us to perform asynchronous data retrieval and update parts of a web page without reloading the entire page. We will learn how to enhance the user experience by implementing AJAX requests and integrating Vue.js components to create reactive and interactive interfaces.

Implementing Real-Time Updates with Laravel Echo and WebSockets

Real-time updates are a game-changer for engaging user experiences. We will explore how to implement real-time updates in our applications using Laravel Echo and WebSockets, enabling instant delivery of new data and updates to connected clients.

© Sivaraj Selvaraj 2024
S. Selvaraj, *Building Real-Time Marvels with Laravel*, https://doi.org/10.1007/978-1-4842-9789-6_16

Throughout this chapter, we will immerse ourselves in the world of advanced frontend development with Laravel. By integrating modern frontend frameworks, building SPAs, and incorporating real-time updates, we can create cutting-edge user interfaces that captivate and delight our users. So let's embark on this journey of advanced frontend development to elevate our Laravel projects to the forefront of modern web applications!

Integrating Laravel with Modern Frontend Frameworks

Integrating Laravel with modern frontend frameworks like React and Vue.js allows you to combine the powerful backend capabilities of Laravel with the dynamic and interactive user interfaces provided by these frameworks.

React

React is a powerful and popular JavaScript library for building user interfaces. Facebook developed it, and a large and active community of developers now maintains it. React is often referred to as a "frontend library" because it focuses solely on the view layer of an application.

It follows a component-based architecture, which means the UI is broken down into reusable and modular components. Each component manages its state and efficiently updates the UI based on changes in data.

Here are ideal scenarios to utilize React:

Large-scale applications with complex UI: React's component-based architecture makes it well-suited for building large-scale applications with complex user interfaces. Components can be organized and managed independently, which enhances code organization and maintainability.

Single-page applications (SPAs): React is an excellent choice for building SPAs, where the application dynamically updates the content on the page without the need for full page reloads. The use of a virtual DOM (a lightweight copy of the actual DOM) allows React to efficiently update only the parts of the UI that have changed, resulting in a smooth user experience.

Data-intensive applications: React's virtual DOM and efficient rendering mechanism make it a good choice for data-intensive applications that require frequent updates to the UI based on changing data. It efficiently handles large datasets and provides seamless user interaction.

Cross-platform development: React can be used with React Native to build mobile applications for iOS and Android using the same codebase. This allows for efficient cross-platform development and code reuse.

Community and ecosystem: React has a vast and active community, which means you'll find plenty of resources, libraries, and tools to support your development needs. The large ecosystem of React-related tools and libraries enables developers to extend and customize their applications easily.

Vue.js

Vue.js is another popular JavaScript framework for building user interfaces. Evan You created it, and its simplicity and ease of use have gained it significant traction. Like React, Vue.js follows a component-based architecture and emphasizes reactivity.

Here are ideal scenarios to utilize Vue.js:

Rapid prototyping and small- to medium-sized projects: Vue.js is known for its ease of use and gentle learning curve. It's an excellent choice for rapid prototyping and smaller projects where a lightweight framework is preferred. Vue.js allows developers to get started quickly and efficiently.

Incremental adoption: Vue.js can be easily integrated into existing projects, allowing developers to incrementally adopt Vue.js components without rewriting the entire application. This makes it a great choice for projects seeking to migrate or add new features without disrupting the current codebase.

Interactive interfaces and real-time applications: Vue.js's reactivity system makes it well-suited for building interactive interfaces and real-time applications where data changes frequently. The framework efficiently updates the DOM based on changes to the underlying data.

SEO-friendly applications: Vue.js supports server-side rendering (SSR), which helps improve search engine optimization and initial load times. SSR ensures that the initial HTML content is served to search engines, which is beneficial for discoverability and SEO rankings.

Documentation and community support: Vue.js has extensive and clear documentation, making it easy for developers to get started and learn the framework. Additionally, Vue.js has a growing community and ecosystem with a wide range of plugins and libraries, offering support and solutions for various use cases.

React and Vue.js are both powerful frontend frameworks with their own unique strengths and ideal use cases. The decision to use one over the other depends on the specific requirements and goals of your project, as well as your team's familiarity with the respective technologies. React is often preferred for large-scale applications with complex UIs and extensive community support.

On the other hand, Vue.js is an excellent choice for rapid prototyping, incremental adoption, or smaller projects, thanks to its simplicity and ease of integration. Ultimately, both frameworks enable developers to build modern and efficient user interfaces, and your choice between React and Vue.js should align with the needs and objectives of your development project.

Here's an overview of how you can integrate Laravel with React or Vue.js.

Setting Up Laravel

Setting up Laravel involves a few steps to get your development environment ready for building Laravel applications. Here's a high-level overview of the process.

Install PHP

Laravel is built on PHP, so you'll need to have PHP installed on your system. You can download the latest stable version of PHP from the official PHP website (`www.php.net/downloads.php`) and follow the installation instructions for your operating system.

Install Composer

Composer is a dependency management tool for PHP, and it is used to install Laravel and its dependencies. You can download Composer from the official Composer website (`https://getcomposer.org/download/`) and follow the installation instructions for your operating system.

Install Laravel

Once you have Composer installed, you can use it to install Laravel globally on your system. Open a terminal or command prompt and run the following command:

```
composer global require laravel/installer
```

This command installs the Laravel installer, which provides a convenient way to create new Laravel projects.

Create a New Laravel Project

With the Laravel installer installed, you can create a new Laravel project by running the following command in your terminal or command prompt:

```
laravel new project-name
```

Replace 'project-name' with the desired name for your project. This command will create a new directory with the specified name and install Laravel and its dependencies into it.

Start the Development Server

Once the project is created, navigate into the project directory by running 'cd project-name' (replace 'project-name' with the actual name of your project). You can start the Laravel development server by running the following command:

```
php artisan serve
```

This command starts a local development server, and you can access your Laravel application by visiting 'http://localhost:8000' in your web browser.

You have successfully set up Laravel on your system. You can now start building your Laravel applications by editing the files in the project directory and exploring Laravel's documentation and features.

Install Dependencies

To install dependencies for a Laravel project, you'll use Composer, which is a dependency management tool for PHP. Here's how you can install dependencies for your Laravel project:

Navigate to the root directory of your Laravel project in a terminal or command prompt.

Run the following command to install the project's dependencies defined in the 'composer.json' file:

```
composer install
```

This command will read the 'composer.json' file, resolve the dependencies, and download them into a 'vendor' directory in your project.

Wait for Composer to download and install the dependencies. This may take a while, depending on the size of the project and the number of dependencies.

Once the installation is complete, Composer will generate an 'autoload.php' file in the 'vendor' directory. This file is responsible for autoloading the classes and files from the installed dependencies.

After installing the dependencies, you can start using them in your Laravel project. Laravel itself and many popular libraries and packages have already defined their dependencies in the 'composer.json' file, so you don't need to worry about manually downloading and managing them.

If you are working on a team project or deploying your Laravel application to a production environment, it is important to include the 'composer.lock' file in your version control system. This file ensures that the exact versions of the dependencies used in the development environment are also used in other environments, providing consistent behavior across different setups.

Additionally, you might have dependencies specific to frontend frameworks like React or Vue.js. To manage those dependencies, you'll typically use npm or Yarn, which are package managers for JavaScript. Laravel Mix, the build tool included with Laravel, simplifies the integration of frontend dependencies into your Laravel project. You can define those dependencies in your project's 'package.json' file and install them using npm or Yarn.

Frontend performance optimization is crucial for delivering a fast and smooth user experience. One of the key techniques to achieve this is by optimizing assets like JavaScript, CSS, and images. In this section, we'll explore how to use asset compilation and minification to improve frontend performance in your web applications.

Configure Laravel Mix

Configuring Laravel Mix allows you to define how your frontend assets, such as JavaScript and CSS files, are compiled and processed. Laravel Mix provides a fluent API that simplifies the build process and asset management in your Laravel project. Here's how you can configure Laravel Mix:

Open your Laravel project's root directory in a text editor.

Locate the 'webpack.mix.js' file. This file is the configuration file for Laravel Mix.

Inside the 'webpack.mix.js' file, you'll see an Illustration configuration. By default, Laravel Mix is set up to compile your application's Sass and JavaScript files.

Specify the entry point for your frontend application. For Illustration, if you're using React, you might have an 'app.js' file that serves as the entry point. If you're using Vue.js, you might have an 'app.js' or 'main.js' file as the entry point. Update the 'mix.js' method call to specify the correct entry point file, for Illustration:

```
mix.js('resources/js/app.js', 'public/js');
```

Optionally, you can configure other asset compilation rules based on your project's needs. Here are some common configuration options:

Compiling Sass or CSS files: Laravel Mix can compile your Sass or CSS files into CSS. You can use the 'mix.sass' or 'mix.css' method to specify the input and output files:

```
mix.sass('resources/sass/app.scss', 'public/css');
```

Versioning: Laravel Mix supports versioning assets to ensure proper cache busting. You can use the 'mix.version()' method to enable versioning. This will append a unique hash to the filenames of your compiled assets:

```
mix.version();
```

Browser compatibility: Laravel Mix includes Autoprefixer by default, which automatically adds vendor prefixes to your CSS rules to ensure compatibility with different browsers.

Additional plugins and customizations: Laravel Mix provides a range of additional plugins and customization options to suit your project's requirements. You can explore the Laravel Mix documentation (`https://laravel-mix.com/docs`) for more advanced configuration options.

Save the changes to the 'webpack.mix.js' file.

Once you have configured Laravel Mix, you can use the Laravel Mix CLI to compile your assets. Open a terminal or command prompt in your project's root directory and run the following command:

```
npm run dev
```

This command will trigger the asset compilation process defined in your 'webpack.mix.js' file. Laravel Mix will compile and bundle your assets based on the specified configuration.

You can also use other commands like 'npm run watch' for real-time asset compilation during development or 'npm run production' for optimized asset compilation for production deployment. These commands are defined in your project's 'package.json' file.

Asset Compilation

Asset compilation involves combining multiple JavaScript and CSS files into a single file to reduce the number of HTTP requests made by the browser. Fewer requests mean faster page loading times. Laravel provides built-in support for asset compilation through Laravel Mix, which is based on the popular Webpack build tool.

Install Laravel Mix by running the following command:

```
npm install laravel-mix --save-dev
```

Configure your asset compilation settings in the 'webpack.mix.js' file at the root of your Laravel project:

```
// webpack.mix.js
const mix = require('laravel-mix');
mix.js('resources/js/app.js', 'public/js')
   .sass('resources/sass/app.scss', 'public/css')
   .version();
```

In this example, we compile the 'app.js' file from the 'resources/js' directory to 'public/js' and the 'app.scss' file from the 'resources/sass' directory to 'public/css'. The '.version()' method adds a version hash to the filenames, enabling cache busting.

Run the following command to trigger asset compilation:

```
npm run dev
```

This will compile your assets and place them in the 'public' directory. You can also use 'npm run watch' to automatically recompile assets during development.

Asset Minification

Minification is the process of removing unnecessary characters and spaces from your JavaScript and CSS files to reduce their size. Smaller files load faster, leading to improved page load times. Laravel Mix also includes built-in support for asset minification.

Install additional dependencies for minification:

```
npm install cross-env cssnano css-loader --save-dev
```

Update your 'webpack.mix.js' file to enable minification:

```
// webpack.mix.js
const mix = require('laravel-mix');
mix.js('resources/js/app.js', 'public/js')
    .sass('resources/sass/app.scss', 'public/css')
    .version()
    .minify(['public/js/app.js', 'public/css/app.css']);
```

In this example, we added the '.minify()' method to minify the compiled 'app.js' and 'app.scss' files.

Run the following command to compile and minify your assets:

```
npm run production
```

The 'npm run production' command is used for generating optimized and minified assets for production use.

Optimizing frontend performance is critical for providing a fast and responsive user experience. By using asset compilation to reduce HTTP requests and asset minification to decrease file sizes, you can significantly improve your application's loading times. Laravel Mix simplifies the process of asset compilation and minification, making it easier for developers to optimize their frontend code.

With these techniques in place, your web application will be better equipped to handle larger user traffic, reduce bounce rates, and provide an overall more enjoyable experience for your users. As you continue to develop and refine your application, be sure to regularly review and optimize your frontend assets to maintain excellent performance.

Create Frontend Components

To create frontend components in your Laravel project, you can use the chosen frontend framework, such as React or Vue.js. Here's a general overview of how you can create frontend components in a Laravel project:

Determine the frontend framework: Decide which frontend framework you want to use, such as React or Vue.js. Make sure you have the necessary dependencies installed, as mentioned earlier.

Choose a location for your components: In Laravel, frontend components are typically stored in the 'resources/js' directory. You can create subdirectories within this directory to organize your components based on your project's structure.

Create a new component file: In the appropriate directory, create a new file with a '.js' or '.vue' extension, depending on the framework you're using.

Define the component: In the component file, define your component using the syntax and conventions of the chosen frontend framework.

If you're using React, define your component using JSX syntax, for Illustration:

```
import React from 'react';
const MyComponent = () => {
  return <div>Hello, World!</div>;
};
export default MyComponent;
```

If you're using Vue.js, define your component using the Vue component options. The following is an illustration of this feature:

```
<template>
  <div>Hello, World!</div>
</template>
<script>
export default {
  name: 'MyComponent',
};
</script>
```

Use the component in your application: Once you've created a component, you can use it in your application by importing it and including it in other components or templates. Depending on the frontend framework, the process of using components may vary.

In React, you can import and use the component in other React components. The following is an illustration of this feature:

```
import React from 'react';
import MyComponent from './path/to/MyComponent';
const App = () => {
  return (
    <div>
      <h1>My App</h1>
      <MyComponent />
    </div>
  );
};
export default App;
```

In Vue.js, you can include the component in the template of other Vue components. The following is an illustration of this feature:

```
<template>
  <div>
    <h1>My App</h1>
    <MyComponent />
  </div>
</template>
<script>
import MyComponent from './path/to/MyComponent';
export default {
  name: 'App',
```

```
  components: {
    MyComponent,
  },
};
</script>
```

Repeat the process for other components: Create additional component files as needed for your application's UI structure and functionality.

Remember to compile your frontend assets using Laravel Mix after creating or modifying components. Run 'npm run dev' to compile the assets during development or 'npm run watch' to watch for changes and automatically recompile them.

This is a basic overview of creating frontend components in a Laravel project using a frontend framework like React or Vue.js. The specific syntax and conventions may differ depending on the framework and your project's requirements. Consult the documentation for the chosen framework for more detailed instructions and best practices when working with components.

Interact with Laravel's Backend

To interact with Laravel's backend from your frontend components, you'll typically make HTTP requests to Laravel's API endpoints. Laravel provides various ways to handle these requests and interact with the backend. Here's an overview of how you can interact with Laravel's backend from your frontend components:

Choosing an HTTP library: To make HTTP requests from your frontend components, you can use JavaScript's built-in 'fetch' API or popular HTTP libraries like Axios. Both options work well with Laravel.

Using 'fetch': The 'fetch' API is built into modern web browsers and provides a simple way to make HTTP requests. Here's an Illustration of making a GET request using 'fetch':

```
fetch('/api/users')
  .then(response => response.json())
  .then(data => {
    // Handle the response data
  })
```

```
  .catch(error => {
    // Handle any errors
  });
```

Using Axios: Axios is a widely used HTTP library that provides a more feature-rich API and additional functionalities. To use Axios, you need to install it in your project using npm or Yarn. Here's an Illustration of making a GET request using Axios:

```
import axios from 'axios';
axios.get('/api/users')
  .then(response => {
    const data = response.data;
    // Handle the response data
  })
  .catch(error => {
    // Handle any errors
  });
```

Choose the HTTP library that best suits your project's needs and follow its documentation for more details on making different types of requests (GET, POST, PUT, DELETE, etc.) and handling response data.

Defining API routes: In Laravel, you'll need to define routes to handle the incoming requests from your frontend components. These routes will map to specific controllers or closures that handle the business logic and return responses.

You can define your API routes in the 'routes/api.php' file. Here's an Illustration of defining a route that responds to a GET request for retrieving user data:

```
<?php
use Illuminate\Support\Facades\Route;
Route::get('/users', 'UserController@index');
```

In this Illustration, the '/users' route is mapped to the 'index' method of the 'UserController'.

Implementing controllers or closures: In your backend, you'll need to implement controllers or closures to handle the requests and return responses.

Controllers provide a structured way to organize your application logic, while closures allow you to define logic inline within your routes.

Using controllers: Create a controller using the 'php artisan make:controller' command or manually in the 'app/Http/Controllers' directory.

In the controller, define methods that correspond to the routes and perform the necessary operations, for Illustration:

```php
<?php
namespace App\Http\Controllers;
use App\Models\User;
class UserController extends Controller
{
    public function index()
    {
        $users = User::all();
        return response()->json($users);
    }
}
```

Using closures: If you prefer using closures, you can define the logic directly within your routes file, for Illustration:

```php
<?php
use Illuminate\Support\Facades\Route;
use App\Models\User;
Route::get('/users', function () {
    $users = User::all();
    return response()->json($users);
});
```

Choose the approach that aligns with your project's structure and requirements.

Handling request data and responses: In your Laravel controllers or closures, you can access the request data, such as query parameters or request bodies, using the 'Request' object. You can also validate the incoming data using Laravel's validation rules.

To return responses, you can use Laravel's response helpers like 'response()->json()' to format the data as JSON and send it back to the frontend.

Here's an Illustration of a controller method that handles a POST request and stores user data:

```php
public function store(Request $request)
{
    $validatedData = $request->validate([
        'name' => 'required',
        'email' => 'required|email',
        // Additional validation rules
    ]);
    $user = User::create($validatedData);
    return response()->json($user, 201);
}
```

This Illustration validates the request data, creates a new user in the database, and returns the created user with a status code of 201 (Created).

By making HTTP requests from your frontend components to Laravel's API endpoints and handling those requests in Laravel's backend controllers or closures, you can establish communication between the frontend and backend.

This allows you to send and receive data, perform CRUD operations, and handle various business logic in your Laravel application.

Routing and Navigation

Routing and navigation play a crucial role in frontend development, especially when building single-page applications (SPAs) or multi-page applications (MPAs).

In a Laravel project, you can handle routing and navigation using various approaches and tools. Here's an overview of how you can manage routing and navigation in your Laravel project.

Laravel Routing Basics

Laravel provides a powerful routing system that allows you to define routes for your application in the 'routes/web.php' file.

These routes handle incoming requests and determine which controller method or closure should be executed.

You can define routes for different HTTP methods (GET, POST, PUT, DELETE) and specify the corresponding URI pattern and associated logic.

Here's an Illustration of defining a basic route in Laravel:

```php
<?php
use Illuminate\Support\Facades\Route;
Route::get('/home', 'HomeController@index');
```

Frontend Routing in SPAs

If you're building a single-page application (SPA) using a frontend framework like React or Vue.js, you'll typically handle routing on the client side.

For React, you can use a library like React Router, and for Vue.js, you can use Vue Router.

Configure your frontend router to handle different routes and map them to specific components. These routes will correspond to the routes defined in your Laravel backend.

Ensure that your Laravel backend has a "catch-all" route that redirects all requests to your SPA's main entry point to prevent conflicts between frontend and backend routes.

Here's an Illustration of configuring React Router to handle routing in a React SPA:

```jsx
import { BrowserRouter as Router, Switch, Route } from 'react-router-dom';
import Home from './components/Home';
import About from './components/About';
const App = () => {
  return (
    <Router>
```

```
    <Switch>
      <Route exact path="/" component={Home} />
      <Route path="/about" component={About} />
      {/* Add more routes */}
    </Switch>
  </Router>
);
};
```

Navigation and Linking

To create navigation links within your application, you can use the appropriate methods or components provided by your frontend framework's routing library.

In React Router, you can use the 'Link' component to create navigation links that trigger client-side routing, for Illustration:

```
import { Link } from 'react-router-dom';
const Navigation = () => {
  return (
    <nav>
      <ul>
        <li>
          <Link to="/">Home</Link>
        </li>
        <li>
          <Link to="/about">About</Link>
        </li>
        {/* Add more navigation links */}
      </ul>
    </nav>
  );
};
```

Generating URLs in Laravel

Laravel provides helper functions and methods to generate URLs for different routes within your application.

The 'url()' helper function generates a fully qualified URL for a given path or route name, for Illustration:

```
$url = url('/path/to/page');
```

Authentication and Route Protection

If you have authentication requirements for certain routes, Laravel offers built-in authentication and authorization features.

You can use middleware to protect routes and ensure that only authenticated users can access them. Laravel provides middleware like 'auth' and 'guest' out of the box.

Here's an Illustration of using the 'auth' middleware to protect a route:

```
Route::get('/profile', 'ProfileController@show')->middleware('auth');
```

Named Routes

Assigning names to your routes in Laravel can simplify the process of generating URLs or redirecting to specific routes.

You can assign a name to a route using the 'name()' method.

The following is an illustration of this feature:

```
Route::get('/about', 'AboutController@index')->name('about');
```

With named routes, you can generate URLs using the 'route()' helper function.
The following is an illustration of this feature:

```
$url = route('about');
```

By properly configuring routing and navigation in your Laravel project, you can ensure that the correct components are rendered for each route, handle client-side routing in SPAs, create navigation links, and secure certain routes based on authentication requirements.

Authentication and Authorization

Authentication and authorization are essential aspects of building secure applications. Laravel provides built-in features and tools to handle authentication and authorization seamlessly. Here's an overview of how you can implement authentication and authorization in your Laravel project.

Authentication

Laravel offers a robust authentication system out of the box, including features like user registration, login, logout, and password reset.

Start by setting up your User model, typically located in the 'app/Models' directory. Laravel provides a default 'User' model, but you can customize it to fit your application's needs.

Configure the database connection and table for storing user information in the 'config/auth.php' configuration file.

Laravel provides authentication routes and controllers that handle the authentication logic. You can use the 'php artisan make:auth' command to generate the necessary authentication scaffolding, including routes, controllers, and views.

Customize the authentication views located in the 'resources/views/auth' directory to match your application's design.

Once set up, you can use Laravel's authentication helpers and methods to manage user sessions, check if a user is logged in, and restrict access to certain routes or actions.

For Illustration, to protect a route, you can use the 'auth' middleware in your route definition:

```
Route::get('/dashboard', 'DashboardController@index')-
>middleware('auth');
```

Refer to Laravel's authentication documentation (`https://laravel.com/docs/authentication`) for detailed instructions and options for customizing authentication features.

Authorization

Laravel also provides robust authorization mechanisms to control access to certain resources or actions based on user roles or permissions.

Laravel's authorization features work in conjunction with authentication. Once a user is authenticated, you can define authorization policies and rules to determine if the user is allowed to perform certain actions.

You can create authorization policies using the 'php artisan make:policy' command or manually in the 'app/Policies' directory. Policies define methods that correspond to specific actions and return 'true' or 'false' based on the user's authorization status.

Associate the policies with the relevant models in the 'AuthServiceProvider' located in the 'app/Providers' directory.

Within your controllers or middleware, you can use Laravel's 'authorize()' method to check if the authenticated user is authorized to perform a specific action:

```
$this->authorize('update', $post);
```

Laravel also provides Blade directives like '@can' and '@cannot' to conditionally display content based on the user's authorization status.

Refer to Laravel's authorization documentation (`https://laravel.com/docs/authorization`) for detailed instructions and Illustrations of implementing authorization in your application.

By implementing authentication and authorization in your Laravel project, you can ensure that only authenticated users have access to certain features, protect routes and resources based on user roles or permissions, and provide a secure environment for your application. Laravel's built-in authentication and authorization features provide a solid foundation, and you can customize them to meet your application's specific requirements.

Compiling and Serving Assets

Compiling and serving assets in a Laravel project involves using Laravel Mix, a build tool that simplifies the compilation and optimization of frontend assets such as JavaScript, CSS, and images. Laravel Mix provides a fluent API for defining asset compilation rules and offers features like asset versioning and code splitting. Here's an overview of how you can compile and serve assets in your Laravel project:

Configure asset compilation.

Open the 'webpack.mix.js' file located in the root directory of your Laravel project. This file serves as the configuration file for Laravel Mix.

Laravel Mix comes pre-configured with some basic compilation rules for JavaScript and CSS. You can customize and add additional rules based on your project's requirements.

For Illustration, to compile a Sass file and output it as a CSS file, you can use the 'mix. sass()' method:

```
mix.sass('resources/sass/app.scss', 'public/css');
```

Similarly, you can use the 'mix.js()' method to compile a JavaScript file:

```
mix.js('resources/js/app.js', 'public/js');
```

Laravel Mix provides many more methods for handling different types of assets, such as images, fonts, and stylesheets. Consult the Laravel Mix documentation (https://laravel-mix.com/docs) for more advanced configuration options.

Define compilation scripts.

In your project's 'package.json' file, you'll find a 'scripts' section. This section defines various scripts for executing commands related to asset compilation.

Laravel Mix provides some default scripts, such as 'dev', 'watch', and 'production'. These scripts are automatically set up for you when you create a new Laravel project.

The 'dev' script compiles your assets for development purposes. The 'watch' script monitors changes to your assets and automatically recompiles them. The 'production' script optimizes and minifies your assets for a production environment.

You can customize or add new scripts to the 'package.json' file based on your needs.

Compile assets.

Open a terminal or command prompt and navigate to the root directory of your Laravel project.

To compile your assets for development, run the following command:

```
npm run dev
```

For automatic recompilation during development, you can run the following command:

```
npm run watch
```

To optimize and minify your assets for a production environment, use the following command:

```
npm run production
```

Serve assets.

After compiling your assets, you can serve them using Laravel's built-in development server or a web server of your choice.

To use Laravel's development server, open a terminal or command prompt and navigate to your project's root directory.

Run the following command to start the development server:

```
php artisan serve
```

Once the server is running, you can access your application in a web browser at 'http://localhost:8000'.

By configuring asset compilation and using Laravel Mix, you can easily compile and optimize your frontend assets in your Laravel project.

Laravel Mix simplifies the build process and provides features like versioning, code splitting, and asset optimization. By following these steps, you can efficiently manage your project's assets and ensure optimal performance.

By following these steps, you can integrate Laravel with React or Vue.js and build powerful web applications that leverage the strengths of both the backend and frontend frameworks.

Remember to refer to the documentation and resources specific to React or Vue.js for more detailed instructions on integrating with Laravel.

Building Single-Page Applications (SPAs) with Laravel and JavaScript

It involves combining the backend capabilities of Laravel with a JavaScript framework like React or Vue.js to create dynamic and interactive user interfaces. Here's an overview of how you can build SPAs with Laravel and JavaScript.

Set Up the Laravel Backend

Start by setting up your Laravel backend, following the steps outlined earlier. Make sure your Laravel project is configured and running properly.

Choose a JavaScript Framework

Select a JavaScript framework like React or Vue.js to build the frontend of your SPA.

You can install React or Vue.js dependencies using npm or Yarn in your Laravel project's root directory.

Create a Frontend Directory

In your Laravel project, create a directory to house your frontend code. Commonly, this directory is named 'resources/js'.

Set Up Routing

Configure Laravel's routing system to allow a single entry point for your SPA.

In the 'routes/web.php' file, define a route that catches all requests and directs them to your SPA's main view or blade file, for Illustration:

```
Route::get('/{any}', function () {
    return view('app');
})->where('any', '.*');
```

In this Illustration, any request will be directed to the 'app.blade.php' view.

Create the Main View

Create the 'app.blade.php' (or a different name of your choice) file in the 'resources/views' directory.

This file will serve as the entry point for your SPA.

Depending on the JavaScript framework you're using, include the necessary script tags to load the framework and your compiled JavaScript assets.

Build Your Frontend Components

In the 'resources/js' directory, start creating your frontend components using the chosen JavaScript framework.

Organize your components into directories based on the structure of your application.

Define and configure your components to handle different parts of your application's UI and functionality.

Handle Client-Side Routing

Utilize the routing system of your chosen JavaScript framework (e.g., React Router or Vue Router) to manage client-side routing within your SPA.

Configure routes, map them to specific components, and handle navigation between different views within your application.

Make API Requests to the Laravel Backend

Use HTTP libraries like Axios or use 'fetch' to make API requests from your frontend components to your Laravel backend.

Send requests to the appropriate Laravel routes and handle the responses in your frontend components.

Use Laravel's built-in APIs and authentication mechanisms to secure the API routes and handle user authentication and authorization.

Compile and Serve Assets

Set up asset compilation and bundling using Laravel Mix, as discussed in a previous section.

Compile and bundle your JavaScript and CSS assets using Laravel Mix's configuration.

Serve the compiled assets using Laravel's development server or a web server of your choice.

Test and Deploy

Test your SPA thoroughly to ensure all functionalities are working as expected.

When ready, deploy your Laravel backend and the compiled frontend assets to a production environment.

Configure your web server to serve the SPA's main view for all routes.

By following these steps, you can integrate Laravel's backend capabilities with a JavaScript framework to build powerful SPAs.

Laravel handles the API and backend functionality, while the JavaScript framework takes care of the frontend rendering and interactivity.

Remember to consult the documentation and resources specific to the chosen JavaScript framework for more detailed instructions and best practices.

Enhancing User Experience with AJAX and Vue.js Components

Enhancing the user experience with AJAX and Vue.js components in a Laravel project allows you to create dynamic and responsive interfaces that can update data without refreshing the entire page.

AJAX (Asynchronous JavaScript and XML) enables you to make asynchronous requests to the server, while Vue.js provides a powerful framework for building reactive components.

Here's an overview of how you can enhance the user experience using AJAX and Vue.js components in your Laravel project.

Install Vue.js

If you haven't already, install Vue.js in your Laravel project using npm or Yarn. Run the following command in your project's root directory:

```
npm install vue
```

This will add Vue.js as a dependency in your project.

Create a Vue Component

In the 'resources/js' directory of your Laravel project, create a new file for your Vue component. For Illustration, create a file named 'IllustrationComponent.vue'.

Define your Vue component in the created file. You can use the Vue Single File Component format, which includes the template, script, and style sections in one file.

For Illustration, a simple Vue component that displays a message could look like this:

```
<template>
  <div>
    <p>{{ message }}</p>
    <button @click="fetchData">Fetch Data</button>
  </div>
</template>
<script>
export default {
  data() {
    return {
      message: '',
    };
  },
```

```
  methods: {
    fetchData() {
      // Perform AJAX request and update the message
    },
  },
};
</script>
<style>
/* Component styles */
</style>
```

Register the Vue Component

Open the 'resources/js/app.js' file and import the created Vue component.

Register the component globally or locally, depending on your needs. For Illustration, here's how to register it globally:

```
import Vue from 'vue';
import IllustrationComponent from './IllustrationComponent.vue';
Vue.component('Illustration-component', IllustrationComponent);
```

Add the Vue Component to a Blade Template

In one of your Blade templates (e.g., 'resources/views/welcome.blade.php'), include the Vue component using the 'Illustration-component' tag or element.

```
<div id="app">
  <Illustration-component></Illustration-component>
</div>
```

Enable Vue.js

In the same 'resources/views/welcome.blade.php' file, add the necessary script tags to enable Vue.js and your compiled JavaScript assets, for Illustration:

```
<script src="{{ mix('js/app.js') }}"></script>
```

Make AJAX Requests

Inside your Vue component's 'fetchData' method, you can make an AJAX request to retrieve data from your Laravel backend.

You can use the 'fetch' API or libraries like Axios to make the request.

For Illustration, here's using Axios:

```
import axios from 'axios';
methods: {
  fetchData() {
    axios.get('/api/data')
      .then(response => {
        this.message = response.data.message;
      })
      .catch(error => {
        console.error(error);
      });
  },
},
```

Configure Laravel API Routes

Define API routes in the 'routes/api.php' file of your Laravel project to handle the AJAX requests from your Vue.js components.

For Illustration, create a route that returns a JSON response:

```php
<?php
use Illuminate\Support\Facades\Route;
Route::get('/data', function () {
    return response()->json([
        'message' => 'Hello from the server!',
    ]);
});
```

Compile and Serve Assets

Compile and bundle your JavaScript assets using Laravel Mix, as discussed earlier.

Use Laravel's development server or a web server of your choice to serve your compiled assets.

By using AJAX and Vue.js components, you can create interactive and responsive user interfaces in your Laravel project. Vue.js components can handle AJAX requests to fetch data from your Laravel backend and update the user interface dynamically.

Remember to refer to the Vue.js and Laravel documentation for more detailed instructions and best practices for working with AJAX and Vue.js components in your project.

Implementing Real-Time Updates with Laravel Echo and WebSockets

Implementing real-time updates in a Laravel project can be achieved using Laravel Echo and WebSockets.

Laravel Echo is a JavaScript library that simplifies subscribing to channels and listening for events, while WebSockets provide a bidirectional communication protocol for real-time updates.

Here's an overview of how you can implement real-time updates using Laravel Echo and WebSockets in your Laravel project:

Install Laravel Echo and Laravel WebSockets.

In your Laravel project's root directory, install Laravel Echo and Laravel WebSockets using npm or Yarn:

```
npm install laravel-echo pusher-js laravel-echo-server
```

Configure Laravel WebSockets.

In your Laravel project, publish the Laravel WebSockets configuration file by running the following command:

```
php artisan vendor:publish --provider="BeyondCode\LaravelWebSockets\
WebSocketsServiceProvider" --tag="config"
```

Open the 'config/websockets.php' file and configure the WebSocket server details, such as host, port, and SSL options.

Set the broadcaster to 'pusher' in your '.env' file:

```
BROADCAST_DRIVER=pusher
```

Start the WebSocket server.

Run the following command to start the Laravel WebSocket server:

```
php artisan websockets:serve
```

The server will be available at the configured host and port.

Subscribe to channels and listen for events in your JavaScript code.

In your frontend JavaScript code, import Laravel Echo and configure it to connect to the WebSocket server.

For Illustration, in your 'resources/js/bootstrap.js' file:

```
import Echo from 'laravel-echo';
window.Pusher = require('pusher-js');
window.Echo = new Echo({
  broadcaster: 'pusher',
  key: process.env.MIX_PUSHER_APP_KEY,
  wsHost: window.location.hostname,
  wsPort: 6001,
  disableStats: true,
});
```

Subscribe to channels and listen for events.
The following is an illustration of this feature:

```
Echo.channel('notifications')
  .listen('NewNotification', (notification) => {
    console.log(notification);
    // Handle the received notification data
  });
```

Trigger events from the Laravel backend.
In your Laravel backend, define events and dispatch them to the appropriate channels.
For Illustration, create an event class 'NewNotification' in the 'app/Events' directory:

```
<?php
namespace App\Events;
use Illuminate\Broadcasting\Channel;
use Illuminate\Contracts\Broadcasting\ShouldBroadcast;
class NewNotification implements ShouldBroadcast
{
    public $notification;
    public function __construct($notification)
```

```
    {
        $this->notification = $notification;
    }
    public function broadcastOn()
    {
        return new Channel('notifications');
    }
}
```

Dispatch the event where necessary, passing the relevant data:

```
event(new NewNotification($notificationData));
```

Authorize channels (optional).

If you want to restrict access to certain channels, you can define channel authorization in your Laravel backend.

Create an authorization class that implements the 'Illuminate\Contracts\Broadcasting\ShouldBroadcast' interface and defines the 'authorize' method to check if the user is authorized to access the channel.

For Illustration, create an authorization class 'NotificationChannel' in the 'app/Broadcasting' directory:

```
<?php
namespace App\Broadcasting;
use App\User;
class NotificationChannel
{
    public function join(User $user)
    {
        // Check if the user is authorized to join the channel
        return true; // or false based on your logic
    }
}
```

Register the authorization class in your 'BroadcastServiceProvider' in the 'app/ Providers' directory.

Test the real-time updates.

With the WebSocket server running and your JavaScript code configured, you can test the real-time updates.

Trigger the necessary events from your Laravel backend, and the subscribed channels in your JavaScript code will receive the events and execute the defined callback functions.

By implementing Laravel Echo and WebSockets in your Laravel project, you can easily add real-time updates and event-driven communication between the backend and frontend. Laravel Echo simplifies the process of subscribing to channels and listening for events, while WebSockets provide the underlying communication protocol. Remember to refer to the Laravel Echo and Laravel WebSockets documentation for more detailed instructions and advanced features.

Summary

In this chapter, you learned advanced frontend programming with Laravel, with a focus on creating strong and dynamic user interfaces. The chapter showed how to integrate new frontend technologies and approaches into the Laravel environment. It introduced you to Laravel Mix, a sophisticated asset compilation tool, and how to use it to manage and optimize frontend assets. We also discussed how to use Vue.js or React.js with Laravel to develop interactive and reactive frontend components, as well as how to use server-side rendering (SSR) to boost SEO and speed.

The next chapter will demonstrate some advanced database optimization techniques.

CHAPTER 17

Advanced Database Techniques and Optimization

In the previous chapter, we explored the exciting realm of advanced frontend development with Laravel, empowering us to create modern and interactive user interfaces that elevate the user experience. As we continue our journey through Laravel's advanced features, we now shift our focus to the heart of every application—the database. In this chapter, we will explore advanced database techniques and optimization strategies to ensure the efficiency, reliability, and scalability of our applications.

Database Indexing and Query Optimization Techniques

In this section, we will delve into the world of database indexing and query optimization. Indexing plays a critical role in improving query performance, and we will explore various indexing techniques to speed up data retrieval and optimize our database queries.

Advanced Database Relationships and Performance Considerations

Database relationships are fundamental to relational databases, but they can have a significant impact on application performance. We will learn how to optimize database relationships and manage performance considerations when dealing with complex relationships.

Implementing Database Replication and Failover Strategies

High availability and data redundancy are essential for mission-critical applications. We will explore how to implement database replication and failover strategies to ensure data availability and recoverability in the event of database failures.

© Sivaraj Selvaraj 2024
S. Selvaraj, *Building Real-Time Marvels with Laravel*, https://doi.org/10.1007/978-1-4842-9789-6_17

Database Partitioning and Sharding for Large-Scale Applications

As applications grow in size and complexity, database partitioning and sharding become crucial techniques for handling large datasets and improving database performance. We will learn how to implement partitioning and sharding strategies to scale our databases for large-scale applications.

Data Migrations and Schema Management in Production Environments

In this final section, we will focus on data migrations and schema management in production environments. We will explore best practices for managing database schema changes without causing disruptions to ongoing operations or data integrity.

Throughout this chapter, we will immerse ourselves in the world of advanced database techniques and optimization in Laravel. By mastering database indexing, query optimization, and advanced database strategies, we can create robust and high-performing applications capable of handling vast amounts of data and delivering a seamless user experience. So let's embark on this journey of database optimization to ensure our Laravel applications are at the peak of efficiency and reliability!

Database Indexing and Query Optimization Techniques

In the world of database management, the efficiency of data retrieval and query performance is paramount to the success of any application. Database indexing and query optimization techniques are essential tools that empower developers and administrators to improve database performance and responsiveness.

This guide will focus on exploring the fundamentals of database indexing and query optimization. We will delve into the concept of indexing, its various types, and how it accelerates data retrieval by reducing query execution time. Understanding how to design and implement efficient database indexes is key to optimizing the performance of large-scale applications.

Moreover, we will examine query optimization techniques to fine-tune SQL queries and reduce resource consumption. By analyzing query execution plans and using profiling tools, developers can identify and address bottlenecks, ensuring optimal query performance.

By the end of this guide, you'll be equipped with the knowledge and insights needed to create high-performing databases and streamline query execution. Whether you are a developer or a database administrator, understanding database indexing and query optimization is critical for building robust and efficient applications. Let's delve into the world of database optimization and harness the power of these techniques to enhance your data-driven systems.

Database Indexing

Database indexing is a technique used to improve the performance of data retrieval operations, such as searching or filtering, in a database system. It involves creating additional data structures called indexes, which store selected columns or fields of a table in a format optimized for efficient searching and retrieval.

Here's an Illustration scenario to illustrate how indexing works.

Suppose we have a database table called "Customers" with the following columns:

CustomerID	FirstName	LastName	Email	Phone
1	John	Smith	john.smith@Illustration.com	123-456-78
2	Emily	Johnson	emily.johnson@Illustration.com	987-654-32
3	David	Brown	david.brown@Illustration.com	456-789-12
...	...	...	...	...

Let's assume we frequently run queries to retrieve customer records based on their email addresses.

Without an index, the database system would need to perform a full table scan, examining each row one by one to find matching email addresses. As the table grows larger, this can become time-consuming and resource-intensive.

To improve the query performance, we can create an index on the "Email" column:

```
CREATE INDEX idx_customers_email ON Customers (Email);
```

The preceding SQL statement creates an index named "idx_customers_email" on the "Email" column of the "Customers" table.

Now, when we execute a query to retrieve customer records based on their email addresses, the database system can leverage the index for faster access.

It will navigate the index data structure, which may be implemented as a B-tree, hash table, or other optimized data structures, to locate the desired email addresses more efficiently.

For Illustration, let's consider the following query:

```
SELECT * FROM Customers WHERE Email = 'john.smith@Illustration.com';
```

With the index in place, the database system can quickly find the relevant customer records by directly accessing the index structure instead of scanning the entire table. This results in significantly improved query performance, especially when the table contains a large number of rows.

It's important to note that indexing comes with certain trade-offs. While indexes improve search and retrieval performance, they also require additional storage space and can slightly impact the performance of write operations (such as insert, update, or delete), as the indexes need to be updated whenever the underlying data changes.

Careful consideration should be given to selecting the columns to index as well as the type of index to use, based on the specific requirements and query patterns of the application.

In practice, a combination of indexing strategies, including B-tree indexes, hash indexes, and bitmap indexes, may be employed to optimize different types of queries effectively.

In summary, database indexing is a powerful technique that enhances query performance by creating additional data structures to facilitate efficient data retrieval.

By creating indexes on frequently accessed columns, the database system can minimize the time and resources required to search for specific values, resulting in significant performance improvements.

Query Optimization

Query optimization is the process of selecting the most efficient execution plan for a given query, aiming to minimize response time and resource utilization. It involves analyzing the query and available database statistics to determine the optimal way to retrieve the required data.

Let's consider an Illustration scenario with a table called "Orders" that contains information about customer orders:

OrderID	CustomerID	ProductID	Quantity	OrderDate
1	101	201	5	2022-05-01
2	102	202	3	2022-05-02
3	101	203	2	2022-05-03
...	...	...	...	...

Suppose we have a query to retrieve the total quantity of products ordered by a specific customer:

```
SELECT SUM(Quantity) FROM Orders WHERE CustomerID = 101;
```

To optimize this query, the database system employs various techniques and strategies:

Indexing: Creating an index on the "CustomerID" column allows the database system to quickly locate the relevant rows without scanning the entire table. The index improves the query's performance by reducing the search space.

Query rewrite: The database system may rewrite the query to a more efficient form based on the available indexes and statistics. For Illustration, it can transform the query to use an index scan instead of a full table scan if an appropriate index exists.

Cost-based optimization: The database system utilizes statistical information about the data and indexes to estimate the cost of different execution plans. It considers factors such as the size of the table, index selectivity, and available system resources. The optimizer evaluates multiple potential execution plans and selects the one with the lowest estimated cost.

Join algorithms: If the query involves joining multiple tables, the optimizer selects the appropriate join algorithm based on the table sizes, indexes, and join conditions. Common join algorithms include nested loop joins, hash joins, and merge joins.

Predicate pushdown: The optimizer may push filtering conditions down the execution plan to reduce the amount of data processed early in the query execution. This helps minimize the data transfer and improve query performance.

By applying these optimization techniques, the database system can generate an efficient execution plan for the query.

The optimizer may determine that using the index on the "CustomerID" column is the most effective approach.

It would then use an index scan to locate the relevant rows and calculate the sum of the "Quantity" column, resulting in optimized query performance.

It's important to note that query optimization is highly dependent on the specific database system and its optimizer capabilities.

The optimizer may employ various strategies and algorithms to find the best execution plan for each query, taking into account factors such as data distribution, available indexes, and system resources.

Query optimization aims to minimize response time and resource utilization by selecting the most efficient execution plan for a given query.

Through techniques like indexing, query rewriting, cost-based optimization, and join algorithms, the database system improves the query's performance and enhances the overall efficiency of the database.

Additional Techniques

Views

A view in a database is a virtual table that is based on the result of a SQL query. It does not physically store data but rather represents a stored query that can be accessed like a regular table. Views provide an abstraction layer, allowing users to interact with complex data structures using simplified and predefined queries.

Here are some key characteristics of views:

Data abstraction: Views hide the underlying complexity of the data model by presenting a simplified and tailored representation of data to users or applications.

Security: Views can be used to restrict access to sensitive data by granting access only to specific columns or rows, providing an additional layer of security.

Ease of use: Views simplify the querying process for end users by predefining complex joins or aggregations, making it easier to retrieve the required data.

No data duplication: Since views do not store data themselves, they eliminate the need for data duplication and reduce storage requirements.

Dynamic data: Views always reflect the most up-to-date data in the underlying tables, ensuring real-time access to information.

Materialized Views

Materialized views, on the other hand, are a physical representation of the result of a SQL query. Unlike regular views, they store data in a separate physical table, which needs to be updated periodically to maintain consistency with the underlying tables. Here are the key characteristics of materialized views:

Data storage: Materialized views physically store the result of the underlying query, which means they require additional storage space.

Precomputed data: The data in a materialized view is precomputed and updated periodically, reducing the need for complex query processing during runtime.

Performance optimization: Materialized views can significantly improve query performance, especially for complex and resource-intensive queries, by providing pre-aggregated or pre-joined data.

Data consistency: Since materialized views are not automatically updated with real-time data changes, there might be a delay between the actual data and the data in the materialized view.

Refresh strategies: Materialized views need to be refreshed periodically to ensure data accuracy. Depending on the requirements, they can be refreshed on demand, at specified intervals, or whenever the underlying data changes.

Comparison

Storage: Regular views do not store data themselves and, therefore, consume minimal storage space. Materialized views, on the other hand, store precomputed data and require additional storage.

Real-time data: Regular views always reflect the real-time data in the underlying tables. Materialized views might not always have the latest data, as they need to be periodically refreshed.

Performance: Materialized views can significantly improve query performance by reducing the need for complex computations during runtime. Regular views, being virtual, might result in slightly slower query performance.

Data updates: Regular views do not require any data updates, as they are based on live data from the underlying tables. Materialized views need to be refreshed or updated periodically to ensure data accuracy.

Use cases: Regular views are suitable for data abstraction, security, and simplifying complex queries. Materialized views are ideal for scenarios where complex queries need to be precomputed and performance optimization is critical.

Materialized Views

Materialized views are precomputed results of queries stored as physical tables. They are particularly useful for complex and frequently executed queries.

By creating and refreshing materialized views, database systems can improve query performance by avoiding expensive computations during query execution.

For Illustration, refer to the following snippet.

Consider a database that stores sales data in a table called "Sales" with columns such as "ProductID", "Date", and "Revenue".

If we frequently execute a query to calculate the total revenue for each product on a daily basis, it can be resource-intensive.

To optimize this query, we can create a materialized view that precomputes the daily revenue for each product and refreshes it periodically:

```
CREATE MATERIALIZED VIEW daily_revenue_mv AS
SELECT ProductID, Date, SUM(Revenue) AS TotalRevenue
FROM Sales
GROUP BY ProductID, Date;
```

Now, instead of executing the complex query on the "Sales" table every time, we can simply query the materialized view:

```
SELECT ProductID, Date, TotalRevenue
FROM daily_revenue_mv;
```

The database system retrieves the precomputed results from the materialized view, reducing query execution time and resource consumption.

Caching

Caching stores frequently accessed data in memory to reduce database queries and improve response times. For example, a web app can cache user profiles, checking the cache first before querying the database, leading to faster performance.

Columnar Storage and Compression

Columnar storage and compression techniques optimize data storage and retrieval for analytical queries on large datasets. Instead of storing data row by row, columnar storage stores the values of each column separately. This improves query performance by reducing the amount of data read from disk.

Additionally, compression techniques can be applied to further reduce the storage size and improve I/O efficiency.

See the following Illustration:

Consider a database table called "StockPrices" that contains columns like "Symbol", "Date", "Open", "High", "Low", and "Close". If we frequently execute queries that analyze the historical prices of a specific stock symbol, columnar storage can be advantageous.

By storing each column separately, the database system only needs to read the "Close" column values for the specified symbol rather than retrieving the entire row. This reduces I/O operations and improves query performance.

Furthermore, applying compression techniques, such as dictionary encoding or run-length encoding, can further reduce the storage footprint and improve data retrieval efficiency.

These additional techniques, including materialized views, caching, and columnar storage, play a significant role in optimizing database performance.

By leveraging these techniques appropriately, database systems can minimize response time, reduce resource utilization, and improve overall efficiency in various scenarios.

By applying these indexing and query optimization techniques, database administrators and developers can enhance the performance of their database systems, reduce response times, and improve overall efficiency.

Advanced Database Relationships and Performance Considerations

This section focuses on advanced database relationships and performance considerations. We'll cover topics such as one-to-one, one-to-many, and many-to-many relationships and discuss their implications for database design and performance.

We'll also explore techniques for optimizing query performance in complex relationships, including denormalization, materialized views, and caching.

In database systems, advanced relationships between tables can impact performance, and it is essential to consider various performance considerations. This section explores advanced database relationships and techniques for optimizing their performance.

Types of Relationships

One-to-one: In a one-to-one relationship, each record in one table is associated with exactly one record in another table. To optimize performance, it is important to minimize unnecessary joins and ensure appropriate indexing on foreign key columns.

One-to-many: In a one-to-many relationship, a record in one table can be associated with multiple records in another table.

To optimize performance, proper indexing, such as creating an index on the foreign key column, is important. Additionally, using efficient join techniques, like nested loop joins or hash joins, can improve performance.

Many-to-many: A many-to-many relationship involves multiple records in one table being associated with multiple records in another table.

It is typically implemented using a junction table. To optimize performance, indexing the foreign key columns in the junction table and using appropriate join techniques are crucial.

Optimization Techniques

Denormalization: Denormalization involves intentionally introducing redundancy into the database schema to improve performance. By duplicating data or introducing derived columns, denormalization can reduce the need for complex joins and improve query performance.

Partitioning: Partitioning involves dividing a large table or index into smaller, more manageable pieces. By distributing data across multiple physical storage devices or servers, partitioning can improve query performance, parallelism, and data management efficiency.

Indexing: Creating appropriate indexes on columns involved in join operations, filtering, or sorting can significantly enhance query performance. Understanding query patterns and using composite indexes or covering indexes can further optimize performance.

Considering these advanced database relationships and implementing suitable optimization techniques can greatly improve the performance and efficiency of database systems.

By understanding the data access patterns, optimizing queries, utilizing appropriate indexing strategies, and employing denormalization or caching, when necessary, database administrators and developers can ensure optimal performance in complex relational scenarios.

Implementing Database Replication and Failover Strategies

Here, we'll delve into the concepts of database replication and failover strategies. We'll discuss various replication techniques, such as master-slave replication, multi-master replication, and synchronous vs. asynchronous replication. Additionally, we'll explore failover strategies like hot standby, cold standby, and automatic failover.

We'll also touch on considerations for ensuring data consistency and handling conflicts in a replicated database environment.

Implementing database replication and failover strategies is crucial for ensuring high availability and fault tolerance in database systems.

Database Replication

First, let's assume we have two database servers: a master server and a slave server. The master server is the primary server that handles write operations, while the slave server replicates data from the master for read operations.

Configure the master server.

In the MySQL configuration file (my.cnf), add the following lines under the [mysqld] section to enable binary logging, which is necessary for replication:

```
server-id = 1
log-bin = mysql-bin
```

Restart the MySQL service to apply the configuration changes.

Create a replication user on the master server.

Connect to the MySQL server as a privileged user and create a dedicated replication user. Grant replication-related privileges to this user:

```
CREATE USER 'replication_user'@'slave_ip' IDENTIFIED BY 'password';
GRANT REPLICATION SLAVE ON *.* TO 'replication_user'@'slave_ip';
FLUSH PRIVILEGES;
```

Replace 'slave_ip' with the IP address of the slave server and 'password' with the desired password.

Configure the slave server.

In the MySQL configuration file (my.cnf) on the slave server, add the following lines under the [mysqld] section to enable replication:

```
server-id = 2
relay-log = mysql-relay-bin
```

Restart the MySQL service to apply the configuration changes.

Start replication on the slave server.

Connect to the slave server's MySQL console and execute the following SQL statements to start replication:

```
CHANGE MASTER TO
  MASTER_HOST='master_ip',
  MASTER_USER='replication_user',
  MASTER_PASSWORD='password',
  MASTER_LOG_FILE='mysql-bin.000001',
  MASTER_LOG_POS=XXX;
START SLAVE;
```

Replace 'master_ip' with the IP address of the master server, 'replication_user' with the replication user, 'password' with the user's password, and 'XXX' with the appropriate log position obtained from the master server.

Once the preceding steps are completed, the slave server will begin replicating data from the master server. Any changes made on the master server will be automatically propagated to the slave server.

It's important to note that this Illustration demonstrates the basic setup of master-slave replication in MySQL.

There are additional considerations and configurations for more advanced replication scenarios, such as configuring replication filters, monitoring replication status, or handling replication failures. Remember to consult the documentation and consider your specific requirements when implementing database replication in your environment.

Failover Strategies

Failover is a crucial aspect of ensuring high availability and reliability in a system. It involves the ability to automatically switch to a backup or standby system when the primary system experiences a failure or becomes unavailable. Here are some common failover strategies:

Active-passive failover: In this strategy, there are a primary (active) system that serves incoming requests and a secondary (passive) system that remains idle until needed. If the primary system fails, the secondary system takes over, becoming the new primary.

Active-active failover: In this approach, multiple systems are active and serving requests simultaneously. If one system fails, the load is distributed among the remaining active systems, ensuring continuous service availability.

Load balancer–based failover: A load balancer can distribute incoming requests across multiple servers. If a server fails, the load balancer redirects traffic to other healthy servers, ensuring seamless failover.

Database replication: Replicating databases across multiple servers can provide failover capabilities. If the primary database fails, the standby database takes over, minimizing data loss.

Cloud provider failover services: Cloud service providers like AWS Relational Database Service (RDS) offer built-in failover and replication options. For example, AWS RDS provides Multi-AZ (Availability Zone) deployment for high availability, automatically replicating data to a standby instance in a different Availability Zone.

Amazon RDS Multi-AZ with One Standby

When using Laravel with Amazon RDS Multi-AZ with one standby, the Laravel application can take advantage of the high availability and automatic failover capabilities provided by the Multi-AZ setup. Laravel's database configuration needs to be properly set up to connect to the Amazon RDS Multi-AZ deployment. Here's how you can do it.

Set Up Amazon RDS Multi-AZ Deployment

Create an Amazon RDS Multi-AZ MySQL or PostgreSQL database using the AWS Management Console.

Laravel Configuration

Open the .env file in your Laravel project and update the database configuration with the Amazon RDS endpoint, username, password, and database name:

```
DB_CONNECTION=mysql
DB_HOST=<your_amazon_rds_endpoint>
DB_PORT=3306
DB_DATABASE=<your_database_name>
DB_USERNAME=<your_database_username>
DB_PASSWORD=<your_database_password>
```

Laravel's database configuration should now point to your Amazon RDS Multi-AZ MySQL or PostgreSQL database.

Use Laravel's Eloquent ORM

With the database configured, you can use Laravel's Eloquent ORM to interact with the database. Define models and use them to perform database operations:

```
// Example Model: User.php
namespace App\Models;
use Illuminate\Database\Eloquent\Model;
class User extends Model
```

```
{
    protected $table = 'users';
    protected $fillable = ['name', 'email', 'password'];
}
```

Laravel Code Snippets

Query data from the database:

```
// Retrieve all users
$users = \App\Models\User::all();
// Retrieve a user by ID
$user = \App\Models\User::find(1);
// Retrieve users by conditions
$users = \App\Models\User::where('age', '>', 25)->get();
```

Insert data into the database:

```
// Create a new user
$user = new \App\Models\User();
$user->name = 'John Doe';
$user->email = 'john@example.com';
$user->password = bcrypt('secret');
$user->save();
```

Update the data in the database:

```
// Update a user by ID
$user = \App\Models\User::find(1);
$user->name = 'Updated Name';
$user->save();
```

Delete data from the database:

```
// Delete a user by ID
$user = \App\Models\User::find(1);
$user->delete();
```

By using Laravel with Amazon RDS Multi-AZ with one standby, you can take advantage of the automatic failover capabilities and ensure high availability for your application's database. Laravel's Eloquent ORM provides a convenient and straightforward way to interact with the database, making it easy to build reliable and performant applications on AWS.

Amazon RDS Multi-AZ with Two Readable Standbys

The Laravel application can leverage the high availability and read scalability provided by the Multi-AZ setup when it uses Laravel with Amazon RDS Multi-AZ with two readable standbys. With two readable standbys, you can offload read traffic from the primary instance and improve overall database performance.

Here's how you can set it up.

Set Up Amazon RDS Multi-AZ Deployment

Create an Amazon RDS Multi-AZ MySQL or PostgreSQL database using the AWS Management Console.

Laravel Configuration

Open the '.env' file in your Laravel project and update the database configuration with the Amazon RDS endpoint, username, password, and database name:

```
DB_CONNECTION=mysql
DB_HOST=<your_amazon_rds_endpoint>
DB_PORT=3306
```

```
DB_DATABASE=<your_database_name>
DB_USERNAME=<your_database_username>
DB_PASSWORD=<your_database_password>
```

Laravel's database configuration should now point to your Amazon RDS Multi-AZ MySQL or PostgreSQL database.

Use Laravel's Eloquent ORM

With the database configured, you can use Laravel's Eloquent ORM to interact with the database. Define models and use them to perform database operations:

```php
// Example Model: User.php
namespace App\Models;
use Illuminate\Database\Eloquent\Model;
class User extends Model
{
    protected $table = 'users';
    protected $fillable = ['name', 'email', 'password'];
}
```

Laravel Code Snippets

Query data from the database:

```php
// Retrieve all users
$users = \App\Models\User::all();
// Retrieve a user by ID
$user = \App\Models\User::find(1);
// Retrieve users by conditions
$users = \App\Models\User::where('age', '>', 25)->get();
```

Insert data into the database:

```
// Create a new user
$user = new \App\Models\User();
$user->name = 'John Doe';
$user->email = 'john@example.com';
$user->password = bcrypt('secret');
$user->save();
```

Update data in the database:

```
// Update a user by ID
$user = \App\Models\User::find(1);
$user->name = 'Updated Name';
$user->save();
```

Delete the data from the database:

```
// Delete a user by ID
$user = \App\Models\User::find(1);
$user->delete();
```

Utilize Readable Standbys for Read Scaling

To offload read traffic from the primary instance, you can configure Laravel to connect to the readable standbys for read-only operations.

In the Laravel database configuration file ('config/database.php'), define additional read connections using the read-only endpoints of the standbys:

```
'connections' => [
    // ...
    'mysql_readonly1' => [
```

```
        'driver' => 'mysql',
        'host' => '<readable_standby_1_endpoint>',
        'port' => '3306',
        'database' => '<your_database_name>',
        'username' => '<your_readonly_username>',
        'password' => '<your_readonly_password>',
        'read' => true,
    ],
    'mysql_readonly2' => [
        'driver' => 'mysql',
        'host' => '<readable_standby_2_endpoint>',
        'port' => '3306',
        'database' => '<your_database_name>',
        'username' => '<your_readonly_username>',
        'password' => '<your_readonly_password>',
        'read' => true,
    ],
    // ...
],
```

Now, you can use the read connections for read-only database operations in your Laravel:

```
// Use the first readable standby for read-only queries
$users = \App\Models\User::on('mysql_readonly1')->get();
// Use the second readable standby for read-only queries
$users = \App\Models\User::on('mysql_readonly2')->get();
```

By using Laravel with Amazon RDS Multi-AZ with two readable standbys, you can achieve high availability, automatic failover, and read scalability for your application's database. The readable standbys allow you to distribute read traffic across multiple instances, providing improved performance and responsiveness for your application users.

Tip for Failover and Replication with AWS RDS

AWS RDS (Relational Database Service) simplifies database management by automating routine tasks like backups, patch management, and scaling. It offers Multi-AZ deployment, which is a failover solution designed to ensure high availability. In Multi-AZ, AWS RDS automatically provisions and maintains a synchronous standby replica in a different Availability Zone. If the primary database becomes unavailable, AWS RDS automatically promotes the standby replica to the primary instance, providing seamless failover with minimal downtime.

Using AWS RDS for failover and replication can be advantageous because it's user-friendly and managed by AWS, reducing the operational burden on users. With AWS RDS Multi-AZ, users can achieve high availability and data durability without complex manual configurations.

By implementing robust database replication and failover strategies, organizations can ensure high availability, fault tolerance, and data consistency in the event of server failures or outages. Careful consideration of replication models, failover mechanisms, network infrastructure, and monitoring can help maintain a resilient database environment.

Database Partitioning and Sharding for Large-Scale Applications

In this section, we'll explore the concepts of database partitioning and sharding, which are essential for scaling databases in large-scale applications. We'll discuss different partitioning techniques, such as range partitioning, hash partitioning, and list partitioning, and their advantages and trade-offs. Additionally, we'll delve into sharding strategies and their implementation considerations, including data distribution, load balancing, and query routing.

In large-scale applications, database partitioning and sharding techniques are employed to handle the increased volume of data and user traffic efficiently. This section explores the concepts of database partitioning and sharding and their application in large-scale environments.

Database Partitioning

Database partitioning is the process of breaking a large database table into smaller, more manageable partitions, each containing a subset of the data. These partitions are distributed across different physical storage devices or servers. Partitioning can be done using various methods, such as range-based partitioning (based on a specific range of values) or hash-based partitioning (based on a hash function).

In Laravel, you can use the "Laravel Partitioning" package to easily implement database partitioning. This package supports both range- and hash-based partitioning. To set up database partitioning, follow these steps:

Install the Laravel Partitioning package.

```
composer require awjudd/laravel-partitioning
```

Prepare the database table.

Modify the migration for the large table that you want to partition, for example:

```
use Illuminate\Database\Migrations\Migration;
use Illuminate\Database\Schema\Blueprint;
use Illuminate\Support\Facades\Schema;
use Awjudd\Partition\Commands\Partition;
class CreateOrdersTable extends Migration
{
    public function up()
    {
        Schema::create('orders', function (Blueprint $table) {
            $table->id();
            $table->unsignedBigInteger('user_id');
            $table->integer('amount');
            $table->timestamp('order_date');
            $table->timestamps();
        });
```

```
        // Add partition for the 'order_date' column
        Partition::add('orders', 'order_date');
    }
    public function down()
    {
        Schema::dropIfExists('orders');
    }
}
```

Configure the partitioning.

Add the partitioning configuration to your `config/partitioning.php` file. For example:

```
return [
    'orders' => [
        'mode' => 'range', // You can also use 'hash' mode
        'column' => 'order_date',
        'partitions' => [
            '2023-01-01' => 'p1',
            '2023-02-01' => 'p2',
            // Define more partition boundaries and names as needed
        ],
    ],
];
```

Database Sharding

Database sharding involves distributing data across multiple database servers, with each server handling a specific subset of the data. Sharding is commonly done using a shard key, which determines the shard (database server) to which the data belongs.

In Laravel, there are various approaches to implementing sharding. One common approach is using the "Laravel Multi-Tenancy" package, which allows you to shard data based on a tenant identifier.

To implement database sharding using the Laravel Multi-Tenancy package, follow these steps:

Install the Laravel Multi-Tenancy package.

```
composer require hyn/multi-tenant
```

Configure Multi-Tenancy.

Configure the package according to your database and tenancy requirements. You'll need to create a new Tenant model, database, and tenant middleware for managing tenants.

Shard the 'orders' table.

Use the tenant identifier (e.g., user ID or account ID) as the shard key, for example:

```php
use Illuminate\Database\Eloquent\Model;
class Order extends Model
{
    // ...
    /**
    * Get the connection name for the shard.
    *
    * @return string
    */
    public function getConnectionName()
    {
        // Get the tenant identifier (user ID) and append it to the default
        connection name.
        return 'tenant_' . $this->user_id % 5; // 5 represents the number
        of shards/servers.
    }
}
```

Update database config.

Update your database configuration in `config/database.php` to include multiple shard connections:

```
return [
    'connections' => [
        'tenant_0' => [
            // Configuration for Shard 0
            // ...
        ],
        'tenant_1' => [
            // Configuration for Shard 1
            // ...
        ],
        // Add more shard connections as needed
    ],
];
```

These explanations and code snippets should give you a good starting point for implementing database partitioning and sharding in your large-scale Laravel applications.

Considerations

Data distribution: The distribution of data across partitions or shards should be carefully planned to ensure even data distribution and a balanced query load. Uneven data distribution can lead to performance issues and hotspots.

Data consistency: Maintaining data consistency in a partitioned or sharded database environment requires special attention. Techniques like distributed transactions, eventual consistency, or consensus algorithms may be employed based on the application's requirements.

Data joins: Performing joins across multiple partitions or shards can be challenging. Techniques like distributed joins, denormalization, or data duplication may be employed to handle join operations efficiently.

System monitoring: Monitoring the performance, health, and resource utilization of individual partitions or shards is crucial to ensuring optimal system performance and identifying potential issues.

By implementing database partitioning and sharding techniques, organizations can achieve scalability and improved performance in large-scale applications. Proper planning of data distribution, careful consideration of data consistency mechanisms, and efficient query routing are key factors in successful implementation.

Data Migrations and Schema Management in Production Environments

This section focuses on data migrations and schema management in production environments. We'll discuss techniques for performing seamless data migrations, including schema changes, data transformations, and data synchronization between different database versions. We'll explore strategies for minimizing downtime and ensuring data integrity during migrations. Additionally, we'll touch upon schema management best practices, version control, and the importance of backward compatibility.

In production environments, data migrations and schema management are critical aspects of managing databases. This section explores the challenges and best practices for performing data migrations and effectively managing database schemas in production.

Data Migrations

Data migrations are used to modify or transform existing data in your production database when deploying changes to the application. Data migrations are different from regular database migrations, which primarily deal with the schema structure.

The need for data migration arises when you need to

Update existing data to conform to new data structures or formats.

Populate newly added columns with default values.

Perform data transformations to adapt to application changes.

Best Practices for Data Migrations

Always create backups: Before running data migrations in production, it's essential to create a backup of the database. This ensures that you can roll back in case something goes wrong during the migration process.

Test data migrations thoroughly: Test the data migration on a staging or development environment first to ensure it works as expected. This helps identify any issues before applying it to the production database.

Atomic migrations: When dealing with complex data migrations, consider wrapping your migration in a transaction to make it atomic. This ensures that the migration either fully succeeds or fully fails, preventing inconsistencies.

Use database transactions: When updating large datasets, consider using database transactions to optimize the migration process and reduce the risk of data corruption.

Version control data migrations: Keep data migrations under version control to track changes over time. This makes it easier to manage and roll back migrations if needed.

Here's an example data migration.

Let's assume that we want to add a new column 'status' to the existing 'users' table and populate it with default values for all existing records.

Create a new data migration:

```
php artisan make:migration add_status_to_users --data
```

Edit the migration file to define the data migration logic:

```php
// database/migrations/20230806120000_add_status_to_users.php
use Illuminate\Database\Migrations\Migration;
use Illuminate\Database\Schema\Blueprint;
use Illuminate\Support\Facades\Schema;
class AddStatusToUsers extends Migration
{
    public function up()
    {
        Schema::table('users', function (Blueprint $table) {
            $table->string('status')->default('active');
```

```
    });
    // Populate the 'status' column with default value 'active'
    DB::table('users')->update(['status' => 'active']);
}
public function down()
{
    Schema::table('users', function (Blueprint $table) {
        $table->dropColumn('status');
    });
}
}
```

Schema Management

Schema management involves creating and modifying database tables and columns to reflect changes in your application's data structure. In Laravel, schema management is achieved through database migrations and the Schema Builder.

Here are best practices for schema management:

Create small migrations: It's generally better to create several small, focused migrations rather than one large migration. This makes it easier to manage and roll back changes if needed.

Use timestamps: By default, Laravel's migrations include timestamps in the migration filename. This ensures that migrations are executed in the order they were created, helping prevent dependency issues.

Avoid direct SQL queries: Use Laravel's Schema Builder methods to define the schema changes. Avoid writing raw SQL queries directly in the migration files to maintain code consistency and cross-database compatibility.

Keep track of table alterations: Be mindful of the impact of altering existing tables with a significant amount of data. Some alterations may require additional downtime or cause performance issues during the migration.

Rollback plan: Always have a plan to roll back migrations in case something goes wrong during the deployment. This involves having backups and testing rollbacks beforehand.

Here's an example schema migration.

Let's create a new migration to modify the orders table by adding a new column, total_amount.

Create a new migration:

```
php artisan make:migration add_total_amount_to_orders
```

Edit the migration file to define the schema changes:

```php
// database/migrations/20230807103000_add_total_amount_to_orders.php
use Illuminate\Database\Migrations\Migration;
use Illuminate\Database\Schema\Blueprint;
use Illuminate\Support\Facades\Schema;
class AddTotalAmountToOrders extends Migration
{
    public function up()
    {
        Schema::table('orders', function (Blueprint $table) {
            $table->decimal('total_amount', 10, 2)->after('amount');
        });
    }
    public function down()
    {
        Schema::table('orders', function (Blueprint $table) {
            $table->dropColumn('total_amount');
        });
    }
}
```

Remember to create backups and thoroughly test the data migrations and schema changes in a staging or development environment before running them in production. Always have a rollback plan in case something goes wrong during the migration process. Following these best practices will help you manage data and schema changes effectively and maintain a healthy database in your production environment.

By following best practices for data migrations and schema management, organizations can minimize disruptions, maintain data integrity, and effectively manage the evolution of their databases in production environments.

Proper planning, thorough testing, version control, documentation, and change management processes are key elements in successful data migration and schema management practices.

Summary

In this chapter, we explored sophisticated database strategies and optimization in the context of Laravel web development with an eye toward increasing the efficiency and performance of database operations. You learned about query optimization, indexing, and caching strategies that can be used to reduce query execution times and increase overall database performance. We covered various approaches for dealing with huge datasets, optimizing database schema design, and enhancing performance with database-specific features. You learned about the importance of database profiling and performance tuning in order to detect and address bottlenecks.

We will cover serverless computing as it relates to Laravel in the next chapter.

CHAPTER 18

Laravel and Serverless Computing

In the previous chapter, we explored the vital realm of advanced database techniques and optimization in Laravel, ensuring the efficiency and scalability of our applications' data layer. As our journey through Laravel's advanced features continues, we now venture into the world of serverless computing—a paradigm that revolutionizes application development and deployment.

Introduction to Serverless Architecture and Function as a Service (FaaS)

In this section, we will delve into the principles and concepts of serverless architecture and Function as a Service (FaaS). Serverless computing allows us to build and deploy applications without the need to actively manage the underlying servers. We will understand how FaaS enables us to focus on writing code for specific functions, relieving us of server maintenance and scalability concerns.

Integrating Laravel with Serverless Platforms

Laravel, known for its versatility and flexibility, can be integrated with serverless platforms. We will explore how to adapt Laravel to work seamlessly in a serverless environment, allowing us to leverage the benefits of serverless computing while leveraging the power of the Laravel framework.

Scaling Laravel with Serverless Auto-scaling and Event Triggers

Serverless platforms offer dynamic scaling capabilities, automatically adjusting resources based on incoming workloads. We will learn how to scale Laravel applications with serverless auto-scaling, ensuring optimal performance and cost efficiency. Additionally, we will explore how event triggers can be utilized to trigger Laravel functions in response to specific events.

© Sivaraj Selvaraj 2024
S. Selvaraj, *Building Real-Time Marvels with Laravel*, https://doi.org/10.1007/978-1-4842-9789-6_18

Monitoring and Debugging Serverless Laravel Applications

In this final section, we will focus on monitoring and debugging serverless Laravel applications. We will explore tools and techniques to monitor the performance of serverless functions and troubleshoot potential issues in the serverless environment.

Throughout this chapter, we will immerse ourselves in the world of serverless computing and its integration with Laravel. By adopting serverless architecture, we can build highly scalable and cost-effective applications that automatically adjust to meet user demands. So let's embark on this journey of serverless computing and Laravel to revolutionize the way we deploy and manage our applications!

Introduction to Serverless Architecture and Function as a Service (FaaS)

Serverless architecture and Function as a Service (FaaS) have emerged as game-changing paradigms in the world of cloud computing. This revolutionary approach allows developers to build and deploy applications without the burden of managing servers and infrastructure. By focusing solely on writing code, developers can enjoy increased agility, reduced operational overhead, and cost efficiency.

In this guide, we will explore the principles of serverless architecture and delve into the world of Function as a Service. We'll discuss how serverless computing enables rapid development, automatic scaling, and event-driven execution of code. Additionally, we'll explore popular serverless platforms, such as AWS Lambda, Google Cloud Functions, and Microsoft Azure Functions, that facilitate a seamless serverless environment.

Understanding the benefits and use cases of serverless architecture empowers developers and organizations to optimize resources, increase scalability, and accelerate application development. Whether you are a developer exploring new possibilities or an organization seeking to streamline your cloud infrastructure, embracing serverless architecture and Function as a Service can elevate your development journey. Let's begin this exploration into the realm of serverless computing and unlock its potential for transforming the way we build and deploy applications.

The Benefits of Serverless Architecture and FaaS

Reduced operational overhead: Developers don't need to worry about server provisioning, scaling, or maintenance.

Cost optimization: You pay only for the compute resources consumed during function execution, rather than paying for idle server time.

Scalability: Serverless platforms automatically scale functions based on incoming requests, ensuring applications can handle varying workloads.

Event-driven approach: Various events, such as HTTP requests, database changes, or time-based schedules, can trigger functions.

Microservices architecture: Serverless promotes a microservices approach, where each function can represent a specific task or feature of the application.

Here are some key characteristics of serverless architecture and FaaS:

Event-driven execution: Specific events, such as HTTP requests, database changes, file uploads, or scheduled tasks, trigger functions in a serverless architecture. Each function performs a specific task and is invoked independently.

Pay-per-use pricing: Serverless platforms charge based on the actual usage of functions, rather than a fixed cost for maintaining servers. Each function invocation consumes execution time and resources, and they bill you only for that.

Automatic scaling: Serverless platforms handle the scaling of functions automatically. They allocate resources dynamically based on the incoming workload. Functions can scale up or down in response to demand, ensuring efficient resource utilization.

Stateless functions: Functions in serverless architectures are typically stateless, meaning they don't store any persistent data between invocations. Any required data or state is passed as input parameters or retrieved from external storage services.

Reduced operational overhead: With serverless architectures, the cloud provider handles infrastructure management, including server provisioning, operating system updates, and load balancing. This allows developers to focus on writing code and delivering functionality.

Overall, serverless architecture and FaaS provide a flexible and scalable approach to building applications, allowing developers to focus on writing code while taking advantage of automatic scaling and reduced operational overhead.

Integrating Laravel with Serverless Platforms

Serverless Providers

Serverless providers are cloud computing platforms that offer Function as a Service (FaaS) capabilities, allowing developers to deploy individual functions that run in response to specific events. These providers manage the underlying infrastructure and scaling automatically, enabling developers to focus solely on writing the code for their functions. Here are some popular serverless providers:

AWS Lambda: Amazon Web Services (AWS) Lambda is one of the leading serverless platforms. It supports multiple programming languages, including Node.js, Python, Java, C#, and Go. Various events, such as HTTP requests, changes to data in AWS services (e.g., S3, DynamoDB), scheduled events, and custom events, trigger Lambda functions.

Google Cloud Functions: Google Cloud Functions is part of the Google Cloud Platform (GCP) and supports Node.js, Python, and Go languages. It integrates seamlessly with other GCP services, such as Cloud Storage, Cloud Pub/Sub, and Cloud Firestore, to trigger functions based on events.

Azure Functions: Microsoft Azure Functions is a serverless offering in Microsoft Azure, supporting C#, JavaScript, Java, Python, and PowerShell. Events from Azure services, HTTP requests, and time-based schedules can trigger it.

IBM Cloud Functions: IBM Cloud Functions, also known as IBM Cloud OpenWhisk, allows developers to write functions in Node.js, Python, Java, and Swift. It integrates well with other IBM Cloud services and external event sources.

Alibaba Cloud Function Compute: Alibaba Cloud Function Compute is part of Alibaba Cloud and supports Node.js, Python, and Java. It is tightly integrated with other Alibaba Cloud services for event triggering.

Vercel: Vercel is a platform optimized for frontend deployment, but it also supports serverless functions. It is designed for building Jamstack applications and supports popular frontend frameworks like React, Vue.js, and Next.js.

Each serverless provider has its own unique features, pricing models, and integrations with other cloud services. Developers can choose the provider that best fits their application requirements, development expertise, and existing cloud infrastructure.

AWS Lambda is commonly used due to its extensive feature set, flexibility, and wide adoption, but other providers may be more suitable for specific use cases or for organizations with existing cloud platform preferences.

Integrating Laravel, a PHP web application framework, with serverless platforms like AWS Lambda can bring several benefits, such as cost optimization, scalability, and simplified deployment. Here's a detailed explanation of how you can integrate Laravel with AWS Lambda.

Decompose Your Laravel Application

Identify the parts of your Laravel application that can be split into smaller, independent functions. For example, you can convert specific API endpoints or background tasks into individual Lambda functions. Let's consider an example where we have an API endpoint in Laravel that handles user registration.

Write a Lambda function.

Create a separate PHP function that will handle the user registration logic. This function should use the necessary Laravel components to perform the registration process. Here's an example of what the Lambda function might look like:

```php
<?php
use Illuminate\Support\Facades\Validator;
require '/path/to/laravel/bootstrap/app.php';
function registerUser($event)
{
    // Retrieve the necessary data from the event
    $name = $event['name'];
    $email = $event['email'];
    $password = $event['password'];
    // Validate the input data
    $validator = Validator::make(
        compact('name', 'email', 'password'),
        [
            'name' => 'required',
            'email' => 'required|email',
            'password' => 'required|min:6',
        ]
    );
```

```
if ($validator->fails()) {
    // Handle validation errors and return a response
    return [
        'statusCode' => 400,
        'body' => $validator->errors(),
    ];
}
// Perform user registration logic using Laravel's ORM or any other
necessary components
// ...
// Return a success response
return [
    'statusCode' => 200,
    'body' => 'User registered successfully',
];
}
```

Package your function.

Use a tool like the Serverless Framework or AWS SAM (Serverless Application Model) to package your Lambda function along with any required dependencies. These tools allow you to define the function's configuration and specify any necessary resources.

Deploy to AWS Lambda.

Deploy your packaged function to AWS Lambda using the chosen deployment tool. This will provision the necessary resources and configure the event triggers for the function. Here's an example configuration using the Serverless Framework:

```
service: my-laravel-service
provider:
  name: aws
  runtime: provided.al2
  region: us-east-1
functions:
  registerUser:
    handler: registerUser
```

```
events:
  - http:
      path: register
      method: post
```

Configure the API gateway.

If you want to expose the Lambda function as an API endpoint, you can use Amazon API Gateway to handle the routing and invocation. Configure the necessary endpoints and map them to the corresponding functions. In the preceding Serverless Framework example, the 'registerUser' function is mapped to the '/register' path with the HTTP POST method.

Handle database connections.

Since AWS Lambda functions are stateless and short-lived, you may need to adapt your Laravel application to handle database connections more efficiently. Consider using connection pooling or caching mechanisms to minimize the overhead of establishing new connections for each function invocation.

Configure environment variables.

Store any necessary configuration values, such as database credentials or API keys, as environment variables in your Lambda function. This allows you to keep sensitive information separate from your code. AWS Lambda provides a mechanism to set environment variables through the console or deployment configurations.

By following these steps, you can integrate Laravel with AWS Lambda and leverage the benefits of serverless computing, such as automatic scaling, cost optimization, and simplified deployment. Remember to refer to the documentation and resources provided by AWS and Laravel for more detailed instructions and best practices.

Scaling Laravel with Serverless Auto-scaling and Event Triggers

Serverless Auto-scaling

One of the key advantages of serverless computing is its inherent auto-scaling capability. Serverless platforms automatically scale the number of function instances in response to incoming requests. We'll explore how Laravel applications can benefit from serverless auto-scaling, ensuring they can handle spikes in traffic while optimizing costs during periods of low usage.

Scaling Laravel with serverless auto-scaling and event triggers allows the application to handle varying workloads efficiently and ensure optimal resource utilization. Here's how you can achieve scaling in a serverless environment.

The Benefits of Serverless Auto-scaling for Laravel

Cost optimization: You only pay for the actual compute time used during function execution, which can lead to cost savings during periods of low traffic.

Performance: With auto-scaling, your Laravel application can handle sudden spikes in traffic without manual intervention, ensuring optimal performance for users.

Scalability: Serverless auto-scaling is highly responsive, quickly adjusting the number of function instances to match the demand, allowing your application to scale seamlessly.

To Take Advantage of Serverless Auto-scaling

Optimize function granularity: Ensure that the individual functions within your Laravel application have a narrow focus and handle specific tasks. This approach allows the platform to scale only the necessary functions and not the entire application.

Configure concurrency limits: Set appropriate concurrency limits for your Lambda functions. This prevents overutilization of resources and ensures that the platform scales smoothly without overwhelming the environment.

Monitor and fine-tune: Monitor the performance of your application and adjust the concurrency settings based on real-world usage patterns. Fine-tuning concurrency limits can help strike a balance between cost and performance.

The platform in AWS Lambda manages auto-scaling automatically. You can set the maximum concurrency for your function to control the number of instances running simultaneously. When the number of incoming requests exceeds the current concurrency limit, AWS Lambda will automatically add more instances to handle the increased load.

Here's an Illustration for scaling Laravel with AWS Lambda auto-scaling.

First, ensure you have the AWS SDK for PHP (AWS SDK) installed as a dependency in your Laravel project:

```
composer require aws/aws-sdk-php
```

Create a Lambda function that executes a simple Laravel task. This example demonstrates a Lambda function that calculates the factorial of a number:

```
// Lambda Function Code
use Aws\Lambda\LambdaClient;
$lambda = new LambdaClient([
    'region' => 'us-east-1',
    'version' => 'latest',
]);
// The handler function to execute when the Lambda is triggered
$handler = function ($event) {
    // Laravel-specific code for factorial calculation
    $number = $event['number'];
    $result = factorial($number);
    return $result;
};
// Register the Lambda handler
$functionName = 'my-laravel-factorial-function';
$lambda->createFunction([
    'FunctionName' => $functionName,
    'Runtime' => 'provided',
    'Role' => 'arn:aws:iam::123456789012:role/service-role/my-lambda-role',
    'Handler' => 'index.handler',
    'Code' => [
        'ZipFile' => base64_encode('Lambda function code here...'),
    ],
    'Timeout' => 30,
    'MemorySize' => 256,
    'Environment' => [
```

```
        'Variables' => [
            // Environment variables can be used for Laravel configuration
            if needed
        ],
    ],
    'Tags' => [
        // Optionally, add tags for better resource management
    ],
]);
```

Configure the concurrency limit for your Lambda function. This limit determines the number of simultaneous function executions:

```
$lambda->putFunctionConcurrency([
    'FunctionName' => $functionName,
    'ReservedConcurrentExecutions' => 100, // Set the maximum concurrency
    limit here
]);
```

Event Triggers and Background Jobs

Event-driven architectures are a natural fit for serverless computing. We'll demonstrate how Laravel applications can use serverless functions to process background jobs and handle event triggers efficiently. For example, we might use a serverless function to process image uploads to S3 or update database records when certain events occur.

To Implement Event Triggers and Background Jobs

Identify suitable tasks: Identify tasks within your Laravel application that can be executed asynchronously without affecting the main request-response cycle.

Event sources: Configure event sources to trigger the corresponding Lambda functions based on events. For example, you can use S3 events to process uploaded files or a message queue like SQS to process queued jobs.

Decoupling: Decouple background tasks from the main application logic to improve responsiveness. This allows your application to return faster responses to users while offloading non-critical tasks to serverless functions.

Error handling: Implement proper error handling and retry mechanisms for event-triggered functions to ensure reliable processing.

By leveraging serverless auto-scaling and event triggers, Laravel applications can efficiently scale to meet varying workloads and ensure high availability. This enables the application to respond dynamically to user demands while minimizing resource waste and operational costs.

Let's assume you have a Laravel application with a background job that sends emails asynchronously using the 'illuminate/queues' package. We'll configure a serverless function to process these queued email jobs.

Here's an Illustration for using AWS Lambda to process queued jobs.

First, ensure you have the 'illuminate/queues' package installed as a dependency in your Laravel project:

```
composer require illuminate/queues
```

Create a Lambda function that processes queued jobs. This example demonstrates a Lambda function that handles email jobs:

```
// Lambda Function Code
use Aws\Lambda\LambdaClient;
$lambda = new LambdaClient([
    'region' => 'us-east-1',
    'version' => 'latest',
]);
// The handler function to execute when the Lambda is triggered
$handler = function ($event) {
    // Laravel-specific code to process queued email jobs
    $job = unserialize($event['job']);
    dispatch($job);
};
```

```
// Register the Lambda handler
$functionName = 'my-laravel-queue-worker';
$lambda->createFunction([
    'FunctionName' => $functionName,
    'Runtime' => 'provided',
    'Role' => 'arn:aws:iam::123456789012:role/service-role/my-lambda-role',
    'Handler' => 'index.handler',
    'Code' => [
        'ZipFile' => base64_encode('Lambda function code here...'),
    ],
    'Timeout' => 30,
    'MemorySize' => 256,
    'Environment' => [
        'Variables' => [
            // Environment variables can be used for Laravel configuration
            if needed
        ],
    ],
    'Tags' => [
        // Optionally, add tags for better resource management
    ],
]);
```

Configure the event source for the Lambda function to trigger it when there are queued jobs:

```
use Aws\Sqs\SqsClient;
$sqs = new SqsClient([
    'region' => 'us-east-1',
    'version' => 'latest',
]);
// Configure the SQS queue URL where the Laravel jobs are placed
$queueUrl = 'https://sqs.us-east-1.amazonaws.com/123456789012/my-queue';
// Create the event mapping to trigger the Lambda function
```

```
$lambda->createEventSourceMapping([
    'FunctionName' => $functionName,
    'EventSourceArn' => $queueUrl,
    'BatchSize' => 5, // Number of jobs to process in each Lambda
    invocation
]);
```

With these configurations, your Laravel application can now automatically scale with serverless auto-scaling based on incoming request rates and handle background jobs efficiently using event triggers.

Load Testing and Performance Optimization

To ensure the serverless Laravel application can handle real-world traffic, we'll perform load testing to understand its scalability and performance limits. Based on load testing results, we can optimize the application to improve response times and resource utilization.

Load Testing

Load testing involves subjecting your application to simulated user traffic to assess its performance under different levels of load. By performing load tests, you can identify potential bottlenecks, measure response times, and determine the maximum capacity your application can handle.

Load Testing Steps

Identify critical scenarios: Determine the key functionalities of your serverless Laravel application that need testing, such as API endpoints, database queries, or specific user actions.

Choose a load testing tool: Select a load testing tool that supports serverless applications. Popular options include the Apache JMeter, Artillery, and Locust.

Write test scenarios: Create test scenarios that simulate different user behaviors, such as concurrent API requests or user sign-ups.

Configure load test parameters: Set the number of virtual users (concurrent requests) and the duration of the load test.

Run the load test: Execute the load test against your serverless Laravel application and monitor its performance.

Analyze the results: Review the test results to identify performance bottlenecks, response times, and error rates. Use the information to optimize your application.

Optimize performance: Performance optimization aims to improve the speed, responsiveness, and efficiency of your serverless Laravel application. Here are some strategies for optimizing your application's performance:

Minimizing cold starts: Mitigate cold starts, which occur when a serverless function is invoked after a period of inactivity. Strategies like warming up functions or using provisioned concurrency can help reduce cold start delays.

Code and dependency optimization: Optimize your Laravel code and remove any unnecessary dependencies. Use AWS Lambda Layers to manage shared libraries, reducing the size of your deployment package.

Caching frequently accessed data: Utilize caching mechanisms like AWS ElastiCache or Redis to store frequently accessed data, reducing the need for repeated computations.

Database optimization: Optimize database queries, use indexes, and employ AWS RDS read replicas to offload read-intensive operations.

Optimizing memory and timeout: Adjust the memory allocation and function timeout settings based on your application's resource requirements.

Load balancing: Implement load balancing and distribute incoming requests across multiple Lambda instances to prevent overloading a single instance.

Concurrency throttling: Set appropriate concurrency limits to control the number of simultaneous function executions and prevent resource overutilization.

Asynchronous processing: Utilize event-driven architectures and background processing for non-critical tasks to improve responsiveness.

Monitoring and fine-tuning: Continuously monitor your application's performance, analyze logs, and fine-tune settings based on real-world usage patterns.

Caching optimization: Optimize caching configurations to balance memory usage and cache hit rates effectively.

By load testing your serverless Laravel application and implementing performance optimization strategies, you can ensure that your application can handle varying workloads efficiently and deliver a fast and responsive user experience. Regularly review and optimize your application to maintain excellent performance and reliability in a serverless environment.

Monitoring and Debugging Serverless Laravel Applications

Serverless Monitoring Tools

Monitoring serverless applications is crucial to ensuring their performance, availability, and reliability. There are various serverless monitoring tools available that can help you track and analyze the behavior of your serverless Laravel application.

Here are some popular serverless monitoring tools:

AWS X-Ray: AWS X-Ray is a distributed tracing service that allows you to analyze the performance of your serverless functions and identify bottlenecks. It provides end-to-end tracing of requests and helps you visualize the flow of requests across different Lambda functions and AWS services.

AWS CloudWatch: AWS CloudWatch is a monitoring and logging service that collects and tracks metrics, logs, and events for various AWS resources, including Lambda functions. You can use CloudWatch to monitor function invocations, error rates, and resource utilization.

Datadog: Datadog is a cloud monitoring platform that supports serverless monitoring, including AWS Lambda. It provides real-time monitoring, alerting, and visualization of Lambda function performance and other AWS resources.

New Relic: New Relic offers a comprehensive monitoring solution for serverless applications. It provides insights into the performance of your Lambda functions, including cold start times, response times, and error rates.

IO Pipe: IO Pipe is a monitoring and observability platform designed specifically for serverless applications. It offers real-time monitoring, tracing, and debugging for Lambda functions.

Thundra: Thundra is another serverless monitoring and observability platform that supports AWS Lambda. It provides detailed insights into function performance, distributed tracing, and root cause analysis.

Epsagon: Epsagon is a distributed tracing and monitoring solution for serverless applications. It automatically traces requests across Lambda functions and other AWS services, providing insights into performance and potential issues.

Dynatrace: Dynatrace is an AI-powered monitoring platform that offers support for AWS Lambda and serverless applications. It provides automatic tracing and analysis of function performance and dependencies.

These monitoring tools offer a range of features, including real-time monitoring, alerting, tracing, and performance analysis, to help you gain insights into the behavior of your serverless Laravel application. Depending on your specific needs and preferences, you can choose a monitoring tool that best fits your requirements for effectively managing and maintaining your serverless application.

Logging and Error Handling

Logging and error handling are critical aspects of managing a serverless Laravel application. Proper logging and error handling practices help in troubleshooting issues, identifying potential problems, and maintaining the overall health of the application. Let's explore how to implement logging and error handling in your serverless Laravel application.

Logging

Logging involves recording information, events, and errors that occur during the execution of your serverless functions. It allows you to keep track of the application's behavior, which is valuable for debugging and monitoring performance.

Logging Best Practices

Use structured logging: Implement structured logging to include relevant data fields in log messages. This helps in the easy parsing and analysis of logs.

Log different levels: Log messages at various severity levels, such as INFO, DEBUG, WARNING, and ERROR. Different levels provide insights into the application's different states.

Include contextual information: Include contextual information in log messages, such as request IDs, function names, and timestamps, to facilitate log correlation and analysis.

Log exceptions and errors: Capture and log exceptions and errors along with relevant stack traces to identify the root cause of issues.

Log external service calls: Log details of external service calls, API requests, and responses to understand the application's interactions with other systems.

Choose the right logging mechanism: Depending on the serverless platform you use, select an appropriate logging mechanism. For example, AWS Lambda supports logging to Amazon CloudWatch.

For Illustration, refer to the following snippet:

```
use Illuminate\Support\Facades\Log;
$handler = function ($event) {
    // Log an INFO message
    Log::info('Lambda function started', ['event' => $event]);
    try {
        // Your Laravel-specific code here...
        // Log a DEBUG message
        Log::debug('Processing data...', ['data' => $someData]);
        // More Laravel-specific code...
    } catch (Exception $e) {
        // Log the ERROR message along with stack trace
        Log::error('An error occurred', ['exception' => $e->getMessage(),
        'stack' => $e->getTrace()]);
        // Optionally, rethrow the exception for Lambda error handling and
        reporting
        throw $e;
    }
    // Log a custom message
    Log::info('Lambda function completed successfully');
    return $result;
};
```

In this Illustration, we used different log levels (**info**, **debug**, and **error**) to log messages at various severity levels. We also included contextual information like the event data and any specific data being processed. This makes it easier to analyze logs and trace the application's behavior.

Error Handling

Error handling involves gracefully dealing with exceptions and errors that may occur during the execution of your serverless functions. Proper error handling ensures that the application remains stable and does not crash unexpectedly.

Error Handling Best Practices

Use try-catch blocks: Wrap potential error-prone code within try-catch blocks to catch exceptions and handle errors gracefully.

Log errors: Log exceptions and errors using the logging mechanism. Include relevant information, such as error messages and stack traces.

Implement custom exception handling: Implement custom exception handling to categorize and handle specific types of errors differently.

Provide fallback mechanisms: Provide fallback mechanisms to handle errors, especially for critical operations, to maintain application stability.

Implement error reporting: Implement error reporting to notify administrators or developers about critical errors via email or other notification services.

Use Dead Letter Queues (DLQs): For asynchronous operations, consider using Dead Letter Queues (DLQs) to store failed messages for further analysis.

For Illustration, refer to the following snippet:

```
use Illuminate\Support\Facades\Log;
use Aws\Sqs\SqsClient;
$handler = function ($event) {
    try {
        // Your Laravel-specific code here...
        if ($someCondition) {
            // Throw a custom exception for demonstration purposes
            throw new Exception('An error occurred while processing
            data.');
        }
        // More Laravel-specific code...
    } catch (Exception $e) {
        // Log the ERROR message along with stack trace
        Log::error('An error occurred', ['exception' => $e->getMessage(),
        'stack' => $e->getTrace()]);
        // Use AWS SDK to publish the failed message to a Dead Letter
        Queue (DLQ)
        $sqsClient = new SqsClient([
            'region' => 'us-east-1',
```

```
        'version' => 'latest',
    ]);
    $queueUrl = 'https://sqs.us-east-1.amazonaws.com/123456789012/
    my-dlq';
    $sqsClient->sendMessage([
        'QueueUrl' => $queueUrl,
        'MessageBody' => json_encode($event),
    ]);
  }
  return $result;
};
```

In this example, we caught the custom exception, logged the error details, and then published the failed message to the Dead Letter Queue (DLQ) using the AWS SDK. The DLQ will store the failed messages for further analysis, and you can set up monitoring and alerting for the DLQ to be notified of failed messages.

By implementing effective logging and error handling practices in your serverless Laravel application, you can proactively identify issues, monitor the application's behavior, and maintain high application availability and performance. Regularly review and analyze logs to ensure the application's smooth functioning and promptly address any arising issues.

Cost Optimization

Cost optimization is a crucial aspect of managing a serverless Laravel application. Serverless computing offers cost-effective benefits, but without proper optimization, costs can escalate, especially when operating at scale.

Here are some strategies for cost optimization in your serverless Laravel application:

Right-sizing Lambda functions

Analyze the memory requirements and performance characteristics of your Lambda functions. Right-size the memory allocation to match the actual needs of the function. Overprovisioning memory can lead to unnecessary costs.

Provisioned concurrency

Consider using provisioned concurrency to reduce cold starts and improve response times. However, carefully choose the number of concurrent instances to avoid overprovisioning.

Use AWS Lambda Layers

Leverage AWS Lambda Layers to share common libraries across multiple functions. This reduces the size of the deployment package and optimizes storage costs.

Optimize function execution time

Efficiently use resources and optimize the execution time of your Lambda functions. Reducing execution time can lead to lower costs.

Choose the optimal memory size

Measure the performance of your Lambda functions at different memory sizes and choose the most cost-effective memory configuration.

Auto-scaling configuration

Set up auto-scaling policies based on actual usage patterns. This ensures that you have enough concurrent executions to handle traffic while avoiding unnecessary costs during idle periods.

Stateless design

Follow a stateless design pattern to avoid unnecessary resource consumption and ensure that functions scale properly.

Use serverless databases

Consider using serverless databases, such as AWS Aurora Serverless or DynamoDB, which automatically scale based on demand and save costs during low-traffic periods.

Use cache effectively

Leverage caching mechanisms like AWS ElastiCache or Redis to minimize redundant calculations and reduce database access, leading to cost savings.

Monitor and analyze costs

Regularly monitor and analyze your AWS Lambda costs using AWS Cost Explorer or other monitoring tools. Identify cost spikes and investigate the reasons to optimize resource usage.

Implement fine-grained permissions

Follow the principle of least privilege and implement fine-grained permissions to avoid unintended access and potential cost overruns.

Use reserved instances

If you have predictable workloads, consider using reserved instances for long-term cost savings on AWS services.

Control request payloads

Minimize the size of request and response payloads to reduce data transfer costs.

Clean up unused resources

Periodically review and clean up unused Lambda functions, API gateway stages, and other resources to avoid unnecessary charges.

By applying these cost optimization strategies, you can ensure that your serverless Laravel application runs efficiently and cost-effectively. Regularly monitor and fine-tune your application to achieve the best balance between performance and cost in a serverless environment.

Summary

In this chapter, you learned about Laravel's interaction with serverless computing, a novel way to deploy applications. We focused on hosting and running Laravel apps using serverless platforms such as AWS Lambda, Google Cloud Functions, or Azure Functions. The benefits of serverless computing were discussed, including autonomous scaling, cost effectiveness, and reduced maintenance overhead. The chapter explained how to package Laravel apps as serverless functions and integrate them with serverless infrastructure. We also covered how to deal with serverless-specific difficulties such as cold start times and the stateless nature of functions.

In the next chapter, we will look at using Laravel to build Progressive Web Applications.

CHAPTER 19

Building Progressive Web Applications (PWAs) with Laravel

In the previous chapter, we explored the groundbreaking world of serverless computing and its integration with Laravel, enabling us to build highly scalable and efficient applications without the burden of server management. As our journey through Laravel's advanced features continues, we now dive into the realm of Progressive Web Applications (PWAs)—a transformative approach to crafting web applications that offer a seamless user experience across various devices and network conditions.

Understanding Progressive Web Applications and Service Workers

In this section, we will delve into the concept of Progressive Web Applications and the role of service workers. PWAs combine the best of web and native applications, delivering app-like experiences directly within a web browser. We will explore how service workers enable offline capabilities and background tasks, revolutionizing the way users interact with web applications.

Converting Laravel Applications into PWAs

Laravel applications can be enhanced with PWA capabilities to provide a consistent and engaging user experience across different platforms. We will learn how to convert Laravel applications into PWAs by integrating the necessary components and manifest files to enable PWA functionalities.

Offline Support and Caching Strategies for PWAs

Offline support is a hallmark of PWAs, allowing users to interact with the application even when they are not connected to the Internet. We will explore caching strategies using service workers to provide seamless offline access to critical resources.

© Sivaraj Selvaraj 2024
S. Selvaraj, *Building Real-Time Marvels with Laravel*, https://doi.org/10.1007/978-1-4842-9789-6_19

Push Notifications and Background Sync in PWAs

Push notifications and background sync are essential features that keep users engaged and informed. We will learn how to implement push notifications and background synchronization in PWAs to deliver timely updates and maintain application synchronization in the background.

Optimizing PWAs for Performance and User Experience

In this final section, we will focus on optimizing PWAs for performance and user experience. We will explore techniques to reduce loading times, enhance responsiveness, and deliver an immersive and user-friendly PWA experience.

Throughout this chapter, we will immerse ourselves in the world of Progressive Web Applications and Laravel, equipping ourselves with the knowledge and skills to build modern web applications that offer a seamless and engaging user experience. By adopting PWA principles, we can deliver high-performance applications that are accessible to users across devices and network conditions. So let's embark on this journey of building Progressive Web Applications with Laravel to elevate our web development expertise to new heights!

Understanding Progressive Web Applications and Service Workers

In the realm of web development, Progressive Web Applications (PWAs) have emerged as a game-changer, offering users a seamless and immersive experience that blurs the lines between web and native mobile applications. At the core of this technology lie service workers, a powerful browser feature that enables developers to take control over caching, network requests, and background synchronization.

In this guide, we will delve into the concept of Progressive Web Applications and the essential role that service workers play in their creation. We'll explore the distinctive features of PWAs, including offline accessibility, fast loading, and responsiveness, all of which contribute to an enhanced user experience.

Service workers, with their ability to cache resources and manage network requests, empower PWAs to function seamlessly, even with low or no Internet connectivity. Understanding the installation, registration, and lifecycle of service workers is key to unlocking the full potential of PWAs.

Throughout this guide, we will also discuss best practices for designing and building Progressive Web Applications. From optimizing performance to ensuring responsive design, we'll cover the essential principles that make PWAs stand out in the ever-evolving world of web development.

Whether you are a web developer seeking to leverage the power of PWAs or a business owner looking to improve user engagement and retention, understanding Progressive Web Applications and service workers is crucial for staying ahead in the modern web landscape. Let's embark on this journey to explore the fascinating world of PWAs and service workers and create web experiences that leave a lasting impact on users.

Key Characteristics of Progressive Web Applications

Progressive enhancement: PWAs are designed to work on any device, regardless of the browser's capabilities. They progressively enhance the user experience based on the features supported by the user's browser.

Responsive design: PWAs are built with responsive design principles, ensuring that the user interface adapts and fits well on various screen sizes, from desktops to mobile devices.

Connectivity independence: PWAs can work offline or in low-quality network conditions. Using service workers to cache essential assets and data achieves this, allowing users to access content even when they're offline.

App-like user experience: PWAs provide an immersive user experience, resembling native mobile applications. They can be launched from the user's home screen and have smooth animations and interactions.

Secure and HTTPS-enabled: PWAs require a secure connection (HTTPS) to ensure data privacy and security. This also allows them to leverage modern browser features like service workers.

Service Workers

Service workers are a crucial technology that powers many of the features in Progressive Web Applications. They are JavaScript files that run in the background, separate from the web page, and act as a proxy between the web application and the network.

Service workers enable the following functionalities in PWAs:

Offline support: Service workers can intercept network requests and cache the responses. This allows the PWA to serve cached content when the user is offline or on a slow network.

Caching strategies: Service workers allow developers to implement various caching strategies, such as cache-first, network-first, or stale-while-revalidate, to optimize the PWA's performance.

Push notifications: Service workers enable push notifications, allowing the PWA to send notifications to the user's device even when the application is not open.

Background sync: With service workers, PWAs can perform background sync, which means they can synchronize data with the server even if the app is not actively being used.

It's important to note that service workers run in a separate context from the web page, which means they are more resilient to failures and can be shut down and restarted as needed without affecting the user experience.

By understanding PWAs and the role of service workers, developers can create web applications that deliver a more reliable and engaging experience to users, closing the gap between web and native applications.

Converting Laravel Applications into PWAs

In this section, the focus will be on taking an existing Laravel web application and converting it into a Progressive Web Application. It will cover the necessary steps to modify the Laravel application to include service workers and other PWA-related features.

Set Up a Manifest File

Create a 'manifest.json' file in the root of your Laravel application. This file provides metadata about the PWA, such as the name, short name, icons, theme colors, and other configuration settings. Here's an example of a simple 'manifest.json' file:

```
// manifest.json
{
  "name": "My Laravel PWA",
  "short_name": "Laravel PWA",
  "start_url": "/",
```

```
  "display": "standalone",
  "background_color": "#f0f0f0",
  "theme_color": "#333333",
  "icons": [
    {
      "src": "/images/icon-72x72.png",
      "sizes": "72x72",
      "type": "image/png"
    },
    {
      "src": "/images/icon-96x96.png",
      "sizes": "96x96",
      "type": "image/png"
    },
    {
      "src": "/images/icon-144x144.png",
      "sizes": "144x144",
      "type": "image/png"
    }
  ]
}
```

Add a Service Worker

Create a service worker file (e.g., 'service-worker.js') in the public directory of your
Laravel project. The service worker will handle caching and offline functionality. Here's a
basic example of a service worker:

```
// service-worker.js
const CACHE_NAME = 'my-laravel-pwa-cache-v1';
const cacheUrls = ['/', '/css/app.css', '/js/app.js'];
self.addEventListener('install', event => {
  event.waitUntil(
    caches.open(CACHE_NAME)
```

```
      .then(cache => cache.addAll(cacheUrls))
  );
});
self.addEventListener('fetch', event => {
  event.respondWith(
    caches.match(event.request)
      .then(response => response || fetch(event.request))
  );
});
```

Then, register the service worker in your main HTML file (e.g., 'resources/views/welcome.blade.php') using the following script:

```
<!-- resources/views/welcome.blade.php -->
<script>
  if ('serviceWorker' in navigator) {
    navigator.serviceWorker.register('/service-worker.js')
      .then(registration => console.log('Service worker registered:',
      registration))
      .catch(error => console.error('Error registering service worker:',
      error));
  }
</script>
```

Enable HTTPS

Ensure your Laravel application is served over HTTPS to unlock PWA features. This may involve setting up SSL certificates for your web server.

Responsive Design

Make sure your Laravel views use responsive design principles so that the PWA adapts to different screen sizes. For example, use CSS media queries to adjust the layout based on screen width:

```
/* Example CSS media query for responsive design */
@media screen and (max-width: 768px) {
  /* Adjust styles for smaller screens */
}
```

Add the Install Prompt

Prompt users to install your PWA using the 'beforeinstallprompt' event. Add the following script to your main HTML file:

```
<!-- resources/views/welcome.blade.php -->
<script>
  window.addEventListener('beforeinstallprompt', event => {
    event.preventDefault();
    const installPrompt = event;
    // Show your custom install banner or popup here
    // For example, display a button or banner to prompt installation
  });
</script>
```

Implement Offline Support

Identify critical assets and data that should be available offline and cache them in the service worker's install event. In our example service worker, we cached the homepage, CSS, and JS files. You can expand this list based on your application's needs.

Optimize Performance

Optimize your Laravel application for better performance. Minimize file sizes, leverage caching strategies, and lazy-load non-essential resources to reduce loading times.

Test on Different Devices and Browsers

Thoroughly test your Laravel PWA on various devices and browsers to ensure compatibility and a consistent user experience.

Register Service Worker Routes

Depending on your Laravel application's structure and caching requirements, you might need to register routes for the service worker to handle specific requests. In Laravel, you can do this in the service worker file or in the application's service provider:

```
// Example of registering service worker routes in Laravel
Route::get('/service-worker.js', 'ServiceWorkerController@serviceWorker');
```

Add PWA Features

Consider implementing additional PWA features like push notifications and background sync using the service worker. For example, to implement push notifications, you'll need to handle the push event in the service worker and request permission from the user.

These are the general steps to convert a Laravel application into a Progressive Web Application. Remember that the specific implementation details may vary depending on your application's complexity and requirements. Always refer to the official documentation and best practices for Laravel and Progressive Web Applications to ensure a smooth conversion process.

Offline Support and Caching Strategies for PWAs

Offline support and caching strategies are crucial aspects of building Progressive Web Applications (PWAs). They enable PWAs to work reliably even when the user is offline or experiencing poor network connectivity. Let's dive into more detail about offline support and various caching strategies that can be employed in PWAs.

Offline Support

Offline support is the ability of a PWA to function even when the user's device is not connected to the Internet. To achieve offline support, PWAs utilize service workers to cache essential assets and data when the application is initially accessed online. Then, when the user goes offline, the cached resources are served from the local cache, enabling the PWA to continue functioning.

Here's a step-by-step guide to implementing offline support in your PWA:

Register the service worker.

As mentioned earlier, the service worker is a JavaScript file that controls the caching and network-related functionality of the PWA. You need to register the service worker in your main HTML file:

```
<!-- In your main HTML file, e.g., resources/views/welcome.blade.php -->
<script>
  if ('serviceWorker' in navigator) {
    navigator.serviceWorker.register('/service-worker.js')
      .then(registration => console.log('Service worker registered:',
      registration))
      .catch(error => console.error('Error registering service worker:',
      error));
  }
</script>
```

Implement the service worker.

Inside your 'service-worker.js' file, implement the caching logic for essential assets that you want to make available offline. The following is an example of caching key resources during the installation of the service worker:

```
// service-worker.js
const CACHE_NAME = 'my-laravel-pwa-cache-v1';
const cacheUrls = ['/', '/css/app.css', '/js/app.js', '/images/logo.png'];
```

```
self.addEventListener('install', event => {
  event.waitUntil(
    caches.open(CACHE_NAME)
      .then(cache => cache.addAll(cacheUrls))
  );
});
```

In this example, we are caching the homepage ('/'), CSS ('/css/app.css'), JavaScript ('/js/app.js') and an image ('/images/logo.png') during the installation of the service worker.

Implement a fetch event for offline fallback.

To ensure that cached resources are served when the user is offline, you need to implement the 'fetch' event in the service worker. This event intercepts all network requests, allowing the service worker to respond with cached data if available:

```
// service-worker.js
self.addEventListener('fetch', event => {
  event.respondWith(
    caches.match(event.request)
      .then(response => response || fetch(event.request))
  );
});
```

In this example, when a fetch event occurs, the service worker tries to find a match in the cache. If a match is found, it responds with the cached resource; otherwise, it fetches the resource from the network.

With these steps, your PWA will have basic offline support, and essential resources will be available even when the user is offline.

Caching Strategies

In addition to offline support, caching strategies are essential for optimizing the performance of PWAs. Different caching strategies can be used to determine how and when resources are cached, retrieved, and updated. Popular caching strategies include

Cache-first strategy

This strategy serves the cached resource first, and if it's not available, then it fetches it from the network. It prioritizes delivering the cached content for faster load times.

Network-first strategy

This strategy fetches the resource from the network first, and if it's not available (e.g., due to poor network connectivity), then it serves the cached version. It ensures users get the latest content when they have a reliable network connection.

Stale-while-revalidate strategy

This strategy serves the cached resource immediately and then fetches the latest version from the network in the background. It ensures the user sees something even if the network request takes longer.

Cache-falling-back-to-network strategy

This strategy serves the cached resource first and then fetches the latest version from the network. If the network request fails, it falls back to the cached version.

To implement these caching strategies, you can modify the fetch event in the service worker accordingly. For example, here's how to use the cache-first strategy:

```
// service-worker.js
self.addEventListener('fetch', event => {
  event.respondWith(
    caches.match(event.request)
      .then(response => response || fetch(event.request))
  );
});
```

To implement other caching strategies, you need to adjust the fetch event logic to match the desired behavior.

Implementing offline support and caching strategies can greatly enhance the user experience of your Laravel PWA, ensuring that it works reliably and efficiently, even under challenging network conditions. Remember to always test thoroughly to ensure that your caching strategies work as expected and provide the best user experience.

Push Notifications and Background Sync in PWAs

Push notifications and background sync are two powerful features that can be implemented in Progressive Web Applications (PWAs) using service workers. They enable PWAs to engage users even when the application is not actively open and allow data synchronization in the background. Let's explore each feature in detail.

Push Notifications

Push notifications are messages sent from a server to a user's device even when the user is not actively using the application. They provide a way to re-engage users and deliver timely updates, promotions, or relevant information. To implement push notifications in your PWA, you need to set up the necessary server-side infrastructure and handle events in the service worker.

Here's an overview of the steps involved in implementing push notifications: Register for push notifications.

In your PWA's frontend code, you'll need to request permission from the user to send push notifications. This is typically done using the 'Notification. requestPermission()' method:

```
// Example code to request push notification permission
if ('Notification' in window) {
  Notification.requestPermission()
    .then(permission => {
      if (permission === 'granted') {
        // Permission granted, proceed to subscribe to push notifications
      }
    });
}
```

Subscribe to push notifications.

Once the user grants permission, you can subscribe to push notifications and obtain a unique endpoint for sending push messages. You'll need to send this endpoint to your server for later use.

Handle push events in the service worker.

In the service worker, listen for push events and show notifications when a push message is received:

```
// service-worker.js
self.addEventListener('push', event => {
  const pushData = event.data.json();
  const title = pushData.title;
  const options = {
    body: pushData.message,
    icon: '/path/to/icon.png',
    // other options...
  };
  event.waitUntil(self.registration.showNotification(title, options));
});
```

With these steps, your PWA will be capable of showing push notifications to users, keeping them informed and engaged even when the application is not open.

Background Sync

Background sync allows PWAs to synchronize data with the server even when the user is offline or has a poor network connection. It ensures that the PWA can perform critical operations in the background and keep the data up to date. Background sync is especially useful for applications that involve form submissions, messaging, or other real-time interactions.

Here's how to implement background sync in your PWA:

Detect support for background sync.

Check if the browser supports background sync before attempting to use it:

```
// Check for Background Sync support
if ('SyncManager' in window) {
  // Background Sync is supported, proceed with registration
}
```

Register a background sync task.

When the user performs an action that requires background synchronization, register a background sync task with the service worker:

```
// In your PWA's front-end code
if ('serviceWorker' in navigator && 'SyncManager' in window) {
  navigator.serviceWorker.ready
    .then(registration => {
      return registration.sync.register('syncData');
    })
    .catch(error => {
      // Registration failed
    });
}
```

Handle background sync events in the service worker.

In the service worker, listen for the 'sync' event and perform the required synchronization with the server:

```
// service-worker.js
self.addEventListener('sync', event => {
  if (event.tag === 'syncData') {
    event.waitUntil(
      // Perform data synchronization with the server
    );
  }
});
```

With background sync implemented, the PWA will attempt to synchronize data with the server whenever a network connection is available, ensuring a seamless user experience.

By implementing push notifications and background sync, a Laravel PWA can keep users engaged with timely updates and allow data synchronization, even when they are not actively using the application or have limited connectivity. These features enhance the overall user experience and make your PWA more powerful and useful.

Optimizing PWAs for Performance and User Experience

Optimizing Progressive Web Applications (PWAs) for performance and user experience is crucial to ensuring that your application is fast and responsive and provides a seamless experience for users across different devices and network conditions. Here are some key strategies to optimize your Laravel PWA.

Performance Auditing

Use Google Lighthouse to perform a performance audit for your Laravel PWA. You can run Lighthouse from the Chrome Developer Tools or use a command-line tool.

Example: In the Chrome Developer Tools, go to the "Audits" tab, select "Performance", and click "Run audits".

Code Splitting

Leverage code splitting to split your JavaScript and CSS into smaller chunks that are loaded only when needed.

Example: Use Webpack's dynamic import to split your JavaScript into multiple bundles.

```
// main.js
const button = document.getElementById('loadMoreButton');
button.addEventListener('click', () => {
  import('./lazy-loaded-module.js').then(module => {
    // Code from the lazy-loaded module is executed when needed
  });
});
```

Lazy Loading

Implement lazy loading for images using the 'loading="lazy"' attribute.

Example: In your Laravel Blade template, add the 'loading="lazy"' attribute to images.

```
<img src="/path/to/image.jpg" alt="Lazy-loaded image" loading="lazy">
```

Responsive Design

Ensure your Laravel views use responsive design principles to adapt to different screen sizes.

Example: Use CSS media queries to adjust the layout based on screen width.

```
/* Example CSS media query for responsive design */
@media screen and (max-width: 768px) {
  /* Adjust styles for smaller screens */
}
```

Minify and Compress Assets

Use Laravel Mix or other build tools to minify and compress your CSS, JavaScript, and other assets.

Example: In your Laravel Mix configuration file ('webpack.mix.js'), enable minification.

```
// Example webpack.mix.js
mix.js('resources/js/app.js', 'public/js')
    .postCss('resources/css/app.css', 'public/css', [
        require('postcss-import'),
        require('tailwindcss'),
    ]);
```

Cache Control Headers

You should set appropriate cache control headers for your assets to control how long the browser caches them.

Example: In your Laravel application, use middleware to set cache control headers for specific routes or asset types.

```php
// Example middleware to set cache control headers for assets
public function handle($request, Closure $next)
{
    $response = $next($request);
    $response->header('Cache-Control', 'public, max-age=86400'); // Cache
assets for 1 day
    return $response;
}
```

Offline Page

Create a custom offline page in your Laravel views to show when the user is offline.

Example: Create an 'offline.blade.php' view that informs the user about the offline status.

```
<!-- resources/views/offline.blade.php -->
<div>
  <h1>You are currently offline</h1>
  <p>Please check your internet connection and try again.</p>
</div>
```

Optimize Images

Use image compression tools and modern image formats like WebP to optimize images.

Example: Use a command-line tool like ImageMagick to convert images to WebP format.

```
Example ImageMagick command to convert PNG to WebP
convert input.png output.webp
```

Background Data Sync

Implement background sync for critical data synchronization in your Laravel PWA.

Example: In your service worker, listen for sync events and handle background data synchronization.

```
// service-worker.js
self.addEventListener('sync', event => {
  if (event.tag === 'syncData') {
    event.waitUntil(
      // Perform data synchronization with the server
    );
  }
});
```

PWA-Specific Caching Strategies

Implement caching strategies in your service worker to optimize resource fetching.

Example: Implement a cache-first strategy for essential assets.

```
// service-worker.js
self.addEventListener('fetch', event => {
  event.respondWith(
```

```
    caches.match(event.request)
      .then(response => response || fetch(event.request))
  );
});
```

Optimize Fonts

Limit the number of font weights and styles used in your PWA to reduce font file sizes.

Example: Use a custom font with only the necessary font weights and styles.

```css
/* Example CSS for custom font */
@font-face {
  font-family: 'CustomFont';
  src: url('/path/to/custom-font-regular.ttf') format('truetype');
  font-weight: 400;
  font-style: normal;
}
```

Use Web Workers

Use Web Workers to offload intensive tasks from the main thread.

Example: Create a Web Worker script to perform complex calculations.

```javascript
// worker.js
self.addEventListener('message', event => {
  const data = event.data;
  // Perform complex calculations with data
  const result = /* calculation result */;
  self.postMessage(result);
});
```

Monitor Performance

Use analytics tools like Google Analytics or other monitoring tools to track your PWA's performance.

Example: Integrate Google Analytics into your Laravel application.

```
<!-- resources/views/welcome.blade.php -->
<script async src="https://www.googletagmanager.com/gtag/js?id=YOUR_GA_
TRACKING_ID"></script>
<script>
  window.dataLayer = window.dataLayer || [];
  function gtag(){dataLayer.push(arguments);}
  gtag('js', new Date());
  gtag('config', 'YOUR_GA_TRACKING_ID');
</script>
```

By applying these optimization techniques with examples, your Laravel PWA will deliver a faster, more responsive, and engaging user experience, ensuring that users stay satisfied and engaged with your application. Remember to regularly test and measure performance to identify further areas for improvement.

Summary

In this chapter, you learned how to create Progressive Web Applications (PWAs) with Laravel. We covered developing web apps that integrate the best of online and mobile experiences, allowing users to interact in a fluid and responsive manner across a variety of devices and network situations. The chapter explained fundamental PWA principles like offline access, push alerts, and fast loading times and demonstrated how to use service workers, the core of PWAs, to cache and provide content offline. You also learned how to include push notification features into your PWAs with Laravel and third-party services.

In the next chapter, we will explore advanced UI/UX design patterns for Laravel.

CHAPTER 20

Advanced UI/UX Design Patterns for Laravel

In the previous chapter, we embarked on the transformative journey of building Progressive Web Applications (PWAs) with Laravel, creating web applications that deliver seamless and engaging user experiences across various devices and network conditions. As we continue our exploration of Laravel's advanced features, we now shift our focus to the user interface and user experience (UI/UX) design aspects of our applications.

Designing User-Friendly Interfaces with Laravel's Blade Templating Engine

In this section, we will delve into the art of designing user-friendly interfaces using Laravel's powerful Blade templating engine. Blade offers a flexible and intuitive way to create dynamic and reusable UI components, streamlining the process of building consistent and visually appealing interfaces.

Implementing Responsive Design and Mobile Optimization Techniques

Responsive design is essential to ensuring our applications adapt seamlessly to different screen sizes and devices. We will explore how to implement responsive design and apply mobile optimization techniques in Laravel to deliver a delightful experience to users on various platforms.

Enhancing User Experience with CSS Animation and Transition Effects

The user experience can be elevated through subtle and engaging CSS animation and transition effects. We will learn how to implement these effects in Laravel applications to captivate users and provide a sense of interactivity and responsiveness.

Designing Accessible Applications with Laravel

Accessibility is a vital aspect of modern web development, ensuring that all users, regardless of their abilities, can access and use our applications. We will explore how to design accessible applications in Laravel, adhering to web accessibility standards and best practices.

© Sivaraj Selvaraj 2024

S. Selvaraj, *Building Real-Time Marvels with Laravel*, https://doi.org/10.1007/978-1-4842-9789-6_20

Implementing User Feedback and Usability Testing in Laravel Applications

User feedback and usability testing are invaluable for refining and improving the user experience. We will discover how to implement user feedback mechanisms in Laravel applications and conduct usability testing to gain insights into user behavior and preferences.

Throughout this chapter, we will immerse ourselves in the world of advanced UI/UX design patterns for Laravel. By mastering the art of user-friendly interfaces, responsive design, and engaging user experience, we can create applications that delight users and keep them coming back for more. So let's embark on this journey of advanced UI/UX design patterns to elevate the aesthetics and usability of our Laravel applications!

Designing User-Friendly Interfaces with Laravel's Blade Templating Engine

User experience is at the heart of every successful web application. A well-designed and user-friendly interface can make a significant difference in how users interact with and perceive your website or web application. Laravel, the popular PHP web framework, offers a powerful templating engine called Blade, which enables developers to craft intuitive and visually appealing user interfaces with ease.

In this guide, we will focus on exploring how to design user-friendly interfaces using Laravel's Blade templating engine. We'll dive into the syntax and features that Blade provides, allowing developers to create dynamic and organized templates efficiently. By leveraging Blade's layout files, partials, and components, you can maintain a consistent design across your application while keeping your codebase clean and maintainable.

Moreover, we will explore techniques for responsive design and accessibility to ensure that your interfaces are accessible and perform optimally on various devices and platforms.

Whether you are a seasoned Laravel developer looking to enhance your user interface design skills or a newcomer eager to learn about the power of Blade, this guide aims to equip you with the knowledge and best practices needed to create delightful user experiences for your web applications. Let's get started on the journey to crafting user-friendly interfaces that captivate and engage your users.

Let's explore some best practices and techniques to design user-friendly interfaces using Blade.

Organizing Blade Templates

Organize your PWA's Blade templates in a directory structure that allows easy navigation and maintenance. Figure 20-1 illustrates Blade templates.

```
resources/
├── views/
│   ├── layouts/
│   │   ├── app.blade.php
│   │   └── ...
│   ├── partials/
│   │   ├── header.blade.php
│   │   ├── footer.blade.php
│   │   └── ...
│   ├── home.blade.php
│   ├── dashboard.blade.php
│   └── ...
└── ...
```

Figure 20-1. *Blade templates*

Using Template Inheritance (Extends)

Leverage Blade's template inheritance to create a consistent layout for your PWA across multiple views:

```
<!-- layouts/app.blade.php -->
<!DOCTYPE html>
<html>
<head>
    <title>@yield('title')</title>
    <!-- Common meta tags and PWA manifest -->
</head>
```

```
<body>
    @include('partials.header')
    @yield('content')
    @include('partials.footer')
    <!-- Common service worker registration script -->
</body>
</html>
```

Using Partials (Includes)

Break down complex views into smaller, reusable partials using Blade's '@include'
directive, including PWA-specific components:

```
<!-- layouts/app.blade.php -->
<!DOCTYPE html>
<html>
<head>
    <title>@yield('title')</title>
    <!-- Common meta tags and PWA manifest -->
</head>
<body>
    @include('partials.header')
    @yield('content')
    @include('partials.footer')
    <!-- Common service worker registration script -->
</body>
</html>
```

Blade Directives for Conditionals and Loops

Use Blade directives for conditionals and loops, even in PWA-specific scenarios:

```
<!-- Example of conditional rendering in Blade -->
@if(auth()->check())
    <div>Welcome, {{ auth()->user()->name }}!</div>
@else
    <div>Welcome, Guest!</div>
@endif
<!-- Example of loop in Blade -->
@foreach($notifications as $notification)
    <div>{{ $notification->message }}</div>
@endforeach
```

Blade Components (Laravel 7+)

Use Blade components to create reusable UI elements for your PWA:

```
<!-- Example of a Blade component for a notification -->
<!-- resources/views/components/notification.blade.php -->
<div class="notification">
   {{ $slot }}
</div>
```

```
<!-- Using the Blade component for a notification -->
<x-notification>
    New message received!
</x-notification>
```

Form Handling with Blade

Use Blade's form directives for easy form handling and CSRF protection:

```
<!-- Example of Blade form handling -->
<form action="/submit" method="POST">
    @csrf
    <input type="text" name="username">
    <button type="submit">Submit</button>
</form>
```

Design Consistency

Maintain design consistency across your PWA using CSS and adhere to PWA design principles.

Mobile-Friendly Design

Ensure your PWA interface is mobile-friendly and responsive by utilizing CSS media queries and responsive design techniques. Test your design on various devices to ensure a seamless user experience.

By incorporating these PWA examples in your Laravel Blade templates, you can create user-friendly and responsive interfaces that are optimized for Progressive Web Applications, leading to a delightful user experience across various devices and network conditions.

Implementing Responsive Design and Mobile Optimization Techniques

Implementing responsive design and mobile optimization techniques is essential to ensuring that your Laravel application provides a seamless and user-friendly experience across different devices and screen sizes. Let's explore some best practices and techniques to achieve responsive design and mobile optimization in your Laravel application.

Use CSS Media Queries

Leverage CSS media queries to make your PWA responsive to different screen sizes and devices:

```css
/* Example of a CSS media query for mobile devices */
@media (max-width: 767px) {
  /* Styles specific to mobile devices */
  .navbar {
    display: none; /* Hide the navbar on small screens */
  }
}
```

Mobile-First Approach

Adopt a mobile-first approach when styling your PWA to prioritize mobile users and then enhance it for larger screens:

```css
/* Example of a mobile-first CSS style */
body {
  font-size: 14px;
}
/* Styles for larger screens */
@media (min-width: 768px) {
  body {
    font-size: 16px;
  }
}
```

Use Responsive Frameworks

Utilize responsive CSS frameworks like Bootstrap or Tailwind CSS to expedite the creation of responsive designs in your PWA:

```
<!-- Example of using Bootstrap's responsive grid system -->
<div class="container">
  <div class="row">
    <div class="col-md-6">
      <!-- Content for the left column -->
    </div>
    <div class="col-md-6">
      <!-- Content for the right column -->
    </div>
  </div>
</div>
```

Optimize Images

Optimize images for mobile devices to reduce page load time. Use responsive image techniques with 'srcset' and 'sizes' attributes to serve appropriately sized images based on the user's device:

```
<!-- Example of using responsive images in a PWA -->
<img src="/path/to/image.jpg" alt="Mobile-friendly image"
     srcset="/path/to/image-small.jpg 480w,
             /path/to/image-medium.jpg 768w,
             /path/to/image-large.jpg 1024w"
     sizes="(max-width: 767px) 100vw,
             (min-width: 768px) 50vw"
>
```

Touch-Friendly Interactions

Design touch-friendly interactions for mobile devices, such as larger tap targets and swipe gestures, to improve the usability of your PWA on touchscreens:

```
/* Example of increasing tap target size in a PWA */
.button {
  padding: 10px 20px;
}
```

Accessibility Considerations

Ensure that your responsive design maintains accessibility. Test your PWA using screen readers and keyboard navigation to ensure a smooth experience for users with disabilities.

Viewport Meta Tag

Add a viewport meta tag to your HTML to control how your PWA is displayed on mobile devices:

```
<!-- Viewport meta tag for mobile optimization in a PWA -->
<meta name="viewport" content="width=device-width, initial-scale=1.0">
```

Performance Optimization

Optimize the performance of your responsive PWA by minimizing CSS and JavaScript, leveraging browser caching, and employing server-side caching techniques.

Test on Various Devices

Thoroughly test your responsive PWA on different devices, including smartphones, tablets, and desktops, to ensure that it adapts correctly to various screen sizes and devices.

By incorporating these responsive design and mobile optimization techniques in your Laravel PWA, you can provide a seamless and user-friendly experience to users across different devices, enhance accessibility, and deliver optimal performance, resulting in increased user engagement and satisfaction with your PWA.

Enhancing User Experience with CSS Animation and Transition Effects

Enhancing the user experience with CSS animation and transition effects can add a touch of interactivity and delight to your Laravel application. CSS animations and transitions make UI elements more engaging, creating smooth and visually appealing interactions. Let's explore how to leverage CSS animation and transition effects to enhance the user experience in your Laravel application.

CSS Animations

Use CSS animations to create dynamic and fluid movements for UI elements in your PWA. For example, animate buttons and icons to provide visual feedback to users:

```css
/* Example of a CSS animation for a button in a PWA */
.button {
  transition: transform 0.2s ease;
}
.button:hover {
  transform: scale(1.1);
}
```

CSS Transitions

Apply CSS transitions to smoothly change an element's properties over time. Use them for dropdown menus, sliding elements, or toggling visibility:

```
/* Example of a CSS transition for a dropdown menu in a PWA */
.dropdown-menu {
  height: 0;
  overflow: hidden;
  transition: height 0.3s ease;
}
.dropdown-menu.active {
  height: 150px; /* Expand the dropdown on activation */
}
```

Keyframe Animations

Leverage keyframe animations to create more complex and custom animations in your PWA. For instance, animate loading spinners or progress bars:

```
/* Example of a keyframe animation for a loading spinner in a PWA */
@keyframes spin {
  0% {
    transform: rotate(0deg);
  }
  100% {
    transform: rotate(360deg);
  }
}
.spinner {
  animation: spin 2s linear infinite;
}
```

Delicate Hover Effects

Apply subtle hover effects to buttons, links, and other interactive elements in your PWA to provide visual feedback to users:

```css
/* Example of a delicate hover effect for a button in a PWA */
.button {
  transition: background-color 0.2s ease;
}
.button:hover {
  background-color: #f0f0f0;
}
```

CSS Transitions for Smooth State Changes

Use CSS transitions to create smooth state changes in your PWA, such as showing/hiding dropdowns or sliding elements in and out of view:

```css
/* Example of a CSS transition for a dropdown menu in a PWA */
.dropdown-menu {
  opacity: 0;
  pointer-events: none;
  transition: opacity 0.2s ease;
}
.dropdown-menu.active {
  opacity: 1; /* Fade in the dropdown on activation */
  pointer-events: auto;
}
```

Animation Timing Functions

Experiment with different timing functions (e.g., ease, ease-in, ease-out, ease-in-out) to control the animation's acceleration and deceleration, providing a more natural feel to the movement:

```
/* Example of using different timing functions for a button animation in
a PWA */
.button {
  transition: transform 0.2s ease-in-out;
}
```

Use Animations Sparingly

While CSS animations and transitions can enhance the user experience, avoid overusing them in your PWA. Use animations where they add value and make interactions more intuitive, but be mindful of their impact on performance and the user experience.

By incorporating these CSS animation and transition techniques in your Laravel PWA, you can create an engaging and interactive user experience, making your PWA feel more dynamic and responsive. However, always consider the performance implications of animations, especially on mobile devices, and ensure they contribute positively to the overall user experience.

Designing Accessible Applications with Laravel

Designing accessible applications is crucial to ensuring that all users, including those with disabilities, can access and use your Laravel application. Accessible applications adhere to web accessibility standards, making them usable by individuals with various impairments, such as visual, auditory, motor, and cognitive disabilities. Let's explore how to design accessible applications with Laravel.

Semantic HTML

Use semantic HTML elements to provide meaningful structure in your Laravel PWA views, enhancing accessibility for all users:

```
<!-- Example of using semantic HTML in a Laravel PWA view -->
<header>
    <h1>Welcome to our PWA</h1>
</header>
<nav>
    <!-- Navigation links -->
</nav>
<main>
    <!-- Main content -->
</main>
<footer>
    <!-- Footer content -->
</footer>
```

ARIA Roles and Attributes

Leverage ARIA roles and attributes to enhance the accessibility of interactive elements in your Laravel PWA:

```
<!-- Example of using ARIA attributes in a Laravel PWA view -->
<button aria-label="Open Menu" aria-controls="menu-items" aria-expanded="false">Menu</button>
<div id="menu-items" role="menu" aria-hidden="true">
    <!-- Menu items -->
</div>
```

Focus Management

Ensure that your Laravel PWA maintains a logical and consistent focus order for keyboard users:

```
<!-- Example of setting tabindex and focus management in a Laravel PWA
view -->
<input type="text" tabindex="1">
<input type="checkbox" tabindex="2">
```

Alternative Text for Images

Always provide descriptive alternative text for images in your Laravel PWA to make visual content accessible to screen readers and users who cannot view images:

```
<!-- Example of using alt text for an image in a Laravel PWA view -->
<img src="/path/to/image.jpg" alt="A scenic view of a mountain landscape">
```

Form Accessibility

Ensure that form elements have clear and concise labels in your Laravel PWA:

```
<!-- Example of using labels and form validation in a Laravel PWA view -->
<label for="username">Username</label>
<input type="text" id="username" name="username" required>
```

Color Contrast

Maintain sufficient color contrast between text and background in your Laravel PWA to improve readability for users with visual impairments.

Test with Assistive Technologies

Regularly test your Laravel PWA using screen readers and other assistive technologies to verify its accessibility and identify any issues that need to be addressed.

Accessibility Auditing Tools

Use accessibility auditing tools, such as Lighthouse in Chrome DevTools, to automatically identify potential accessibility issues in your Laravel PWA.

Provide Transcripts and Captions

Include transcripts for audio and video content and captions for videos in your Laravel PWA to make them accessible to users with hearing impairments.

Implementing User Feedback and Usability Testing in Laravel Applications

Implementing user feedback and conducting usability testing are essential steps in enhancing the user experience and improving the overall usability of your Laravel application. Gathering feedback from users and testing your application with real users can help identify pain points, discover usability issues, and gather insights for making informed improvements. Let's explore how to implement user feedback and usability testing in your Laravel applications.

Feedback Collection Mechanisms

Implement a feedback form in your Laravel PWA where users can provide their thoughts, suggestions, and bug reports:

```
<!-- Example of a feedback form in a Laravel PWA view -->
<form action="/submit-feedback" method="POST">
    @csrf
```

```html
<textarea name="feedback" placeholder="Please provide your feedback"></
textarea>
    <button type="submit">Submit</button>
</form>
```

Error Reporting

Set up error reporting and logging in your Laravel PWA to capture any errors or issues users may encounter. Log critical errors with context information:

```php
// Example of error reporting and logging in Laravel
try {
    // Code that may throw an error
} catch (Exception $e) {
    Log::error('Critical Error: ' . $e->getMessage(), ['context' =>
$additionalContext]);
}
```

Analyze User Behavior

Utilize analytics tools in your Laravel PWA to track user behavior, interactions, and navigation patterns:

```html
<!-- Example of adding Google Analytics tracking to a Laravel PWA -->
<script async src="https://www.googletagmanager.com/gtag/js?id=YOUR_GA_
TRACKING_ID"></script>
<script>
    window.dataLayer = window.dataLayer || [];
    function gtag() { dataLayer.push(arguments); }
    gtag('js', new Date());
    gtag('config', 'YOUR_GA_TRACKING_ID');
</script>
```

Usability Testing

Conduct usability testing with real users to evaluate your Laravel PWA's effectiveness. Observe their interactions and gather feedback on usability and the user interface.

A/B Testing

Perform A/B testing in your Laravel PWA to compare different design or feature variations and determine which performs better with users:

```
// Example of A/B testing in a Laravel PWA
if (rand(0, 1) === 0) {
    // Show variation A
} else {
    // Show variation B
}
```

User Surveys

Create user surveys in your Laravel PWA to gather specific feedback on usability, user satisfaction, and perceived performance:

```
<!-- Example of a user survey in a Laravel PWA view -->
<form action="/submit-survey" method="POST">
    @csrf
    <label>How satisfied are you with the application?</label>
    <input type="radio" name="satisfaction" value="1"> Very Satisfied
    <input type="radio" name="satisfaction" value="2"> Satisfied
    <input type="radio" name="satisfaction" value="3"> Neutral
    <input type="radio" name="satisfaction" value="4"> Dissatisfied
    <input type="radio" name="satisfaction" value="5"> Very Dissatisfied
    <button type="submit">Submit</button>
</form>
```

Feedback Analysis and Action Plan

Analyze the collected feedback and usability testing results. Create an action plan to address the feedback and prioritize improvements.

Iterative Improvement

Iteratively implement the identified improvements in your Laravel PWA based on user feedback and test results.

Accessibility Testing

Conduct accessibility testing to ensure that your Laravel PWA is usable by users with disabilities. Test with screen readers and other assistive technologies.

Performance Testing

Perform performance testing to assess your Laravel PWA's speed and responsiveness. Optimize critical areas to improve the overall user experience.

User Support and Communication

Provide clear channels for users to reach out for support or assistance in your Laravel PWA. Promptly respond to user queries and communicate updates on resolved issues.

Bug Tracking and Issue Management

Use a bug tracking system in your Laravel PWA to record and manage reported issues. Prioritize and resolve bugs based on their impact on users.

By implementing user feedback mechanisms and conducting usability testing in your Laravel PWA, you can continuously improve the user experience and create a user-centric application. User feedback and usability testing allow you to identify pain points, optimize workflows, and make data-driven decisions to enhance your Laravel PWA based on real user needs and preferences. This approach promotes inclusivity, ensures accessibility, and provides a more positive and valuable experience for all users of your Progressive Web Application.

Summary

Over the course of this chapter, you learned sophisticated UI/UX design patterns for Laravel web apps. We focused on developing interfaces that are intuitive, visually appealing, and user-friendly, improving the entire user experience. We covered responsive design principles and how to efficiently use them in Laravel applications to offer a consistent experience across multiple devices and screen sizes. We also discussed sophisticated UI components and design principles for optimizing page loading speeds and increasing interactivity, such as endless scrolling, lazy loading, and dynamic content loading. We also delved into how to use animations and transitions to create interesting user interfaces.

In the next chapter, we'll explore advanced analytics and reporting in Laravel.

CHAPTER 21

Advanced Analytics and Reporting in Laravel

In the previous chapter, we delved into the captivating realm of advanced UI/UX design patterns for Laravel, mastering the art of creating user-friendly interfaces and enhancing user experiences. As our journey through Laravel's advanced features continues, we now shift our focus to another critical aspect of application development—advanced analytics and reporting.

Integrating Analytics Tools with Laravel

In this section, we will explore the integration of powerful analytics tools with Laravel. Analytics tools provide invaluable insights into application performance, user behavior, and other essential metrics. We will learn how to integrate popular analytics platforms with Laravel, enabling us to track and analyze critical data.

Collecting and Analyzing Application Metrics and User Behavior

Data collection and analysis are crucial for understanding how our applications are performing and how users interact with them. We will discover how to collect and analyze application metrics and user behavior data, gaining valuable insights to make data-driven decisions.

Building Custom Dashboards and Reports with Laravel

Custom dashboards and reports provide a comprehensive view of application performance and user engagement. We will learn how to build custom dashboards and reports in Laravel, presenting data in a visually appealing and meaningful manner.

Implementing A/B Testing and Conversion Tracking

A/B testing is a powerful technique for comparing two different versions of a feature or design to determine which performs better. We will explore how to implement A/B testing and conversion tracking in Laravel applications, optimizing our applications based on real-world user feedback.

© Sivaraj Selvaraj 2024
S. Selvaraj, *Building Real-Time Marvels with Laravel*, https://doi.org/10.1007/978-1-4842-9789-6_21

Using Data Visualization Libraries with Laravel

Data visualization plays a crucial role in making complex data understandable and actionable. We will discover how to use data visualization libraries with Laravel to create interactive and informative charts, graphs, and visual representations of our data.

Throughout this chapter, we will immerse ourselves in the world of advanced analytics and reporting in Laravel. By integrating analytics tools, collecting and analyzing data, and building custom reports, we can gain valuable insights into application performance and user behavior. So let's embark on this journey of advanced analytics and reporting to unlock the full potential of our Laravel applications and make data-driven decisions for success!

Integrating Analytics Tools with Laravel

Data-driven insights play a crucial role in understanding user behavior, monitoring application performance, and making informed business decisions. Analytics tools offer valuable metrics and statistics that help developers and business owners gain actionable insights into their Laravel applications.

In this guide, we will explore how to integrate analytics tools with Laravel to track user interactions, monitor key performance indicators (KPIs), and identify areas for improvement.

We'll cover the process of integrating popular analytics platforms such as Google Analytics, Mixpanel, and Segment, leveraging their APIs and SDKs to capture and analyze user data effectively.

Additionally, we'll discuss how to set up event tracking, custom dimensions, and conversion tracking to measure the success of specific user actions and marketing campaigns.

Understanding the data provided by analytics tools empowers developers to optimize user experiences, identify potential bottlenecks, and tailor marketing strategies to specific user segments.

Throughout this guide, we'll also explore privacy considerations and compliance with data protection regulations to ensure responsible data handling and user privacy.

Whether you are a developer or a business owner, integrating analytics tools with Laravel can provide valuable insights that drive your application's success. Let's dive into the world of analytics integration and harness the power of data to optimize your Laravel application and make informed decisions for your business.

Let's Explore How to Integrate Google Analytics with Laravel

Create a Google Analytics account.

If you don't have a Google Analytics account, sign up for one at `https://analytics.google.com/`. Once you create your account, you'll get a unique tracking ID for your website.

Install the Laravel analytics package.

To simplify the integration process, you can use the "spatie/laravel-analytics" package. Install it using Composer:

```
composer require spatie/laravel-analytics
```

Configure.

After installing the package, add the service provider and alias to your config/app.php file:

```php
// config/app.php
'providers' => [
    // ...
    Spatie\Analytics\AnalyticsServiceProvider::class,
],
'aliases' => [
    // ...
    'Analytics' => Spatie\Analytics\AnalyticsFacade::class,
],
```

Authenticate with Google Analytics.

To authenticate your Laravel application with Google Analytics, you need to add the required configuration in config/analytics.php. You can either use a service account or OAuth. For simplicity, let's use OAuth:

```
// config/analytics.php
return [
    // ...
    'view_id' => 'YOUR_VIEW_ID', // Replace with your Google
    Analytics view ID
    'oauth_credentials' => [
        'client_id' => 'YOUR_CLIENT_ID',
        'client_secret' => 'YOUR_CLIENT_SECRET',
        'redirect_uri' => 'YOUR_REDIRECT_URI',
        'refresh_token' => 'YOUR_REFRESH_TOKEN',
    ],
];
```

Obtain OAuth credentials.

To get the client_id, client_secret, and redirect_uri, you need to create a project in the Google Developer Console and enable the Analytics API. Then, set up the OAuth 2.0 credentials and get the necessary credentials.

Retrieve and display analytics data.

Now that you've integrated Google Analytics with Laravel, you can retrieve and display analytics data in your application. For example, you can fetch the number of pageviews for the current day:

```
use Spatie\Analytics\AnalyticsFacade as Analytics;
public function index()
{
    // Get the pageviews for today
    $pageviews = Analytics::fetchTotalVisitorsAndPageViews(1)->first();
    return view('dashboard', compact('pageviews'));
}
```

Display the data.

In your view (e.g., dashboard.blade.php), you can display the analytics data:

```html
<!-- dashboard.blade.php -->
@extends('layouts.app')
@section('content')
    <div class="container">
        <h1>Dashboard</h1>
        <p>Total Pageviews Today: {{ $pageviews['pageViews'] }}</p>
    </div>
@endsection
```

By following these steps, you can successfully integrate Google Analytics with your Laravel application and start tracking user behavior and website metrics. You can further explore the "spatie/laravel-analytics" package documentation for additional functionalities and more advanced analytics tracking in your Laravel application.

Collecting and Analyzing Application Metrics and User Behavior

Collecting and analyzing application metrics and user behavior is crucial for understanding how users interact with your Laravel application and identifying areas for improvement. Here's how you can collect and analyze this data.

Logging

Laravel provides a built-in logging system that allows you to record various events, errors, and activities in your application. You can use the logging system to capture important events and data, such as user actions, API requests, or critical errors:

```
// Example of logging in Laravel
Log::info('User logged in', ['user_id' => $user->id]);
Log::error('Critical error occurred', ['exception' => $exception]);
```

Custom Event Listeners

Create custom event listeners in Laravel to capture specific events within your application. For example, you can listen for user registration, login, or product purchase events and record them in your database or log file:

```
// Example of custom event listener in Laravel
class UserRegisteredListener
{
    public function handle(UserRegisteredEvent $event)
    {
        // Record the user registration event
        UserActivity::create([
            'user_id' => $event->user->id,
            'action' => 'registered',
            'timestamp' => now(),
        ]);
    }
}
```

Database Queries

Use Laravel's Eloquent ORM or database queries to collect relevant data from your application's database. For example, you can retrieve information about user activities, product views, or orders:

```
// Example of collecting user behavior data using database queries
in Laravel
$userActivities = UserActivity::where('user_id', $user->id)-
>orderBy('timestamp', 'desc')->get();
```

User Tracking and Cookies

Implement user tracking using cookies or sessions to monitor user behavior, such as the number of pageviews, time spent on the website, or actions taken within a session:

```
// Example of tracking user behavior with cookies in Laravel
public function trackUserBehavior(Request $request)
{
    $userData = [
        'ip_address' => $request->ip(),
        'user_agent' => $request->userAgent(),
        'last_activity' => now(),
        // Add other relevant data
    ];
    $request->session()->put('user_data', $userData);
}
```

Third-Party APIs

Integrate with third-party APIs or analytics tools to gather more comprehensive data. For example, you can integrate Google Analytics or Mixpanel to track user behavior and interactions.

Analyzing the Data

Store the collected data in a database or external storage (e.g., Elasticsearch) for analysis. Use data visualization tools like Kibana or Grafana to create meaningful reports and visualizations. Identify patterns, trends, and user preferences to make data-driven decisions.

Improving User Experience

Based on the insights from data analysis, implement improvements in your Laravel application to enhance the user experience, optimize performance, and address pain points.

By collecting and analyzing application metrics and user behavior, you can gain valuable insights into how users interact with your Laravel application. This data-driven approach empowers you to make informed decisions, optimize your application, and provide a better experience for your users.

Building Custom Dashboards and Reports with Laravel

Building custom dashboards and reports with Laravel allows you to present application metrics and analytics data in a user-friendly and visually appealing manner. Custom dashboards enable you to monitor key performance indicators (KPIs), track trends, and gain valuable insights into your application's performance. Figure 21-1 illustrates custom dashboards.

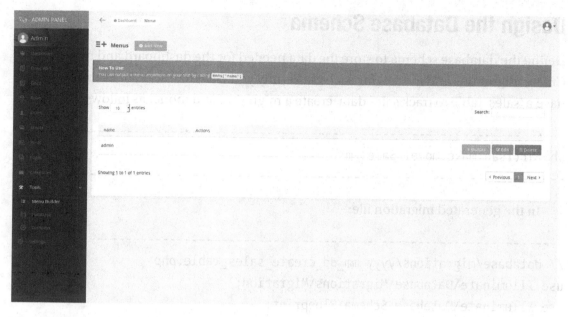

Figure 21-1. *Custom dashboard*

Here's a step-by-step guide on how to build custom dashboards and reports with Laravel.

Define Dashboard Requirements

Before you start building the dashboard, it's essential to define the requirements and the data you want to present. Identify the key performance indicators (KPIs) and metrics you want to display on the dashboard. Consider the types of charts, graphs, and visualizations that will best represent the data.

Set Up a Laravel Project

Create a new Laravel project or use an existing one to start building your custom dashboard. If you haven't already installed Laravel, you can do so using Composer:

```
composer create-project laravel/laravel my-dashboard-project
cd my-dashboard-project
```

Design the Database Schema

Define the database schema to store the data needed for the dashboard and reports. Create migrations and models for each data entity you want to track. For example, if you have a 'sales' table to track sales data, create a migration and model as follows:

```
php artisan make:model Sale -m
```

In the generated migration file:

```php
// database/migrations/yyyy_mm_dd_create_sales_table.php
use Illuminate\Database\Migrations\Migration;
use Illuminate\Database\Schema\Blueprint;
use Illuminate\Support\Facades\Schema;
class CreateSalesTable extends Migration
{
    public function up()
    {
        Schema::create('sales', function (Blueprint $table) {
            $table->id();
            $table->string('product');
            $table->integer('quantity');
            $table->decimal('amount', 8, 2);
            $table->timestamps();
        });
    }
    public function down()
    {
        Schema::dropIfExists('sales');
    }
}
```

Seed the Database with Sample Data

To test and develop your dashboard, seed the database with some sample data. You can use database seeders to populate the tables with test data:

```
php artisan db:seed
```

Create a seeder to populate the 'sales' table with sample data:

```
php artisan make:seeder SalesSeeder
```

In the generated seeder file:

```
// database/seeders/SalesSeeder.php
use Illuminate\Database\Seeder;
use App\Models\Sale;
class SalesSeeder extends Seeder
{
    public function run()
    {
        Sale::create([
            'product' => 'Widget A',
            'quantity' => 10,
            'amount' => 100.00,
        ]);
        Sale::create([
            'product' => 'Widget B',
            'quantity' => 5,
            'amount' => 75.50,
        ]);
        // Add more sample data as needed
    }
}
```

In the DatabaseSeeder.php file, call the SalesSeeder:

```
// database/seeders/DatabaseSeeder.php
use Illuminate\Database\Seeder;
class DatabaseSeeder extends Seeder
{
    public function run()
    {
        $this->call(SalesSeeder::class);
    }
}
```

Run the seeder to populate the database:

```
php artisan db:seed
```

Create Routes and Controllers

Define routes in `routes/web.php` to handle requests for the dashboard and reports. Create controllers to fetch the data from the database and pass it to the views for rendering, for example:

```
// routes/web.php
Route::get('/dashboard', 'DashboardController@index');
Route::get('/reports', 'ReportsController@index');
```

Define routes and a controller to handle the dashboard:

```
// routes/web.php
use App\Http\Controllers\DashboardController;
```

```
Route::get('/dashboard', [DashboardController::class, 'index']);
Create a controller:
```

---

php artisan make:controller DashboardController

In the generated controller file:

```php
// app/Http/Controllers/DashboardController.php
use App\Models\Sale;
use Illuminate\Http\Request;
class DashboardController extends Controller
{
    public function index()
    {
        $salesData = Sale::all();
        return view('dashboard.index', compact('salesData'));
    }
}
```

Create Dashboard and Report Views

Design and create the dashboard and report views in the `resources/views` directory.
You can use Blade templates to render the data in HTML format and include charts and
visualizations using JavaScript libraries like Chart.js or D3.js.

For example, in the `dashboard.index` view:

```php
<!-- resources/views/dashboard/index.blade.php -->
@extends('layouts.app')
@section('content')
    <h1>Dashboard</h1>
    <div id="sales-chart"></div>
@endsection
```

```
@section('scripts')
    <script>
        // Use JavaScript to render the sales chart using Chart.js or other
        libraries
    </script>
@endsection
```

Styling and Enhancements

Apply CSS styles and customizations to improve the appearance of your dashboard and reports. You can also add additional features, such as date filters, data aggregation, and export options.

Authentication and Authorization

If your dashboard contains sensitive data or is intended for specific users, implement authentication and authorization to control access to the dashboard and reports.

Deploy the Dashboard

Finally, deploy your Laravel dashboard to your preferred hosting environment. Ensure that the database and server configurations are set up correctly for production.

Implementing A/B Testing and Conversion Tracking

Implementing A/B testing and conversion tracking in your Laravel application allows you to compare different versions of your website or specific features to measure user engagement and conversion rates. Conversion tracking helps you monitor user actions and measure the effectiveness of specific call-to-action (CTA) elements. Here's how you can implement A/B testing and conversion tracking in Laravel:

Define the A/B testing experiment.

Let's say you want to test two different button colors (blue and green) on your website's call-to-action (CTA) button to see which one leads to more sign-ups.

Generate a random test group.

You can generate a random test group for the A/B test by using Laravel's session to store the assigned group (A or B). We'll use a simple example of randomizing the button color for each user visit:

```
// Example of generating a random test group (A or B)
public function index(Request $request)
{
    $testGroup = mt_rand(0, 1); // 0 for A, 1 for B
    $request->session()->put('test_group', $testGroup);
    // Other logic for the dashboard view
}
```

Track user actions.

To track conversions, set up a custom event to record user sign-ups as conversions. For this example, let's assume we have a user registration event and we want to track successful sign-ups as conversions:

```
// Example of custom event listener in Laravel for conversion tracking
class UserRegisteredListener
{
    public function handle(UserRegisteredEvent $event)
    {
        if ($event->isConversion) {
            // Record the conversion event
            Conversion::create([
                'user_id' => $event->user->id,
                'goal_name' => 'Sign Up',
                'timestamp' => now(),
            ]);
        }
    }
}
```

Measure and compare results.

Collect data on the number of sign-ups from both test groups (A and B) over a set period. Calculate the conversion rate for each group by dividing the number of successful sign-ups by the total number of visitors in that group:

```
// Example of calculating conversion rate for A/B test groups
$groupAVisitors = User::where('test_group', 0)->count();
$groupBVisitors = User::where('test_group', 1)->count();
$groupAConversions = Conversion::where('goal_name', 'Sign Up')-
>where('user_id', 'test_group', 0)->count();
$groupBConversions = Conversion::where('goal_name', 'Sign Up')-
>where('user_id', 'test_group', 1)->count();
$groupAConversionRate = $groupAVisitors > 0 ? ($groupAConversions /
$groupAVisitors) * 100 : 0;
$groupBConversionRate = $groupBVisitors > 0 ? ($groupBConversions /
$groupBVisitors) * 100 : 0;
```

Choose the winning variation.

Compare the conversion rates for both groups. The variation with the higher conversion rate is the winner and should be implemented as the default option.

Ensure statistical significance (optional).

To ensure statistical significance, you may use statistical tools or libraries to analyze the results. For simplicity, we'll skip this step in the example.

Use A/B testing libraries (optional).

There are A/B testing libraries available for Laravel, such as "laravel-ab," which can simplify the process of setting up and managing A/B tests.

Visualize results (optional).

Use data visualization libraries like Chart.js or Laravel Charts to create visual representations of the A/B test results.

By implementing A/B testing and conversion tracking in your Laravel application, you can measure the effectiveness of different variations and make data-driven decisions to optimize your website for improved user engagement and conversion rates.

Using Data Visualization Libraries with Laravel

Using data visualization libraries like D3.js with Laravel allows you to create dynamic and interactive visualizations to present complex data in a user-friendly and engaging manner. D3.js is a powerful JavaScript library for manipulating documents based on data and creating stunning visualizations. Figure 21-2 illustrates data visualization in D3.js.

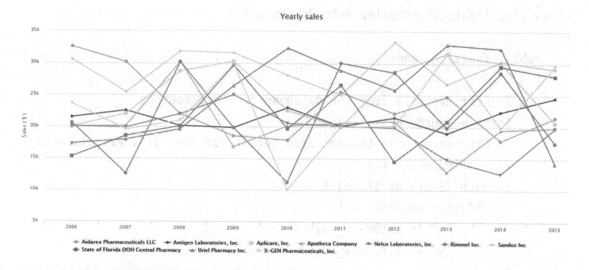

Figure 21-2. *Data visualization in D3.js*

Here's how you can use D3.js with Laravel:

Include the D3.js library.

First, include the D3.js library in your Laravel application. You can download the library or use a CDN to include it in your views:

```
<!-- Example of including D3.js from a CDN -->
<script src="https://d3js.org/d3.v7.min.js"></script>
```

Prepare data in the Laravel controller.

In your Laravel controller, prepare the data you want to visualize using D3.js. You can fetch data from the database or other sources and format it into the required format for the visualization:

```php
// Example of preparing data in Laravel controller
class VisualizationController extends Controller
{
    public function index()
    {
        // Retrieve data from the database or other sources
        $data = YourModel::all();
        // Prepare data in the required format for the D3.js visualization
        $formattedData = [];
        foreach ($data as $item) {
            $formattedData[] = [
                'x' => $item->x_value,
                'y' => $item->y_value,
            ];
        }
        // Pass the formatted data to the view
        return view('visualization.index', compact('formattedData'));
    }
}
```

Create visualizations in the view.

In the view (e.g., 'visualization.blade.php'), use D3.js to create the data visualization. You can use various D3.js functions and methods to render different types of visualizations, such as bar charts, line charts, scatter plots, and more:

```php
<!-- Example of creating a bar chart with D3.js in the Laravel view -->
@extends('layouts.app')
@section('content')
    <div class="container">
        <h1>Data Visualization with D3.js</h1>
```

```
        <div id="chart"></div>
    </div>
    <script>
        // D3.js code to create the bar chart
        var data = {!! json_encode($formattedData) !!};
        var svg = d3.select("#chart")
            .append("svg")
            .attr("width", 500)
            .attr("height", 300);
        var xScale = d3.scaleBand()
            .domain(data.map(d => d.x))
            .range([0, 400])
            .padding(0.1);
        var yScale = d3.scaleLinear()
            .domain([0, d3.max(data, d => d.y)])
            .range([300, 0]);
        svg.selectAll("rect")
            .data(data)
            .enter()
            .append("rect")
            .attr("x", d => xScale(d.x))
            .attr("y", d => yScale(d.y))
            .attr("width", xScale.bandwidth())
            .attr("height", d => 300 - yScale(d.y))
            .attr("fill", "steelblue");
    </script>
@endsection
```

Style and customize the visualization.

You can further style and customize the visualization to match your application's
design and requirements. D3.js provides a wide range of options for customizing visual
elements like colors, labels, axes, and more.

Responsive visualization (optional).

To make the visualization responsive to different screen sizes, you can use CSS and D3.js to adjust the chart dimensions based on the container's width.

By using D3.js with Laravel, you can create impressive data visualizations that enhance the presentation of complex data and enable users to gain insights from the data with interactive and engaging charts and graphs. Remember to optimize the performance of your visualizations for a smooth user experience.

By leveraging advanced analytics and reporting techniques in Laravel, you can make data-driven decisions, gain valuable insights into your application's performance, and provide users with an exceptional experience. Custom dashboards, A/B testing, and data visualization empower you to optimize your application for improved user engagement and conversion rates.

Summary

In this chapter, we delved into advanced analytics and reporting in Laravel web apps. We covered how to use data to get valuable insights and make sound decisions and how to include analytics tools and frameworks, including Google Analytics and Chart. js, into your Laravel apps in order to measure and visualize user activity and application performance. The chapter also demonstrated data collection and processing strategies, as well as how to produce custom reports and interactive dashboards. You also saw how to use data visualization to display complex data in an understandable and interesting manner.

In the next chapter, we will cover advanced third-party integrations.

CHAPTER 22

Advanced Third-Party Integrations

In the previous chapter, we explored the captivating world of advanced analytics and reporting in Laravel, leveraging data-driven insights to optimize application performance and user engagement. As our journey through Laravel's advanced features continues, we now turn our attention to the realm of advanced third-party integrations—a crucial aspect of extending the functionality and integration reach of our applications.

Integrating Laravel with Payment Gateways

In this section, we will delve into the seamless integration of Laravel with popular payment gateways. Enabling secure and smooth payment processing is essential for any ecommerce or subscription-based application. We will learn how to integrate payment gateways into Laravel applications, facilitating transactions and providing a seamless checkout experience for users.

Implementing Social Media and Authentication (OAuth) Integrations

Social media integration and OAuth authentication have become integral parts of modern web applications. We will explore how to implement social media logins and OAuth integrations in Laravel, enabling users to authenticate with their social media accounts and interact with our applications.

Integrating Laravel with Email Marketing Services

Email marketing is a powerful tool for engaging with users and promoting products or services. We will learn how to integrate Laravel with popular email marketing services like Mailchimp, allowing us to manage email campaigns, collect subscriber data, and deliver targeted content to users.

© Sivaraj Selvaraj 2024
S. Selvaraj, *Building Real-Time Marvels with Laravel*, https://doi.org/10.1007/978-1-4842-9789-6_22

Integrating Laravel with Cloud Storage Providers

Cloud storage providers offer scalable and cost-effective solutions for managing and serving media files and assets. We will explore how to integrate Laravel with cloud storage providers like AWS S3, streamlining file uploads, storage, and retrieval in our applications.

Building Custom API Integrations with Laravel

Custom API integrations allow us to connect with external services and fetch or push data from and to our applications. We will discover how to build custom API integrations with Laravel, expanding the functionalities of our applications by leveraging external data and services.

Throughout this chapter, we will immerse ourselves in the world of advanced third-party integrations in Laravel. By seamlessly integrating with payment gateways, social media platforms, email marketing services, cloud storage providers, and custom APIs, we can unlock new possibilities and offer enhanced services to our users. So let's embark on this journey of advanced third-party integrations to take our Laravel applications to greater heights of functionality and efficiency!

Integrating Laravel with Payment Gateways

Laravel provides robust support for integrating with popular payment gateways like Stripe, PayPal, and Razorpay.

When integrating payment gateways like Stripe, PayPal, and Razorpay into your Laravel application, it is essential to follow the official documentation provided by these platforms. Their documentation will always contain the most accurate and up-to-date instructions on how to implement the payment gateway correctly. Here are some important points to consider:

Official documentation: Always refer to the official documentation of the payment gateway you are integrating. Each platform provides detailed guides, API references, and code samples to help you implement the integration correctly.

Documentation links are as follows:

Stripe: `https://stripe.com/docs`

PayPal: `https://developer.paypal.com/docs/api/overview/`

Razorpay: `https://razorpay.com/docs/`

Version compatibility: Ensure that your Laravel application uses the correct version of the payment gateway's SDK or API, which aligns with the supported version.

Security and compliance: Payment gateways have strict security measures and compliance requirements. Follow the security guidelines provided by the payment platform to ensure that customer data and payment transactions are handled securely.

API keys and credentials: Protect your API keys, secret keys, and other credentials. Store them securely, preferably in environment variables, and avoid exposing them in your codebase.

Sandbox environment: Use sandboxes or test environments provided by payment gateways for initial development and testing. This allows you to test transactions without using real money.

Error handling: Implement proper error handling for payment processing. Handle potential errors gracefully and provide clear error messages to users when necessary.

Confirmation and notification: Notify users of successful payments, order confirmations, and any transaction status updates using the payment gateway's webhooks or IPN (Instant Payment Notification) mechanisms.

Refunds and disputes: Familiarize yourself with the refund and dispute resolution processes of the payment gateway to handle customer requests efficiently.

Remember that payment gateways may update their APIs and features over time. Always stay informed about any changes or updates to ensure that your integration remains functional and compliant with the latest standards.

By following the official documentation and staying up to date with the latest instructions, you can create a seamless and secure payment experience for your users, increasing customer trust and satisfaction.

To integrate these payment gateways into your Laravel application, you can follow these steps:

Install the required packages.

First, you need to install the necessary packages for integrating Laravel with Stripe and PayPal. Use Composer to install the official packages: 'laravel-stripe' for Stripe and 'laravel-paypal' for PayPal.

```
composer require stripe/stripe-php
composer require srmklive/paypal
```

Configure the package.

After installing the packages, configure them with your API credentials. Open the '.env' file and add the following lines:

```
STRIPE_KEY=your_stripe_key
STRIPE_SECRET=your_stripe_secret
PAYPAL_CLIENT_ID=your_paypal_client_id
PAYPAL_SECRET=your_paypal_secret
```

Set up routes and controllers.

Create routes to handle payment-related actions. Open the 'routes/web.php' file and define the necessary routes, for example:

```php
use App\Http\Controllers\PaymentController;
Route::get('/payment', [PaymentController::class, 'create'])-
>name('payment.create');
Route::post('/payment/process', [PaymentController::class, 'process'])-
>name('payment.process');
Route::post('/payment/webhook/stripe', [PaymentController::class,
'stripeWebhook'])->name('payment.stripe.webhook');
```

Implement payment processing logic.

Create a controller called 'PaymentController' to handle the payment processing. In the 'create' method, initiate the payment and display the payment form. In the 'process' method, handle the payment response. Here's an example:

```php
namespace App\Http\Controllers;
use Illuminate\Http\Request;
use Stripe\PaymentIntent;
class PaymentController extends Controller
{
    public function create()
```

```
    {
        return view('payment.create');
    }
    public function process(Request $request)
    {
        // Process the payment response from the gateway (e.g., Stripe
or PayPal)
    }
}
```

Handle payment responses.

In the 'process' method of the 'PaymentController', handle the payment response from the gateway. For example, in the case of Stripe, you can use the 'stripe-php' package to handle the response:

```php
use Stripe\PaymentIntent;
public function process(Request $request)
{
    $paymentIntentId = $request->input('payment_intent');
    $paymentIntent = PaymentIntent::retrieve($paymentIntentId);
    if ($paymentIntent->status === 'succeeded') {
        // Payment succeeded, update order status, store transaction
        details, etc.
        return redirect()->route('payment.success');
    } else {
        // Payment failed, handle error, display error message, etc.
        return redirect()->route('payment.failure');
    }
}
```

Implement webhooks.

Payment gateways often send webhook notifications for events like successful or failed payments. Set up webhook routes and corresponding methods in the 'PaymentController' to handle these notifications, for example, in the case of Stripe:

```
-----------------------------------------------------------------------
use Illuminate\Http\Request;
use Stripe\Webhook;
public function stripeWebhook(Request $request)
{
    $payload = $request->getContent();
    $signature = $request->header('Stripe-Signature');
    try {
        $event = Webhook::constructEvent($payload, $signature,
        $yourWebhookSigningSecret);
        // Handle the specific event type (e.g., payment succeeded,
        failed, etc.)
        switch ($event->type) {
            case 'payment_intent.succeeded':
                // Handle successful payment event
                break;
            case 'payment_intent.failed':
                // Handle failed payment event
                break;
            // Handle other event types as needed
        }
    } catch (Exception $e) {
        // Handle and log any webhook verification or processing errors
    }
    return response('Webhook received');
}
-----------------------------------------------------------------------
```

These code snippets demonstrate the integration of Laravel with payment gateways like Stripe and PayPal. You can customize the code based on your specific requirements and payment gateway of choice.

Implementing Social Media and Authentication (OAuth) Integrations

Laravel offers built-in support for implementing social media authentication using OAuth providers such as Facebook, Twitter, Google, and GitHub. Here's how you can integrate social media authentication into your Laravel application:

Set up OAuth providers.

To implement social media authentication, you need to register your application with the desired OAuth providers (e.g., Facebook, Twitter, Google, and GitHub) to obtain API credentials such as the client ID and client secret.

Configure Laravel.

In the Laravel configuration files, typically located at 'config/services.php', you can add the credentials for each OAuth provider you want to integrate with. This allows Laravel to authenticate and authorize users using the OAuth providers' APIs. Here's an example configuration for integrating with Facebook and Twitter:

```
'facebook' => [
    'client_id' => env('FACEBOOK_CLIENT_ID'),
    'client_secret' => env('FACEBOOK_CLIENT_SECRET'),
    'redirect' => env('FACEBOOK_REDIRECT_URI'),
],
'twitter' => [
    'client_id' => env('TWITTER_CLIENT_ID'),
    'client_secret' => env('TWITTER_CLIENT_SECRET'),
    'redirect' => env('TWITTER_REDIRECT_URI'),
],
```

Create routes and controllers.

Define routes to handle OAuth authentication and authorization callbacks. These routes will redirect users to the OAuth provider's authentication page and handle the response from the provider. Open the 'routes/web.php' file and add the necessary routes. Here's an example:

```
use App\Http\Controllers\Auth\SocialAuthController;
use Laravel\Socialite\Facades\Socialite;
Route::get('/login/{provider}', [SocialAuthController::class,
'redirectToProvider'])->name('social.login');
Route::get('/login/{provider}/callback', [SocialAuthController::class,
'handleProviderCallback']);
```

Implement authentication logic.

Create a controller called 'SocialAuthController' to handle the authentication logic. In the 'redirectToProvider' method, redirect the user to the OAuth provider's authentication page. In the 'handleProviderCallback' method, handle the response from the provider and authenticate the user. Here's an example:

```
namespace App\Http\Controllers\Auth;
use App\Http\Controllers\Controller;
use Illuminate\Http\Request;
use Laravel\Socialite\Facades\Socialite;
class SocialAuthController extends Controller
{
    public function redirectToProvider($provider)
    {
        return Socialite::driver($provider)->redirect();
    }
    public function handleProviderCallback(Request $request, $provider)
    {
        $socialUser = Socialite::driver($provider)->user();
        // Check if the user is already registered in your application
        $user = User::where('email', $socialUser->getEmail())->first();
        if (!$user) {
            // User is not registered, create a new user record
            $user = User::create([
                'name' => $socialUser->getName(),
                'email' => $socialUser->getEmail(),
```

```
            // Set other user attributes as needed
        ]);
    }
    // Log in the user
    auth()->login($user);
    // Redirect the user to the desired page
    return redirect('/home');
    }
}
```

Handle authenticated users.

Once the user is authenticated, you can create or update a user record in your application's database based on the OAuth provider's response. In the preceding example, we check if the user is already registered using their email. If not, we create a new user record. Finally, we log the user in using Laravel's authentication system.

These code snippets demonstrate the integration of Laravel with social media authentication using OAuth providers. You can customize the code to handle additional OAuth providers and incorporate your application's specific user registration and login logic.

Integrating Laravel with Email Marketing Services

To integrate Laravel with email marketing services like Mailchimp, you can follow these steps:

Install the required package.

Start by installing the 'spatie/laravel-newsletter' package using Composer. This package provides a Laravel wrapper for interacting with popular email marketing services, including Mailchimp:

```
composer require spatie/laravel-newsletter
```

Configure the package.

After installing the package, add the service provider and alias in the 'config/app. php' file:

```
'providers' => [
    // ...
    Spatie\Newsletter\NewsletterServiceProvider::class,
],
'aliases' => [
    // ...
    'Newsletter' => Spatie\Newsletter\NewsletterFacade::class,
],
```

Set up Mailchimp credentials.

Obtain your Mailchimp API key from your Mailchimp account. Open the '.env' file and add the following line with your Mailchimp API key:

```
MAILCHIMP_API_KEY=your_mailchimp_api_key
```

Define mailing list and subscription logic.

Determine which mailing lists you want to manage and the corresponding subscription logic. Create routes and controller methods to handle operations such as subscribing users, unsubscribing users, or updating their preferences. Here's an example:

```
namespace App\Http\Controllers;
use Illuminate\Http\Request;
use Newsletter;
class NewsletterController extends Controller
{
    public function subscribe(Request $request)
    {
        $email = $request->input('email');
```

```
        if (!Newsletter::isSubscribed($email)) {
            Newsletter::subscribe($email);
        }
        // Redirect or show success message
    }
    public function unsubscribe(Request $request)
    {
        $email = $request->input('email');
        if (Newsletter::isSubscribed($email)) {
            Newsletter::unsubscribe($email);
        }
        // Redirect or show success message
    }
}
```

Integrate with your application's logic.

You can integrate the email marketing service with your application's existing logic. For example, you can add an option for users to subscribe to a newsletter during the registration process or send automated emails to subscribers based on specific events. Here's an example of adding the subscription option during user registration:

```
<form action="{{ route('newsletter.subscribe') }}" method="POST">
    @csrf
    <label for="email">Email:</label>
    <input type="email" name="email" id="email" required>
    <button type="submit">Subscribe</button>
</form>
```

```
// Routes
Route::post('/newsletter/subscribe', [NewsletterController::class,
'subscribe'])->name('newsletter.subscribe');
// Controller method
public function subscribe(Request $request)
```

```
{
    $email = $request->input('email');
    // Subscribe the user to the mailing list
    Newsletter::subscribe($email, ['name' => $request->input('name')]);
    // Redirect or show success message
}
```

These code snippets demonstrate the integration of Laravel with an email marketing service like Mailchimp. You can customize the code based on your specific requirements and the email marketing service you are integrating with.

Integrating Laravel with Cloud Storage Providers

To integrate Laravel with cloud storage providers like AWS S3, you can follow these steps:

Install the required package.

To integrate Laravel with cloud storage providers, you can use the 'league/flysystem-aws-s3-v3' package. Install it using Composer:

```
composer require league/flysystem-aws-s3-v3
```

Configure the package.

After installing the package, you need to configure it with your AWS S3 credentials. Open the '.env' file and add the following lines:

```
AWS_ACCESS_KEY_ID=your_access_key
AWS_SECRET_ACCESS_KEY=your_secret_access_key
AWS_DEFAULT_REGION=your_aws_region
AWS_BUCKET=your_bucket_name
```

Set up cloud storage logic.

Determine how you want to handle file uploads and retrievals in your Laravel application. Create routes and controller methods to handle file uploads, file deletions, and serving files to users. Here's an example:

```
--------------------------------------------------------------------------

namespace App\Http\Controllers;
use Illuminate\Http\Request;
use Illuminate\Support\Facades\Storage;
class FileController extends Controller
{
    public function upload(Request $request)
    {
        $file = $request->file('file');
        $path = Storage::disk('s3')->put('uploads', $file);
        // Store the file path in your database or perform other operations
    }
    public function download($filename)
    {
        $path = 'uploads/' . $filename;
        if (Storage::disk('s3')->exists($path)) {
            return Storage::disk('s3')->download($path);
        }
        abort(404);
    }
}

--------------------------------------------------------------------------
```

Integrate with your application's logic.

You can integrate the cloud storage functionality with your application's existing logic. For example, you can store user-uploaded files in the cloud storage provider's database and save the file URLs or keys in your application's database for later retrieval. Here's an example:

```
use Illuminate\Support\Facades\Storage;
public function upload(Request $request)
{
    $file = $request->file('file');
    $path = Storage::disk('s3')->putFile('uploads', $file, 'public');
    // Store the file path or URL in your database for later retrieval
    $fileUrl = Storage::disk('s3')->url($path);
    // Perform other operations and return a response
}
```

These code snippets demonstrate the integration of Laravel with a cloud storage provider like AWS S3. You can customize the code based on your specific requirements and the cloud storage provider you are integrating with.

Building Custom API Integrations with Laravel

Laravel makes it easy to build custom API integrations with external services. Here's an overview of the steps involved:

Define the API endpoints.

Determine the endpoints you need to interact with the external service. Create routes in Laravel to handle these endpoints, for example:

```
use App\Http\Controllers\Api\ExternalServiceController;
Route::get('/external-service/resource', [ExternalServiceController::class,
'getResource'])->name('external-service.get-resource');
Route::post('/external-service/resource', [ExternalServiceController::class
, 'createResource'])->name('external-service.create-resource');
```

Implement the API logic.

Create a controller called 'ExternalServiceController' to handle the API logic. In the controller methods, implement the logic to interact with the external API. You can use Laravel's built-in HTTP client or packages like Guzzle to send requests to the API, handle responses, and process data. Here's an example:

```php
namespace App\Http\Controllers\Api;
use Illuminate\Http\Request;
use Illuminate\Support\Facades\Http;
class ExternalServiceController extends Controller
{
    public function getResource()
    {
        $response = Http::get('https://api.external-service.com/resource');
        if ($response->successful()) {
            $data = $response->json();
            // Process and return the retrieved resource
            return response()->json($data);
        }
        // Handle unsuccessful API response
        abort($response->status());
    }
    public function createResource(Request $request)
    {
        $response = Http::post('https://api.external-service.com/
        resource', [
            'data' => $request->input('data'),
        ]);
        if ($response->successful()) {
            $data = $response->json();
            // Process and return the created resource
            return response()->json($data);
        }
        // Handle unsuccessful API response
        abort($response->status());
    }
}
```

Authenticate with the API.

If the external API requires authentication, you need to implement the authentication process. This may involve obtaining API keys, tokens, or credentials and passing them in the request headers or query parameters. Here's an example of adding an API key to the request headers:

```php
use Illuminate\Support\Facades\Http;
public function getResource()
{
    $response = Http::withHeaders([
        'Authorization' => 'Bearer your_api_key',
    ])->get('https://api.external-service.com/resource');
    // Handle the API response as before
}
```

Handle API responses.

Handle the responses received from the external API. You can parse the response data, transform it if necessary, store it in your application's database, or present it to the user. Here's an example of parsing and transforming the API response:

```php
use Illuminate\Support\Facades\Http;
public function getResource()
{
    $response = Http::get('https://api.external-service.com/resource');
    if ($response->successful()) {
        $data = $response->json();
        // Transform the API response data
        $transformedData = $this->transformApiResponse($data);
        // Store the transformed data in your application or present it to
        the user
        // ...
        return response()->json($transformedData);
    }
```

```
    // Handle unsuccessful API response
    abort($response->status());
}
private function transformApiResponse($data)
{
    // Transform the API response data here
    // ...
    return $transformedData;
}
```

Implement error handling and logging.

Implement error handling mechanisms to handle API errors and exceptions. You can log errors for debugging purposes and provide appropriate error responses to the user.

Here's an example of logging API errors:

```
use Illuminate\Support\Facades\Http;
use Illuminate\Support\Facades\Log;
public function getResource()
{
    try {
        $response = Http::get('https://api.external-service.com/resource');
        if ($response->successful()) {
            $data = $response->json();
            // Process and return the retrieved resource
            return response()->json($data);
        }
        // Handle unsuccessful API response
        abort($response->status());
    } catch (\Exception $e) {
        // Log the API exception for debugging
        Log::error('API Error: ' . $e->getMessage());
```

```
    // Handle the error and return an appropriate response
    // ...
  }
}
```

These code snippets demonstrate the process of building custom API integrations with Laravel. You can customize the code based on your specific requirements and the external API you are integrating with.

By following these steps, you can build custom API integrations within your Laravel application, allowing seamless communication with external services.

Summary

In this chapter, we focused on advanced third-party integrations in the context of Laravel web development. The chapter explained how to integrate external services and APIs into Laravel applications to increase their functionality. We also covered numerous integration mechanisms, such as RESTful APIs, OAuth, and webhooks, that will allow them to communicate smoothly between their apps and other platforms. We discussed approaches for dealing with third-party authentication, authorization, and data exchange, as well as how to integrate popular APIs into your Laravel apps, such as social media networks, payment gateways, and cloud services.

In the next chapter, we will cover how to secure Laravel applications.

CHAPTER 23

Securing Laravel Applications

In the previous chapter, we delved into the crucial realm of advanced third-party integrations in Laravel, expanding the functionalities of our applications through seamless integration with payment gateways, social media platforms, email marketing services, cloud storage providers, and custom APIs. As we continue our exploration of Laravel's advanced features, we now shift our focus to an equally essential aspect—securing Laravel applications.

Implementing Two-Factor Authentication (2FA) in Laravel

In this section, we will explore the implementation of two-factor authentication (2FA) in Laravel applications. 2FA adds an extra layer of security to user accounts by requiring users to provide a second authentication factor, usually through a one-time code sent to their mobile devices. We will learn how to implement 2FA to protect user accounts from unauthorized access.

Securing User Input and Form Validation

Securing user input and validating form submissions is vital for preventing security vulnerabilities and data breaches. We will discover how to implement robust form validation in Laravel to ensure that user-submitted data is accurate and safe and meets the required criteria.

Preventing Cross-Site Scripting (XSS) and Cross-Site Request Forgery (CSRF) Attacks

Cross-Site Scripting (XSS) and Cross-Site Request Forgery (CSRF) attacks are common security threats that target web applications. We will explore how to prevent these attacks in Laravel by implementing security measures such as escaping output and using CSRF tokens.

© Sivaraj Selvaraj 2024
S. Selvaraj, *Building Real-Time Marvels with Laravel*, https://doi.org/10.1007/978-1-4842-9789-6_23

Securing API Endpoints with API Keys and Rate Limiting

APIs play a significant role in modern web applications, but they are also susceptible to security breaches. We will learn how to secure API endpoints in Laravel by implementing API keys and rate limiting to control access and prevent abuse.

Implementing Content Security Policies (CSPs) and SSL/TLS Encryption

Content Security Policies (CSPs) and SSL/TLS encryption are essential components of web application security. We will explore how to implement CSPs to mitigate security risks from malicious scripts and enforce secure connections using SSL/TLS encryption.

Throughout this chapter, we will immerse ourselves in the world of securing Laravel applications. By implementing robust security measures such as two-factor authentication, form validation, XSS and CSRF prevention, API security, and encryption techniques, we can fortify our applications against common security threats and protect user data and sensitive information. So let's embark on this journey of securing Laravel applications to ensure they stand strong against potential security risks and vulnerabilities!

Implementing Two-Factor Authentication (2FA) in Laravel

In the realm of web security, two-factor authentication (2FA) has become an essential safeguard against unauthorized access and data breaches. Laravel, the popular PHP web framework, provides developers with robust tools to seamlessly implement 2FA in their applications.

This guide will focus on the process of implementing two-factor authentication in Laravel. We'll explore the importance of 2FA and its various methods, such as Time-based One-Time Passwords (TOTP) and SMS-based verification.

By leveraging Laravel's built-in 2FA features and integrating third-party packages, developers can enhance the security of user accounts and protect sensitive data effectively.

Throughout this guide, we'll cover the steps to set up and configure 2FA, handle user enrollment, and customize the user interface for a seamless experience.

By the end of this guide, you'll be equipped with the knowledge and techniques needed to implement robust two-factor authentication in your Laravel applications, bolstering the security of your web projects. Let's dive into the world of 2FA in Laravel and elevate the protection of your user accounts.

Here's How 2FA Typically Works

Username and password

The first step remains the same as the traditional login process. The user provides their username/email and password to log into their account.

Second authentication factor

After entering the correct username and password, the system prompts the user to provide a second authentication factor. This can fall into one of the following three categories:

- a. Something you know: This could be a PIN, passphrase, or the answer to a security question.

- b. Something you have: This is typically a physical device such as a smartphone, security token, or smart card.

- c. Something you are: This refers to biometric factors like fingerprints, facial recognition, or iris scans.

Delivery of the 2FA code

The system generates a one-time code (OTP) associated with the user account and sends it to the user via a secondary communication channel. Common delivery methods include SMS, email, authenticator apps, or hardware tokens.

User verification

The user receives the OTP and enters it into the login interface. The system verifies the provided code against the one generated for the user's account.

Access granted

If the OTP matches and the second factor is successfully verified, the user gains access to their account.

Benefits of 2FA

Increased security: 2FA significantly reduces the risk of unauthorized access, as an attacker would need both the user's password and access to their second factor to break in.

Protection against password breaches: Even if passwords are compromised in a data breach, the attacker still needs the second factor to access the account.

User-friendly: Many 2FA methods are relatively easy for users to set up and use regularly, providing an additional layer of security without complicating the login process too much.

Keep in mind that, while 2FA improves security, it is not entirely foolproof. Sophisticated attackers may still find ways to bypass it. Therefore, it is crucial to implement other security measures such as regular password updates, strong password policies, and monitoring for suspicious account activity. Additionally, users should be educated about the importance of 2FA and encouraged to enable it whenever possible to protect their online accounts.

To Enable 2FA in Laravel, You Can Follow These Steps

Install the Laravel 2FA package.

```
composer require pragmarx/google2fa-laravel
```

Publish the package configuration file.

```
php artisan vendor:publish --provider="PragmaRX\Google2FALaravel\
ServiceProvider"
```

Generate the migration to add the 2FA secret key column to the users table.

```
php artisan migrate
```

Update the User model.

Open the 'User' model (typically located at 'app/Models/User.php') and add the 'TwoFactorAuthenticatable' trait and the 'Google2FAUser' contract:

```
use PragmaRX\Google2FA\Google2FA;
use PragmaRX\Google2FA\Contracts\Google2FAUser;
use PragmaRX\Google2FA\Google2FAInterface;
```

```php
use Illuminate\Foundation\Auth\User as Authenticatable;
use Illuminate\Database\Eloquent\Factories\HasFactory;
use Illuminate\Notifications\Notifiable;
use Laravel\Fortify\TwoFactorAuthenticatable;
class User extends Authenticatable implements Google2FAUser
{
    use HasFactory, Notifiable, TwoFactorAuthenticatable;
    // ...
    /**
     * Get the Google2FA Secret Key for the user.
     *
     * @return string
     */
    public function getGoogle2FASecretKey(): string
    {
        return $this->google2fa_secret;
    }
}
```

Enable 2FA middleware.

In your 'app/Http/Kernel.php' file, add the '2fa' middleware to the
'$routeMiddleware' array:

```php
protected $routeMiddleware = [
    // ...
    '2fa' => \PragmaRX\Google2FA\Vendor\Laravel\Middleware::class,
];
```

Enable 2FA in the login process.

In your 'app/Http/Controllers/Auth/LoginController.php' file, update the 'login'
method to include the 2FA check:

```php
use Illuminate\Http\Request;
use Illuminate\Support\Facades\Auth;
use PragmaRX\Google2FA\Support\Authenticator;
class LoginController extends Controller
{
    // ...
    /**
     * Handle a login request to the application.
     *
     * @param  \Illuminate\Http\Request  $request
     * @return \Illuminate\Http\RedirectResponse|\Illuminate\Http\
       Response|\Illuminate\Http\JsonResponse
     *
     * @throws \Illuminate\Validation\ValidationException
     */
    public function login(Request $request)
    {
        $this->validateLogin($request);
        // Check if 2FA is enabled for the user
        if ($this->is2FAEnabled($request)) {
            return $this->validate2FA($request);
        }
        // Continue with regular login process
        // ...
    }
    /**
     * Check if 2FA is enabled for the user.
     *
     * @param  \Illuminate\Http\Request  $request
     * @return bool
     */
    protected function is2FAEnabled(Request $request): bool
    {
        $user = $this->guard()->user();
```

```
        return $user instanceof Google2FAUser && $user-
        >twoFactorAuthEnabled();
    }
    /**
     * Validate the user's 2FA code.
     *
     * @param  \Illuminate\Http\Request  $request
     * @return \Illuminate\Http\RedirectResponse
     */
    protected function validate2FA(Request $request)
    {
        $user = $this->guard()->user();
        $authenticator = app(Authenticator::class)->boot($user);
        if ($authenticator->verifyKey($user, $request->input('2fa_
        code'))) {
            $this->guard()->login($user, $request->filled('remember'));
            return $this->authenticated($request, $user)
                ?: redirect()->intended($this->redirectPath());
        }
        return redirect()->back()
            ->withErrors(['2fa_code' => __('Invalid authentication
            code.')])
            ->withInput($request->except('2fa_code'));
    }
}
```

Update your login view.

In your login view ('resources/views/auth/login.blade.php'), add the 2FA code input field if 2FA is enabled for the user:

```
@if ($show2FAField)
    <div>
        <label for="2fa_code">{{ __('Two-Factor Code') }}</label>
```

```
            <input id="2fa_code" type="text" name="2fa_code" required
            autofocus>
        </div>
    @endif
```

Enable 2FA for users.

To enable 2FA for users, you can add an option in your user settings where users can scan a QR code using an authenticator app (e.g., Google Authenticator) and store the generated secret key. You can use the 'Google2FA::generateSecretKey()' method to generate the secret key and the 'Google2FA::getQRCodeInline()' method to generate the QR code image.

Here's Illustration code for enabling 2FA:

```php
use PragmaRX\Google2FA\Google2FA;
use Illuminate\Support\Facades\Auth;
class UserController extends Controller
{
    // ...
    /**
     * Enable Two-Factor Authentication for the user.
     *
     * @param  \Illuminate\Http\Request  $request
     * @return \Illuminate\Http\RedirectResponse
     */
    public function enable2FA(Request $request)
    {
        $user = Auth::user();
        $google2fa = app(Google2FA::class);
        $user->google2fa_secret = $google2fa->generateSecretKey();
        $user->save();
        $qrCode = $google2fa->getQRCodeInline(
            config('app.name'),
            $user->email,
            $user->google2fa_secret
        );
```

```
        return view('2fa.enable', compact('user', 'qrCode'));
    }
}
```

In the view ('resources/views/2fa/enable.blade.php'), you can display the QR code for the user to scan and configure their authenticator app.

That's it! You have now implemented two-factor Authentication (2FA) in your Laravel application. Users will be prompted to enter a verification code from their authenticator app during the login process if 2FA is enabled for their account.

Securing User Input and Form Validation

Securing user input and performing proper form validation are essential to protecting your Laravel application from potential security vulnerabilities. Here's how you can secure user input and implement form validation in Laravel.

Use Laravel's Validation Rules

Laravel provides a comprehensive set of validation rules that you can use to validate user input. These rules ensure that the data entered by users meets the expected criteria. Some commonly used validation rules include 'required', 'email', 'numeric', 'unique', and more.

For Illustration, refer to the following snippet:

```
use Illuminate\Http\Request;
use Illuminate\Support\Facades\Validator;
class UserController extends Controller
{
    public function store(Request $request)
    {
        $validator = Validator::make($request->all(), [
            'name' => 'required|string',
            'email' => 'required|email|unique:users',
            'password' => 'required|min:8',
        ]);
```

```
        if ($validator->fails()) {
            return redirect()->back()
                ->withErrors($validator)
                ->withInput();
        }
        // Process valid input
        // ...
    }
}
```

Sanitize user input.

In addition to validation, it's crucial to sanitize user input to prevent common security vulnerabilities such as SQL injection or Cross-Site Scripting (XSS) attacks. Laravel provides various helper functions and methods that you can use to sanitize user input.

For Illustration, refer to the following snippet:

```
$name = $request->input('name');
$sanitizedName = filter_var($name, FILTER_SANITIZE_STRING);
```

Implement form request validation.

Laravel allows you to define form request classes that handle the validation logic. These classes automatically validate incoming requests before your controller methods are invoked.

Generate a form request class using the Artisan command:

```
    php artisan make:request StoreUserRequest
```

Open the generated form request class ('app/Http/Requests/StoreUserRequest.php') and define the validation rules in the 'rules' method.

Update your controller method to type-hint the form request class.

```
use App\Http\Requests\StoreUserRequest;
class UserController extends Controller
{
    public function store(StoreUserRequest $request)
    {
        // Form request validation passed, process valid input
        // ...
    }
}
```

Validate uploaded files.

If your application accepts file uploads, it's crucial to validate them properly to prevent potential security risks. Laravel provides convenient methods for validating file uploads, including checking the file size, MIME type, and extension.

For Illustration, refer to the following snippet:

```
use Illuminate\Http\Request;
use Illuminate\Support\Facades\Validator;
class UserController extends Controller
{
    public function store(Request $request)
    {
        $validator = Validator::make($request->all(), [
            'avatar' => 'required|image|mimes:jpeg,png,jpg,gif|m
            ax:2048',
        ]);
        if ($validator->fails()) {
            return redirect()->back()
                ->withErrors($validator)
                ->withInput();
        }
```

```
        // Process valid input
        // ...
    }
}
```

By leveraging Laravel's validation features, implementing proper input sanitization, and validating uploaded files, you can enhance the security of your Laravel application and protect against common vulnerabilities associated with user input.

Preventing Cross-Site Scripting (XSS) and Cross-Site Request Forgery (CSRF) Attacks

Preventing Cross-Site Scripting (XSS) and Cross-Site Request Forgery (CSRF) attacks is crucial to ensuring the security of your Laravel application. Here's how you can mitigate these vulnerabilities.

Preventing Cross-Site Scripting (XSS) Attacks

Escaping output

When rendering user-generated content in your views, use the '{{ $variable }}' syntax or the '@escape' Blade directive. This automatically escapes the output, preventing it from being interpreted as HTML or JavaScript.

For Illustration, refer to the following snippet:

```
<p>{{ $userInput }}</p>
```

Sanitizing user input

Use Laravel's 'strip_tags' function or the 'htmlspecialchars' function to sanitize user input and remove any HTML or JavaScript tags.

For Illustration, refer to the following snippet:

```
$sanitizedInput = strip_tags($userInput);
```

Content Security Policies (CSPs)

Implement a Content Security Policy (CSP) to restrict the types of content that can be loaded on your web pages. A CSP allows you to define trusted sources for scripts, stylesheets, images, and other resources, thereby mitigating the risk of XSS attacks.

For Illustration, refer to the following snippet:

```
// Set the Content-Security-Policy header in your middleware or web
server configuration
$response->header('Content-Security-Policy', 'script-src \'self\'');
```

Preventing Cross-Site Request Forgery (CSRF) Attacks

CSRF protection middleware

Laravel provides built-in CSRF protection middleware that automatically generates and validates CSRF tokens for each user session.

The CSRF token is included in forms and AJAX requests, and Laravel verifies its authenticity on each non-GET request.

Including CSRF tokens in forms

In your HTML forms, include the CSRF token by using the '@csrf' Blade directive. This adds a hidden input field with the CSRF token value.

For Illustration, refer to the following snippet:

```
<form method="POST" action="/submit">
    @csrf
    <!-- form fields -->
</form>
```

AJAX requests with CSRF tokens

For AJAX requests, include the CSRF token in the request headers or within the request body.

You can retrieve the CSRF token value using the 'csrf_token()' function and send it along with the AJAX request.

Here's an Illustration using jQuery:

```javascript
$.ajax({
    url: '/api/endpoint',
    type: 'POST',
    data: {
        _token: '{{ csrf_token() }}',
        // other data
    },
    success: function (response) {
        // handle success
    },
    error: function (xhr) {
        // handle error
    }
});
```

By implementing these measures, you can significantly reduce the risk of XSS and CSRF attacks in your Laravel application and ensure the security of user data and interactions.

Securing API Endpoints with API Keys and Rate Limiting

Securing API endpoints is crucial to preventing unauthorized access and abuse. Laravel provides mechanisms such as API keys and rate limiting to secure your API endpoints effectively. Here's how you can implement these security measures.

Securing API Endpoints with API Keys

Generate API keys.

Generate a unique API key for each user or client that needs access to your API.

Store the API keys securely in your application or database.

API key authentication middleware.

Create a middleware to authenticate API requests using API keys.

In the middleware, validate the API key sent with the request against the stored API keys.

Return a 401 Unauthorized response if the API key is invalid or missing.

Apply the middleware.

Apply the API key authentication middleware to the routes or controllers that require API key protection.

You can apply the middleware to specific routes or create a middleware group for API routes.

Here's an Illustration of API key authentication middleware:

```
namespace App\Http\Middleware;
use Closure;
class APIKeyMiddleware
{
    public function handle($request, Closure $next)
    {
        $apiKey = $request->header('X-API-KEY');
        if (! $this->isValidApiKey($apiKey)) {
            return response()->json(['error' => 'Unauthorized'], 401);
        }
        return $next($request);
    }
    private function isValidApiKey($apiKey)
    {
        // Validate the API key against the stored keys
        // Return true if the API key is valid, false otherwise
    }
}
```

Securing API Endpoints with Rate Limiting

Enable rate limiting middleware.

Laravel provides a built-in rate limiting middleware that allows you to define rate limits per route or per user.

Enable the rate limiting middleware in your API routes or in a middleware group.

Configure rate limits.

Configure the rate limits for your API endpoints based on your application's requirements.

You can set the maximum number of requests allowed within a specific time period (e.g., requests per minute, per hour).

Handle rate limit exceeded responses.

When a user exceeds the rate limit, you can customize the response returned by the rate limiting middleware.

The response can include relevant information, such as the remaining time until the rate limit resets.

Here's an Illustration of a rate limiting configuration:

```
namespace App\Http\Middleware;
use Closure;
use Illuminate\Cache\RateLimiter;
use Symfony\Component\HttpFoundation\Response;
class ThrottleRequests
{
    protected $limiter;
    public function __construct(RateLimiter $limiter)
    {
        $this->limiter = $limiter;
    }
    public function handle($request, Closure $next, $maxAttempts = 60,
    $decayMinutes = 1)
    {
        $key = $this->resolveRequestSignature($request);
        if ($this->limiter->tooManyAttempts($key, $maxAttempts)) {
            $response = $this->buildRateLimitExceededResponse($maxAttempts,
            $decayMinutes);
            throw new HttpResponseException($response);
        }
        $this->limiter->hit($key, $decayMinutes * 60);
        $response = $next($request);
```

```
    return $this->addHeaders(
        $response,
        $maxAttempts,
        $this->calculateRemainingAttempts($key, $maxAttempts)
    );
    }
    // ...
}
```

These measures of implementing API keys and rate limiting help secure your API endpoints by ensuring that only authorized clients have access and limiting the number of requests they can make within a specific time frame.

Implementing Content Security Policies (CSPs) and SSL/TLS Encryption

A Content Security Policy (CSP) is a security feature implemented by web browsers to mitigate certain types of attacks, such as Cross-Site Scripting (XSS) and data injection. A CSP allows web developers to specify which sources of content are considered trusted and can be executed or loaded on a web page. By restricting the allowed content sources, a CSP helps prevent malicious scripts and unauthorized content from running, reducing the risk of security vulnerabilities.

The Main Goals of the Content Security Policy

Mitigate XSS attacks: XSS attacks occur when an attacker injects malicious scripts into a web page, which then execute in the context of a user's browser. A CSP helps prevent such attacks by allowing only scripts from trusted sources to be executed.

Reduce data injection risks: A CSP helps protect against data injection attacks, where attackers try to inject unauthorized data into a web page, leading to data leaks or unauthorized actions.

Prevent clickjacking: A CSP can prevent clickjacking attacks, where an attacker tricks a user into clicking a hidden or disguised element, potentially leading to unintended actions.

Implementing Content Security Policies (CSPs) and SSL/TLS encryption are essential security measures to protect your Laravel application. Here's how you can implement them.

Implementing Content Security Policies (CSPs)

Enable CSP middleware.

Laravel does not provide a built-in CSP middleware, but you can create a custom middleware to set the Content-Security-Policy header.

Create the CSP middleware.

Create a new middleware class, such as 'CspMiddleware', using the 'php artisan make:middleware CspMiddleware' command.

Configure the CSP rules.

In the 'handle' method of the 'CspMiddleware' class, define the CSP rules based on your application's needs.

Specify allowed sources for various types of content, such as scripts, styles, images, fonts, and more.

Here's an Illustration of CSP middleware:

```
namespace App\Http\Middleware;
use Closure;
class CspMiddleware
{
    public function handle($request, Closure $next)
    {
        $response = $next($request);
        $response->header('Content-Security-Policy', "default-src 'self'");
        return $response;
    }
}
```

Apply the middleware.

Apply the 'CspMiddleware' to the desired routes or globally to secure your entire application.

You can apply the middleware in the 'web' middleware group or specify it explicitly for specific routes.

Here's an Illustration of applying the CSP middleware globally:

```
// app/Http/Kernel.php
protected $middlewareGroups = [
    'web' => [
        // ...
        \App\Http\Middleware\CspMiddleware::class,
    ],
    // ...
];
```

By applying the CSP middleware, you can define a Content Security Policy that restricts the types of content that can be loaded on your web pages, mitigating the risk of various web attacks.

Implementing SSL/TLS encryption is a crucial aspect of web security. SSL (Secure Sockets Layer) and its successor TLS (Transport Layer Security) are cryptographic protocols that provide secure communication over a network, most commonly used to secure web traffic between a client (e.g., a web browser) and a server (e.g., a web server).

SSL/TLS Standard

SSL was introduced in the 1990s to secure communication on the Internet. However, TLS succeeded SSL due to the vulnerabilities found in it. The terms SSL and TLS are often used interchangeably, but in modern implementations, TLS is the standard used to secure web connections.

TLS works by encrypting data transmitted between the client and server, ensuring that sensitive information, such as login credentials, credit card numbers, and personal data, remains confidential and secure. It also provides authentication, verifying that the server the client is connecting to is indeed the correct one.

TLS operates at the Transport Layer of the OSI model, sitting between the Application Layer (e.g., HTTP) and the Network Layer (e.g., TCP/IP).

Implementing SSL/TLS Encryption

Obtain an SSL/TLS certificate.

Obtain an SSL/TLS certificate from a trusted certificate authority (CA).

You can acquire a certificate through paid CAs or use services like Let's Encrypt, which provides free certificates.

Configure your web server.

Install the SSL/TLS certificate on your web server. The process varies depending on the web server software you are using (e.g., Apache, Nginx, etc.).

Update your web server configuration to listen on the HTTPS (port 443) protocol and configure the SSL/TLS certificate and private key.

Enforce HTTPS redirection.

Configure your Laravel application to enforce HTTPS by redirecting all HTTP requests to HTTPS.

You can do this by adding a middleware or modifying your web server configuration.

Here's an Illustration of HTTPS redirection middleware:

```
namespace App\Http\Middleware;
use Closure;
use Illuminate\Support\Facades\App;
use Illuminate\Support\Facades\URL;
class ForceHttpsMiddleware
{
    public function handle($request, Closure $next)
    {
        if (!App::environment('local') && !$request->secure()) {
            URL::forceScheme('https');
        }
        return $next($request);
    }
}
```

Apply the HTTPS redirection middleware.

Apply the 'ForceHttpsMiddleware' to the desired routes or globally to enforce HTTPS.

You can apply the middleware in the 'web' middleware group or specify it explicitly for specific routes.

Here's an Illustration of applying the HTTPS redirection middleware globally:

```
// app/Http/Kernel.php
protected $middlewareGroups = [
    'web' => [
        // ...
        \App\Http\Middleware\ForceHttpsMiddleware::class,
    ],
    // ...
];
```

By implementing SSL/TLS encryption and enforcing HTTPS, you ensure that the communication between your application and clients is encrypted, enhancing the security and privacy of data transmitted over the network.

It's important to note that the configuration of CSPs and SSL/TLS encryption may vary depending on your specific application and server environment.

It's recommended to consult the documentation of your web server software and review security best practices to ensure proper implementation.

By implementing CSPs and SSL/TLS encryption, you can protect your Laravel application from various security risks, including XSS attacks, data injection, and eavesdropping.

Self-Signed Certificates

Self-signed certificates are SSL/TLS certificates that are generated and signed by the entity that owns the website or server, rather than a trusted third-party certificate authority (CA). These certificates are often used in testing and development environments, as well as in closed systems where public trust is not required. However, they are not suitable for production environments or public-facing websites, as they lack the third-party validation and trust that come with certificates issued by reputable CAs.

Some Key Points to Understand About Self-Signed Certificates

Self-signed certificate generation

To create a self-signed certificate, the website owner generates a public-private key pair using a tool like OpenSSL. The private key remains with the server, while the public key is used to create the certificate.

Certificate signing

The entity's private key signs self-signed certificates, not those issued by trusted CAs. This means there is no external verification of the certificate's authenticity.

Browser warnings

When a user visits a website secured with a self-signed certificate, their web browser will display a warning indicating that the certificate is not trusted. This is because the browser cannot verify the authenticity of the certificate through a trusted CA.

No public validation

Self-signed certificates do not undergo the rigorous validation process that certificates from trusted CAs go through. They lack the public trust and assurance that come with CA-issued certificates.

Security risks

While self-signed certificates provide encryption, they do not offer protection against Man-in-the-Middle (MITM) attacks. An attacker could intercept communication between the client and server and present a fake self-signed certificate, leading to potential security risks.

Use cases

Self-signed certificates are mainly used in development and testing environments to enable encrypted connections for internal or closed systems. They are not suitable for public-facing websites or applications where trust and security are critical.

Let's Encrypt as an alternative

For publicly accessible websites, it is recommended to use certificates from trusted CAs, such as Let's Encrypt, which provides free SSL/TLS certificates. Major web browsers trust Let's Encrypt certificates and offer a secure and reliable solution for encrypting web traffic.

Self-signed certificates are a quick way to enable encryption for development or testing purposes, but they are not recommended for production environments. For public-facing websites, it is crucial to use SSL/TLS certificates from reputable CAs to establish trust and ensure secure communication between clients and servers.

Summary

This chapter explored the critical issue of securing Laravel apps. We covered how to put strong security mechanisms in place to safeguard web applications from potential threats and vulnerabilities. We also reviewed typical security concerns, including Cross-Site Scripting (XSS), Cross-Site Request Forgery (CSRF), and SQL injection, as well as how to avoid them in Laravel apps. We discussed approaches for integrating user authentication and authorization, securing APIs, and encrypting sensitive data. You also learned standard practices for protecting database connections, validating user input, and securely handling user sessions.

The next chapter focuses on advanced DevOps and infrastructure automation.

Summary

CHAPTER 24

Advanced DevOps and Infrastructure Automation

In the previous chapter, we explored the critical aspect of securing Laravel applications, fortifying them against common security threats and vulnerabilities. As our journey through Laravel's advanced features continues, we now shift our focus to the realm of DevOps and infrastructure automation—essential aspects of modern application development and deployment.

Infrastructure as Code (IaC) with Laravel and Tools like Terraform

In this section, we will delve into the concept of Infrastructure as Code (IaC) and its application with Laravel. IaC allows us to manage and provision infrastructure through code, making it easier to maintain, version, and reproduce. We will explore how to use tools like Terraform to automate the creation and management of Laravel application infrastructures.

Automating Deployment Pipelines with Laravel and CI/CD Tools

Automating deployment pipelines streamlines the process of releasing new features and updates to production. We will learn how to set up continuous integration/continuous deployment (CI/CD) pipelines for Laravel applications, ensuring that code changes are automatically tested, built, and deployed to production environments.

Implementing Application Monitoring and Log Management

Application monitoring and log management are critical for gaining insights into application performance and detecting issues. We will explore how to implement application monitoring and log management solutions to proactively identify and resolve potential problems.

© Sivaraj Selvaraj 2024

S. Selvaraj, *Building Real-Time Marvels with Laravel*, https://doi.org/10.1007/978-1-4842-9789-6_24

Continuous Performance Optimization and Auto-scaling

Continuous performance optimization is crucial to maintaining high application performance and responsiveness. We will discover how to continuously monitor and optimize Laravel applications, ensuring they can handle varying workloads with auto-scaling capabilities.

Building Highly Available and Fault-Tolerant Laravel Infrastructures

In this final section, we will focus on building highly available and fault-tolerant Laravel infrastructures. We will explore strategies to design resilient architectures that can withstand failures and provide uninterrupted service to users.

Throughout this chapter, we will immerse ourselves in the world of advanced DevOps and infrastructure automation with Laravel. By adopting Infrastructure as Code, automating deployment pipelines, implementing monitoring and optimization strategies, and building resilient infrastructures, we can streamline development processes and deliver reliable and performant applications. So let's embark on this journey of advanced DevOps and infrastructure automation to elevate the efficiency and reliability of our Laravel projects!

Infrastructure as Code (IaC) with Laravel and Tools like Terraform

In the rapidly evolving world of software development, advanced DevOps practices and infrastructure automation have become crucial for building modern, scalable, and efficient applications. Infrastructure as Code (IaC) stands at the forefront of this movement, enabling developers to manage infrastructure resources through code, ensuring consistency, version control, and automation.

This guide will focus on the advanced integration of Infrastructure as Code with Laravel using powerful tools like Terraform. We'll explore how IaC empowers developers and operations teams to effortlessly define, deploy, and manage infrastructure, streamlining application deployments and promoting environment consistency.

With Terraform as a leading IaC tool, we'll delve into its capabilities for defining Infrastructure as Code and leveraging Terraform providers for seamless integration with various cloud platforms.

Throughout this guide, we'll explore advanced concepts of infrastructure automation, including configuration management, continuous integration and continuous deployment (CI/CD) pipelines, and best practices for handling sensitive data and secrets securely.

By the end of this guide, you'll be equipped with advanced DevOps and infrastructure automation knowledge, empowering you to optimize your Laravel projects with Infrastructure as Code and Terraform. Let's embark on this journey of advanced DevOps practices and explore the power of infrastructure automation in the context of Laravel applications.

In the context of Laravel applications, using Infrastructure as Code with tools like Terraform can bring several benefits:

Reproducibility: With Terraform, you can define your Laravel application's Infrastructure as Code in configuration files. These files can be version-controlled and shared across the team, ensuring that everyone works with the same infrastructure setup. This reduces configuration drift and the risk of discrepancies between environments.

Scalability: Terraform allows you to define and manage cloud resources and infrastructure components like servers, databases, load balancers, and more. You can easily scale up or down your infrastructure based on demand by modifying the Terraform configuration and applying the changes.

Automated provisioning: Terraform automates the provisioning process, meaning you can create and configure the entire infrastructure stack with just a few commands. This saves time and reduces the potential for human errors that often occur in manual setup.

Portability: Since Terraform abstracts the underlying infrastructure providers (e.g., AWS, Azure, and GCP), you can easily switch between cloud providers or use a multi-cloud strategy without rewriting the entire infrastructure code.

Collaboration: Infrastructure as Code enables collaboration between developers and operations teams. Developers can define infrastructure requirements in the same version-controlled repositories as their code, making it easier for the operations team to understand and deploy the application with the required infrastructure.

Here's How Terraform Plan Acts as an Advisory

Preview changes: Running Terraform Plan generates a detailed plan of the actions Terraform will take based on the current state and the changes in your configuration files. It shows the resources that will be added, modified, or deleted.

Verification: By reviewing the plan output, you can verify that Terraform is going to make the desired changes. It helps ensure that your infrastructure will be provisioned or destroyed as you expect.

Safety check: Before any changes are applied, Terraform Plan allows you to catch errors, typos, or misconfigurations that might lead to issues or unintended consequences. It provides an opportunity to correct any mistakes before they affect your living environment.

Cost estimation: For cloud-based infrastructure, Terraform Plan can estimate the costs associated with the planned changes. It helps you understand the financial impact of the modifications before they are applied, preventing unexpected expenses.

Collaboration: When working in a team, Terraform Plan becomes a way to share the proposed changes with other team members. They can review and discuss the plan before applying it, ensuring that everyone is aware of the upcoming changes.

To Use Terraform with Laravel, You Would Typically

Install Terraform: Download and install Terraform on your development machine or your continuous integration/continuous deployment (CI/CD) server.

Write configuration: Create Terraform configuration files (usually with a '.tf' extension) that define the desired infrastructure state. This includes resources like virtual machines, databases, networks, and any other components needed for your Laravel application.

Initialize Terraform: Run 'terraform init' in the directory containing your Terraform configuration files. This command initializes Terraform and downloads the required provider plugins.

Plan and apply: Use 'terraform plan' to preview the changes Terraform will make to your infrastructure. After reviewing the plan, run 'terraform apply' to create or modify the infrastructure according to the configuration.

Version-control: Store your Terraform configuration files in version control (e.g., Git) along with your Laravel application code. This ensures that changes to the infrastructure can be tracked and reviewed over time.

Manage state: Terraform keeps track of the infrastructure state in a state file. It's essential to manage this state file carefully, especially in a collaborative environment, to prevent conflicts and inconsistencies.

To Perform a Destroy Operation (e.g., Removing Resources)

Before running terraform destroy, use Terraform Plan --destroy to preview the resources that will be destroyed. This step allows you to verify that you are indeed deleting the correct resources.

Review the destruction plan and confirm that it aligns with your intention.

If everything looks good, execute terraform destroy to remove the specified resources.

Setting Up Terraform for Laravel

It involves several steps. Before you begin, make sure you have the following prerequisites in place:

Installing Terraform: Download and install Terraform on your local development machine or the server where you plan to manage your Laravel infrastructure.

Cloud provider account: You'll need an account with a cloud provider (e.g., AWS, Azure, or GCP) where you'll deploy your Laravel application. Ensure you have the necessary access credentials (access keys and secret keys) with the required permissions to create and manage resources.

Steps to Set Up Terraform for Your Laravel IaC

Project Structure

Create a new directory for your Terraform project. Inside this directory, organize your Terraform files. A common Terraform project structure might look like Figure 24-1.

```
terraform/
|-- main.tf
|-- variables.tf
|-- outputs.tf
|-- terraform.tfvars
|-- .terraform/
|-- .terraform.lock.hcl
|-- .terraformrc
|-- terraform.tfstate
```

Figure 24-1. *Terraform project structure*

'main.tf': This is the main Terraform configuration file where you define your infrastructure resources.

'variables.tf': Define input variables that can be used to parameterize your Terraform configuration.

'outputs.tf': Specify output variables that you want to be displayed after applying the Terraform configuration.

'terraform.tfvars': Store your variable values here. This file should be added to '.gitignore' to avoid sharing sensitive information.

'.terraform/': Terraform will create this directory, which will contain downloaded provider plugins.

'. terraform.lock.hcl': Lock file to track the provider versions used in the project.

'. terraformrc': Optional file for configuring Terraform settings.

'terraform.tfstate': A state file that keeps track of the infrastructure's current state.

Configure a Provider

In your 'main.tf', configure the cloud provider you'll be using, for example, for AWS:

```
provider "aws" {
  region = "us-west-2"  # Replace with your desired region
  # Other provider-specific configurations like access keys can be set here.
}
```

Define Resources

Within 'main.tf', you'll define the specific infrastructure resources required for your Laravel application. This can include virtual machine configurations, lines, databases, load balancers, security groups, etc., for example, to create an AWS EC2 instance:

```
resource "aws_instance" "laravel_instance" {
  ami           = "ami-0c55b159cbfafe1f0"
  instance_type = "t2.micro"
  # Other instance configurations
}
```

Configure Variables

In 'variables.tf', define input variables that can be used to parameterize your Terraform configuration. This allows you to provide values from 'terraform.tfvars' or via command-line flags:

```
variable "aws_access_key" {}
variable "aws_secret_key" {}
variable "region" {
  default = "us-west-2"  # Replace with your desired default region
}
```

Configure Outputs

In 'outputs.tf', define any output variables that you want to see after applying your Terraform configuration:

```
output "public_ip" {
  value       = aws_instance.laravel_instance.public_ip
  description = "The public IP address of the Laravel instance."
}
```

Initialize Terraform

Navigate to your project directory and run 'terraform init'. This command will initialize Terraform and download the required provider plugins.

Plan and Apply

Run 'terraform plan' to see a preview of the changes Terraform will make. Review the plan to ensure it aligns with your expectations. If everything looks good, run 'terraform apply' to create the infrastructure based on your Terraform configuration:

```
terraform plan
terraform apply
```

Manage State

Terraform keeps track of the infrastructure state in the 'terraform.tfstate' file. It's crucial to manage this file carefully. If you're working with a team, consider using remote state storage (e.g., Terraform Cloud, AWS S3) for collaboration and to prevent state file conflicts.

With these steps, you should have Terraform set up for your Laravel Infrastructure as Code project. Remember to follow best practices, keep your Terraform configuration version-controlled, and ensure that sensitive information is handled securely (e.g., using environment variables or a secure configuration management solution).

Automating Deployment Pipelines with Laravel and CI/CD Tools

Automating deployment pipelines for Laravel applications using CI/CD (continuous integration/continuous deployment) tools is a fundamental practice that enhances software delivery efficiency and reliability. Figure 24-2 illustrates a CI/CD pipeline.

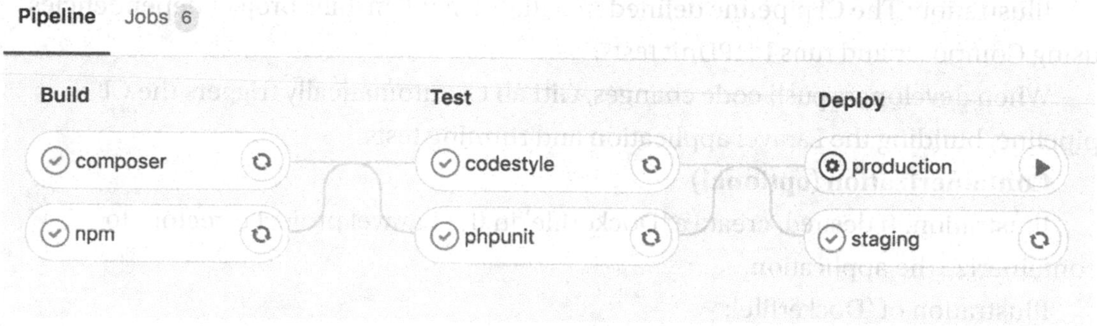

Pipeline	Jobs 6		
Build		**Test**	**Deploy**
⊘ composer ↻		⊘ codestyle ↻	⊛ production ▶
⊘ npm ↻		⊘ phpunit ↻	⊘ staging ↻

Figure 24-2. *CI/CD pipeline*

Let's walk through an Illustration of setting up a CI/CD pipeline for a Laravel project using GitLab CI/CD:

Source control management

Illustration: Create a Git repository on GitLab to manage the Laravel project's source code. All developers can collaborate, push changes, and create feature branches.

Continuous integration (CI)

Illustration: In GitLab, create a '.gitlab-ci.yml' configuration file at the root of the repository.

Illustration for '.gitlab-ci.yml':

```
stages:
  - build
  - test
build:
  stage: build
  script:
    - composer install
```

```
test:
  stage: test
  script:
    - vendor/bin/phpunit
```

Building and testing a Laravel application

Illustration: The CI pipeline defined in '.gitlab-ci.yml' installs project dependencies using Composer and runs PHPUnit tests.

When developers push code changes, GitLab CI automatically triggers the CI pipeline, building the Laravel application and running tests.

Containerization (optional)

Illustration: If desired, create a 'Dockerfile' in the Laravel project directory to containerize the application.

Illustration of 'Dockerfile':

```
FROM php:8.0-apache
COPY . /var/www/html
RUN chown -R www-data:www-data /var/www/html/storage
RUN docker-php-ext-install pdo pdo_mysql
EXPOSE 80
CMD ["apache2-foreground"]
```

Image registry (optional)

Illustration: Set up the GitLab Container Registry to store the Docker image built from the Laravel application.

The Docker image can be tagged and pushed to the GitLab Container Registry for later use in the CD process.

Continuous deployment (CD)

Illustration: Extend the '.gitlab-ci.yml' to include CD stages for deploying to different environments.

Illustration for '.gitlab-ci.yml' with CD stages:

```
stages:
  - build
  - test
  - deploy_staging
  - deploy_production
# ... Build and test stages as before ...
deploy_staging:
  stage: deploy_staging
  script:
    - echo "Deploying to staging server"
    # Additional commands to deploy to staging environment
deploy_production:
  stage: deploy_production
  script:
    - echo "Deploying to production server"
    # Additional commands to deploy to production environment
```

Environment configuration

Illustration: Utilize GitLab CI/CD variables to manage environment-specific configurations securely.

Store sensitive data like database credentials and API keys as CI/CD variables, which can be accessed during deployment.

Quality checks (optional)

Illustration: Add additional jobs in '.gitlab-ci.yml' to perform code quality checks.

Use tools like PHP CodeSniffer and PHPStan to analyze code style and detect potential issues.

Manual approvals (optional)

Illustration: Implement manual approvals using GitLab CI/CD for production deployments.

A designated user or group must approve deployments to the production environment.

Rollback mechanism (optional)

Illustration: Set up version control with tags or branches to enable easy rollbacks.
In the case of critical issues, revert to a previous version and redeploy.

Monitoring and logging

Illustration: Use Laravel's logging features or third-party tools to collect and analyze application logs.

Implement monitoring tools like New Relic or Prometheus to track application performance.

Notifications and alerts

Illustration: Configure GitLab CI/CD to send notifications and alerts via email or chat channels.

Receive immediate alerts for build or deployment failures.

By setting up a comprehensive CI/CD pipeline, development teams can automate the build, test, and deployment processes for their Laravel applications, ensuring rapid, reliable, and error-free delivery. This Illustration demonstrates how GitLab CI/CD can be utilized to implement a professional deployment pipeline for Laravel projects, offering seamless collaboration and efficient software delivery.

Implementing Application Monitoring and Log Management

Implementing application monitoring and log management is essential for maintaining the health, performance, and security of your Laravel application. Monitoring allows you to track important metrics and detect issues early, while log management helps you gain insights into application behavior and troubleshoot problems effectively. Figure 24-3 illustrates log monitoring/feedback flow.

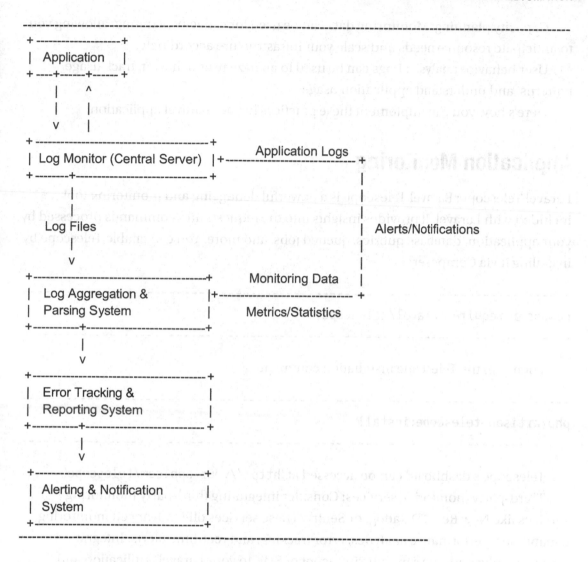

Figure 24-3. Log monitoring/feedback flow

Why implement application monitoring and log management?

Application monitoring and log management offer several benefits to Laravel developers and DevOps teams:

Proactive issue detection: Monitoring allows you to detect issues and potential bottlenecks in real time, enabling you to take corrective actions before they escalate.

Performance optimization: Monitoring data provides insights into your application's performance, helping you identify areas that require optimization.

Incident response: Log management helps you troubleshoot incidents and identify the root causes of errors or issues quickly.

Capacity planning: Monitoring data can be used for capacity planning, allowing you to anticipate resource needs and scale your infrastructure accordingly.

User behavior analysis: Logs can be used to analyze user behavior, track usage patterns, and understand application usage.

Here's how you can implement these practices in your Laravel application.

Application Monitoring

Laravel Telescope: Laravel Telescope is a powerful debugging and monitoring tool included with Laravel. It provides insights into the requests and commands processed by your application, database queries, queued jobs, and more. You can enable Telescope by installing it via Composer:

```
composer require laravel/telescope
```

Then, run the Telescope installation command:

```
php artisan telescope:install
```

Telescope's dashboard can be accessed at 'http://your-app.com/telescope'.

Third-party monitoring services: Consider integrating third-party monitoring services like New Relic, Datadog, or Sentry. These services offer advanced monitoring capabilities, performance analytics, error tracking, and real-time alerts. Integration usually involves adding a monitoring agent or SDK to your Laravel application and configuring it with your service provider's API keys.

Log Management

Laravel logging: Laravel comes with robust logging capabilities out of the box. The application logs are usually stored in the 'storage/logs' directory. Laravel's logging configuration can be found in the 'config/logging.php' file, where you can define log channels and specify where logs should be stored, log levels, etc.

Daily log rotation: To manage log files effectively, enable daily log rotation to prevent log files from growing indefinitely. This is set up in the logging configuration:

```
'channels' => [
    'daily' => [
        'driver' => 'daily',
        'path' => storage_path('logs/laravel.log'),
        'level' => 'debug',
        'days' => 14,
    ],
],
```

Log aggregation: For large-scale applications or distributed systems, centralizing logs becomes crucial. Consider using log aggregation tools like the Elasticsearch, Logstash, and Kibana (ELK) stack or services like Papertrail, Loggly, or Graylog to collect and analyze logs from multiple servers.

Error reporting: Implement error reporting services like Sentry or BugSnag to capture and report exceptions and errors that occur within your Laravel application. These services can provide detailed error information, stack traces, and user context, enabling you to resolve issues proactively.

Log security: Be mindful of log security, especially if you're logging sensitive information. Avoid logging sensitive data like passwords or credit card details. Instead, use masked or obfuscated versions of the data to maintain compliance with security standards.

By implementing application monitoring and log management, you can gain valuable insights into your Laravel application's behavior, identify performance bottlenecks, and quickly resolve any issues that arise. Regularly review the monitoring data and logs to ensure your application's stability and performance.

Continuous Performance Optimization and Auto-scaling

Continuous performance optimization and auto-scaling are critical components of managing and maintaining a high-performing Laravel application. In this section, we will explore how to continuously optimize the performance of your application and leverage auto-scaling to dynamically adjust resources based on demand.

Let's explore these concepts with examples.

Continuous Performance Optimization

Caching

Example: Using caching to store frequently accessed data and reduce database queries

```
// Caching a query result for 5 minutes
$users = Cache::remember('users', 300, function () {
    return DB::table('users')->get();
});
```

Database optimization

Example: Using eager loading to optimize database queries

```
// Without eager loading (N+1 problem)
$posts = Post::all();
foreach ($posts as $post) {
    echo $post->user->name;
}
// With eager loading
$posts = Post::with('user')->get();
foreach ($posts as $post) {
    echo $post->user->name;
}
```

Queues and job processing

Example: Offloading time-consuming tasks to a background queue

```
php artisan make:job SendEmailJob
```

```
// Inside SendEmailJob.php
public function handle()
{
    // Code to send the email
}
// Dispatching the job to the queue
SendEmailJob::dispatch($user)->delay(now()->addSeconds(10));
```

Profiling and benchmarking

Example: Using Laravel Telescope for application monitoring

```
composer require laravel/telescope
php artisan telescope:install
```

After installation, you can access Telescope's dashboard at 'http://your-app.com/telescope'.

Auto-scaling

Auto-scaling allows your application to automatically adjust its resources to handle varying workloads. This is particularly useful during traffic spikes or when demand increases. Here's an example of auto-scaling with AWS Elastic Beanstalk:

Set up Elastic Beanstalk.

Package your Laravel application into a ZIP file.

Create an Elastic Beanstalk environment with PHP as the platform.

Upload and deploy the ZIP file to Elastic Beanstalk.

Configure auto-scaling.

Access your Elastic Beanstalk environment in the AWS Management Console.

Go to Configuration ⟨?⟩ Scaling.

Set up scaling triggers based on CPU utilization or other metrics to add or remove instances automatically.

Conduct load testing.

Before enabling auto-scaling, conduct load testing to simulate high-traffic conditions. Tools like Apache JMeter or Loader.io can help you assess how well your application performs under different loads.

Keep in mind that auto-scaling can be used in combination with other cloud providers like Google Cloud Platform (GCP) or Microsoft Azure, each with their own auto-scaling solutions.

By continuously optimizing your Laravel application and implementing auto-scaling, you can ensure a smooth user experience even during traffic spikes or increased workloads. These practices help you stay prepared for varying demands and maintain high application performance.

Building Highly Available and Fault-Tolerant Laravel Infrastructures

Building highly available and fault-tolerant Laravel infrastructures is crucial to ensuring that your application remains resilient and accessible even in the face of hardware failures or unexpected issues. To explain this concept in detail, let's first break down the components of a highly available and fault-tolerant infrastructure and then create an ASCII diagram to illustrate it.

Components of a Highly Available and Fault-Tolerant Laravel Infrastructure

Load balancer: A load balancer sits between the users and the application servers. It distributes incoming traffic across multiple application instances, ensuring that each server receives an equal share of requests. This prevents any single server from being overwhelmed by traffic.

Application servers: These are the servers that host your Laravel application. They handle incoming requests, process business logic, and return responses to the users.

Having multiple application servers ensures redundancy and allows the system to handle higher loads.

Database servers: The database servers store and manage the application's data. For fault tolerance, it's common to have a database replication setup, where data is replicated to multiple database servers. This ensures that if one database server fails, another can take its place without losing data.

Content Delivery Network (CDN): A CDN is a network of servers distributed geographically. It caches and serves static assets, such as images, CSS, and JavaScript files, closer to the users. This reduces the load on the application servers and improves the overall performance for users across different locations.

File storage: Highly available infrastructures usually use cloud-based file storage solutions (e.g., Amazon S3 or Google Cloud Storage) to store user-uploaded files and assets. This ensures data durability and accessibility even if an application server goes down.

Auto-scaling: Auto-scaling enables the infrastructure to dynamically adjust the number of application servers based on traffic or workload. When the traffic increases, new instances can be automatically provisioned, and when the demand decreases, instances can be scaled down, optimizing resource utilization and cost. Figure 24-4 illustrates a highly available and fault-tolerant Laravel infrastructure.

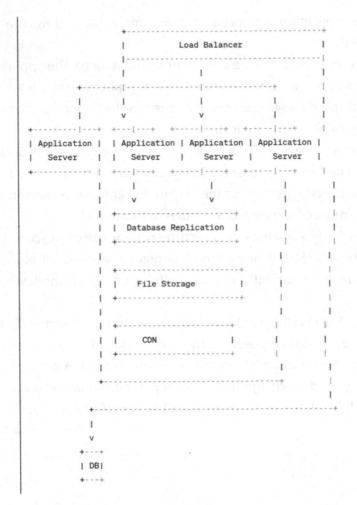

Figure 24-4. *Highly available and fault-tolerant Laravel infrastructure*

This highly available and fault-tolerant Laravel infrastructure ensures that the application remains robust, even during peak traffic or unexpected failures. It provides users with a seamless experience, enhances performance, and minimizes downtime.

Building a highly available and fault-tolerant Laravel infrastructure on AWS involves utilizing various services and implementing best practices. Let's break down each component and provide detailed explanations along with example code snippets.

Web Application Layer

Elastic Beanstalk

Elastic Beanstalk provides an easy way to deploy, manage, and scale web applications. Start by creating an Elastic Beanstalk environment for your Laravel app:

```
eb init -p php-7.4 my-laravel-app
eb create my-laravel-env
```

Deployment configuration ('laravel.config')

Create a configuration file in your Laravel project to customize deployment settings and environment variables:

```
# .ebextensions/laravel.config
option_settings:
  aws:elasticbeanstalk:container:php:phpini:
    document_root: public
    memory_limit: 512M
  aws:elasticbeanstalk:application:environment:
    APP_ENV: production
    APP_KEY: YOUR_APP_KEY
    # Add other Laravel environment variables
```

Auto-scaling

Enable auto-scaling to handle traffic fluctuations. In the Elastic Beanstalk configuration, update the number of instances:

```
option_settings:
  aws:autoscaling:asg:
    MinSize: 2
    MaxSize: 4
```

Load Balancing

Application load balancer (ALB)

Create an ALB to distribute traffic across instances:

```
aws elbv2 create-load-balancer --name my-laravel-alb --subnets subnet-xxx
subnet-yyy
```

Target group and listener

Configure a target group and listener for the ALB:

```
aws elbv2 create-target-group --name my-laravel-tg --protocol
HTTP --port 80
aws elbv2 create-listener --load-balancer-arn YOUR_ALB_ARN --protocol
HTTP --port 80 --default-actions Type=forward,TargetGroupArn=YOUR_TARGET_
GROUP_ARN
```

Database Layer

Amazon RDS

Set up an RDS instance for your Laravel application:

```
aws rds create-db-instance --db-instance-identifier my-laravel-db --engine
mysql --allocated-storage 20 --db-instance-class db.t2.micro --master-
username admin --master-user-password mypassword
```

Multi-AZ deployment

Enable Multi-AZ deployment for automatic failover:

```
aws rds modify-db-instance --db-instance-identifier
my-laravel-db --multi-az
```

Caching

Amazon ElastiCache (Redis)

Create an ElastiCache Redis cluster:

```
aws elasticache create-cache-cluster --cache-cluster-id
my-laravel-cache --cache-node-type cache.m4.small --engine redis
```

Laravel caching configuration

Configure Laravel to use Redis for caching in 'config/cache.php':

```
'default' => env('CACHE_DRIVER', 'redis'),
```

File Storage

Amazon S3

Set up an S3 bucket for file storage:

```
aws s3api create-bucket --bucket my-laravel-bucket --create-bucket-
configuration LocationConstraint=YOUR_REGION
```

Laravel filesystem configuration

Configure Laravel to use S3 for file storage in 'config/filesystems.php':

```
'disks' => [
    's3' => [
        'driver' => 's3',
        'key' => env('AWS_ACCESS_KEY_ID'),
        'secret' => env('AWS_SECRET_ACCESS_KEY'),
        'region' => env('AWS_DEFAULT_REGION'),
```

```
        'bucket' => env('AWS_BUCKET'),
    ],
],
```

Content Delivery

Amazon CloudFront

Set up a CloudFront distribution for content delivery:

```
aws cloudfront create-distribution --origin-domain-name my-laravel-bucket.
s3.amazonaws.com
```

Monitoring and Logging

Amazon CloudWatch

Set up CloudWatch alarms for monitoring:

```
aws cloudwatch put-metric-alarm --alarm-name my-laravel-cpu --alarm-
description "High CPU usage" --metric-name CPUUtilization --namespace AWS/
EC2 --statistic Average --period 300 --threshold 90 --comparison-operator
GreaterThanOrEqualToThreshold --dimensions Name=InstanceId,Value=YOUR_
INSTANCE_ID --evaluation-periods 2 --alarm-actions arn:aws:sns:YOUR_
REGION:YOUR_ACCOUNT_ID:YOUR_SNS_TOPIC
```

Security

Virtual Private Cloud (VPC)

Create a VPC and subnets:

```
aws ec2 create-vpc --cidr-block 10.0.0.0/16
aws ec2 create-subnet --vpc-id YOUR_VPC_ID --cidr-block
10.0.1.0/24 --availability-zone YOUR_AZ
```

Security groups and network ACLs

Configure security groups and network ACLs to control inbound and outbound traffic.

AWS IAM

Create IAM roles and policies for least privilege access.

Backup and Disaster Recovery

Amazon RDS automated backups

Enable automated backups for your RDS instance:

```
aws rds modify-db-instance --db-instance-identifier my-laravel-db --backup-
retention-period 7
```

Logging and Error Tracking

AWS CloudTrail

Enable CloudTrail to track API activity and resource changes.

AWS X-Ray

Implement AWS X-Ray for distributed tracing.

Third-party error tracking services

Integrate third-party error tracking services like Sentry or BugSnag.

By implementing these AWS services and best practices, you can build a highly available and fault-tolerant Laravel infrastructure. Regularly test failover scenarios and ensure you have

Summary

In this chapter, you learned advanced DevOps strategies and infrastructure automation for Laravel web apps. The chapter explained how to optimize the deployment process and efficiently manage the infrastructure. It introduced continuous integration and continuous deployment (CI/CD) pipelines to automate the build, test, and deployment processes. We also discussed how to containerize and orchestrate Laravel applications using Docker and Kubernetes, maintaining consistency across environments. You learned core Infrastructure as Code (IaC) principles and how to use tools like Terraform and Ansible to automate server and cloud resource provisioning and setup.

In the next and final chapter, we will cover the new and updated features of Laravel 10.

CHAPTER 25

New Features and Updates in Laravel 10

There's an undeniable thrill that accompanies the unveiling of new features in any software release, and Laravel 10 is no exception. In this chapter, we will explore the exciting additions and enhancements that come with the latest version of this powerful PHP framework.

The Central Role of PHP 8.1 in Laravel 10

Laravel 10 embraces the latest technology by making PHP 8.1 the minimum-required version. This move allows developers to leverage the fantastic features introduced in PHP 8.1 within their Laravel applications. One noteworthy feature that finds application in Laravel 10 is "readonly properties," which ensure that specific object properties cannot be modified after their initial assignment. Additionally, Laravel 10 utilizes "array_is_list," which conveniently determines if an array is a simple list with sequential integer keys, making it easier to manage and manipulate arrays within the framework.

Readonly Properties

PHP 8.1 introduces the concept of 'readonly' properties, allowing developers to define class properties that can only be set once during the object's initialization. Once set, these properties become immutable and cannot be modified afterward, ensuring data integrity and preventing accidental changes.

In Laravel 10, certain classes and properties take advantage of the 'readonly' feature to enhance code safety and prevent unintended modifications.

© Sivaraj Selvaraj 2024

S. Selvaraj, *Building Real-Time Marvels with Laravel*, https://doi.org/10.1007/978-1-4842-9789-6_25

For example, in previous Laravel versions, a class property may have been defined like this:

```
class User {
    public $name;
    // ...
}
```

In Laravel 10, using PHP 8.1's 'readonly' feature, we can define the property as

```
class User {
    public readonly string $name;
    // ...
}
```

Now, the '$name' property can only be set once during the object's construction, and any attempts to modify it after initialization will result in a runtime error.

For Illustration, refer to the following snippet:

```
class User {
    public readonly string $name;
    public function __construct(string $name) {
        $this->name = $name;
    }
}
```

Array Is List

PHP 8.1 introduces the 'array_is_list()' function, which allows developers to determine if an array is numerically indexed (list) or associative. This function is useful when dealing with arrays and ensures more precise handling of list and associative array data.

In Laravel 10, this function is used in certain scenarios to improve code readability and ensure proper data handling when dealing with arrays.

For example, you can use 'array_is_list()' to check if an array is numerically indexed:

```
$array = [1, 2, 3];
if (array_is_list($array)) {
    // It's a list
} else {
    // It's an associative array
}
```

This feature enhances the predictability and reliability of array-related operations in Laravel 10.

Enhancements to Laravel's Official Packages

One of the many reasons Laravel remains at the forefront of PHP frameworks is its commitment to maintaining and updating not just the core framework but also its official packages and the entire ecosystem. With the release of Laravel 10, a host of official Laravel packages have received timely updates, ensuring seamless compatibility and enhanced functionalities. Let's take a closer look at the most recent packages that have been updated to support Laravel 10:

Breeze

Laravel Breeze, a minimal and lightweight starter kit, has been updated to align perfectly with Laravel 10. Breeze simplifies the process of setting up a new Laravel application with authentication scaffolding, making it an excellent starting point for developers to kickstart their projects.

Cashier Stripe

Cashier Stripe, an indispensable package for handling subscription billing and managing Stripe integrations within Laravel applications, has received a much-anticipated update. The latest version ensures smooth integration with Laravel 10, allowing developers to effortlessly handle subscription-related tasks.

Dusk

Laravel Dusk, the beloved browser automation and testing tool, has been fine-tuned to support Laravel 10. This means developers can continue to conduct end-to-end browser tests with confidence, ensuring their applications function flawlessly across different environments.

Horizon

Horizon, Laravel's exceptional Redis-based queue monitoring solution, is fully compatible with Laravel 10. Developers can take advantage of Horizon's intuitive dashboard and monitoring capabilities to manage their application's queued jobs efficiently.

Installer

The Laravel installer, responsible for bootstrapping new Laravel applications, has received necessary updates to cater to Laravel 10's requirements. Developers can now enjoy the seamless installation of fresh Laravel projects with the updated installer.

Jetstream

Laravel Jetstream, a robust application scaffolding designed for Laravel applications, has been upgraded to provide full support for Laravel 10. Jetstream continues to serve as an essential toolkit for developers seeking to build powerful and feature-rich applications quickly.

Passport

Passport, the comprehensive OAuth2 server implementation, has been updated for compatibility with Laravel 10. With Passport, developers can effortlessly add secure and convenient authentication mechanisms to their Laravel APIs.

Pint

Pint, Laravel's API rate limiter, has been revamped to complement Laravel 10's features seamlessly. Pint helps developers maintain control over API requests and responses, ensuring efficient API usage.

Sail

Laravel Sail, the lightweight command-line interface for coordinating development environments, is fully compatible with Laravel 10. Sail makes it effortless for developers to set up and manage development environments using Docker.

Scout

Scout, Laravel's full-text search package, is now geared up to support Laravel 10. Developers can continue to use Scout to implement powerful and fast search functionality in their Laravel applications.

Valet

Valet, a development environment tailored for macOS users, has been updated to sync perfectly with Laravel 10. Developers on macOS can take advantage of Valet's simplicity and speed to build Laravel applications effortlessly.

Improved Predis Version Compatibility

Predis, the robust Redis client for PHP used in Laravel for caching, receives a version upgrade in Laravel 10. While Laravel formerly supported both Predis versions 1 and 2, Laravel 10 discontinues support for Predis 1. However, developers can still utilize the official PHP extension for communicating with Redis servers, as it provides an API for this purpose.

For Illustration, refer to the following snippet:

```
// Laravel configuration using Redis version 2
'redis' => [
    'client' => 'predis',
    'default' => [
        'host' => env('REDIS_HOST', '127.0.0.1'),
        'password' => env('REDIS_PASSWORD', null),
        'port' => env('REDIS_PORT', 6379),
        'database' => 0,
    ],
],
```

Native Type Declarations

In Laravel 10, a significant enhancement is introduced with native type declarations, revolutionizing the way developers define parameter and return types. This improvement simplifies code structure, eliminates the reliance on DocBlocks for type hinting, and enhances the overall developer experience. Let's explore a different example to understand the impact of this change.

Before Laravel 10, a method might have been defined as follows, using DocBlocks to specify parameter and return types:

```
/**
 * Calculate the total price of items in the shopping cart.
 *
 * @param array $items
 * @return float
 */
public function calculateTotalPrice(array $items)
{
    $total = 0;
    foreach ($items as $item) {
        $total += $item['price'];
    }
    return $total;
}
```

With the introduction of native type declarations in Laravel 10, the same method can now be expressed as follows:

```
/**
 * Calculate the total price of items in the shopping cart.
 */
public function calculateTotalPrice(array $items): float
{
    $total = 0;
    foreach ($items as $item) {
        $total += $item['price'];
    }
    return $total;
}
```

The difference is evident. In Laravel 10, you no longer need DocBlocks to specify that the parameter '$items' must be an array and that the return type is a 'float'. Instead, you can directly define the parameter type and return type using native type declarations in the method signature.

This change in Laravel 10 greatly improves the readability and maintainability of the codebase. It allows IDEs to better understand the expected types, enabling them to provide accurate auto-completion suggestions, code hints, and error checks during development.

Developers can now focus more on writing clean and concise code, confident that the native type declarations will enhance the clarity and correctness of their functions. This improvement fosters a smoother and more productive coding experience, making Laravel 10 a go-to choice for modern web development.

Default Invokable Validation Rules

In Laravel 10, a significant improvement has been made to the way validation rules are handled. Unlike Laravel 9, where you needed to add an --invokable flag when using the Artisan command to create an invokable validation rule, Laravel 10 simplifies the process by making all validation rules invokable by default. Let's explore this change and see how easy it is to create a new invokable rule in Laravel 10.

In Laravel 9, to create an invokable rule, you would use the following Artisan command:

```
php artisan make:rule --invokable CustomRule
```

However, thanks to the enhancements in Laravel 10, you no longer need to specify the --invokable flag. Instead, you can directly run the following command to create your custom invokable rule:

```
php artisan make:rule CustomRule
```

Laravel 10 treats all validation rules as invokable by default, streamlining the rule creation process and simplifying the overall development workflow. With this improvement, creating custom validation rules becomes more intuitive and requires less effort.

Enhanced Database Operations with Native Column Modification Support

In Laravel 10, an exciting new feature has been introduced to enable column modifications without the need for external packages like DBAL (doctrine/dbal). This enhancement allows developers to use the 'change()' method to modify columns effortlessly in MySQL, PostgreSQL, and SQL Server databases, reducing dependencies and simplifying the development process. Let's explore an example to grasp the power of this feature.

Imagine we have a table named 'users' with a column called 'email_frequency'. Initially, the column is defined as follows:

```
$table->string('email_frequency')->default('weekly')->comment('Frequency of email notifications');
```

Now, let's say we want to change the data type of the 'email_frequency' column to accommodate longer strings. In Laravel 10, this task becomes a breeze:

```
$table->text('email_frequency')->change();
```

The preceding code snippet successfully modifies the 'email_frequency' column to use the 'text' data type, which can handle longer textual content. However, it's essential to note that the 'change()' method will remove the previous attributes such as 'DEFAULT' and 'COMMENT'. To retain these attributes when changing the column type, we can do the following:

```
$table->text('email_frequency')->default('weekly')->comment('Frequency of
email notifications')->change();
```

By including the desired attributes, we ensure that the 'email_frequency' column retains its previous specifications while adapting to the new 'text' data type.

For scenarios where your application involves multiple database connections and you've already installed DBAL, Laravel 10 offers the 'useNativeSchemaOperationsIfPossible()' method. By calling this method within the 'boot' method of the 'AppServiceProvider', you can take advantage of native schema operations when available, falling back to the package's functionality as needed. Here's how you can use it:

```
use Illuminate\Support\Facades\Schema;
class AppServiceProvider extends ServiceProvider
{
    public function boot()
    {
        Schema::useNativeSchemaOperationsIfPossible();
    }
}
```

By leveraging this approach, you optimize database operations and utilize native schema operations efficiently, even when working with multiple database connections.

Native Retrieval of Column Types

In Laravel 10, a remarkable feature awaits developers who seek to obtain column types with enhanced accuracy and efficiency. Unlike previous versions that relied on the doctrine/dbal package to retrieve column types, Laravel 10 introduces an improved 'Schema::getColumnType' method that provides direct access to the actual column types without any mapping to DBAL equivalents. This advancement simplifies database operations and ensures support for a wider array of column types across various databases.

Let's explore this feature with a different example. Imagine we have a table named 'employees' with a column called 'hire_date'. Previously, using DBAL, you might have retrieved the column type as follows:

```
use Illuminate\Support\Facades\DB;
use Illuminate\Support\Facades\Schema;
$columnType = DB::getDoctrineColumn('employees', 'hire_date')->getType()->getName();
```

However, with the introduction of Laravel 10, you can now directly obtain the native column type without the need for DBAL:

```
use Illuminate\Support\Facades\Schema;
$columnType = Schema::getColumnType('employees', 'hire_date');
```

This improved approach returns the actual column type itself, such as 'date', providing more precise and accurate information about the column's data type.

Moreover, this feature proves especially beneficial when writing integration tests for the new native column modifying functionality in Laravel 10. It allows you to verify the column type modifications directly, ensuring that your database schema changes are correctly applied.

Furthermore, you have the flexibility to choose whether to retrieve just the data type name or the complete type definition of the specified column, for instance:

```
use Illuminate\Support\Facades\Schema;
$columnType = Schema::getColumnType('employees', 'hire_date');
// Returns 'date'
```

This enhanced method empowers developers with greater control over their database schema, enabling seamless integration testing and leading to more robust and reliable applications.

Enhanced Support for the whereExists() Method in the Eloquent Builder

In Laravel 10, an exciting enhancement has been made to the 'whereExists()' method of the Eloquent Builder, providing improved support for using an Eloquent Builder as a nested query. Prior to Laravel 10, setting up the nested query required a closure. However, with this update, developers can directly include an Eloquent Builder, simplifying complex queries and making them more concise.

Let's explore this feature with a different example. Consider two models, 'Post' and 'Comment', with a one-to-many relationship, where a post can have multiple comments. Previously, using the 'whereExists()' method with a closure, you might have written code like this:

```
Post::whereExists(function ($query) {
    $query->from('comments')->whereColumn('comments.post_id', 'posts.id');
});
```

However, with Laravel 10, you can now leverage the improved support for an Eloquent Builder as follows:

```
Post::whereExists(
    Comment::whereColumn('comments.post_id', 'posts.id')
);
```

This enhancement simplifies the process of constructing nested queries and eliminates the need for nested closures, resulting in more readable and maintainable code.

Moreover, this update allows you to use custom builder methods and model scopes directly within the 'whereExists()' method, enabling you to fine-tune your nested query with ease. For instance, you can apply any custom scopes or methods defined on the 'Comment' model to further refine the nested query:

```
Post::whereExists(
    Comment::whereColumn('comments.post_id', 'posts.id')->approved()-
>recent()
);
```

By embracing this feature in Laravel 10, developers can streamline complex query building, making it more manageable and efficient when dealing with relationships between models.

Optimizing Eager Loading

In Laravel 10, an intriguing enhancement awaits developers dealing with eager-loading relations that don't have any keys to be loaded. This improvement tackles an existing issue where eager loading would result in unnecessary queries being executed, leading to performance inefficiencies.

Before Laravel 10, when eager-loading relations without any keys to be loaded, Laravel would still execute a query similar to the following:

```
select * from 'orders' where 0 = 1
```

However, with the introduction of Laravel 10, the eager loading process is optimized. Instead of executing redundant queries, the framework now verifies whether any keys are available before proceeding. If no keys are found, Laravel provides an empty collection right away, bypassing the unnecessary database queries.

For instance, suppose we have two models, 'User' and 'Role', with a relationship defined between them. Previously, eager-loading relations without keys would have caused unnecessary queries:

```
$users = User::with('roles')->get();
```

With Laravel 10, this optimization ensures that if there are no keys to be loaded, an empty collection is returned directly:

```
$users = User::with('roles')->get(); // Returns an empty collection if
there are no keys to be loaded
```

By eliminating the execution of futile queries, Laravel 10 significantly enhances the performance of eager loading operations, reducing database overhead and improving the overall efficiency of the application.

$path Is Optional for Filesystem Methods

Laravel 10 introduces a notable improvement by making the '$path' parameter optional for certain filesystem methods, enhancing the flexibility and ease of managing uploaded files and file operations within the application.

Previously, when utilizing methods like 'putFile', 'putFileAs', 'store', 'storeAs', 'storePublicly', and 'storePubliclyAs', developers were required to explicitly provide the '$path' parameter along with the uploaded file, for instance:

```
Storage::disk('s3')->putFile('post/images', $uploadedFile);
```

However, with the introduction of Laravel 10, the '$path' parameter is no longer mandatory for these methods. Instead, you can take advantage of predefined constants from the 'Disk' class to specify the desired storage location:

```
Storage::disk(Disk::PostImages)->putFile($uploadedFile);
```

By using predefined constants like 'Disk::PostImages', developers can effortlessly manage the storage locations without the need to explicitly provide the '$path' parameter. This simplification streamlines the code and minimizes the risk of errors when specifying file storage locations.

Enhanced Database Expressions and Grammar-Specific Formatting

Laravel 10 introduces a game-changing feature that addresses a significant challenge faced when working with multiple databases. This enhancement allows developers to handle database-specific expressions and formatting more efficiently, eliminating the need for repetitive raw database code.

In previous versions of Laravel, when dealing with multiple databases, developers had to resort to raw database code to achieve specific outcomes. For instance, consider the need to return the first value of a list as an alias when working with PostgreSQL and MySQL:

```
DB::table('visitors')
->when(isPostgreSQL(), fn ($query) => $query-
>select(DB::raw('coalesce(NULL, "user", "guest") AS "First Visitor"')))
->when(isMySQL(), fn ($query) => $query->select(DB::raw('coalesce(NULL,
'user', 'guest') AS 'First Visitor'')))
```

The preceding code uses the 'COALESCE()' function to return the first non-null value as an alias named "First Visitor". However, this approach necessitates writing raw database code for each database type, resulting in less maintainable and less portable code.

With the arrival of Laravel 10, developers can now create reusable expression classes that implement raw expressions and statements for queries, providing a much cleaner and more flexible solution. This new approach eliminates the need to write raw database code repeatedly, ensuring a consistent and standardized experience across multiple databases.

Let's explore the new approach by creating two classes—'Alias' for aliasing and 'Coalesce' for utilizing the 'COALESCE()' function:

```
class Alias implements Expression
{
  public function __construct(
    public readonly Expression|string $expression,
    public readonly string $name,
```

```
) { }
  public function getValue(Grammar $grammar): string
  {
    return match ($grammar->isExpression($this->expression)) {
      true => "{$grammar->getValue($this->expression)} as {$grammar->
      wrap($this->name)}",
      false => $grammar->wrap("{$this->name} as {$this->name}"),
    };
  }
}
class Coalesce implements Expression
{
  public function __construct(
    public readonly array $expressions,
  ) { }
  public function getValue(Grammar $grammar): string
  {
    $expressions = array_map(function ($expression) use($grammar): string {
      return match ($grammar->isExpression($expression)) {
        true => $grammar->getValue($expression),
        false => $grammar->wrap($expression),
      };
    }, $this->expressions);
    $expressions = implode(', ', $expressions);
    return "coalesce({$expressions})";
  }
}
```

Now, we can achieve the same outcome for both MySQL and PostgreSQL databases using the new approach:

```
DB::table('visitors')->select(new Alias(new Coalesce([NULL, 'user',
'guest']), 'First Visitor'));
```

Enhanced SQL Server Query Performance with FETCH and OFFSET for Queries Without orderBy

In Laravel 10, an exciting update has been introduced for SQL Server users, optimizing query performance when using 'skip' and 'take' without an explicit 'orderBy' clause. This enhancement significantly improves query execution and pagination efficiency, resulting in faster and more responsive database interactions.

In previous versions of Laravel, queries without an 'orderBy' clause would employ a fallback method involving subqueries and the 'row_number()' function to achieve pagination. However, this approach could lead to slower execution and increased overhead.

Let's consider the following example using 'skip', 'take', and 'orderBy' in a query:

```
$builder->select('*')->from('users')->skip(11)->take(10)->orderBy('email',
'desc');
```

In previous versions, Laravel would generate SQL with 'FETCH' and 'OFFSET' for pagination:

```
select * from [users] order by [email] desc offset 11 rows fetch next 10
rows only
```

However, when the 'orderBy' clause was omitted, the fallback method involved a subquery with 'row_number()':

```
select * from (select *, row_number() over (order by (select 0)) as row_
num from [users]) as temp_table where row_num between 11 and 20 order
by row_num
```

In Laravel 10, the new update enables the use of 'FETCH' and 'OFFSET' even when the 'orderBy' clause is not present in the query, resulting in more efficient execution:

```
select * from [users] order by (SELECT 0) offset 10 rows fetch next 10
rows only
```

This enhancement offers a remarkable 33% improvement in query speed and reduces the number of execution steps, delivering a more streamlined and optimized pagination process.

Laravel Pennant

In the ever-changing landscape of web applications, introducing new features and managing feature flags can be challenging tasks. To simplify this process, Laravel introduces its first-party package, Laravel Pennant, designed to streamline feature flag management.

Laravel Pennant provides an easy-to-use solution for handling feature flags within your web application. The package offers support for both in-memory array drivers and databases, making it versatile and adaptable to your specific requirements.

Defining a new feature using Laravel Pennant is straightforward:

```
use LaravelPennantFeature;
Feature::define('new-color-button', function () {
    // Define the conditions for enabling the new color button feature
});
```

With this simple code snippet, you have created a new feature named 'new-color-button' and specified the conditions that trigger its activation.

To check whether a user has access to a particular feature, you can use the following code:

```
use LaravelPennantFeature;
if (Feature::active('new-color-button')) {
    // Implement the logic for the new color button feature
}
```

This streamlined approach allows you to enable or disable features based on specific conditions, such as user roles, permissions, or any other custom criteria.

In Laravel Blade templates, checking feature flags becomes even more concise and elegant:

```
@feature('new-color-button')
    // Display the new color button feature
@endfeature
```

Laravel Pennant empowers developers to manage feature flags effortlessly, making it a valuable tool for continuous updates and A/B testing in web applications. With this package, you can confidently experiment with new features, control their activation, and deliver a seamless user experience.

Laravel Process Interaction

With the release of Laravel 10, a groundbreaking feature called Process Interaction has been introduced, revolutionizing the way CLI processes are handled and tested. This feature comes with a user-friendly API that makes testing and running CLI processes a breeze, significantly simplifying the development process.

Let's explore an example from the original PR for this feature by Taylor Otwell:

```
use Illuminate\Support\Facades\Process;
$result = Process::run('ls -la');
$result->successful();
$result->failed();
$result->exitCode();
```

```
$result->output();
$result->errorOutput();
$result->throw();
$result->throwIf($condition);
```

As you can see, the code is concise and straightforward. Building processes become even more convenient with additional options:

```
$result = Process::timeout(60)->path(base_path())->env([...])-
>run('ls -la');
$result = Process::forever()->run('ls -la');
```

To leverage this powerful feature for testing purposes, you can easily create a new fake process:

```
Process::fake([
    'ls *' => Process::result('Hello From Laravel 10'),
]);
```

Now, you can run the fake process and take advantage of the newly available assertions:

```
$result = Process::run('ls -la');
Process::assertRan(function ($process, $result) {
    return $process->command == 'ls -la';
});
Process::assertRanTimes(function ($process, $result) {
    return $process->command == 'ls -la';
}, times: 1);
Process::assertNotRan(function ($process, $result) {
    return $process->command == 'cat foo';
});
```

Laravel 10's Process Interaction offers developers an elegant and efficient way to handle CLI processes, enabling smooth execution and robust testing. Embrace this powerful feature to simplify your CLI interactions, efficiently run processes, and ensure seamless testing of CLI functionalities in your Laravel 10 application.

Pest Scaffolding

When creating new Laravel projects in Laravel 10, the test scaffolding with Pest is now enabled by default. Pest is a delightful testing framework that simplifies and enhances the testing experience for developers. To take advantage of this feature, simply use the '--pest' flag when building a new Laravel app with the Laravel installer:

```
laravel new example-app --pest
```

By using the '--pest' flag, you ensure that Pest is set up and ready to go for your project, making testing a seamless and enjoyable process. With Pest, you can write expressive and readable tests that bring joy to the development experience.

Pest provides a more natural and elegant testing syntax that is designed to resemble plain English. This makes it easy for developers of all levels to write clear and concise tests that are easy to understand and maintain.

Summary

In this chapter, we covered the newest and updated features of Laravel 10.

Index

A

A/B testing, 514, 517, 530–532, 536
Amazon Web Services (AWS), 17, 289, 458
Analytics
    A/B testing/conversion
      tracking, 530–532
    collecting/analyzing application
      custom event listeners, 522
      data analyze, 524
      database queries, 522
      logging, 521
      third-party APIs, 523
      user experience, 524
      user tracking/cookies, 523
    data collection, 517
    data visualization libraries, 533–535
    tools, 517, 518
Angular, 391
Application Programming Interfaces (API)
    authentication, 86, 103
    authentication/security
      cross-origin requests, 114, 115
      JWT method, 111–113
      Laravel Sanctum, 110
      throttling, 114
      token, 110
    compatibility, 105
    definition, 104
    development, 103
    endpoints, 214, 215
    error handling, 104
    error responses, 120

    exception handling, 118, 119
    external services, 215
    format error responses, 119
    handling validation errors, 121
    integration, 104
    logging/debugging, 120
    mocking system, 215–217
    modularity, 104
    rate limiting, 116, 117
    rate limiting and throttling, 103
    RESTful (*see* RESTful APIs)
    running process, 217
    scalability, 104
    throttling, 116, 117
'array_is_list()' function, 606
'asset()' helper function, 385
Asynchronous JavaScript and XML
    (AJAX), 274, 391, 416, 417, 419,
    420, 567
Authentication
    API development, 103, 110–115
    broadcasting events, 175
    guards
      actions/resources, 84
      components, 84
      customization options, 88
      definition, 85, 89
      mobile applications/API-driven
        systems, 86
      sessions, 85
      token driver, 85
    login process, 76

F

G

M

Printed in the United States
by Baker & Taylor Publisher Services

Printed in the United States
by Baker & Taylor Publisher Services